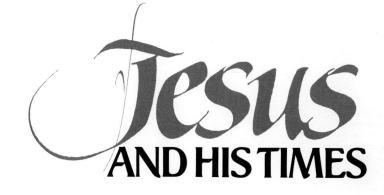

Jesus
AND HIS TIMES

Reader's Digest

Jesus
AND HIS TIMES

The Reader's Digest Association, Inc.
Pleasantville, New York   Montreal

Jesus AND HIS TIMES

Editor: Kaari Ward
Art Editor: Evelyn Bauer

Senior Editor: James Dwyer
Associate Editor: Robert V. Huber
Research Editors: Hildegard Anderson, Mary Jane Hodges
Picture Researcher: Margaret O. Mathews
Associate Art Editor: Larissa Lawrynenko
Art Associate: Nancy Mace
Editorial Assistant: Jean Ryan

Contributors

Writers: Charles Bricker
Lionel Casson
Charles Flowers
Wendy Murphy
Bryce Walker
Bernard Weisberger
Researcher: Mary Lyn Maiscott
Copy Editor: Susan Converse Winslow
Indexer: Sydney Wolfe Cohen

READER'S DIGEST GENERAL BOOKS
Editorial Director: John A. Pope, Jr.
Managing Editor: Jane Polley
Art Director: David Trooper
Group Editors: Norman B. Mack, John Speicher,
Susan J. Wernert

Marble statue of the Good Shepherd,
fourth–sixth century A.D..

Principal Adviser and Editorial Consultant

Thomas L. Robinson, *Department of Biblical Studies, Union
Theological Seminary*

Board of Consultants

David Graf, *Department of History, University of Miami*

George MacRae, *The Divinity School, Harvard University*

Bruce M. Metzger, *Princeton Theological Seminary*

Nahum M. Sarna, *Professor Emeritus, Department of Near Eastern
and Judaic Studies, Brandeis University*

Gerald Sheppard, *Department of Biblical Studies,
Emmanuel College, University of Toronto*

The scriptural quotations in this publication are from The New
Oxford Annotated Bible with the Apocrypha, Revised Standard
Version, Copyright © 1973, 1977 by Oxford University Press, Inc.

The acknowledgments and credits that appear on pages 322–324
are hereby made a part of this copyright page.

Library of Congress Cataloging in Publication Data

Jesus and his times.

Bibliography: p.
Includes index.
1. Jesus Christ—Biography. 2. Christian
biography—Palestine. 3. Bible. N.T. Gospels—
History of contemporary events. 4. Palestine—
Social life and customs. 5. Names in the Bible.
I. Reader's Digest Association.
BT301.2.J46   1987   232.9   86-24857
ISBN 0-89577-257-4

Printed in the United States of America

Contents

Introduction

Jesus and the Four Gospels

At the time, the birth of Jesus was nearly as obscure an event as is possible to imagine. But his ministry and death set off a chain reaction of proclamation and interpretation of his life that quickly elevated his story from obscurity to cosmic significance.

Among the forces that have shaped Western civilization the story of Jesus ranks as one of the most powerful. Since it first began to be told—in the days, perhaps hours, following Jesus' death—it has wielded influence impossible to calculate. The story has shaped the entire course of Christianity and its understanding of the world and of God. And even those who are part of the rich non-Christian traditions that make up the patchwork of Western culture have inevitably been touched by the great historical forces set in motion by the story of Jesus.

The telling of the story was an enterprise of Christian believers long before anyone thought of them as Christians. It began after Jesus' crucifixion, when one of his followers had to explain to himself or to a questioner just who this Jesus was and why his followers did not disband after he was executed. It has never stopped.

Since then, in the multitudes of Christian communities throughout the centuries and across the continents, the story has been read and retold in scores of languages. It has been dramatized and sung and preached and danced and celebrated and interpreted myriads of times. It has provided proverbs and moral examples for daily life and

hope at the brink of death. The rhythm of the whole Christian year has been organized around the celebration of crucial moments in the life of Jesus. In spite of the great diversity that has divided Christian communities, this story has been shared by all. For all, this is the story of salvation that made Christianity what it was and is.

In relatively recent times another kind of interest in Jesus has arisen. It focuses on Jesus not as the center of a cosmic drama of incarnation and redemption but as a historical figure—a person who has had a vast impact on subsequent events, no matter what one may believe about him religiously. Hundreds of books have been written with some variation of this historical aim.

Within this library of biographies, a reader can find practically every kind of portrayal of Jesus imaginable. Some accounts are spare and cautious reconstructions of events. Many are more imaginative creations that combine elements of history with large doses of the writer's own interests. There are portrayals of Jesus that range from meek and mild to militant revolutionary, from rabbinical teacher to quiet mystic to wild-eyed eccentric. Jesus has been seen as the prototype of the American salesman and as the instigator of proletarian class struggle. In short, people have looked at Jesus and seen something of themselves reflected.

Then, too, there are the many iconoclasts who claim to reveal what "really happened"—that Jesus was only a mythical figure created by early Christians or that Jesus survived his execution or that Jesus was completely misunderstood by everyone until now, and so on.

The great variety of interpretation is remarkable, especially since all the many portrayals are based on the same few sources. Practically everything that is known about Jesus comes from the four Gospels in the New Testament. True, there are a few references to Jesus in non-Christian sources, but the information they provide amounts to little more than that Jesus lived, was a teacher with disciples, and was executed. There are also a few pieces of information in other books of the New Testament and early Christian literature outside the Gospels, but very little that is not also in the four Gospels. Thus everyone who wishes to tell about Jesus in any detail must fall back on the stories told by Matthew, Mark, Luke, and John.

When the historian examines the period in which Jesus lived, however, the situation is quite different. A vast treasury of sources opens up, including hundreds of ancient texts in Greek, Hebrew, Aramaic, Latin, and other languages. There are private documents—letters, school exercises, contracts, invitations, invoices—all of which help to illuminate the world in which the events of the Gospels took place. The historian can also draw information from archeological excavations, including the study of ancient inscriptions, manuscripts, coins, pottery, architecture, and underwater finds.

In JESUS AND HIS TIMES all these sources of information have contributed to our account of the world in which Jesus lived. This book will not try to present another new or startling interpretation of Jesus; rather, it will provide modern eyes with a view of the vibrant and fascinating and turbulent period in which Jesus was on earth. As for the life of Jesus, the narrative will stay close to the sources, namely, the four Gospels.

To a great extent the four Gospels are just what the name implies: the word *gospel* is a translation of the Greek word *euangelion*, meaning "good news" or "proclamation." The Gospels were originally written by Christians to proclaim the news of Jesus as the Christ. They were directed both to believers, to confirm and instruct them in their faith, and to nonbelievers, to lead them to faith. The Gospel writers never tried to be objective in the way a modern journalist might wish to be. The Gospels are documents of faith from first to last, enlivened by the belief that they are telling the story not of ordinary occurrences but of miraculous events in which God has intervened in the world. Mark expressed well the commitment of all the Gospels when he began his narrative with a confession of faith: "The beginning of the Gospel of Jesus Christ, the Son of God" (Mark 1:1).

Why are there four Gospels? There is no simple answer to this question. Luke began his Gospel by remarking that "many" had already undertaken to write an account of the events he wished to narrate. No one knows exactly what writings Luke was including in his "many," but clearly our four Gospels were not the only such documents in the early church. In fact, dozens of gospels circulated at various times in the first few centuries. Of most of these so-called apocryphal, or hidden, gospels only fragments have survived till today.

Perhaps the best known of these texts is the gospel of Thomas, probably written near the beginning of the second century. Only a few fragments of the original Greek text have ever been found, but its content became known when a number of manuscripts were discovered by chance in Egypt some 40 years ago. One contained a translation of the entire gospel of Thomas in the Coptic language. This gospel differed from the New Testament

Gospels in that it included only the words of Jesus with practically no narrative of events, not even the story of the crucifixion and resurrection. Many of the sayings of Jesus in Thomas' gospel are similar to those in the New Testament Gospels. Indeed, numerous scholars have argued that in some instances they may be closer to the original words of Jesus than the corresponding sayings in the New Testament.

When there is more than one Gospel text, it is inevitable that differences in wording will occur. Questions arise: Which is right? Can any of the texts be trusted if they differ among themselves? Why is there not a single authoritative text that can avoid all the problems?

The force of such questions was clearly felt in the early church. In the mid-second century a Christian author named Tatian overcame the diversity among the four Gospels by weaving them all into a single continuous narrative called the Diatessaron (meaning "through four"). His work was used for several centuries in his native Syria as the authoritative Gospel. Another solution was proposed during the same period by a highly influential self-styled reformer named Marcion. Since the Gospels differ among themselves, he believed, only one of them can be authoritative. A choice must be made, and for Marcion the choice fell on the Gospel of Luke, in his own somewhat revised version.

In contrast to either of these solutions, the great majority of the church rejected attempts to have a single Gospel text and came to recognize all four, side by side, with all their variations, as authoritative. It seemed inevitable that all four should be recognized as authoritative sacred texts, though sometimes the reasons given seem remarkable to modern ears. For example, toward the end of the second century Irenaeus, the Christian bishop of Lyons in southern Gaul, wrote: "It is not possible that the Gospels can be either more or fewer in number than they are. For since there are four zones of the world in which we live, and four principal winds, while the church has been scattered throughout all the world, and the pillar and ground of the church is the gospel and the spirit of life; it is fitting that she should have four pillars, breathing incorruption on every side, and vivifying men afresh."

Whatever the reasons, the focus on four authoritative Gospels had profound effects. Nearly all the other gospel texts that were in circulation fell into disuse, and most were lost forever. Inevitably the view of Jesus in all later generations was shaped by the fact that these canonical texts became practically the only available source of knowledge. And because there were four Gospels rather than one, a certain variety of interpretation of Jesus was built into the New Testament from the start.

All four Gospels share a single basic intention: to proclaim the story of Jesus as a message of divine salvation. They also share many elements of content. It is important, for example, that all four, in contrast to works like the gospel of Thomas, not only provide the teachings of Jesus but also narrate events of his life. The overlap is most extensive in the passion narrative, the account of Jesus' suffering and death. That fact has been very important not only for our understanding of events but also for Christian theology. It means that each of the Gospels bears witness—again, in contrast to a work like the gospel of Thomas—that Jesus' life and teachings cannot be properly understood alone, but only as they are seen through the prism of his death and resurrection.

By far the greatest similarities occur among the first three Gospels—Matthew, Mark, and Luke. These are commonly called the Synoptic Gospels, from the Greek word meaning "to view together." Although the Synoptic Gospels were composed by different writers, they share a common basic order of events that is distinct from the Gospel According to John. They also include similar types of materials, and indeed, in passage after passage, their very wording is exactly or nearly identical. The extent of these similarities is best seen by reading the Gospels in a "synopsis," an edition in which the parallel texts of the Gospels are printed side by side. (The table below offers a brief survey of certain events in Jesus' life and shows where they are covered in the Gospels.)

The extent of the similarities has convinced most scholars—even going as far back as Saint Augustine in the fourth century A.D.—that the Gospel writers made use of one another's texts. The explanation of their relationships that is most common today is that Mark's Gospel, the shortest of the four, is also the earliest. Both Matthew and Luke knew and used Mark's Gospel in writing their own, and thus their Gospels share the basic outline of events in Mark. Both were aware of many other traditions about Jesus that were available in the early church, including an early collection of his teachings.

Events in the life of Jesus as recorded in the Gospels

		Matthew	Mark	Luke	John
EARLY YEARS	Birth	1:18–25		2:1–7	
	Visit of the Wise Men	2:1–12			
	Flight into Egypt	2:13–21			
	Teaching in the Temple			2:41–51	
	Jesus' baptism	3:13–17	1:9–11	3:21–22	
	Changing water into wine				2:1–11
	Temptation in the Wilderness	4:1–11	1:12–13	4:1–13	
JESUS' MINISTRY	Start of the Galilean ministry	4:12–17	1:14–15	4:14–15	
	Summoning the first disciples	4:18–22	1:16–20	5:1–11	1:35–51
	Sermon on the Mount	5:1–7:29		6:20–49	
	Naming the Apostles	10:1–42	3:13–19; 6:7–19	9:1–6	
	Feeding 5,000	14:13–21	6:32–44	9:10–17	6:1–14
	Walking on water	14:22–33	6:45–52		6:16–21
	Peter declares Jesus to be the Christ	16:16	8:29	9:20	
	Transfiguration of Jesus	17:1–13	9:2–8	9:28–36	
	Raising of Lazarus				11:1–44
FINAL DAYS	Entry into Jerusalem	21:1–11	11:1–10	19:28–44	12:12–19
	Cleansing of the Temple	21:12–13	11:15–17	19:45–46	2:13–17
	Judas betrays Jesus	26:14–16	14:10–11	22:3–6	
	Preparations for Passover	26:17–19	14:12–16	22:7–13	
	Last Supper	26:20–29	14:17–25	22:14–18	13:1–30
	Arrest	26:47–56	14:43–52	22:47–53	18:2–12
	Trial	26:57–27:26	14:53–15:15	22:54–23:25	18:13–19:16
	Crucifixion and death	27:33–54	15:22–39	23:33–47	19:17–37
	Burial	27:57–61	15:42–47	23:50–56	19:38–42
	Resurrection	28:1–10	16:1–8	24:1–11	20:1–18
	Appearances to disciples	28:16–20	16:12–18	24:13–49	20:19–21:23
	Ascension		16:19	24:50–51	

Both wanted to ensure that these early traditions would not be lost, and each therefore combined them with the basic narrative that the Gospel of Mark provided. In addition, each Gospel writer was directing his narrative toward the needs of the Christian community in which he lived. Thus there are important variations of detail, emphasis, and interpretation.

Although the differences among the Gospels are often viewed as a historical problem, those differences provide much of the richness of the Gospels' witness and make them the greatest treasure of Christianity. Each Gospel has its distinct voice. No one can be replaced by another. Their varying contours have helped to keep the New Testament witness from becoming rigid.

The divergences great and small even among the Synoptic Gospels are on every page and were built into the texts from the beginning. Matthew and Luke were certainly well aware—and apparently unconcerned—that they were often not simply repeating Mark's words unchanged. They evidently felt no requirement to do so. Sometimes they chose to shift the order of events in the narrative. For example, in the Gospel of Luke, Jesus' rejection at Nazareth is told as the first major event of his ministry, but that event is narrated considerably later in his ministry in Matthew and Mark. Sometimes two Gospels preserve two separate early Christian traditions about the same event, as, for example, the narratives of Jesus' birth in Matthew and Luke. Often the sayings of Jesus or the details of a particular story vary from one Gospel to another.

The most striking differences appear, however, when the reader moves from the Synoptic Gospels to the Gospel of John. The change is profound on every level. One way of seeing the differences is to look at how the Gospels describe the way people respond to Jesus. Although each Gospel makes clear who Jesus is, the Synoptics carry the reader through a long process of observing the disciples and others gradually coming to faith—often the faith is shown to be inadequate. A high point comes in each of the Synoptics when the Apostle Peter at a point well along in Jesus' ministry finally confesses Jesus to be the Christ. The climax comes only with the death and resurrection of Jesus. In many ways the Gospel of John starts where the Synoptics leave off. Within the very first chapter of John several different people confess Jesus. He is described as "the Lamb of God who takes away the sin of the world," the "Messiah," "Christ," the "Son of God," the "King of Israel." In effect John begins with all these titles and then explores what they mean through the rest of the story. Many scholars therefore have seen the Gospel of John as a profound theological reflection on the church's traditions about Jesus.

A perceptive reader will notice the way Jesus regularly speaks in extended theological discourses in John rather than in the brief sayings or parables that are most typical in the Synoptic Gospels. Jesus' language is punctuated by self-revelations: "I am the bread of life"; "I am the light of the world"; "I am the good shepherd"; "I am the resurrection and the life." The discourses in John are so distinctive that even a casual acquaintance with the texts enables the reader to distinguish much of John's material from that in the Synoptic Gospels. Numerous familiar elements of the Synoptic narratives simply do not occur in John's Gospel. Some examples: Jesus' baptism and temptation, his transfiguration, his casting out demons, his teaching in parables, his institution of the Lord's Supper, and his prayer in the garden of Gethsemane.

The important fact, however, is that in spite of all these very real differences, the early church recognized in all four Gospels a common witness to the central belief of Christian communities. The early Christians might have avoided all the problems arising from these differences. They might have excluded the Gospel of John from the New Testament, or they might have included only John;

but they did neither. Each Synoptic Gospel affects the interpretation of the others, and all three are affected by the Gospel of John. No other source offers us more information about Jesus than the four Gospels.

Who wrote the Gospels? The names Matthew, Mark, Luke, and John are well known, and thus this question might seem to be completely answered. Many scholars, however, have pointed out that the traditional titles that give the names of the authors were attached to the Gospels in the second century. Whether any or all of the traditional authors' names are correct remains disputed. Within themselves, all four Gospels are content to be anonymous. Even the Gospel of John, which in its last verses attributes its witness to "the disciple whom Jesus loved," at no point names that disciple. In tradition, of course, the "beloved disciple" has been identified with John the son of Zebedee, and thus the Gospel is called the Gospel of John. The earliest second-century tradition about the writing of Matthew is from Papias, bishop of Hierapolis in Asia Minor, who says that the Apostle Matthew wrote in Hebrew. Our Gospel of Matthew was almost certainly written in Greek, however, and thus it is not clear whether Papias was describing the document we know.

In many ways scholarly disputes about the authorship of these texts make little difference. Whether the Gospel of Luke was written by Luke, Paul's companion, as many believe, or by some other early Christian, will in no way increase or diminish its importance. What matters is that the Gospels have given Christian communities—and indeed the whole world—access to a person and a series of events that have profoundly affected all subsequent history. That story, unfolding in its historical context, is the subject of JESUS AND HIS TIMES. Whether one shares the faith of the Gospel writers in the divine importance of this story or not, every person who is an heir of Western civilization has been shaped by its power.

Early in Christianity, the "four living creatures" of Revelation 4:6 were linked with the four Gospel writers. Matthew is represented by man, Mark by a lion, Luke by an ox, and John by an eagle, as shown in these sixth-century A.D. mosaic portraits from Ravenna.

Chapter One

The Birth of the Savior

According to the Gospel of Luke, "In those days a decree went out from Caesar Augustus that all the world should be enrolled. . . . And all went to be enrolled, each to his own city." Thus Joseph and Mary went to Bethlehem, home of Joseph's ancestors, and Jesus was born in the city of David.

Jesus was born into a world at peace. It was a Roman peace, watched over by the vigilant Roman legions whose very presence discouraged any brewing revolt in the remote corners of the empire. For the most part, peace brought prosperity and even a measure of luxury to the far-flung provinces. This was not true, however, of tiny Palestine, a region of some 8,000 square miles on the eastern edge of Rome's vast domain. The million or so Jews living there, who had come under the yoke of Rome when Pompey's legions took Jerusalem in 63 B.C., were little more than taxpaying units in one of history's most extensive systems of taxation—a system dependent on the contributions of conquered populations from all over the empire. The great works of Roman government—straight roads and soaring aqueducts, marble buildings and spacious public plazas—were partly funded by taxes, which proved most burdensome on the lowliest members of society. In taxation as in everything else, Rome was a strong-arm overlord. Provincial governors were periodically empowered to conduct a census to organize Rome's tax rolls. It was such a mandate that sent Joseph and Mary on a 90-mile journey to Bethlehem.

From time to time, Rome ordered a census of the peoples under its rule so that it could increase the tax rolls and thus raise additional revenue to carry out imperial projects. It is likely that Roman soldiers were assigned the task of announcing news of these events in the provinces, which at the time of Jesus included Palestine.

This cameo portrait of Emperor Augustus is part of an elaborate gem-studded cross that was created in the 10th century at the request of the Holy Roman Emperor Otto II. After the assassination of Julius Caesar in 44 B.C., the young, ambitious future emperor, then called Octavian, came to power as one of a triumvirate that included Mark Antony. Thirteen years later, Octavian ruled alone. In 27 B.C. the Senate bestowed on him the honorary title Augustus. Rome and its empire prospered under Augustus and entered a long era of relative peace.

The Gospel of Luke tells us that the Roman emperor Caesar Augustus had ordered all subject peoples of Palestine to return to the place of their family origin to be enrolled and that Quirinius was governor of Syria at the time. Historians, however, have not found reference to precisely the census mentioned by Luke. Records reveal that the former Roman consul Publius Sulpicius Quirinius was in charge of Syria, including Palestine, during at least one census, but the date is A.D. 6, a decade after the death of King Herod the Great. Yet it is during Herod's reign that Matthew and Luke place the birth of Jesus.

Did Luke, and perhaps other writers of the New Testament, sometimes confuse the facts of Jesus' life? The Gospels were not written until 70 to 100 years after Jesus' birth. The stories beloved by the earliest followers of Jesus could easily have changed as they were told and retold, thousands of times, during those early years.

Or did Luke use poetic license? The journey to Bethlehem has become one of our most treasured stories. Part of the reason is surely that one's heart goes out to the innocent expectant mother forced to face the hardships of the road—it was a five-day walk from the tiny country village of Nazareth in Lower Galilee to the town of Bethlehem, home of Joseph's ancestors, on the edge of the Judean Wilderness.

Or is the story of the census quite literally true, an event that was not considered worthy of notice by the chroniclers of the Roman Empire, an immense realm of 30 provinces covering 2 million square miles? Palestine, after all, was far removed from the center of worldly power.

Whether owing to inaccuracy, poetic license, or a gap in the historical record, this kind of ambiguity will recur as we look at the life of Jesus. To most readers, such imprecision will not detract from the essence of the story. It is understandable, consider-ing the circumstances in which the New Testament was written. The recording of history with literal exactness of detail is a fairly modern development. At the time, precise fact was far less important than the spiritual message of the stories shared by disciples who still remembered the living Jesus.

For these early believers, only Luke and Matthew set down the story of Jesus' birth—in the first two chapters of their Gospels. Even though the two writers do not relate the same surrounding events, and sometimes may even seem to contradict each other, their common aim is clear: to show that Jesus was indeed the Messiah prophesied. For example, both writers tell us that Jesus was born in Bethlehem, but they do so from different points of view. As told by Matthew, the birth in Bethlehem fulfills an Old Testament prophecy, found in Micah 5:2, but he says nothing about how Mary and Joseph came to be in Bethlehem. Luke, by telling how an imperial census was used to bring Joseph and Mary to Bethlehem, shows God using the greatest powers on earth in order to bring about the birth of Jesus in that town in accordance with the Scriptures.

In the central, most important matters, Matthew and Luke concur. Both stress the intervention of divine warnings and promises. Both show the ordinariness of Jesus' beginnings. Luke shows, for example, that it was only the purity of her soul that distinguished Mary from any other anonymous villager of the day, and Matthew demonstrates that it was Joseph's faith and courage, not his earthly station, that singled him out for his difficult assignment. Thus both writers show that the choice of Jesus' parents revealed that inner truth, not outward show, would be a major theme of the New Testament.

Two annunciations

Luke begins his account of the birth of Jesus a little more than a year before the trip to Bethlehem, with the conception and birth of John, who was to be called the Baptist. Zechariah (Zacharias) and Elizabeth, a devout elderly couple living in the hills of Judea, were childless, even though "they were both righteous before God, walking in all the commandments and ordinances of the Lord blameless." Luke stresses this point because, according to traditional Jewish beliefs, a woman's infertility indicated God's displeasure. Elizabeth lived daily with the sign of divine reproach, or so she might have thought, and had lost all hope of ever bearing a child.

Zechariah, who was a priest, was burning incense in the Temple one day, according to prescribed ritual. Suddenly, an angel appeared beside the holy altar and announced that Elizabeth would at last conceive. She would give birth to a son "filled with the Holy Spirit." This child, who should be named John, would have the spiritual gifts of the revered Old Testament prophet Elijah. John would grow up to win many Jews back to God and would prepare the people for the Lord's purposes.

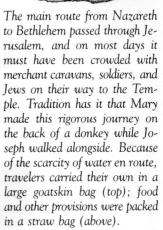

The main route from Nazareth to Bethlehem passed through Jerusalem, and on most days it must have been crowded with merchant caravans, soldiers, and Jews on their way to the Temple. Tradition has it that Mary made this rigorous journey on the back of a donkey while Joseph walked alongside. Because of the scarcity of water en route, travelers carried their own in a large goatskin bag (top); food and other provisions were packed in a straw bag (above).

Abraham

Isaac

Jacob

Judah

Perez

Hezron

Ram

Amminadab

Nahshon

Salmon

Boaz

Obed

Jesse

David

Solomon

Rehoboam

Abijah

Asa

Jehoshaphat

Joram

Pious as Zechariah was, his natural reaction was disbelief. He desired some proof, since common sense told him that his wife was too old. She could become pregnant only by a miracle. That, of course, was just the point. The angel, who revealed himself as Gabriel, said that as a sign against his lack of faith, Zechariah would be struck dumb and remain silent until the day his son was born. When Elizabeth discovered that she was pregnant, she was overjoyed at the great blessing she had been given by God.

The story of Zechariah and Elizabeth is strikingly similar to miraculous births earlier in the Bible. Abraham and Sarah and Manoah and his wife remained childless because of the wife's seeming barrenness (Sarah until she was 90 years old). They then became the parents of Isaac and Samson respectively. In both instances the births were miraculous, overcoming barrenness and old age, and were announced by an angel of the Lord or the Lord himself. The person hearing the announcement expressed fear or prostrated himself and was told of the child to be born and his future life. In regard to Isaac, the child's name was also given. The story of John's birth fits this pattern exactly and prepares us for the greatest of all births—not a birth to a barren woman, but even more remarkable, a birth to a virgin.

In the sixth month of Elizabeth's pregnancy, Gabriel went to Nazareth. In a poignant moment, which has inspired artists throughout the centuries of the Christian Era, he appeared before the young virgin. Mary, who had been betrothed to Joseph, was stunned at the greeting, "Hail, O favored one, the Lord is with you!" (This is the "Ave Maria" of the Latin version of the Bible, the basis for more than one hymn of celebration.)

The heavenly messenger's announcement, known as the Annunciation, promised that Mary would conceive a son to be called Jesus, who was destined to be "Son of the Most High," to reign upon the throne of David, "and of his kingdom there will be no end."

Mary's reaction was down-to-earth. She had no husband. How was she to conceive? Gabriel explained that "the Holy Spirit will come upon you, and the power of the Most High will overshadow you."

The angel also told Mary that her kinswoman Elizabeth had conceived a child in her old age, commenting in a phrase that is a favorite quotation of many Christians in times of confusion or despair, "For with God nothing will be impossible." Mary believed the word of the angel, affirming that she was the handmaiden of the Lord.

Joseph and his mission

From Matthew we learn that Joseph was distressed when he discovered that his betrothed was pregnant. A "just man," who was "unwilling to put her to shame," Joseph determined to have a quiet divorce. In fact, all he needed to do was to write his intention to divorce Mary in a letter witnessed by two people, perhaps even Mary's parents, and not involve the authorities or any other outsiders.

Today divorce would simply not apply to an engaged couple, but according to the customs of Jewish marriage in those days, betrothal was usually considered practically as binding as the marriage that would follow. If her fiancé died before the wedding, for example, a betrothed woman was considered a widow. Betrothal generally lasted about a year, and during that time unfaithfulness on the part of one's betrothed was everywhere regarded as tantamount to adultery. So Joseph had every right to end his betrothal in divorce. Whatever he might feel toward Mary, all visible evidence suggested that she had betrayed him.

Before he could act, Joseph had a dream in which an angel, hailing him as "Joseph, son of David," explained that the child Mary had conceived was of the Holy Spirit. The angel said that the son was to be named Jesus. The name *Jesus* is the Greek form of the Hebrew name *Yeshua*, which in turn is a contraction of the name *Yehoshua* (commonly believed to mean "Yahweh, or Jehovah, saves"), or *Joshua* in English. Although the name was a common one, it is significant because Jesus would "save his people from their sins." The virgin birth, the angel concluded, would fulfill a prophecy about the coming of the Messiah. Joseph therefore took Mary as his wife, but he did not consummate their marriage.

Since Joseph was a descendant of King David, as the angel's greeting and Matthew's genealogy remind us, his marriage to Mary made it possible for Jesus to be born into the House of David.

David is one of the most beloved of all Jewish heroes. He was born in Bethlehem about 1,000 years before Jesus and tended sheep in the surrounding hill country. A noteworthy poet and harpist, he probably composed at least some of the psalms attributed to him. David was also a mighty warrior and leader. He is said to have begun his military career while he was still a youth by slaying the giant Goliath with a slingshot during the struggles between the Philistines and the Hebrews. He went on to be victor in many subsequent battles. Upon the death of Saul, Israel's first king, David was crowned as Saul's successor. His days were a time of independence, expansion, and prosperity for Israel. Most important for the future hopes of his people was the covenant that is described in 2 Samuel 7 between God and David and his descendants. God promised that David's kingdom and throne "shall be established for ever" in Israel. Even later, when no descendant remained upon the throne, many hoped that a descendant of David would rise to fulfill the promise. Both Matthew and Luke emphasize Jesus' birth in the Davidic lineage as the ultimate realization of those hopes and of God's promise.

The name Jesus *is the Greek form of the Hebrew name Yeshua. The name was inscribed on a first-century* B.C. *ossuary, which held bones of the dead.*

The Visitation

Prior to Jesus' birth, Mary acted on some other good news that Gabriel had given her, the pregnancy of her "kinswoman" Elizabeth. Luke, who tells the story, does not disclose what the exact blood relationship might have been between the two women, although tradition has often portrayed them as cousins. Whatever the relationship, Mary and Elizabeth are seen as close friends, for Mary immediately set out to visit this older woman so strangely blessed by God. The unnamed Judean town where Zechariah and Elizabeth lived was perhaps as much as 90 miles south of Nazareth, a journey of at least five days.

When Mary entered Zechariah's house, she greeted Elizabeth. As soon as Elizabeth heard Mary's greeting, John "leaped" in his mother's womb, and Elizabeth, "filled with the Holy Spirit," cried out: "Blessed are you among women, and blessed is the fruit of your womb!" Mary responded joyously, beginning, "My soul magnifies the Lord." In this response, known as the "Magnificat," Mary not only praised, or magnified, the mercy, strength, and generosity of God toward herself, but also celebrated the way God in these events had overwhelmed the proud and mighty and lifted up the weak and poor: "For behold, henceforth all generations will call me blessed."

Mary stayed with her kinswoman for about three months. Although Luke tells us nothing of what happened in that time, it is reasonable to guess that Mary helped Elizabeth with the routine work of the household, which would have been constant and demanding. Every day, water had to be drawn from the village well, bread had to be baked, and curds had to be made from goat's milk. Provisions had to be bought on market days, and cloth had to be made by spinning and weaving.

Uzziah
Jotham
Ahaz
Hezekiah
Manasseh
Amos
Josiah
Jechoniah
Shealtiel
Zerubbabel
Abiud
Eliakim
Azor
Zadok
Achim
Eliud
Eleazar
Matthan
Jacob
Joseph

Jesus

Mary and Elizabeth probably performed many of these tasks together, almost automatically carrying out the homespun obligations of their simple way of life while, we may imagine, discussing over and over again the profound mystery of the blessings God had conferred upon them. For all their faith and joy, though, surely they must have been puzzled. Kneading, spinning, and cooking, obscure in their station like many a mere servant at the great courts of Rome and Jerusalem, they were to be instruments of God's salvation of the world.

The birth of John the Baptist

Shortly after Mary returned to Nazareth, Elizabeth's son was delivered, to the joy of the many friends and relatives who had always loved and respected the admirable Elizabeth. In accordance with Jewish law, the boy was circumcised on the eighth day after his birth; a festive celebration probably followed.

The Jews were not the only ones who practised circumcision; it had long been a custom of the Egyptians as well as other Semitic peoples. Historians do not agree about the origins of the practice or its significance; but for the Jews it was a fundamental sign of the covenant God had made with Abraham, and it served to distinguish them from their ancient enemies, the Philistines, and, later, from the Babylonians, Greeks, and Romans.

Some ancient writers theorized that hygiene was a factor in the origin of the rite of circumcision; others suggested that the original aim was fertility or a lessening of sexual desire. But whatever the reason, for the Jews circumcision was God's law.

It was usually at the ritual of circumcision that a son's name would be announced. There was some bewilderment when Elizabeth called her child John. The choice was unusual because, contrary to custom, the name was not associated with the family; according to Luke, no relative had ever been called John. At this point, old Zechariah, still unable to speak, signaled for a writing tablet and firmly wrote, "His name is John." Onlookers were astonished, but they were to be even more amazed when, after all the months of silence, Zechariah suddenly opened his mouth and began to praise the Lord aloud. His prayer, which recalls the long history of God's relationship with the Jewish people and predicts John's career as "the prophet of the Most High," is the hymn known as the "Benedictus."

With the story of Elizabeth and Zechariah, Luke masterfully laid the groundwork for the even more remarkable events surrounding the birth of Jesus. The attention to local detail, to everyday customs, and to the individual traits of the principals conveys the reality of the scene. As a writer, Luke is able to convince the reader, effectively contrasting recognizable human qualities with the incomprehensible power of divinity.

No room at the inn

Luke begins the story of Jesus' birth by telling of the census and the trip from Nazareth to Bethlehem. He does not give details about the journey. Most likely the couple traveled by day, when the sun was burning hot, and rested at night, probably seeking shelter in the homes of strangers—in those days one was expected to extend hospitality to travelers.

Bethlehem is situated on a low but steep ridge in the rocky hills just south of Jerusalem. The town is surrounded by green fields and lush olive groves, but close to the east is a harsh wilderness, beyond which lies the Dead Sea. Since the time of David, there had been a caravansary, or inn, near Bethlehem because the town was on the main route between Jerusalem and Egypt.

When they arrived at Bethlehem, Mary and Joseph found no place at the inn. At that point they probably looked for available space in someone's home. We are not told by Luke why no one took them in for the night.

Continued on page 22

A flowering field in fertile Galilee.

Hills in Samaria (above) and the Judean desert (below).

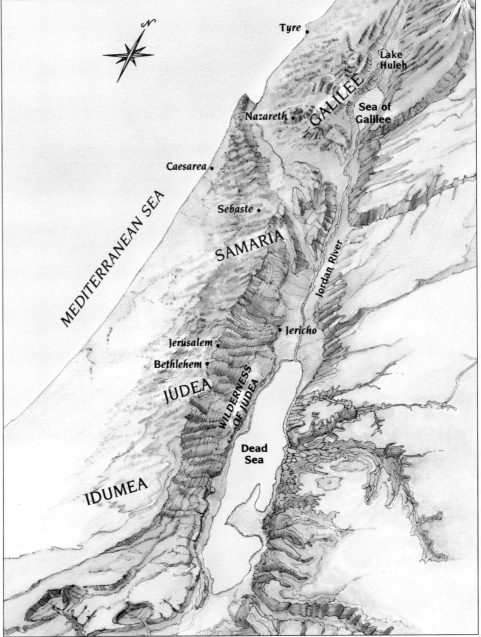

Joseph and Mary traveled from Nazareth, in Galilee, through Samaria to Bethlehem.

A Caravansary

The inn on the outskirts of Bethlehem looked much like this typical caravansary, one of the many similar hostelries along the major trade routes of the time. It served road-weary travelers in the same way that motels do today. In addition to lodging, a caravansary provided protection. Built of local stone or sun-dried brick and walled to keep out brigands, an inn looming on the horizon must have been a welcome sight at the end of a day of dusty travel. Such havens were always built around a source of water, and travelers could feed and water their animals in the open courtyard and fill their water bags from the well. Poor guests probably slept in the courtyard too, but in bad weather they took shelter with their animals in the arcade that constituted the ground floor. A stone staircase led up to an open corridor fronting on a series of tiny, bare rooms available to those who could afford them. Shaded by blankets and mats hung up to air, the more affluent could be somewhat removed from the clatter and stench of the dirty courtyard.

The fact that Luke says there was no place at the inn for Mary and Joseph does not necessarily mean that the inn was unusually crowded. As an ongoing business, and because of its proximity to Jerusalem, Bethlehem's caravansary would have catered to merchants, pilgrims, and other travelers. It is possible that Joseph preferred to seek lodging in the quiet of a secluded stable to spare his pregnant wife the hurly-burly of a night among camel drivers and muleteers.

In any event, Joseph and Mary eventually bedded down somewhere in or around Bethlehem. The location and exact nature of the lodging are unknown. The only clue Luke gives us is that there was a manger, or feeding trough for domestic animals, in the place. Whether the manger was in a courtyard, a stable, or a cave Luke does not say. In later centuries the tradition developed that the birth took place in a cave used as a stable. Habitable caves are found throughout the Bethlehem hills, and it is known that they were used as stables in ancient times.

It would not have been shocking or peculiar for these simple people to spend the night sheltered in a cave where animals often slept. After all, domesticated animals lived very closely with people in those days. Most houses were built so that people occupied a raised area or upper floor, and their animals were penned or tethered on the ground floor.

Jesus is born

All Luke records of this very special night is that Jesus was born. An experienced midwife may have been called to help Mary through her labor, as later tradition described. If so, it was this unknown Bethlehem midwife who cut the baby's umbilical cord. Following typical procedures, the midwife would have brought water, or asked Joseph to fetch some, and then bathed the child. To prevent infection, she would have rubbed salt all over Jesus' body.

We can reasonably surmise that the manger would then have been filled with straw. But before the child was laid in his comfortable, utilitarian crib, Mary bound him in swaddling clothes.

Swaddling was not just a matter of wrapping a child in warm clothing. It was a method of restraining an infant's movements to ensure that its arms and legs would grow straight and strong. Tradition-

The limestone hills that stretch from Galilee to Sinai are pocked with habitable caves. In ancient times shepherds made use of these natural chambers to shelter their flocks from wind, rain, or cold and might even carve a manger, or trough, into the limestone wall for feeding their animals. Such mangers can still be seen in the Bethlehem hills. Though the Bible never says, Jesus may have been born in such a modest shelter.

ally, for at least the first six months of life, long linen strips were tightly wound around an infant's body, preventing the infant from thrashing its arms and legs. Perhaps once a day, the baby was loosed from the swaddling, washed, and gently rubbed with olive oil or dusted with powdered dried myrtle leaves, and then securely wrapped again. Although the practice is disappearing, swaddling is still customary today in some rural areas of the Near East and in parts of the Soviet Union.

Certain poor shepherds

While Jesus lay sleeping in the manger, shepherds were spending the night in the fields with their flocks of sheep somewhere in the countryside around Bethlehem. They would be the first people other than those present at the birth to learn that a miracle had occurred that night.

Shepherds play a significant part in the story of Jesus. They not only remind us that Jesus is descended from David, who was himself a shepherd from Bethlehem, they also symbolize the loving care that was to be central to Jesus' ministry. Jesus would later describe himself as the Good Shepherd, knowing that anyone in Palestine would understand that the relationship between a shepherd and his sheep was one of trust and care, as immortalized in the 23rd Psalm, which begins, "The Lord is my shepherd, I shall not want."

It was customary for shepherds to lead their flocks instead of driving them, as is done in the West. Even today, shepherds in the hills of Judea can be heard calling in a strange language to their sheep, which hasten to follow. The relationship of shepherd to sheep was so close that the shepherd of a small flock could distinguish among his sheep, and any sheep could recognize its master's voice.

The shepherd's lot was not an easy one. He was almost always outdoors, with only a camel-hair cloak and a simple head veil to protect him from the wind

The 14th-century stone-relief Nativity scene above depicts the infant Jesus wrapped in swaddling clothes and lying in a manger, as reported by Luke. The stable animals, the donkey and the ox, watch gently over the baby. The manger could either be carved into a cave wall or stand free, like the one shown below, which was found in the ruins of an ancient stable.

and the rain and from the burning heat of the midday sun. Generally, a shepherd ate only what he could carry with him—bread, cheese, olives, figs, dates, and raisins.

The sheep had to be led to forage and water, and if a sheep fell into a rocky crevice, the shepherd had to climb down to it or pull it to safety with his curved staff. If the sheep was hurt in the fall, the shepherd stretched the animal over his shoulders, carried it to a safe place, and tended its injuries. At night the sheep had to be protected from thieves and from wild animals.

The hills around Bethlehem were full of predators, including bears, leopards, jackals, and occasionally hyenas. The shepherd, usually armed with a sling-

Since the days of Abraham and the other Patriarchs, shepherds have been a familiar sight in the Holy Land. Their lives have changed little over the centuries. Shepherds are mentioned often in the New Testament, and during his ministry Jesus described himself as a shepherd of souls in John 10:14–15:"I am the good shepherd; I know my own and my own know me, as the Father knows me and I know the Father; and I lay down my life for the sheep."

shot and a rod (a wooden club embedded with flint or nails), was the sheep's sole protection against sudden and violent death. In fighting off wild animals or thieves, a shepherd might lose his own life.

To help them protect the animals under their care, shepherds often built a sheepfold. This was an enclosure of high, mortarless stone walls topped with thorn branches to keep out wild animals. The fold had no gate; so the shepherd acted as a human gate by lying across the open entryway. When shepherds shared a sheepfold, they could take turns sleeping.

Date of the Nativity

During the winter (generally from November until Passover), when pasturage became slim and the rain and cold weather threatened, the sheep could no

longer be kept outdoors and so were placed under cover. Because Luke mentions that the shepherds were "out in the field, keeping watch over their flock by night," it is very likely that the traditional date for Christmas is inaccurate.

December 25, celebrated as Christmas only since the fourth century A.D., was chosen by early Christian leaders for both practical and symbolic reasons. In the pagan Roman Empire it had been the date of the beginning of the year's most popular feast, the Saturnalia, a time of wild holiday abandon. It was also astronomically significant, occurring as the winter sun began to move back toward its zenith in the summer heavens. It was the day, in other words, when all could see that the cycle of the seasons would continue and that life would begin again after the symbolic and literal death of winter. The birth of Jesus indicated, on another plane, that life had been renewed and that spiritual rebirth, too, was possible for mankind.

According to Matthew, Jesus was born during the reign of King Herod the Great. Since Herod died in 4 B.C., the date of the Nativity must surely have been earlier. Most scholars choose 6 B.C., or possibly 7 B.C. In the sixth century A.D. calculations were made to institute the Christian Era in our calendar and to begin numbering the years based on the year of Jesus Christ's birth. Because of insufficient historical data, Dionysius Exiguus, the monk doing this work, erred in fixing the time of the birth. The error persists in our calendar to this day.

Angels heard on high

Whatever the date of that first Christmas, Luke tells us that on that night an angel of the Lord appeared to a group of Bethlehem shepherds, bathing them in terrifying brightness. "Be not afraid," said the heavenly visitor, who then explained that "a Savior, who is Christ the Lord," had just been born nearby. The angel instructed the shepherds to seek out, as a sign,

The city of Bethlehem, as it appears today, is seen in the distance through a grove of olive trees. Called Ephrath in the Book of Genesis, Bethlehem has been continuously inhabited for about 33 centuries. The name Beth-lehem is usually translated as "House of Bread." It was the home of Joseph's ancestor David, who established his kingdom in about 1000 B.C.. Every year on Christmas Eve pilgrims gather in the fields on the broad valley east of the city to celebrate the birth of Jesus.

"a babe wrapped in swaddling cloths and lying in a manger." Instantly, a multitude of angels appeared, chanting the lines that are so profoundly linked with Christmas: "Glory to God in the highest, and on earth peace, good will toward men."

When the angels vanished into the heavens, the shepherds lost no time rushing back to Bethlehem to find the infant Jesus. They believed what they had been told. The sight of Mary and Joseph and the baby in the manger confirmed their amazement. Convinced that the Almighty had worked a miracle, they spread the news, according to Luke, and brought wonder to those who heard them—but little more than wonder. It was not yet time for Jesus to be noticed by the crowds.

The adoration of the shepherds corroborated for Mary what she already knew, and she "kept all these things, pondering them in her heart." The glorious incident, however, went unnoticed by the larger world outside. While under Roman rule, Palestine had many unhappy Jews waiting for deliverance at

the hands of an expected Redeemer. Luke reports that the Redeemer had come, but only a few people knew, for the time being, and they were not people to whom Jewish leaders would readily give ear.

Fulfilling the law

Eight days after his birth, like John before him, Jesus was circumcised, in accordance with Jewish law. As Luke reminds us, there were other rituals associated with a birth. Mary, according to Jewish law, was to remain separate from all religious rites for 40 days, the first 7 of which she was considered unclean. Had the child been female, the period of uncleanness and ritual separation would have been twice as long.

When Mary's time of separation drew to a close, the family traveled the five miles north to Jerusalem for the rites of purification and sacrifice at the Temple. There, Jesus, the firstborn, had to be presented before God, in accordance with the law that a firstborn son must be redeemed in memory of God's sparing the firstborn of the Israelites when he

The Wise Men's "star" might have been a conjunction of two planets, a nova or supernova, or a comet. Some associate it with Halley's comet (above), one of the most predictable of all the comets periodically seen from earth. The comet has become a traditional symbol of the birth in Nativity paintings.

slew the firstborn of the Egyptians at the time of the Exodus. Also, it was required that Mary sacrifice two pigeons, or doves, which Joseph probably would have purchased in the courtyard of the Temple. Had he been wealthier, Joseph might have bought and sacrificed a sheep, but he was a carpenter and the price of the doves plus the five shekels he had to pay to redeem his firstborn must have been a hardship.

The Temple itself, an immense structure of cream-colored limestone adorned with marble colonnades, golden gates, and multicolored hangings, was a monument of surpassing magnificence. The religious life of the Jews was centered there. When Jesus was brought to be presented, the Temple was swarming with hundreds of paid priests, sacrificers, musicians, treasurers, and the like.

All the more astonishing, then, are the encounters reported by Luke. An old man named Simeon, informed by the Holy Spirit that he would not die before seeing with his own eyes the promised Redeemer, approached Jesus' family and took the baby in his arms. Blessing God, Simeon prayed, "Lord, now lettest thou thy servant depart in peace." He realized that he had indeed seen "a light for revelation to the Gentiles, and for glory to thy people Israel." Similarly, an 84-year-old widow named Anna, a prophetess who fasted and prayed continually in the Temple, approached and thanked God and spoke about the child to everyone who was waiting for the redemption of Jerusalem.

At this point, Luke leaves the story of Jesus' beginnings and simply states that following these sacrifices, the family returned to Nazareth. The next event he chronicles does not occur until 12 years after Jesus' birth.

Star in the East

From Matthew, however, we receive the impression that Jesus may have spent as much as the first two years of his life in Bethlehem. When Jesus was born,

we are told, "wise men from the East came to Jerusalem, saying, 'Where is he who has been born king of the Jews? For we have seen his star in the East, and have come to worship him.' "

Matthew does not fully describe the star the Wise Men followed but portrays it as a miraculous phenomenon. It is a star that moves ahead of the Wise Men and comes to rest directly over the house where Jesus was. Those who look for historical evidence have found none that exactly fits. Nothing indicates that a major comet would have naturally appeared at the time of Jesus' birth, although the well-known Halley's comet could have been seen in 12 B.C. Many comets appear throughout history with dependable regularity but so infrequently as to seem ominous or portentous.

Two other kinds of rare occurrence in the night sky are the nova and the supernova, exploding stars whose brightness is temporarily greatly increased. However, the occurrence of these phenomena, too, can generally be traced in history because they are likely to be chronicled, but none have been found in the annals of Rome, even though Roman astrologers were very active at the time of Jesus.

A third natural possibility is the conjunction of two planets, which would also have been of great significance to astrologers. It has been calculated that Jupiter and Saturn moved unusually close to each other three times in 7 B.C. Seen from time to time in the modern era, this pairing is not a single "star," but it does create a bright display. Some have speculated that Matthew, who was no astronomer, might easily have described such a remarkable phenomenon as simply a "star."

Whatever this heavenly phenomenon was, when the Wise Men who had seen it arrived in Jerusalem and asked the whereabouts of him "who has been born king of the Jews," they troubled everyone, particularly Herod the Great, who was in fact king of the Jews, a position granted him by Roman power.

We do not really know where the Wise Men came from; Scripture says merely "from the East." But the three most likely places are Persia, Babylon, and the desert regions east of Palestine. Routes commonly taken from these lands are shown on the map below. Able to travel for days without water, camels were the most practical means of transportation across deserts (left). The Wise Men could have formed their own caravan or joined caravans of merchants, which offered protection against the bandits who often threatened small groups of travelers.

"In the days of Herod"

The birth of a new king of the Jews posed an obvious threat to Herod. More than once the tyrant's reign had almost been curtailed by plots against his life. Retaining his power required the subtlest diplomacy toward his superiors, the powerful politicians of Rome, as well as continual vigilance against enemies at home, even in his own family.

Herod was accustomed to crushing potential rivals and would stop at nothing to do so. Though old and weary and perhaps half-crazed by the pain of disease, he would use any means at his disposal to find out what he wanted to know.

First, he turned to the most important priests and scribes (scholars) of Jerusalem for information. Where, he asked them, was the Christ to be born? They told him that, according to prophecy, the Christ would be born in Bethlehem; God had prom-

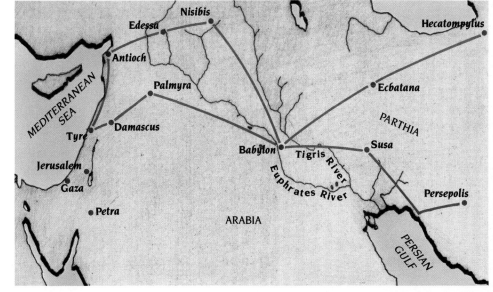

Herod had become king of Judea through political maneuvering, and he jealously guarded his crown by resorting to intrigue and violence. News of the birth of a "king of the Jews" filled him with fear that he might lose his throne. The Bible says that he secretly summoned the Wise Men, who were seeking the newborn king, to his court and questioned them about the whereabouts of this child, pretending to want to worship him. In reality Herod wanted to kill Jesus. Warned in a dream after they had found Jesus, the Wise Men never returned to Herod.

ised from that village "a ruler who will govern my people Israel." This was not what Herod wanted to hear. He had been born in the province of Idumea, south of Judea, and his ancestors had been forced to convert to Judaism. He could hardly claim that the prophecy legitimized his rule.

Secretly, Herod called the Wise Men to him for close questioning. He learned that the extraordinary "star" had first appeared about two years earlier. Dripping with hypocrisy, Herod urged the visitors to

"search diligently for the child" and to inform him when they had found the infant so that he too could worship this heir to the throne of Israel.

Adoration of the Magi

Continuing on their way, the Wise Men were led by the star to Bethlehem. But who were these men, and from what faraway lands had they come? Over the centuries many traditions have arisen around these mysteriously attractive figures. Legend has placed their number variously from 3 to 12. In later tradition they have been referred to as "kings." In medieval times they were even given names: Gaspar (Casper), Melchior, and Balthasar. Most believe that they came from Persia or Babylon; but some have suggested that they might have come from the desert regions of Arabia or perhaps even from the land once ruled by the queen of Sheba.

Matthew's term for the eastern visitors is "Magi" (translated as "Wise Men"). As described in other literature, the Magi were experts in astrology and magic. They considered themselves disciples of Zoroaster, or Zarathushtra, an important Persian religious leader, who believed in one God. By this time, however, Zoroaster's followers had become dualistic, believing in gods of good and evil and incorporating the practice of astrology into their religion.

As hereditary priests of Zoroastrianism, the Magi would have been sensitive to any unusual events in the heavens. Throughout the Mediterranean world at that time astrology was highly regarded as a science. Roman emperors, Greek philosophers and scientists, Persian magi, and ordinary farmers—all were convinced of its efficacy, which appeared to have been demonstrated by the extensive body of astronomical observations built up over generations. The priests of Zoroaster were accustomed to scanning the heavens for messages of importance to human beings. It was only natural to them that deeply significant news would be announced by a rare and startling celestial phenomenon.

But Matthew concentrates, for his purposes, on the visit itself. Whoever they were, whatever they followed, the Wise Men found Jesus with Mary. They fell down and worshiped him, presenting gifts that would be surprising to a family living modestly in Bethlehem, gifts that have often been interpreted symbolically: gold, as the sign of kingship; frankincense, a symbol of divinity; and fragrant myrrh, a substance indicating that one is destined for death.

The Gifts of the Magi

The Magi were the first Gentiles to worship Jesus, just as the shepherds were the first Jews to do so. The gifts the Magi brought probably inspired our custom of giving Christmas gifts. (In some countries gifts are given on January 6, the feast of the Epiphany, which celebrates the visit of the Magi.) According to tradition, the gold brought by the Magi honored Jesus as King and symbolized virtue. The frankincense acknowledged him as God and symbolized prayer. The myrrh indicated that he was to die (that he was human) and symbolized suffering.

The gold that the Magi brought to the Christ Child might have been in any form. This magnificent bowl is an example of ancient Persian goldwork.

The trunk and branches of the Boswellia tree, which grows in Arabia and Africa, are covered with a thin bark. When the bark is cut, a whitish resin (frankincense) emerges. In ancient times this resin was collected and burned in homage to gods.

Myrrh was an aromatic gum derived from a shrub or small tree that is a species of Commiphora. It was used in perfumes and for embalming.

Matthew tells us no more about the details of the occasion. He is more interested, it would seem, in showing his readers that the birth of Jesus had attracted the attention of experts in prophecy. In Luke the witness to this miraculous birth came from the psalms of joyous angels and from awestruck shepherds; in Matthew the testimony is strengthened by an appeal to "wise men" with access to ancient knowledge.

Slaughter of the Innocents

As the Wise Men departed, they left one request of Herod's unfulfilled and so opened the story for its next tragic episode. Warned in a dream not to return to Herod, they left for home without giving the monarch information about the baby's identity and location. In another dream, an angel warned Joseph to take his wife and son and escape to Egypt, for Herod in his rage would soon try to destroy the child even without any information from the Wise Men.

That same night, the endangered family left Bethlehem quietly and headed south. Matthew interprets their departure as a fulfillment of the prophecy, "Out of Egypt have I called my son," Here, Matthew quotes from Hosea 11:1, although the obvious original reference of the prophecy was to Israel.

Furious with the Wise Men, Herod ordered that every Bethlehem boy two years old or younger be killed—that is, every male child born there since the date when the "star" was first seen. Judging from estimates of the likely population and birth rate in Bethlehem during the first century A.D., about 25 children might have been killed. Matthew comments on this slaughter by quoting Jeremiah 31:15: "A voice was heard in Ramah, wailing and loud lamentation, Rachel weeping for her children; she refused to be consoled, because they were no more." Rachel, wife of Jacob, died in childbirth and—according to one tradition, which was probably known to Matthew—was buried near Bethlehem.

The children Rachel is weeping for in the Old Testament passage are the exiled tribes who were descended from her son, Joseph. Matthew seems to be extending their number to include—at least spiritually—the slaughtered infants of Bethlehem.

Secular history, which takes ample note of Herod and his rule, does not mention this particular massacre. Perhaps the reason is that this Slaughter of the Innocents was only one of several other massacres attributed to Herod. Whatever the reason for its not being recorded elsewhere, it nonetheless helped create Herod's reputation in history as an unusually cruel tyrant. The figure of the aging King Herod and the shocking stratagem he employed for protecting his throne have fired the imaginations of Christians through the last 2,000 years. Interest in Herod reached its climax when he was portrayed as the ultimate villain of medieval dramas, ranting and raging about the stage to the delight of audiences.

The Flight into Egypt

Herod's fury in Bethlehem failed of its intention. The Holy Family slipped through his grasp, protected by the angelic warning. In doing so, they had resorted to a traditional Jewish remedy in times of distress, for Egypt had for centuries been a land of refuge. Whenever drought and famine struck, thousands would emigrate to the fertile farms along the life-giving Nile River. The best-known example in the Old Testament is the journey undertaken by the brothers of Joseph to buy grain in time of famine. Centuries later, at the time of the Babylonian conquest, a large company of Jews, including the prophet Jeremiah, migrated to Egypt.

By the first century A.D., about a million Jews were living in Egypt. They were concentrated in Alexandria but were also found in smaller communities throughout Egypt. They must have participated successfully in the economic life of Egypt, despite opposition by the Greeks and heavy taxation.

On their flight into Egypt, Joseph and his family would have had to pass through Sinai, a large triangular wedge of land jutting into the Red Sea. It is a savage wasteland of rocky mountains and barren plateaus, with high sand dunes to the north, along the Mediterranean shore. This is the desert wilderness where the Hebrews wandered after being led out of Egypt by Moses, as told in the Book of Exodus.

To reach this haven would have required a lengthy journey across sun-baked desert wastes. Joseph would probably have taken his family from Bethlehem west to the shores of the Mediterranean, then followed a coastal road to the borders of Egypt.

The trip and the stay in the foreign land have been the subject of folk tales and ancient writings that are not considered accurate, but the New Testament does not offer any facts about the episode. We know that a young Jewish family could have found a welcome in Egypt. We can suppose that Joseph could have found work as a carpenter or as a laborer, if necessary, in that rich land. We can assume that these unsophisticated villagers, Mary and Joseph, would have been homesick for the country of their birth, for their close relatives, and for the customs of home. In short, we can use our imaginations, based upon what historians know about the period.

After the death of Herod in 4 B.C., Joseph and his family returned to their home in southern Galilee. Once more they crossed the bleak Sinai and Negev deserts, but this time they avoided going through Judea, which had passed into the hands of Herod's power-hungry son Archelaus.

"I bring you good news of a great joy ... for to you is born this day in the city of David a Savior, who is Christ the Lord."

Since the dawn of Christianity, artists have translated their impressions of the events in the life of Jesus into paintings, sculpture, and other forms of art. Here is a tiny sampling of works inspired by the birth of Jesus.

"And the angel said to her, 'Do not be afraid, Mary, for you have found favor with God. And behold, you will conceive in your womb and bear a son.'" Luke 1:30–31. Glazed terra-cotta altarpiece by Italian sculptor Andrea della Robbia (1435–1525).

"When Joseph woke from sleep, he did as the angel of the Lord commanded him; he took his wife, but knew her not until she had borne a son; and he called his name Jesus." Matthew 1:24–25. Detail from a 15th-century German painting.

"And she gave birth to her first-born son and wrapped him in swaddling cloths, and laid him in a manger, because there was no place for them in the inn." Luke 2:7. Painting by the 16th-century Italian artist Federico Barocci.

"And in that region there were shepherds out in the field, keeping watch over their flock by night. And an angel of the Lord appeared to them." Luke 2:8–9. Illuminated page from a 15th-century Book of Hours.

+SCS BALTHASSAR +SCS MELCHIOR +SCS CASPAR

"And when the time came for their purification according to the law of Moses, they brought him up to Jerusalem to present him to the Lord." Luke 2:22. Detail from a painting by the Dutch artist Jan van Scorel (1495–1562).

"And going into the house they saw the child with Mary his mother, and . . . offered him gifts, gold and frankincense and myrrh." Matthew 2:11. A 6th-century Italian mosaic (top) and a 19th-century English stained glass window (left).

"Behold, an angel of the Lord appeared to Joseph in a dream and said, 'Rise, take the child and his mother, and flee to Egypt, and remain there till I tell you; for Herod is about to search for the child, to destroy him.' And he rose and took the child and his mother by night, and departed to Egypt."
Matthew 2:13–14. Fresco attributed to the pre-Renaissance Italian master Giotto.

Chapter Two

A Troubled Land

Flanked by the Mediterranean on the west and wide stretches of desert on the east, the Holy Land served as a vital link between Asia and Africa. Throughout history powerful empires fought to control this strategic ribbon of land.

Southeast of Jerusalem, in the wilderness near the Dead Sea, an immense outcrop of reddish-brown stone lifts high above the surrounding desolation. At the top, some 1,300 feet up and commanding the horizon in all directions, the rulers of Judea had placed a military post. This was the mesalike bastion of Masada, the country's southernmost citadel. It was to this sanctuary, in 40 B.C., that the most skillful and ambitious politician in Palestine was fleeing for his life.

Herod had left Jerusalem under cover of darkness, slipping out of the palace with a number of his relatives and armed retainers. Somehow the fugitives had managed to elude the detachment of mercenaries assigned to guard them. They threaded their way through the city's dark, narrow streets, past splintered market stalls and the hulks of burned-out buildings—the detritus of riot and civil war. Beyond Jerusalem's gates this small band skirted the tents of the invading Parthians, fierce mounted warriors of the Persian Empire, who had galloped in from across the eastern deserts to capture Jerusalem.

Having been named king of Judea by the Romans, Herod had to use force to take Jerusalem from Antigonus, who himself had taken it by force just three years earlier. In 37 B.C. Herod's armies stormed the fortress in Jerusalem with catapults and battering rams. Using logs, they rolled towering siege engines up to the walls to meet the enemy face to face. Antigonus' troops retaliated with showers of arrows and missiles and with fire. Herod's siege was just one of many such attacks on Jerusalem, for whoever held the city also controlled Judea.

Flight to Masada

All through that night and well into the next day the group fled southward, stopping from time to time to fend off assaults from Parthian horsemen. The women were mounted on pack animals; only Herod's mother, too aged to ride, traveled in a donkey cart. At one point its wheel hit a rock, overturning the cart and throwing the old lady to the ground. She lay motionless, and for one brief moment Herod's resolve seemed to falter. Thinking her dead, and fearful that any delay would mean capture, he drew his sword as if to hurl himself upon it. Only the pleas of his lieutenants stayed his hand. The cart was heaved upright, and his mother, ruffled but relatively unhurt, was lifted back inside. By daybreak they had passed Bethlehem. Eventually, the company reached the sun-baked landscape of Idumea, Palestine's southernmost region, where Masada was located, and Herod's ancestral home.

Much of what we know about Herod and his times comes down to us from Josephus, the first-century A.D. Jewish soldier and historian who chronicled the history of the Jews from the Creation to the fall of Masada in A.D. 73 after the Jewish revolt against Rome. According to Josephus, Herod was clever and quick-tempered, with a reputation for efficient and sometimes brutal action.

Although Herod was not a Jew by ancestry, he was one by "conversion." About 125 B.C., after Idumea was brought under Jewish control, John Hyrcanus, the Hasmonean ruler and high priest, had forcibly converted all its inhabitants to Judaism to gain their loyalty. By age 25, Herod, son of Idumea's governor, had achieved a high position in the complex hierarchy of the Jewish state: the governorship of Galilee, followed by that of Samaria and of Coele-Syria to the north. Now, less than a decade later, he found himself with nothing. It was the lowest ebb of his mercurial career.

The reason for this turnabout was the defeat of the then high priest, the aging Hyrcanus II, by his rebellious nephew, Antigonus. Antigonus had raised an army in Syria to the north and had marched through Galilee and down to Jerusalem. Thousands of Judeans, unhappy with Hyrcanus' regime, had rallied to the younger man's banner. To augment his forces, Antigonus had called in the Parthians, enticing their monarch with a promise of 1,000 silver talents and 500 well-born women for the harem. Overcome by the powerful enemy, Jerusalem fell and

Masada, Herod's stronghold in the Idumean wilderness, is situated atop an isolated rock that rises dramatically 1,300 feet above the western shore of the Dead Sea. The remains of the fortress complex were excavated in the 1950's and 1960's.

Judea's government collapsed. Hyrcanus was taken prisoner by the Parthians, along with Herod's older brother, Phasael. Bereft of his titles, stripped bare of worldly powers and resources (except for some money and personal effects he had prudently sent ahead to Idumea), Herod had only one option—to flee.

Once Herod had made certain that his family and followers were safely installed in Masada, he journeyed alone to Nabatea, home of his mother's Arab kinsmen, to seek help. He needed money—for arms, for mercenaries, and in particular as ransom for Phasael, whom he hoped to free from his captors.

Destination Rome

The Nabateans wanted no part of Herod's quarrels. They saw no reason to provoke the victorious Parthians by giving him refuge; besides, they owed Herod's family a large sum that they had no intention of repaying. Turned away empty handed, the clever leader devised a new plan. He would cross the deserts to Egypt and sail to Rome, where he would lay his case before the rulers of the mightiest power in the known world.

Egypt's queen, the wily Cleopatra, greeted the fugitive with lavish hospitality. She had an eye for strong men, particularly men of proven military skill. Would Herod become a commander in her army? she reportedly asked. It was a seductive offer, but Herod declined. He had just heard some shocking news regarding his brother and the captive ruler and high priest Hyrcanus. A messenger from Judea had arrived with word that Hyrcanus had been savagely mutilated; Antigonus had slashed off both his ears so that he would be banned from the office of high priest (only a person without physical deformities was worthy of the honor). Phasael, fearful that he would be the next victim, and too proud to suffer abuse from the enemy, had taken matters into his own hands; he had "dashed his head against a rock and removed himself from the world of the living."

The Historian Josephus

Our most extensive record of the politics and life of the Jews at the time of Jesus and his followers comes from the Jewish historian known as Flavius Josephus, whose Hebrew name was Joseph ben Mattathias. A man of immense confidence with a strong instinct for self-preservation, Josephus survived the troubled times he lived in and wrote two major works about the period: *The Jewish War*, which ends with the capture of Jerusalem in A.D. 70, and *Jewish Antiquities*, the story of the Jewish people up to the fall of Masada in A.D. 73.

Josephus was born in Jerusalem of a wealthy priestly family about A.D. 37.

A 19th-century etching of Josephus

His native language was Aramaic, though he knew Hebrew and some Greek. As a young man he studied with the various Jewish sects and even lived as an ascetic for three years in the desert. In A.D. 64, at the age of 27, he went to Rome to plead the cause of some priests who had been sent to Emperor Nero for trial. He returned to Judea with a lasting impression of the glory and power of Rome. As war fever grew he was put in command of the Jewish forces in Galilee, but he was overwhelmed by the Roman general Vespasian. Josephus surrendered and with daring presence of mind predicted that Vespasian would become emperor. When the prediction came true, Josephus' future was secure. He adopted the emperor's family name, Flavius, and was granted the rights of Roman citizenship. After the war, he was taken to Rome where he composed his histories and where he died about A.D. 100.

Josephus says very little directly about Jesus or his followers, a movement that was still of little consequence in his day. A passage that describes Jesus in some detail was, in the opinion of many scholars, added or substantially altered about two centuries after Josephus' death. Josephus does, however, discuss most of the major political figures of the time, including an extensive portrayal of Herod the Great, whom he depicts as both an astute politician and an oppressive tyrant.

Cleopatra　　　　Mark Antony　　　　Octavian

Yet, as the messenger reported, "Phasael bore his death with cheerfulness, for he left behind one who would avenge his death." So Herod's purpose was set. He embarked for Rome, bound on retribution—and unimagined future glory.

When Herod arrived in Rome, the republic was recovering from a civil upheaval of its own—a sequence of battles and power grabs that had followed the assassination four years earlier, in 44 B.C., of its great leader, Julius Caesar. Among the victors in this strife was Mark Antony, one of Caesar's generals, who commanded Rome's forces in the east. Antony happened to be in Rome when Herod rode into the city. Antony received the visitor as an old family friend, as indeed he was. In years past, as Rome's unstoppable legions were extending the city's power into the region of Palestine, Herod's father had contributed provisions to Antony's troops in one of his campaigns.

King of Judea

The assistance and authority Herod sought were promptly assured him. Then Antony introduced him to Octavian, Caesar's adopted heir, soon to rule as the emperor Augustus. Both men together escorted Herod into the Senate. There were lofty speeches full of praise for the young visitor's loyalty and prowess—and pointed references to Antigonus' treachery and the Parthian menace. Thus prompted, the senators rose as a body to proclaim the Idumean refugee king of Judea. The Senate's vote was sealed when Antony, Octavian, and the Roman magistrates, accompanied by the newly appointed king of the Jews, offered a sacrifice to Jupiter. They then deposited the decree in the Capitol, and the day ended with a lavish banquet given by Antony. Within seven days of his arrival in Rome, Herod was on his way home to claim his throne.

Herod's territories

The land that by title was now his lay in a narrow, ragged strip along the Mediterranean's eastern shore. Its borders were in constant flux, shifting in and out through the centuries in response to the lines of political force that time and again rippled over them. A local ruler might switch allegiance, or a city break away, or an imperious neighbor take over an adjoining region. As the borders changed, so, often, did the names by which this land was known. In the days of Abraham and Moses, it was called Canaan; its inhabitants were the Canaanites, who by tradition descended from the biblical Ham, one of the sons of Noah. After the Hebrew tribal territories were united under one ruler, it was called Israel. When the kingdom was divided after the rule of Solomon there were two kingdoms—Israel and Judah (later named Judea). It was the fifth-century B.C. Greek historian Herodotus who dubbed the land Palestine, in reference to the Philistines, who had taken the seacoast of Canaan and engaged in trade with the Greeks.

Herod's territory stretched from the flanks of Mt. Hermon in the north, its shimmering 9,232-foot-high snowcap rising just beyond the border, to the

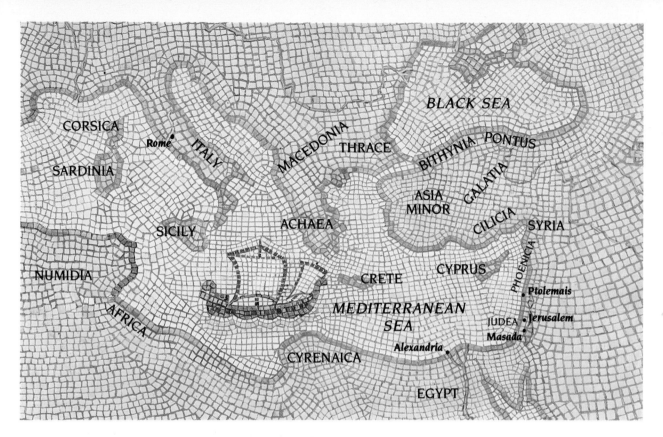

Stripped of his territories, in 40 B.C. Herod embarked on a year-long journey to get help in his quest for kingship. First he fled to Masada. Then he proceeded over wide deserts to Cleopatra's Egypt. From there he sailed across the Mediterranean to Rome for his crown, and finally returned to Ptolemais—a voyage of some 3,000 miles.

To celebrate being named king of Judea, Herod joined with Octavian, Mark Antony, and others in offering a sacrifice to the Roman god Jupiter. A first-century B.C. Roman frieze (below) shows what the sacrifice might have entailed: a bull, a sheep, and a boar, which would have been an anathema to Jews, are about to be slain as part of a lustrum, or purification rite.

The sweep and scope of the biblical lands, as they appear today, are shown in this map made from satellite images. The images were taken from the NASA satellite Landsat 4 by detectors that read the relative brightness of small segments of the terrain at different locations and translate them into numerical values that are stored in a computer. The numbers are processed by the computer and made into a map with color added. The colors help distinguish different features, but they are not the true colors of the land. Red indicates vegetation. White indicates areas of high light reflection, such as sand or the snow on the tip of Mount Hermon. Black represents areas of low light reflection, or high light absorption, such as the deep waters of the Mediterranean, the Sea of Galilee, and the northern basin of the Dead Sea; the shallower waters of the southern basin appear more blue. Green shows plowed soil, and gray indicates urban areas.

salt and alkaline wastes of the Dead Sea, 1,290 feet below sea level and thus the lowest body of water on earth. In less than 150 miles, the land descends from well-watered lushness of fertile fields to stark desolation of the desert.

The fertile soils of Galilee, the northernmost province, yielded wheat and barley, along with vegetables, flax for making linen, walnuts, figs, grapes—also used for wine—and other fruits. Crops were plentiful enough to support hundreds of mountain villages in relative comfort. Timber grew in the rugged northern highlands, and the Sea of Galilee sustained a thriving fresh-water fishing industry. The richest part of the region was the Valley of Jezreel, about 20 miles at its broadest point and rippling with grain.

A similar agricultural profusion, though somewhat diminished, extended south from Jezreel to the region of Samaria. Along the coast, the well-watered Plain of Sharon was heavily forested, even marshy in places. Then inland, as the country ascends in rounded limestone hills to a central moun-

tainous spine, the land becomes steadily drier. Still, there were isolated fertile areas suitable for garden plots, vineyards, and olive groves. Flocks of sheep and goats grazed on the scrubby grasses of the uplands. Beyond the hills, the land dips sharply to the valley of the Jordan, which cuts its way south toward the Dead Sea and offers pockets of fertile soil for growing cereal crops.

South of Samaria the rainfall lessens, the hillsides become stonier, and the gardens are smaller and more scattered. Such was the aspect of the country-side around Jerusalem, in Judea. The city perched in isolation atop a projecting limestone spur, overlooking a semiarid moorland of scrub and thorn bush, cut by steep gorges and narrow defiles. Few roads led down to the coastal plain; only in periods of its greatest expansion could Judea lay claim to this richly productive region. Eastward toward the Jordan the land tumbles down in yellow, waterless hills—the Wilderness of Judea. One sudden patch of greenery relieved its starkness, and that was the Jordan Valley. The oasis at Jericho, the oldest in-

Mount Hermon, crowned with perpetual snow, rules serenely over the verdant hills and valleys of Galilee. The awesome splendor of its presence stands in sharp contrast to the frenetic activity of men like Herod who have ruled in its mighty shadow. Mount Hermon formed a natural boundary to Herod's kingdom; all of Herod's lands were south of it, and it is from the south that it is seen above.

habited city known to man, was famous for its date palms and for the sap of its balsam trees—the Balm of Gilead, fragrant and medicinal, with a reputation for curing headaches and cataracts. But in the south the desert increasingly takes over until in Idumea, part of the land of the Old Testament Edomites, descendants of Esau, it could support only a hard-scrabble populace of nomadic herdsmen.

Land of contrasts

Such were the principal areas of Herod's territory—rugged, compact, more or less agricultural depending on local conditions of soil and rainfall. Many of its villagers lived in relative isolation, because of the rugged, hilly terrain. It was virtually landlocked,

despite the nearby Mediterranean, for its smooth coastline offered no natural harbors. There is no word for port in biblical Hebrew.

In times of political strength, Palestine's boundaries might edge out across the Jordan to contain some minor kingdoms to the east: Gaulanitis (today's Golan Heights), its gray escarpment rising directly east of the Sea of Galilee; beyond this, the lava-strewn tableland of Batanea and Trachonitis; then farther south Perea, the ancient tribal hill country of Ammon and Moab, where a persistent farmer could scratch a living from the sun-baked ground. At its greatest extent it covered some 8,000 square miles. But overall, with the exception of Galilee and parts of Samaria, the land scarcely overflowed with milk and honey—unless seen from the vantage of a desert wanderer who had even less.

Herod's new kingdom might seem a poor prize for larger powers to squabble over, but its value lay elsewhere—in an accident of geography. Palestine was a strategic bonanza to whoever could control it. This ribbon of land, with the sea on one side and the desert on the other, provided the single viable land route for both trade and conquest between the vastly more powerful states that bordered it. Century after century, millennium upon millennium, processions had trekked across it: the armies of the pharaohs, caravans from Arabia, chariots from Assyria and horsemen from Babylonia, the Persians, the Macedonians, Greeks, and later the Romans and the Parthians. Here they met and mingled. And as waves build up a sandbar, each sweeping influx left its residue of population and custom.

The story of Hebrew settlement begins sometime in the 13th century B.C., when a group of Semitic tribesmen, descendants of the Patriarch Abraham, migrated up from Egypt into the land of Canaan. To all appearances they were no different from any other seminomads—living in goat-hair tents, herding their livestock from oasis to oasis, much like the

The flowering hillside above is typical of the rolling countryside in Galilee. The Sea of Galilee itself is seen above right. Actually an inland lake through which the Jordan flows, this peaceful body of water is 12 miles long and 8 miles across at its widest point. It is teeming with fish, and in Jesus' time its shores were dotted with tiny villages whose inhabitants made a living from the lake's bounty.

Mount Tabor, shown at right, lies about five miles southeast of Nazareth. In Psalm 89:12, the domelike mountain, along with Mount Hermon, is said to praise the name of God and thus demonstrate God's might, and in Jeremiah 46:18 Tabor is seen as a sign of the surety of God's judgment.

Bedouin families that still trek through parts of Israel and the Sinai region. But in their hearts they carried a single, overwhelming belief that they alone enjoyed a special relationship with the Deity and, furthermore, that this Deity was the one, only, supreme and universal God.

It was not an entirely new idea, their belief in a single god. Monotheism had surfaced, briefly, in Mesopotamia (Abraham's place of origin) and again in Egypt during the 14th century B.C. But no people clung to it with such tenacity as the Hebrews. And none claimed so personal a bond or such a sense of God-appointed destiny. The Book of Genesis tells us that the Lord promised Abraham to "make of you a great nation, and I will bless you, and make your name great. . . ." In the Book of Exodus the Lord reaffirmed the promise by telling Moses: "Depart, go up hence, you and the people whom you have brought up out of the land of Egypt, to the land of which I swore to Abraham, Isaac, and Jacob. . . ."

And so sometime in the 13th century B.C. the Hebrews moved north into Canaan, battling their way against the peoples already settled there. It was never a continuous or unified effort. The newcomers were divided into 12 proudly independent tribes, each by tradition descended from the sons and grandsons of Jacob, and each fought to secure its own land. Throughout the next two centuries while Canaan was in a state of anarchy, the seafaring Philistines, Israel's neighbors to the west, were gathering strength. After generations of military threats by the Philistines, the Hebrew tribes finally banded together under their most vigorous military leader, Saul, who became Israel's first king.

At the southern end of Herod's kingdom was the Dead Sea, the lowest lying body of water in the world, its surface almost 1,300 feet below sea level. The Dead Sea stretches 49 miles from north to south and 10 miles across. Although no trace of them remains today, some scholars speculate that Sodom and Gomorrah were located at a site that is now beneath the shallow waters of the southern end of the sea. The Dead Sea marks the most dramatic plunge of the Great Rift Valley, a major geological fault line in the earth's crust that runs northward parallel to the Mediterranean coast and southward to the Red Sea and into Africa.

The Jordan River, seen at far left, linked the northern and southern parts of Herod's kingdom. Rising at the base of Mount Hermon, it flows through the Sea of Galilee and then south into the Dead Sea. The Dead Sea is characterized by desolate salt flats (like the ones shown below at far left) created by heavy evaporation of the sea. East of Jerusalem is the Wilderness of Judea, a desert watered only by springs and by wadis, streams that become torrents when rain falls but that are dry most of the year. Shown at left and below are two oases on the Wadi Qilt. A route for wilderness travelers ran along the wadis.

Anointing with Oil

Oils were used to cleanse the skin and protect it from the dry climate. Some were perfumed with plants, flowers, or barks from India and other far-off lands. Because these oils were expensive, they were kept in alabastrons, small alabaster or clay containers, with narrow necks that restricted the flow, like the one shown at right. Oils were also used for ceremonial purposes. Kings were anointed with holy oil at their coronation to show that they were consecrated to God. The term *Messiah* comes from the Hebrew *mashi'ah* ("anointed one"). A third-century A.D. wall painting in the synagogue at Dura-Europus, Syria, shows Samuel anointing David.

House of David

When Saul died, sometime around the year 1000 B.C., David took command of the kingdom. He completed the conquest of Philistia, cleared out pockets of Canaanite resistance, established a new capital at Jerusalem, and unified the contentious tribes into a single people.

This was the supreme turning point, the trumpet blast of destiny announcing God's promise fulfilled, in which the sons of Abraham and Moses saw themselves transformed from nomadic warriors into rulers of a kingdom. Under King David and his son Solomon, the power of the Israelites reached its historical apogee. The kingdom stretched from the Gulf of Aqaba in the south, west to the Mediterranean, and north past Damascus. Tribute poured in, bringing a sudden infusion of wealth. Solomon, who had a particularly quick head for business, took large revenues from copper mines at Ezion-geber, at the head of the Gulf of Aqaba, and set up a lucrative trade monopoly, exchanging horses from Asia Minor for chariots from Egypt.

Much of this wealth went into the embellishment of Jerusalem. After Solomon built a splendid palace, he went to work on the Temple, so memorably lavish that it strained even his large treasury—and required a drastic increase in taxes. The literary arts, too, flourished. For the first time, the oral traditions that had sustained the Hebrews in the desert, the laws of Moses and the stories of the Patriarchs, were set down. Although no documents from this period have survived, this body of writings, augmented by later additions, eventually evolved into the first five books of the Old Testament, the Torah, or the Pentateuch, regarded as the core document of the Jewish faith.

The united kingdom lasted less than a century, but seen in retrospect it was a golden age, and it glowed with a shimmering luster that burned itself into the memory of each subsequent generation of

Jews. The Second Book of Samuel describes God's promise of permanence to David and his line of royal successors. For many Jews in other, troubled times that promise meant that God's annointed, his Messiah, must come from the House of David.

Divided kingdom

Trouble began immediately upon Solomon's death about 922, when his son Rehoboam refused the people's entreaty to lighten the yoke of labor and taxes and indeed promised to add to it. The northern 10 tribes rebelled, led by Jeroboam, an opponent of Solomon who had returned from political asylum in Egypt. And so two Jewish states—Judah in the south and Israel in the north—now confronted each other in bitter opposition.

From this point on, the destiny of the Jews as an independent, united political force went steadily downhill. Israel, richer in land and more populous than its southern neighbor, enjoyed two centuries of relative influence and prosperity. Its capital, Samaria, grew in size and sophistication. Yet all the while a great new power, Assyria, was gathering strength beyond the northern border. When Israel tried to resist its bullying, the armies of Assyria exploded out of Mesopotamia, overran Damascus, and in 721 B.C., after a three-year siege, captured Samaria. The city was laid waste, and Assyrian documents tell us that 27,290 of its leading citizens were carried off by the conquerors. (According to tradition, these became Israel's so-called Ten Lost Tribes, and they simply vanished, swallowed up in the vast reaches of Mesopotamia.) A migration of foreign settlers surged in to take their place. Israel became a province of the Assyrian Empire, its Jewish heritage for the time being largely obscured.

Judah clung on precariously, its territories sharply curtailed. The Assyrian armies marched through on their way to battle Egypt and in passing extracted a heavy tribute from the Jerusalem government. But with the proud tenacity of hill people the world over, the Judahites managed to keep their independence. Then, as Assyria's vigor waned in the following century, there was hope that the nation would regain something of its former glory. But a new imperial force arose in Mesopotamia, the Babylonians, and about 612 B.C. their armies took the Assyrian capital, Nineveh. Their old enemy smashed by a seeming political ally—surely this augured well for Judah. But once set rolling, the chariots of empire do not easily stop. The Babylonian cohorts under Nebuchadnezzar II swarmed down into Palestine, following the general invasion route marked out by their Assyrian predecessors. This time Judah's king refused to pay tribute. Nebuchadnezzar responded by storming Jerusalem. He exacted a cruel punishment. His soldiers ravaged the city, then turned against Solomon's magnificent Temple, stripping it of gold and demolishing it stone by stone. And the most prominent Judahites and their families, numbering many thousands of people, were taken in chains to Babylonia.

Return from captivity

The Babylonian Captivity lasted only 48 years, from 586 through 538 B.C., but the impact on the Jewish soul was such that it might as well have been a thousand. The response was a massive outpouring of religious eloquence—some of it poignantly lyrical, some visionary and apocalyptic. "By the waters of Babylon," a psalmist sang, "there we sat down and wept, when we remembered Zion . . . .If I forget you, O Jerusalem, let my right hand wither." A leading exile figure was the prophet Ezekiel, whose utterances foretold the destruction of Judah's enemies by fire and earthquake, a return to Israel, and in tones that are openly messianic, the reappearance of King David and the revival of his kingdom.

The return soon did take place, following another upheaval in Mesopotamia. In 539 B.C. Cyrus the

In one of the pivotal battles in the ancient world, Alexander the Great defeated the seemingly invincible Persian king Darius III in 333 B.C. at Issus, near the northeastern corner of the Mediterranean. The battle is depicted at right in a mosaic of the first century B.C. found in Pompeii. Alexander is seen attacking a Persian soldier with his lance, while the terrified Darius looks on from his chariot, ready to flee. Having conquered Asia Minor in a year's time, Alexander went on to take Tyre, Gaza, and nearby Jerusalem. Alexander continued his march to Egypt, where he founded Alexandria, the grandest city of the many he established in the course of his conquest. But his empire was short-lived. Just a decade after the battle, Alexander died in Babylon of an undiagnosed disease.

Great of Persia conquered Babylon, and a year later he issued a decree restoring the Jewish state under imperial patronage. When the exiles arrived in Jerusalem, they found the city and their Temple in ruins. The painful task of rebuilding was begun. By 515 B.C. the capstone of the Temple was set in place; for the next 585 years it would stand as the physical center of Jewish faith, a living symbol of God's favor and future promise. In the fifth century B.C. another wave of returnees left Babylon under Ezra and Nehemiah, sparking a religious revival and an even stronger sense of religious mission.

For the next few centuries the Jewish state continued as a tiny theocracy in the hills, its laws modeled strictly on the precepts of the Torah. It owed an overall allegiance to Persia, whose emperor appoint-ed a resident governor to watch over his interests. But most local matters were left in the hands of an hereditary priesthood, with the high priest representing the supreme exponent of Jewish political authority. For the most part Jerusalem was untouched by big power concerns. Then, in 332 B.C., an event took place that once again swept the Jewish people into the mainstream of world affairs.

Rise of Alexander the Great

Throughout its earlier history the main external influences on Palestine had come from Africa and the east; now, 1,000 miles to the northwest, in Macedonia, a new force was stirring. Suddenly, as though touched by divine lightning, the young Alexander the Great, scarcely out of his teens, collected an army, roared into Asia Minor, defeated the last, enfeebled Persian ruler, assumed all his territories, and in just a dozen years amassed the largest empire the Mediterranean world had yet seen. Alexander marched through Palestine in 332 B.C., where he met no resistance, and continued south to gather up Egypt. He marched back through Palestine again on his way northeast to Persia and on toward India. In his wake he confirmed the rights of local independence that had been granted under the Persians and put in his own governors. For the next thousand years the main currents of power and influence would flow from the west.

Alexander's stellar career burned out as quickly as it had begun. Sojourning in Babylon in 323 B.C., he came down with a fever and died in his 33rd year. His generals fell to squabbling over the lands in his vast realm, which they eventually parceled out among them. As a result, much of the ancient world, from Greece in the west through Afghanistan in the east, came under the rule of rival Greek-speaking Macedonian overlords. The period known by historians as the Hellenistic Age, dominated by the culture of Hellas, or Greece, had begun. Syria and Babylonia went to Seleucus, as did eventually a large portion of Asia Minor. Ptolemy I took Egypt and also staked out Palestine and its surrounding area. He had to fight to win it, but by 301 B.C. he had established his supremacy.

Ptolemy and his successors proved to be relatively benign despots. Palestine was joined with Phoenicia (on the Mediterranean coast northwest of Galilee), southern Syria, and the lands across the Jordan (Transjordan) into a single administrative district, all incorporated into greater Egypt. But within this framework individual states were given wide latitude to govern themselves. Thus in Judea, as Judah was now called, the hereditary high priest acted as day-to-day ruler, presiding over an advisory council of elders, seeing to such matters as security, the water

supply, and the collection of taxes—all in addition to his duties as the religious leader of his people. The Jews enjoyed freedom of worship and the right to follow their ancestral laws as they saw fit.

At the same time, the pervading Hellenistic civilization brought about another massive redistribution of ethnic groups. Thousands of Greek settlers swarmed into Samaria and Galilee, mingling with the already mixed population. The Ptolemies were tireless builders of cities, and they founded urban centers on the Greek pattern all along the Mediterranean coast, in lower Galilee, and in the desert beyond the Jordan. Gaza, Ascalon (which gave its name to the shallots, grown locally), Ptolemais—all took on a notably Hellenistic flavor. Prosperous, they attracted large numbers of the more enterprising and outward-looking Jews.

The lure of Hellenism

The same migratory urge worked in the opposite direction, as many thousands of Jewish families moved away from Palestine to Hellenistic communities in other lands. A thriving expatriate colony sprouted in Alexandria, Ptolemies' Egyptian capital, where Jews basked in an enlightened favoritism that set them well above the native Egyptians. The Alexandria settlement grew in wealth and prestige, eventually numbering a million souls. It was the site of an early synagogue, and its scribes produced a Greek translation of the Old Testament that became standard throughout the ancient world. Other Jewish émigrés flocked to Antioch in Syria, to Corinth in Greece, and to various outposts in Asia Minor. Along with the exile community that still remained in Babylonia, and another founded in Persian times at Hyrcania on the Caspian Sea, the number of Jews living abroad, Jews of the Diaspora, came to outnumber those in Palestine.

The increasing enchantment with Greek culture was bound to incense the more devout in Jerusalem.

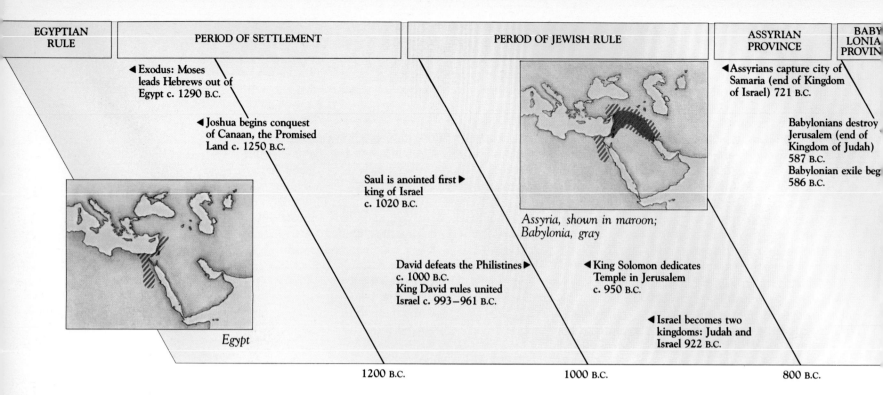

◀ **Exodus: Moses leads Hebrews out of Egypt c. 1290 B.C.**

◀ **Joshua begins conquest of Canaan, the Promised Land c. 1250 B.C.**

Saul is anointed first ▶ king of Israel c. 1020 B.C.

David defeats the Philistines ▶ c. 1000 B.C. King David rules united Israel c. 993–961 B.C.

◀ **King Solomon dedicates Temple in Jerusalem c. 950 B.C.**

◀ **Israel becomes two kingdoms: Judah and Israel 922 B.C.**

◀ **Assyrians capture city of Samaria (end of Kingdom of Israel) 721 B.C.**

Babylonians destroy Jerusalem (end of Kingdom of Judah) 587 B.C. Babylonian exile beg 586 B.C.

Assyria, shown in maroon; Babylonia, gray

Egypt

1200 B.C. 1000 B.C. 800 B.C.

From its earliest history, the Holy Land was ruled time and time again by a foreign power, beginning with the Egyptians, as indicated in the chronology above. In the two millennia from the age of the Patriarchs about 2000 B.C. to the birth of Jesus, the Jews experienced only two periods of self-rule: from the time of Saul to the fall of Jerusalem early in the sixth century B.C. and once more during the nearly eight decades after the Maccabean revolt.

Its material benefits to Judaism were obvious. By religious duty, each adult male, no matter where he lived, was expected to donate a half-shekel a year for the upkeep of the Temple in Jerusalem. Expatriot urban Jews had grown prosperous through trade and craftsmanship; given the number of overseas Jews, they were a major source of state revenue. At the same time, however, Hellenism was seen by many Jews as a dangerous subversion of Jewish tradition and identity.

While the conflicting sentiments of worldliness and religious conservatism simmered quietly, the main threat to Palestine's serenity came from the Seleucid rulers in Syria, who had designs on their neighbors to the south. The dynasty's intentions became bloodily overt in the century's final years when a new Syrian king, Antiochus III, moved down the coast and crossed into Samaria and Judea. The reigning Ptolemy hurried up from Egypt and

drove him out. But Antiochus tried again, and in 198 B.C. he succeeded.

At first the change of potentates hardly seemed to affect the fortunes of the Jews. Local autonomy and religious freedom were reaffirmed. Taxes went north to Antioch instead of south to Alexandria. That was all, but in time it would be enough. The Seleucids were ambitious empire builders, and Antiochus made the mistake of invading Greece. Rome responded by defeating Antiochus at Magnesia in 190 B.C., and he was forced to abandon his newly won territories in Asia Minor. The Romans imposed a punishing tribute, and to meet it, the Seleucids had to raise taxes. Not only that, it seems a Seleucid deputy broke into the Temple at Jerusalem and attempted to steal the treasury.

The Seleucids' appetite for empire continued unslaked under Antiochus' son, Antiochus IV, who took the grandiose title *Epiphanes*—"God made

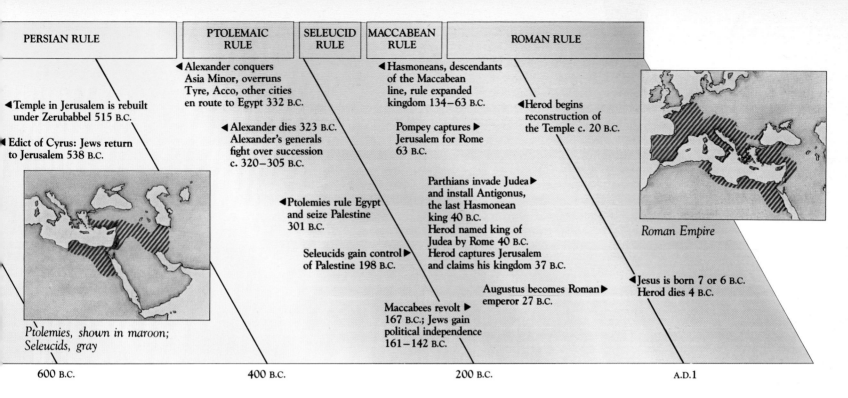

◀ Alexander conquers Asia Minor, overruns Tyre, Acco, other cities en route to Egypt 332 B.C.

◀ Hasmoneans, descendants of the Maccabean line, rule expanded kingdom 134–63 B.C.

◀ Herod begins reconstruction of the Temple c. 20 B.C.

◀ Temple in Jerusalem is rebuilt under Zerubbabel 515 B.C.

◀ Edict of Cyrus: Jews return to Jerusalem 538 B.C.

◀ Alexander dies 323 B.C. Alexander's generals fight over succession c. 320–305 B.C.

Pompey captures ▶ Jerusalem for Rome 63 B.C.

◀ Ptolemies rule Egypt and seize Palestine 301 B.C.

Parthians invade Judea ▶ and install Antigonus, the last Hasmonean king 40 B.C.
Herod named king of Judea by Rome 40 B.C.
Herod captures Jerusalem and claims his kingdom 37 B.C.

Seleucids gain control ▶ of Palestine 198 B.C.

Augustus becomes Roman ▶ emperor 27 B.C.

◀ Jesus is born 7 or 6 B.C.
Herod dies 4 B.C.

Maccabees revolt ▶ 167 B.C.; Jews gain political independence 161–142 B.C.

Ptolemies, shown in maroon; Seleucids, gray

Roman Empire

600 B.C.   400 B.C.   200 B.C.   A.D.1

---

manifest." This in itself must have scandalized his Jewish subjects. Antiochus IV Epiphanes marched through Judea in an attempt to conquer Egypt, was rebuffed, and marched back out again. He faced a challenge from other imperialistic newcomers, the Parthians, who had emerged from their Caspian homeland to chop away at his territories in Mesopotamia. Before confronting them, Antiochus deemed it wise to secure his position in Palestine. His method for doing this, besides bringing in soldiers, was to promote Hellenized Jews, whom he considered his cultural and political allies. Jerusalem was transformed into a virtually Greek city. Renamed Antioch (at Jèrusalem), it was given a Greek administration, a Greek code of law, and a number of other Greek civic institutions.

As if all this were not enough, at one juncture the Syrian monarch, returning from an Egyptian campaign, decided to help himself to the Temple gold. It was the final insult. The city turned out in protest, and Antiochus, panicking, responded by ordering a massacre. Believing that he had a rebellion on his hands and that the purpose of the rebellion was the restoration of the earlier form of government under the Torah, Antiochus banned the Torah. Furthermore, anyone caught observing the Sabbath, or circumcising his son, or refusing to eat pork, was put to death. The Temple sanctuary was splattered in swine's blood and rededicated to the Olympian Zeus. Many Jews chose to die rather than give in.

Then, in 167 B.C., in the hamlet of Modein, a dusty day's march northwest of Jerusalem, the king's officers set up an altar to a Hellenic deity. They gathered the townspeople and commanded the priest, Mattathias, aged and devout, to sacrifice a pig. Mattathias refused. When an apostate Jew stepped up to do the evil work, the enraged priest killed him at the altar. Then Mattathias called out:

"Let every one who is zealous for the law and supports the covenant come out with me!" With his five sons and a company of fellow rebels, he fled into the hills to wage guerrilla war against the Seleucid tyrant.

The Maccabean revolt

From their upland sanctuaries the rebels swooped down to liberate village after village from the alien yoke. Led by the daring Judas Maccabeus, the old priest's third son and successor, they marched into battle and, though outnumbered, put the enemy to flight. (The very name *Maccabeus* rings out in triumph; it is probably Hebrew for "hammer," instrument of God's avenging might.) Soon the entire Judean countryside was in the rebels' hands, with the Syrian presence eroded to a few isolated garrisons and the capital itself. Then in December 164 B.C. Judas delivered his master stroke. He stormed Jerusalem and recaptured the Temple. The priests

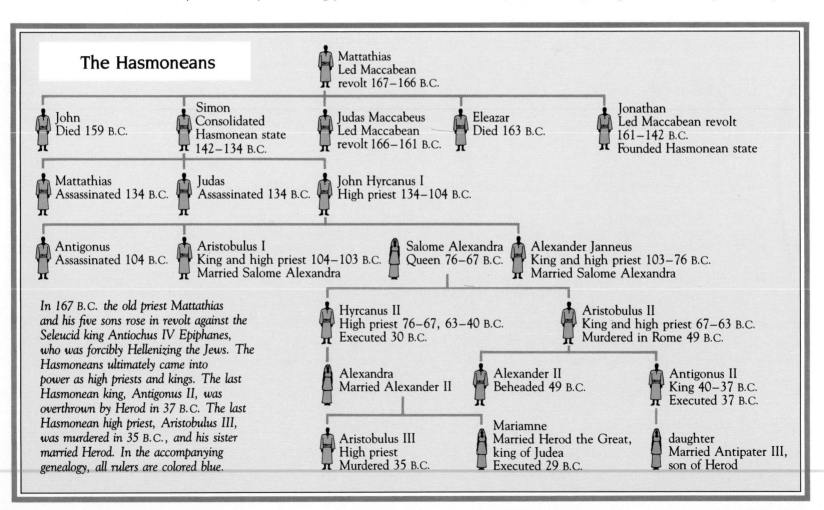

The Hasmoneans

Mattathias
Led Maccabean revolt 167–166 B.C.

John
Died 159 B.C.

Simon
Consolidated Hasmonean state 142–134 B.C.

Judas Maccabeus
Led Maccabean revolt 166–161 B.C.

Eleazar
Died 163 B.C.

Jonathan
Led Maccabean revolt 161–142 B.C.
Founded Hasmonean state

Mattathias
Assassinated 134 B.C.

Judas
Assassinated 134 B.C.

John Hyrcanus I
High priest 134–104 B.C.

Antigonus
Assassinated 104 B.C.

Aristobulus I
King and high priest 104–103 B.C.
Married Salome Alexandra

Salome Alexandra
Queen 76–67 B.C.

Alexander Janneus
King and high priest 103–76 B.C.
Married Salome Alexandra

In 167 B.C. the old priest Mattathias and his five sons rose in revolt against the Seleucid king Antiochus IV Epiphanes, who was forcibly Hellenizing the Jews. The Hasmoneans ultimately came into power as high priests and kings. The last Hasmonean king, Antigonus II, was overthrown by Herod in 37 B.C. The last Hasmonean high priest, Aristobulus III, was murdered in 35 B.C., and his sister married Herod. In the accompanying genealogy, all rulers are colored blue.

Hyrcanus II
High priest 76–67, 63–40 B.C.
Executed 30 B.C.

Aristobulus II
King and high priest 67–63 B.C.
Murdered in Rome 49 B.C.

Alexandra
Married Alexander II

Alexander II
Beheaded 49 B.C.

Antigonus II
King 40–37 B.C.
Executed 37 B.C.

Aristobulus III
High priest
Murdered 35 B.C.

Mariamne
Married Herod the Great, king of Judea
Executed 29 B.C.

daughter
Married Antipater III, son of Herod

returned to purify the sanctuary, the statue of Zeus was flung down, and the ancient rites began anew. If the exile in Babylonia stands as the low ebb of Judea's fortunes, the revolt of the Maccabees must be seen as their renaissance.

Over the next several decades Judea moved steadily toward full independence. After Judas' death, power coalesced in the hands of his two surviving brothers, Jonathan and Simon, who ruled in succession. A formal treaty signed with Antioch in 142 B.C., the first year of Simon's reign, snapped the last tattered bonds of Seleucid control. Shortly thereafter, in a great assembly at Jerusalem, the people by clamorous acclaim raised Simon and his heirs after him to the exalted triple office of "High Priest and General and Ruler of the Jews." A new dynasty had come into being, known as the Hasmoneans after the old priest Mattathias' tribal surname. For the first time since the fall of the Kingdom of Judah, nearly 450 years earlier, the sons of Israel were masters of their own destiny.

The new dynasty began to extend its power over the lands once held by David and Solomon. From the tiny mountain bastion of central Judea, Hasmonean armies moved south to conquer Idumea, as far as the Negev desert. The Idumeans, who throughout the Scriptures are seen as enemies of Israel, were forcibly converted en masse to Judaism. Next, the army turned toward Samaria, which had been openly hostile to the Hasmonean revolt. Jewish soldiers pillaged the capital and destroyed the Samaritan shrine at Mount Gerizim. Parts of Transjordan were taken, including some of its Greek cities, and the Hellenized cities of the coastal plain. Then Galilee fell, and its cosmopolitan, ethnically mixed citizenry was gathered into Judaism.

The sudden ascent to worldly power placed the Hasmoneans in a key political role in eastern Mediterranean affairs; at the same time, as they took on the trappings of monarchy, the new rulers fell prey to all the secular vices and to the bloody court intrigues that characterized many ancient regimes. When the ruler John Hyrcanus died in 104 B.C., he left the realm to his wife. But his eldest son, Aristobulus, staged a palace coup, threw his mother into a dungeon—where she starved to death—and also, for good measure, imprisoned three of his brothers. Suspecting a fourth brother of staging a counter-coup, the new king had him murdered. The king died soon afterward—of natural causes. His successor was one of his jailed brothers, Alexander Janneus—who, to secure his new position, killed off one of the two remaining jailed brothers.

Decline of the Hasmoneans

Alexander Janneus openly flaunted the despised Hellenistic tastes that his ancestors had fought so hard to eradicate. During a celebration of the Feast of the Tabernacles at the Temple, conducted by Janneus in his capacity as high priest, a sect of Pharisees staged a riot. They pelted the king with lemons and called him unfit for his priestly office. Janneus called in troops, 6,000 protesters died, and a rebellion broke out that lasted nine years and cost another 50,000 lives. It ended with the capture of 800 Pharisee leaders. Janneus had them all crucified near the palace during an open-air public banquet, which he attended with his concubines.

Janneus lived on, his body ravaged by vice and drunkenness, until his 49th year. Then, in 76 B.C., the kingdom passed to his long-suffering wife, Salome Alexandra. To avoid further trouble, the queen made peace with the Pharisees and in fact promoted many of them to high posts in her government. A brief era of miraculous prosperity ensued, when "grains of wheat were as large as kidneys, the grains of barley like olives, and lentils like golden denarii"—as later stories told it. This idyll could not last, of course. After reigning nine years, the queen died, sparking a quarrel for succession between her two

Antigonus II, last of the Hasmonean kings (40–37 B.C.), had this bronze coin struck to commemorate the Maccabean revolt, which had taken place more than a century earlier. The revolt marked the return of Jewish rule and freedom of religion. The coin bears the seven-branched candelabrum, or menorah, a symbol of the Jewish faith and the Temple.

The Roman general Pompey, shown above in a late portrait, arbitrated in the quarrel between the Hasmonean brothers Hyrcanus II and Aristobulus II over the rule of Palestine. Taking advantage of the political turmoil in the land, in 63 B.C. Pompey seized Jerusalem and made Hyrcanus high priest and prince with limited powers over a reduced kingdom that was subject to Rome. Palestine was to remain under Roman control for about four centuries.

sons, Hyrcanus II and Aristobulus II. Once again the country was plunged into war.

Enter Pompey the Great

Throughout the period of Hasmonean rule the map of the ancient world was undergoing a profound readjustment. The principal agent of change was Rome. Since their victory over Antiochus III in 190 B.C., the tightly disciplined armies of Rome had spread the city's banner over most of the lands that bordered the Mediterranean. They took Carthage and parts of Spain, then Macedonia and Greece, and all of North Africa. Egypt became an independent vassal. Now Rome's great general Pompey was rampaging through the eastern Mediterranean area. Asia Minor gave in to him, and then, finally, Syria went down. Only Parthia remained to challenge him. In the face of this threat, the turbulence in Palestine could not be allowed to continue. So it seemed like a tailor-made opportunity when Hyrcanus and Aristobulus, Queen Salome's two squabbling sons, remembered their country's friendship treaty with Rome and appealed for help. Pompey was only too glad to move in.

Pompey led his legions to Jerusalem. In the third month of the siege the Romans breached the massive walls and stormed into the Temple, slaughtering anyone who stood in their path, including priests, who continued their sacrifices even as the battle flooded over them.

Unlike most previous conquerors, Pompey left the Temple treasury untouched. But he did commit one terrible breach, which caused more lasting hatred than any loss of life. Curious, perhaps, to see what it was the Jews really worshiped, Pompey and some of his men entered the inner sanctuary. In the holy precinct accessible only to priests they found the golden furniture and vessels used in religious rites. But in the Holy of Holies itself, accessible only to the high priest once a year, the center of God's

presence among his people, they found nothing at all, bare walls. His curiosity satisfied, Pompey had the priests purify the sanctuary after his desecration and reinstate the regular sacrifices. That desecration was enough, however; among pious Jews Pompey's name had become an abomination.

The Romans placed Hyrcanus II back on the throne as high priest and subject prince, curtailing his power and sharply cutting back his territory. Judea including southern Samaria, Perea in the Transjordan, and Galilee were all that remained to him. At the same time he was made an independent vassal to the governor of Syria, now officially a Roman province. Thousands of Jewish war prisoners found themselves packed into ships bound for Rome, where they joined an expatriate colony of other Jews. Aristobulus, too, was taken to Rome, where he was later imprisoned.

Young Herod

It was in a world dominated by Rome that Herod came to manhood. As a youth, he suffered no lack of privilege. His father, Antipater, as governor of Idumea and later Hyrcanus' principal adviser was for all practical purposes the most important man in the land. So the young Herod, growing up close to the seat of power, watching as his father rode out the shifting gusts of palace politics, received a lasting object lesson in political survival. When Julius Caesar, fresh from his conquests in Gaul, rode into the Latin capital to the thunderous welcome of an adoring populace, defeated the aging Pompey, and took over the government, Antipater quickly found a way to ingratiate himself with the new ruler. Sensing a firm ally in a notoriously unstable quarter of Rome's domains, Caesar made Antipater a Roman citizen, promoted him to chief minister of all Judea, and exempted him from taxes. (Hyrcanus remained as nominal prince and as high priest.) In turn, Antipater found posts for his two elder sons: Herod, age 25,

The Roman Soldier

The Roman Army was able to conquer much of the Western world because it was well equipped, well disciplined, and skilled in both fighting and building. Roman troops not only had the latest, most efficient tools for destruction and conquest; they had the engineering skill to build great roads, bridges, and aqueducts in the lands they conquered.

A Roman soldier was equipped with armor and a long shield to protect him from attack. At left is an example of some scale armor and a helmet worn by Roman soldiers of the first century A.D. The small pick ax head below was used for digging and cutting timbers for fortifications.

A detail from the Column of Marcus Aurelius shows a Roman legion on the march. Soldiers carried their own equipment. Heavier supplies were packed into carts drawn by mules.

Spearheads and slingers' missiles, like the ones shown above, are relics of Roman battles. The first-century A.D. fragment of pottery tile, at left, was found in Jerusalem. It is stamped with the image of a boar, symbol of the Roman Tenth Legion that was garrisoned in the city until the third century.

The Herodian Family

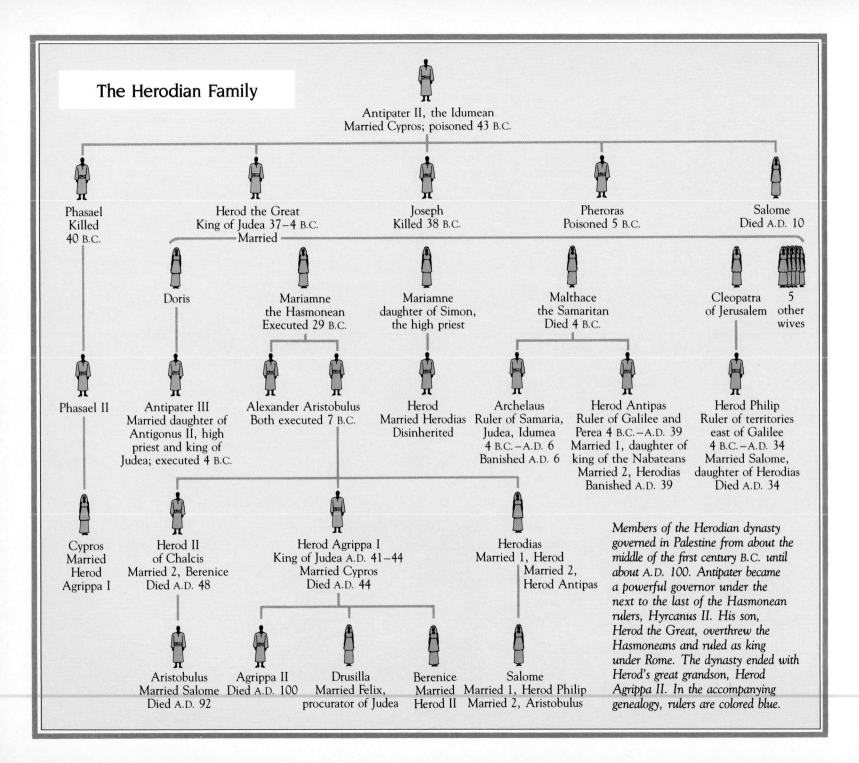

Antipater II, the Idumean
Married Cypros; poisoned 43 B.C.

Phasael
Killed
40 B.C.

Herod the Great
King of Judea 37–4 B.C.
Married

Joseph
Killed 38 B.C.

Pheroras
Poisoned 5 B.C.

Salome
Died A.D. 10

Doris

Mariamne
the Hasmonean
Executed 29 B.C.

Mariamne
daughter of Simon,
the high priest

Malthace
the Samaritan
Died 4 B.C.

Cleopatra
of Jerusalem

5
other
wives

Phasael II

Antipater III
Married daughter of
Antigonus II, high
priest and king of
Judea; executed 4 B.C.

Alexander Aristobulus
Both executed 7 B.C.

Herod
Married Herodias
Disinherited

Archelaus
Ruler of Samaria,
Judea, Idumea
4 B.C.–A.D. 6
Banished A.D. 6

Herod Antipas
Ruler of Galilee and
Perea 4 B.C.–A.D. 39
Married 1, daughter of
king of the Nabateans
Married 2, Herodias
Banished A.D. 39

Herod Philip
Ruler of territories
east of Galilee
4 B.C.–A.D. 34
Married Salome,
daughter of Herodias
Died A.D. 34

Cypros
Married
Herod
Agrippa I

Herod II
of Chalcis
Married 2, Berenice
Died A.D. 48

Herod Agrippa I
King of Judea A.D. 41–44
Married Cypros
Died A.D. 44

Herodias
Married 1, Herod
Married 2,
Herod Antipas

Aristobulus
Married Salome
Died A.D. 92

Agrippa II
Died A.D. 100

Drusilla
Married Felix,
procurator of Judea

Berenice
Married
Herod II

Salome
Married 1, Herod Philip
Married 2, Aristobulus

*Members of the Herodian dynasty
governed in Palestine from about the
middle of the first century B.C. until
about A.D. 100. Antipater became
a powerful governor under the
next to the last of the Hasmonean
rulers, Hyrcanus II. His son,
Herod the Great, overthrew the
Hasmoneans and ruled as king
under Rome. The dynasty ended with
Herod's great grandson, Herod
Agrippa II. In the accompanying
genealogy, rulers are colored blue.*

became governor of Galilee, and Phasael was given Jerusalem.

Thrust into power, Herod moved boldly to take control. "His youth in no way hindered him," Josephus wrote, " . . . being a young man of high spirit." Spirit was clearly needed, and a certain ruthless streak as well, for Galilee was a region with a reputation for lawlessness. Taking the law into his own hands, Herod captured the leader of a gang of bandits that roamed the hills and executed him, along with many of his followers. This gave certain factions in Jerusalem an opportunity to act. Herod was summoned to Jerusalem to stand trial for murder.

Jerusalem's highest court was the Sanhedrin, a body of religious elders and wealthy landowners who by Jewish law held supreme power of life and death. Most men stood before it in a guise of extreme humility, clad in a black tunic, their hair long and unkempt. But Herod showed up in lavish purple robes, attended by his bodyguard. This demeanor frightened many in court but loosed a tirade from the assembly's most respected and courageous rabbi, who cried out against both Herod and all his Idumean relatives. On orders from the Roman governor of Syria, Hyrcanus had tried to arrange the trial's outcome in advance. But when the Sanhedrin proved intractable, he suspended the session and advised Herod to leave the city.

Herod found refuge with the Roman governor in Damascus, who put him in charge of southern Syria. His loyalty and skill soon won him the governorship of Samaria, followed by that of Galilee and Coele-Syria. He became Rome's most ardent supporter in Palestine, following in his father's footsteps.

Then in 40 B.C. came the Parthian invasion that sent Herod fleeing to Masada. When the fugitive Herod appeared in Rome, desperate for support, Mark Antony saw the bold young Idumean as his single best hope for reviving Roman dominance in the eastern regions of the empire.

Herod claims his lands

Herod lost no time sailing back to Palestine. He landed early in 39 B.C. at Ptolemais on the Phoenician coast, conscripted an army, and fought his way south through Samaria and Judea, gathering volunteers as he went. His first priority was to reach his family and relatives at Masada, which was under siege by Antigonus' troops. Their plight was desperate: no rain had fallen for a while and the cisterns were low. But suddenly the skies opened, rain streamed down, and the people were able to hold out until Herod and his forces could save them.

Herod's next objective was Jerusalem. He had

Of all Herod the Great's many descendants, perhaps the most colorful and best known was his son Herod Antipas. Upon his father's death in 4 B.C., Herod Antipas became tetrarch, or ruler, of Galilee and Perea. During his reign he had John the Baptist beheaded and figured in the trial of Jesus. In the French stone carving shown at left he is seen tickling the chin of his stepdaughter, Salome.

A silver Roman coin from the time of Caesar Augustus shows Capricorn, the goat. Capricorn was the astrological sign that was often associated with Emperor Augustus.

A coin issued in A.D. 39 under Herod Antipas bears the image of a graceful date palm. Herod's coins could not carry his portrait because of a Jewish law against "graven images."

already made a thrust in this direction, but he had to give up the idea when some expected support from the Romans failed to materialize. The reason was frustratingly clear. Antigonus, Josephus tells us, had offered a generous bribe to a Roman general, who suddenly decided it was time to send his troops to winter bivouac. So for the time being, Herod had to content himself with pacifying the countryside.

All the while Herod kept waiting for the imperial reinforcements he needed to assault Jerusalem. They came in the spring of 37 B.C. Together with Herod's own troops, the total strength of the army was 11 full battalions of infantry and 6,000 cavalry, along with Syrian auxiliaries. This immensely powerful array now spread out before the city gates. Two massive outer limestone walls protected much of Jerusalem; inside them a labyrinth of inner-city alleyways led to the heavily fortified Temple Mount.

The Roman armies set up their war machines—catapults and battering rams—and started pounding the fortress wall (the scene is illustrated on pages 36–37). They made little progress at first. In daring raids the defenders would dash out to burn the catapults. Through tunnels beneath the walls they raided the Roman encampment. Sometimes battles raged in these underground passages. It took the Romans nearly eight weeks to break through the walls and seize the mount where the Temple stood.

The attackers then laid energetic siege to the inner city. Herod, hoping to induce a settlement and thus avoid more bloodshed, tried to call off the main body of Roman troops. Victory, he suspected, might prove to be as disastrous as failure, leaving him, as he said, "king of a desert." Each day he sent sacrificial animals up over the Temple wall so that the proper rituals could continue. All to no effect. When the inner city fell, the legions cut loose in an orgy of slaughter and pillage—burning houses, killing matrons and maidens alike, striking down citizens of all ages and both sexes. Herod managed to take the Temple himself, thus heading off the sacrilege of an assault by Gentiles. Only by paying a sizable ransom of his own money did he finally persuade the Romans to depart and leave him with the smoldering remains of his new capital. Herod's position was delicate in the extreme. Owing his victory to Roman support, he was a so-called client-king of the empire: free to run the internal affairs of his kingdom but subject to dismissal should he ever incur Rome's displeasure. He must carefully court whoever held the imperial scepter, nurturing imperial favor and assuaging imperial fears, until he came to be seen as irreplaceable. Never again must Rome's destroying legions be allowed to trample uninvited through the land. And then there was the problem of the region's highly diverse and difficult populace—part Jew and part Gentile, torn by inner factionalism, unpredictably rebellious. Somehow Herod must balance these various forces and lead his new kingdom into an era of reasonable prosperity and peace.

The new regime

His first step was to strengthen his grip on the throne. After the collapse of Jerusalem, the pretender, Antigonus, was taken by the Romans and executed. Many Jewish leaders had supported Antigonus, however, and Herod dealt just as harshly with them. He sent hundreds to their deaths and confiscated their estates—thereby adding greatly to his own wealth. Among his victims were 45 members of the Jerusalem nobility who had supported Antigonus and most members of the Sanhedrin, the council of elders, which a decade earlier had brought him to trial for his repressions in Galilee. Surprisingly, he spared the rabbi who had spoken out against him, for Herod admired the old man's courage.

One basic charge against Herod's right to rule could never be erased, however. "One from among your brethren you shall set as king over you; you may not put a foreigner over you. . . ." so it was written in Deuteronomy 17:15. To traditional Jews Herod was clearly a foreigner, an upstart Idumean of questionable lineage, whatever his nominal religion.

Herod adopted a stance of gingerly tolerance toward Judea's more zealous religious groups. From most of his subjects he required an oath of loyalty, first to himself and eventually to the Roman emperor. But the Pharisees and Essenes on conscientious grounds refused the oath. Herod, out of regard for past favors, exempted them, provided they kept to themselves and stayed out of politics. Pharisee preachers might rail against him, pronouncing him God's scourge, a judgment sent from heaven for the people's sins, but at the same time they warned that Herod's rule must be endured. Some continued to prophesy the coming of an apocalyptic age, Judaism triumphant under a messiah from the House of David. Herod simply pretended not to hear. It was never an easy relationship.

Within Palestine Herod set up his administration in ways that led to efficient and tight control. Mostly this meant restricting the sphere of traditional Jewish institutions, such as the law courts, and assuming their powers himself. Having purged the Sanhedrin, he packed this august body with his own followers and reduced its role to ceremonial, rubber-stamp endorsement of his own policies. The king's most important advisers were Greeks; his army, like much of Rome's, consisted largely of foreign mercenaries. He developed a powerful secret police and a network of spies to report from every corner of the realm. Yet all the while he never forgot the fragility of his authority, the sudden turn of events that had brought him to power and that could just as quickly throw him down again. For Palestine could never be a comfortable seat for any ruler, racked as it was by dynastic tensions and old religious fevers, steeped in memory and discontent, and subject to messianic rumblings that never quite grew still.

After the death of Mark Antony, Herod switched his allegiance to Augustus. Realizing that Herod was an important client king of Rome and that it was to his advantage to keep him happy, Augustus restored the territories that Antony had taken from Herod and given to Cleopatra: Jaffa, Gaza, and the oasis city of Jericho. Herod also received the cities of Gadara and Hippus, east and southeast of the Sea of Galilee. In addition Augustus gave Herod areas of the Transjordan, making the Jewish kingdom almost as large as it had been in the Hasmonean golden age. Herod then embarked on a building program to make his kingdom as splendid as it was extensive. In the above map Herod's domain is shown in brown.

Chapter Three

Classes and Masses

The reign of Herod the Great saw change and confrontation. New cities were built and old ones reconstructed, giving work to thousands of craftsmen and laborers. A new, cosmopolitan ruling class arose beside Judea's traditional aristocracy.

Anyone passing through the Judean hills south of Jerusalem during the second decade of King Herod's reign might have seen a remarkable structure taking shape. An entire hill had been truncated, its crest leveled flat to form a volcanolike cone, and on the summit, as though sprouting from the volcano's crater, there arose a massive cylinder of cut limestone.

This was the fortress Herodium, Herod's newest desert sanctuary, named after himself and commemorating a battle he had fought against a party of Jews on this site in 40 B.C. Its construction employed thousands of skilled and unskilled workers. Cadres of master stonecutters quarried huge blocks of limestone from the bedrock; choosing cracks carefully, they drove in wooden wedges and doused them with water so that they would swell and split the rock. Regiments of workers labored to move the huge blocks, and stonemasons chiseled them to precise shape so that, when they were hoisted into place, not even a knife blade could be slid between them. Carpenters shaped doors and

The extensive building projects that marked Herod's reign employed local laborers as well as Roman engineers and Greek architects. Here, one of the king's representatives reviews the plans for a peristyle court with an architect as laborers go about their work—a master stonemason sculpts a capital, day laborers move a paving stone, and slaves ready a crane to position a section of column. The columns, raised a section at a time, were joined by pins.

Seen from a distance across the stark Judean Wilderness south of Jerusalem, the conical hill that contains Herodium, King Herod's namesake citadel, looks like a quiescent volcano. In fact, the hill's distinctive shape is man-made—the result of a remarkable feat of construction. First the existing hill was truncated; next the towers and double walls of the cylindrical fortress were erected on the flat top; then the soil that had been removed was reused as landfill, along with earth from a nearby hill. The slope was built up, creating a "crater" some 45 feet deep, and made smooth, rendering it virtually unscalable. The only entry was by a flight of stone steps built into the hill. The spiral road, clearly visible in the photo at center, was added in later times.

window frames from great logs, and slaves and unskilled day laborers were busy digging, heaving, carrying, hauling water, and carting off debris. There were glassmakers, plasterers and fresco painters, workers in stucco and mosaic, inlay workers, ivory carvers, and goldsmiths and silversmiths to add finishing brilliance.

Their tunics of rough sackcloth pulled forward between their legs and tucked up into their waists for freedom of movement, the workers toiled in the desert wind and heat. At night they probably retired to goat-hair tents, much like those of present-day Bedouins. They subsisted largely on a gruel of lentils or barley, living lives of poverty that stood in stark contrast to the opulence of the project on which they labored.

Monumental and aloof, Herodium was the very embodiment of arrogant power—a clear statement to the Judeans that they now had a master who would brook no challenge to his authority and a demonstration to Judea's Arab and Syrian neighbors of the unassailable might with which this king,

placed on his throne by Roman decree, would defend his territory. By the same token, Herod's display of power served to assure his Roman masters that their trust in him was not misplaced.

Herodium: *palace-fortress*

Herodium's site had been chosen for both military and political reasons. It was to be a link in the early warning system against outside attack—one of a line of fortresses commanding Judea's southern and eastern borders. Some of these fortresses, inherited from previous rulers, were being refurbished. Others, like Herodium, were being built from the ground up. Each was close enough to its nearest neighbors so that a sentry stationed atop the highest turret (Herodium's was some 2,460 feet above sea level) could see a signal and pass the alarm along. And, because Herod had good reason to fear internal rebellion as well as attack from without, the citadel was also a place to which the monarch could flee, should Jerusalem slip from his control.

Whoever the attackers might have been, they

The remains of Herodium are seen in the aerial view at center. Although everything above the landfill has been lost to time and weather, archeologists have pieced together a picture of how the four-tower fortress might have looked. The three semicircular towers were five or six stories high, with each story opening onto a double-walled corridor that girded the fortress. The fourth, the round eastern tower, was probably 45 to 60 feet higher than the others, with upper levels of luxurious apartments where Herod and his entourage could enjoy a gentle breeze and gaze out upon a view that stretched across the Dead Sea to the mountains of Moab. At its base, shown at near left, was a 90-foot-long colonnaded court where footpaths wound among shrubs and flowerbeds.

would have needed extraordinary measures to pry the defenders out. Herodium was virtually impregnable. There was only one entry, a steep staircase of 200 steps of "hewn stone," according to Josephus. At the cardinal points of the compass four rounded towers, one much larger than the others, bulged outward from the massive circular wall. Their bases were sunk deep within a conical skirt of landfill: much of the soil had been brought from a nearby hill that had been partly demolished for the purpose. The covering slope, banked over at the top with stones, was steep and slippery; only a very foolish enemy would attempt to climb it.

For all its strength, Herodium was designed to be palatially livable in the luxuriant style that Herod favored. Inside its walls the architects placed a sunken, colonnaded courtyard with niches for statuary and beds for flowering plants and ornamental shrubs. There was a large reception hall, a Roman bath, and lavish private quarters for the king and his retinue. At the bottom of the hill was another palace complex, whose outstanding feature was a huge artificial

pool fed by aqueduct from Solomon's Pools, a spring near Bethlehem. In the center of this nine-foot-deep pool was an elegant, colonnaded island pavilion, reachable only by boat. Altogether, Herodium's various buildings and their landscaping covered some 45 acres (about the same area as the later Taj Mahal and its gardens), making it one of the largest groupings of royal buildings in the ancient world.

The new regime benefitted from prosperity the like of which Palestine could hardly remember. The king himself grew monumentally rich. Revenues poured in from his vast estates, from high-priced loans to foreign rulers, and from his own astute business dealings. Most of this royal wealth flowed into a building program of gigantic scale. Herod put up monuments as though he were the emperor himself. Herodium was but a small part of the ambitious and wide-ranging construction program that marked his long reign. In addition to the fortresses, many of which included luxurious royal quarters, Herod commissioned several fortified palaces for himself in various corners of the land. A winter palace at

Jericho, which came to be a favorite home, included formal gardens, pools, and an elaborate irrigation system (see the reconstruction on page 68). Atop Masada, the great rock bastion where Herod's family had taken refuge when he had fled Judea in 40 B.C., two palaces were built. A heavy casement wall, one with rooms inside, was built around the rim of the mesa and fortified with towers. One of the palaces, known as the Hanging Palace, was a trilevel structure, its topmost level incorporated into the wall on the mesa's northern rim. Close by stood a large bath, an administrative building, and enormous storerooms. The palace's other two levels were built into the cliff face, descending like steps, sheltered from the blazing sun, and overlooking one of the most spectacularly austere views on earth. Remembering how his family had suffered from thirst in this desert land while he was seeking financial and political support in Rome, Herod created an ingenious water-storage system capable of holding about 10.5 million gallons: two nearby ravines were dammed up, and the water that collected behind them during the brief rainy season was carried by aqueduct to a series of cisterns that were scooped into the bedrock on Masada's northern flank; from there, the water was carried in jars by hundreds of slaves and beasts of burden to massive cisterns atop the citadel.

Western influences

In Galilee and Samaria and along the Mediterranean coast, Herod commissioned scores of monuments, temples, public works, and even entire cities in the same Hellenistic style—in which Greek classicism was combined with Roman grandeur.

The non-Jewish people of these regions had lived for centuries in an uneasy relationship with the Jewish population. In spite of Palestine's long coastline, the Jews had never been notable seafarers. They lived, as it were, with their backs to the sea and their faces toward Jerusalem, their lives shaped

Continued on page 70

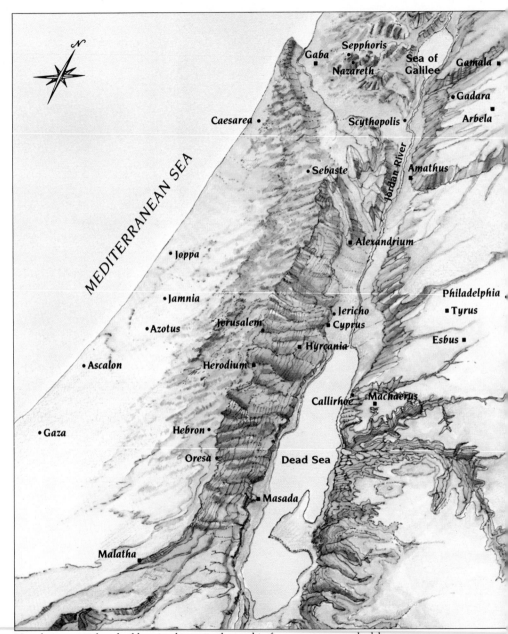

Herod was a tireless builder; in the map above, his fortresses are marked by squares.

Stairs of the temple in Sebaste dedicated to the emperor Augustus.

In addition to the fortresses that Herod built or enlarged and the luxurious palaces that he constructed in Jericho, Masada, Ascalon, Sepphoris, Jerusalem, and elsewhere, he commissioned monuments and buildings in many cities throughout his realm. He created at least two whole new cities: Sebaste (on the site of ancient Samaria) and the port of Caesarea. Remnants of Herodian stonework are plentiful, but almost nothing remains of his most ambitious project, the Temple in Jerusalem.

Tomb built over the traditional burial site of the Patriarchs in Hebron.

Water was carried 13 miles to Caesarea in this aqueduct from the springs beneath Mount Carmel.

Wave-pattern mosaic in the baths at Masada.

Herod's Palace at Jericho

Hot, sun-drenched Jericho was a winter haven for the wealthy, and Herod built three palaces there. Seen at right is the northern wing of the third palace, which overlooks the Wadi Qilt. The reconstruction is based on an aerial view of the site, above. This country retreat, just 15 miles from the hustle and bustle of Jerusalem, was planned as a place of rest and relaxation for Herod and his family. From left to right, there was a 60- by 90-foot reception hall with painted walls resembling marble and a mosaic floor of imported marble and local stone. An 18-foot-wide opening provided a view of the huge sunken garden on the southern bank. Next to the reception hall was an open, colonnaded courtyard; another court, farther right, led into a five-room Roman-style bath. Service rooms and a smaller reception hall were along the northern and eastern sides. The Jericho estate was valuable property. An elaborate irrigation system, begun by the Hasmoneans and improved by Herod, brought water from springs as far as 10 miles away. In the distance at left is Herod's second palace, built on the foundation of a Hasmonean palace. The buildings at right rear included a factory for processing balm and dates.

The houses of the rich were distinguished by elaborate bathing facilities. The arrangement of the rooms varied, just as the views of physicians varied regarding which combination of heat and cold was most beneficial to health. At Herod's Jericho palace, a bather entered the complex through the dressing room in the middle of the line and passed through a tepidarium, or warm room, that might have held a shallow pool of tepid water, on the way either to the caldarium, or hot room, at one end of the line or to the frigidarium, or cold room, at the other. In the frigidarium, shown at right, a large basin or pool of cold water probably rested on the central pedestal and surrounding ring. Bathers might have reclined in the six-foot-wide niches around it.

by the religious and ethnic exclusivity that the Torah demanded. Along the coast, in the regions of ancient Philistia and northward, predominantly pagan communities flourished independent of the Jewish culture. During the centuries of direct rule by the Ptolemies and Seleucids in the wake of Alexander the Great's brief custody of the area, these cities were very receptive to Greek religion and culture. Following the Maccabean revolt in 167 B.C. and the return of Jewish leaders to power, many of these cities fell before the armies of John Hyrcanus and Alexander Janneus, often with great destruction. For these people the coming of the Romans in 63 B.C. was cause for celebration, for it meant liberation from the hated domination of the Hasmoneans, even though liberation meant subjection to Rome.

Greek cities, old and new

With the ascension of Herod, many of these Greek cities—Gaza, Azotus, Jamnia, Joppa, Strato's Tower (later Caesarea), Samaria (later Sebaste), Gadara, and others—found themselves once again under the rule of a king of the Jews. Many of the people chafed at the idea, in spite of Herod's Hellenized outlook. In 20 B.C., for example, Gadara appealed unsuccessfully to the emperor Augustus to be removed from Herod's sway and placed under direct Roman rule. Other Greek cities, such as Ascalon on the coast, Scythopolis between Galilee and Samaria, and most of cities of the Decapolis east of the Jordan, remained free city-states even during Herod's rule.

Naturally, all these cities were centers of Hellenistic culture—full participants in the cosmopolitan intellectual and cultural life that flourished around the Mediterranean. They produced noteworthy philosophers, orators, dramatists, and poets. Ascalon, for example, had over the decades generated at least four leading Stoic philosophers, including Antiochus of Ascalon, a teacher of Cicero. Gadara produced a leading Epicurean philosopher, several poets and satirists, and the rhetorician Theodorus of Gadara, who tutored the young Tiberius, the future Roman emperor.

The gods of Greece were at home in all of these places, though they were often identified with indigenous deities. Local legends in Scythopolis, for example, evidently linked the city's origin to the myths of the Greek god Dionysus. Greek cultural and political institutions were not only accepted in such communities, they were demanded. Gymnasiums, theaters, stadiums, temples, festival games—all the typical aspects of Greek city life—could be found in Palestine. And so Herod, in pursuing his building program, was able to indulge his own Hellenistic tastes to the fullest.

On the site of the ancient, war-ravaged capital of Samaria, he built a lavish new city, which he called Sebaste—from the Greek for Augustus, to whom the whole enterprise, including a magnificent temple, was dedicated. He gave land grants in the nearby countryside to several thousand militiamen from other regions, who could be called into service at any time. On the Mediterranean shore some 25 miles to the northwest, he built an even grander city, Caesarea, also named for the emperor Augustus Caesar. This city, built around an artificial harbor protected by two massive breakwaters, became the kingdom's first true seaport. There were altars on which to sacrifice to pagan gods, whose statues stood alongside a statue of the emperor himself—unacceptable features to the Jewish community, unthinkable in the holy city of Jerusalem.

Rebuilding Jerusalem

Herod's cosmopolitan tastes were not entirely welcome in Jerusalem, and his building program was a source of constant tension. The rebuilding of the

In Masada's Roman bath, the caldarium was heated from below. The floor rested on pillars made of stone and clay brick, and the space beneath it was heated by a furnace. In steam baths, clay pipes were used instead of solid pillars.

city began the moment he took office and continued until well after his death, giving steady employment to thousands of craftsmen and common laborers. In the course of a little over 30 years, the war-torn community, scarred by ruins of the ancient and recent past, became an international showplace. The city's walls, badly damaged during Herod's siege in 37 B.C., were restored and strengthened, and towers were added. Some of these were part of a new fortress—called the Antonia after Herod's then patron Mark Antony—which was begun that same year to replace an older castle that had fallen into ruin. Sumptuous, grand, the Antonia was palatial enough for a royal residence, and Herod probably lived there himself for a time.

But the Antonia's position overlooking the Temple Mount—once the site of the spectacular Temple of Solomon and now of the comparatively modest second Temple built after the exile—presented certain political problems; Herod could not yet safely make such an overt display of his own dominance over the religious authorities. Moreover, the fortress's name lost its political luster after Antony was overwhelmed by Octavian's forces in the Battle of Actium in 31 B.C. and shortly thereafter committed suicide. So Herod decided to build an enormous new palace for himself on a hilltop in Jerusalem's western sector, the elite Upper City. This area, into which the city's population had spread a century earlier, was already marked by mansions where the upper classes lived; Herod's palace put them all to shame.

Around 27 B.C. Herod instituted a Roman-style festival of games in honor of his new Roman patron Augustus and conceived of three impressive public buildings to house them. The first was a theater, which Josephus describes as being in Jerusalem, although some experts now identify it with ruins that have been found about a half-mile south of the city. There were also an amphitheater for gladiatorial shows, which was built somewhere outside the walls

This fragment of stucco decoration from Herod's palace at Jericho was made in the same way the capitals of columns were. Carved small stones were plastered or stuccoed over; then the surface was carved to resemble true stonework.

("in the plain," Josephus says), and a U-shaped hippodrome in which chariot races were held.

The people loved to watch the thrilling and dangerous chariot races, in which opposing charioteers, each driving as many as four pairs of horses, would thunder around the track, trying to crowd their rivals into the rail at the turns; and the sport was not particularly offensive to pious sensibilities. In the amphitheater, however, athletes would take part in wrestling matches, foot races, and other events in the Greek manner—in the nude. This affront to Jewish propriety was reason enough to separate the amphitheater from the city; when Jewish athletes felt obliged to disguise the effects of their circumcision, thus renouncing their faith in the eyes of the devout, the games sparked bitter controversy. The addition of bloody confrontations in which slaves and condemned criminals would fight to the death against each other or against lions, tigers, elephants, and other animals, made such an arena thoroughly distasteful to many Jews.

The new theater, a grandly ornate structure in the Greek style, decorated with marble inlays and imported fabrics, was used for competitions in music and drama. It, and the events it housed, were always felt to be foreign intrusions in Jewish life. Jewish plays were rare indeed, and Greek fare was unacceptable to pious Jews; the comedies reeked of bawdiness, and the ancient tragedies, although among the world's most gripping works of literature, were offensive because they celebrated the exploits of pagan gods and heroes.

Confrontation, when it came, focused on the building's ornamentation. The way in which Herod dealt with it was a demonstration of his heavy-handed but effective methods. In all his buildings around Jerusalem, Herod avoided the use of any decorations that could be construed to break the Commandment against graven images, but the style of the times throughout the Roman world demanded that classical theaters be embellished with statuary. As reports circulated that statues were, indeed, being erected in the theater, many Jews fastened on the issue and used it to raise an outcry against the theater, and by extension, against Herod himself. With great ceremony, he escorted the leaders to the theater and unveiled the "statues" for what they were—artistic assemblages of military trophies and wooden frames with not a graven image of a human or a deity in sight. To the sound of royal laughter, the red-faced protesters retired.

Finally, around 20 B.C., Herod turned his attention to the Temple Mount and the Temple itself, ordering the most ambitious and costly renovations in that structure's long history, outdoing even the legendary grandeur of Solomon's Temple (see Chapter 5). The work was to continue long after Herod's death; the Gospel of John tells us that when Jesus drove the money changers from the Temple, it had been under construction for 46 years.

Challenge to tradition

Great buildings are more than mortar and stone. They represent the hopes, aspirations, and ambitions of the builders. Their construction requires the concerted, organized effort of many laborers and skilled craftsmen over long periods of time. And when they are finished, such buildings stand as public statements of the way a people views itself and wishes to be viewed by others.

There was an inherent contradiction between Herod's view of his kingdom and his subjects' views, and in reconstructing the ancient seat of Jewish faith, Herod met this contradiction head-on. The pious Jews over whom he ruled believed that their nation should be a theocracy, obedient to laws that had been given by God and preserved by strict tradition. But Herod was a ruler in the classical mold: not *of* the people but *over* them. His true community was the Greco-Roman world at large, and particularly the elite of that world—other rulers, their families, and their courts—and the architecture he commissioned reflected the Hellenistic culture, both in concept and in execution.

On the one hand, Herod's new buildings—and especially the new Temple—were designed to boost the king's standing among the populace. They kept more than a generation of workers employed and brought wealth to the city. On the other hand, the building program served to edge Palestine into the modern era of the Roman Empire, thus diluting Jewish influence and incurring the animosity of those who sought to preserve traditional values.

Through their sheer size and scope, Herod's new buildings brought about a general restructuring of Jerusalem's society, turning the city for the first time in its long history into a true urban center, with the king himself at the top of a vast, tax-supported hierarchy of public officials, soldiers, and builders. Moreover, the upper tiers of this hierarchy were largely foreign to Judean culture—by education, philosophy, and religious conviction, if not by birth. As must be the case in any such massive social upheaval, tensions arose between the new order and dispossessed members of the old. The final outcome of the incident of the new theater illustrates the depth of these tensions.

Some of the humiliated Jews nursed their resentment of Herod's violations of ancient customs, and a number of them plotted to strike him down. They arranged for 10 assassins to meet him with daggers as he was to enter the theater during the games. A paid informer exposed the plot, and Herod's police swooped down to arrest the would-be death squad as they were poised to strike. The 10 were tortured and executed, but the informer fared no better—a short time later, a crowd seized him and tore him limb from limb. Herod struck back. Based on eyewitness accounts of this incident, he had the perpetrators and their families punished.

The Art of Carving Stone

Using compass and straightedge, even an unlettered craftsman could create sophisticated geometric designs. For a hexagonal rosette, as on the sundial fragment at right, a stoneworker would incise a circle and then make six equal arcs within it. Bisecting the arcs yielded a 12-point rosette, as on the large ossuary below. For the whorls on the small ossuary, he incised two concentric circles, one half the size of the other, and used the circumference of the smaller circle to guide the placement of the 12 equally spaced arcs. The large ossuary's 16-point rosettes required dividing the circle into quarters, then subdividing them. A similar 16-part division guided the design of the capital at the lower right.

All that remains of a limestone sundial from Jerusalem is this fragment. Even this ordinary object provided an opportunity for the stone carver to show his skill.

These intricately carved ossuaries (or bone chests), found near Jerusalem, display geometric rosettes and other typical designs such as the lilies and grape vines.

In this Corinthian capital, from Jerusalem's Upper City, the artist combined delicate lily scrolls with a band of stylized acanthus leaves.

There was little space for gardens in the teeming city of Jerusalem, so many residents bought fruits and vegetables in the open marketplaces. The fruit vendor depicted in the stone relief above used an umbrella to shield herself and protect her wares from the withering sun.

Butchers, like many other merchants and craftsmen in Jerusalem, conducted their businesses in a single part of town, known as the Street of Butchers. Their number may well have included respected scribes and teachers, many of whom also worked at trades. Their customers would have been well-to-do, for fresh meat was a rarity for the poor.

A *tapestry of stress*

Such violent eruptions were rare—prevented in large part by the ruthless efficiency of Herod's secret police—but they tell us much about the threads of animosity that were woven all through the social fabric of the time, threatening to rend it apart. The gulf between rich and poor was abysmally deep. One wealthy widow is reported to have complained bitterly because her widow's maintenance allowed her only 400 denarii a day for luxuries. A laborer would be happy with a single such coin for a day's wage, part of which would go back to the state to help pay for the buildings upon which he labored, and part of which would find its way to the Temple personnel through various channels of religious taxation. But though the pay was low, working for it was better than joining the gaggle of beggars that clustered in front of the city gates and in the market square of every provincial town.

A strong thread of respect for personal dignity ran through the traditional Jewish culture. It sprang in large part from a shared respect for productive work, seen as a divinely imposed privilege meant to raise the sons of Adam above the beasts. The disruption of this traditional value by a foreign-dominated new

order, which turned productive work into state-organized labor, frayed the fiber of respect that bound the community. Old, festering social stresses became more intense, while new ones occupied the minds of the leaders.

The upper classes were themselves deeply divided. The old-line Temple priests—those who held firmly to ancient tradition—distrusted and were distrusted by those who came to terms with Herod and his court. When Herod had assumed the throne, most of the leading priestly families, staunchly allied to the previous Hasmonean dynasty, had opposed him; to them he was an upstart Idumean of uncertain religious faith and clear Roman loyalties. Early in his reign the king purged and executed many of the opposition and began rewarding his supporters. In due time, much of the resentment of the old upper classes was muted and repressed, though it was never altogether eliminated.

The wide gulf between the priestly aristocracy, from whom the Sadducee party drew its numbers, and the sages, scribes, and teachers, from whom the Pharisees largely filled their ranks, became wider still as the surviving priests made concessions to the new order and were absorbed into it. Few Pharisaic teachers and scribes were wealthy, and many followed rather lowly trades—one a charcoal burner, another a stonemason, and still another a public letter writer, and so forth. Once, the story goes, as a teacher named Joseph was perched on a scaffold, a disciple approached with a religious question. "Wait until this evening," the sage replied. ". . . I am paid by the day and I may not give a minute that belongs to my master away."

For their part, the Pharisees of Jerusalem based their piety not on observance of Temple ritual (the priests' domain) but on careful, day-by-day adherence to a detailed set of religious laws, along with continual discussion and argument about interpretation and application of those laws. Though they worked among the people and were devoted to just implementation of the law and to social welfare, many kept themselves separate from those they called *am ha-aretz*, or "people of the land"—those who did not follow the prescribed procedures of ritual purity in their day-to-day lives or did not tithe their food and earnings in the proper manner. Judgments varied about who were *am ha-aretz*, and so did the degrees of separation from them. Indeed, there were Pharisees who considered themselves defiled as a result of touching an *am ha-aretz*, and thus could not eat until they had taken a ritual bath. Although the *am ha-aretz* could include Jews of all economic strata, most were probably of the lower classes.

Crushed by poverty and taxation, the great mass of urban rabble were largely unable to live by all the Pharisees' precepts regarding purity and tithing, or by the priests' rules of ritual and sacrifice. Their existence was frugal at best and could easily slide off into grinding, impoverished misery. They returned the most pedantic Pharisees' contempt, resented the Sadducees' wealth and privilege, sought the opportunity to labor in Herod's new work force, yet clung for dear life to the usages of piety and fairness that the traditional culture represented.

City life

Life teemed and jostled in the steep, narrow streets and among the bewildering maze of alleys and courtyards in the cities' older sections, such as Jerusalem's Zion district and the central valley, called by Josephus the Valley of the Cheesemakers, between the Temple Mount and the Upper City. Here the common people lived: artisans and craftsmen, who were the backbone of traditional culture; tradesmen, who served the growing urban needs for goods and services; day laborers, who awoke each morning freshly unemployed. Here, too, were the chronic unemployables, beggars, who no longer dreamed of useful work—the crippled, the diseased (except for lepers,

who were not allowed within the city walls), the blind, the insane, the unloved old—all those for whom there was no hospital, no aid, no hope.

Time-honored Jewish tradition provided a measure of care for the downtrodden, counseling the "haves" to share freely with the "have-nots." Highminded Pharisees might urge a return to these humanitarian traditions, but such precepts meant little to most members of the upper classes, who controlled the wealth of the cities. Few others had anything substantial to share. Aside from some master craftsmen who operated small industries and a handful of merchants who had prospered in overseas trade, there were few middle-class Jews: if you were not rich, you were probably poor. And in the cities, divorced from the productive land, that meant that you were very poor indeed.

This Roman relief shows a cloth and cushion merchant displaying his wares to a customer in a colonnaded marketplace. Public markets were found in every large city of the Roman world, although their styles varied from place to place. Jerusalem's were generally open shops, connected with the merchant's home. Palestine's wool market was largely centered in Jerusalem. Galilee produced linen, but precious silk was imported from the Orient.

Divorce was uncommon among Jews, even though a man could divorce his wife simply because she did not please him. To legalize the divorce he had to present her with a bill of divorce, or get, such as the one shown here—although the terms might vary depending on the cause. In this get, Yehosef, son of Yehosef son of Naqsan, declares to Miriam, daughter of Jonathan of Nablata, " . . . that you be enabled yourself to go and be wife to any Jewish man that you desire. And herewith unto you from me a bill of divorce and deed of release. So I grant . . . and all that is destroyed and damaged and . . . I shall recompense you as due, and pay quarterly."

Most city families, like the families in country villages, lived in one- or two-room cubes of white-washed, oven-dried brick with dirt floors and flat roofs of hard-packed clay. Some houses had second floors, where married children lived or space was rented out. (It was in such an upper room that Jesus and the disciples were to share the Passover feast known as the Last Supper.) These houses were not arranged in tidy squares, but bunched around small, hectic courtyards where women did the laundry and cooked over charcoal or wood fires, where children played and life's busy hubbub blended. Toilets were in these courtyards, and so were chicken coops, dovecotes, woodsheds, strawsheds, and other small storehouses. There was no plumbing—water came from public wells to be stored in courtyard cisterns (the trade of water carrier was an urban specialty), no sewage system save open gutters that ran along alleys connecting the courtyards to the streets, no garbage collection, and no gardens to absorb organic wastes. In every house an earthenware lamp burned oil, adding its rancid, fatty odor to what must have been an overpowering stench.

Tradesmen, laborers, and slaves

Cut off from the land, town people looked to shopkeepers and street vendors for their food, and there was a lively trade in staple items. Barley or lentil porridge was the common fare, along with barley bread and perhaps some onions or cucumbers. Nuts, olives, and fruit rounded out the typical diet—and on the Sabbath, a little salted fish. Except in the most affluent houses, meat was reserved for feast days. Only the olives and some of the fruits and nuts were local products. The area around Jerusalem was rich in olive groves, such as those that covered the Mount of Olives, where Jesus went to pray before his arrest. (Olive oil was probably the city's only export, in fact, and many people were employed at commercial oil presses, or *gethsemanes.*)

Craftsmen wore the badges of their trade with pride. A stroll through an urban marketplace might reveal a dyer sporting a brightly colored tag of cloth, a tailor with a large bone needle in his cloak, or a carpenter with a wood chip tucked behind his ear. Among the most secure were the stonecutters, masons, woodworkers, sculptors, and others who formed the heart of Herod's work force; and these were also the proudest professions.

Some other callings, though not dishonorable, were not so well thought of. Among the few grounds upon which a woman could divorce her husband was the fact that he made his living as a copper smelter, tanner, or dung collector—all highly odiferous trades. (The latter two were connected; the dung collector's stock in trade was used for tanning hides.) She could even be granted a divorce if she had known his trade before they were married, on the theory that she hadn't imagined how terrible the smell would be. At the other end of the scale, perfumers, although their jobs were clean and their clientele rich, were despised by the pious because they often came in contact with women of questionable reputation.

The Temple provided work for a privileged few: one family had the right to manufacture incense, another baked the shewbread for the offering, still others were entrusted with annual replacement of the curtains that hung in the Temple. During the great festivals, when the city was aswarm with pilgrims, who were allowed by law to spend 10 percent of their yearly earnings in Jerusalem, there was a busy market in sacrificial animals, from doves to fatted calves. Innkeepers did well then, too, and so did those who sold small, crafted souvenir items.

Most trades were family enterprises, passed down through generations. A boy would acquire his father's skills, as a girl learned her mother's, by helping from early childhood. Members of the same trades tended to live and conduct their businesses in

Smiths were highly respected craftsmen. The relief above illustrates three steps of coppersmithing: weighing raw material, shaping hot metal, and decorating the finished products.

the same areas. In Jerusalem, there was a street of butchers, one of bakers, and another of ironsmiths. The towns of Hebron and Marisa, blessed with particularly fine clay, were known for their pottery. At Sepphoris, near Nazareth in Galilee, the center of the flax country, linen makers predominated. Jerusalem's carders and spinners produced wool thread, and the busy wool market was located in the suburban district called New City. Weavers, however, were in the least desirable neighborhood, near the Dung Gate overlooking the Valley of Hinnom, where refuse was commonly dumped. Because their craft was traditionally regarded as women's work, they were among the so-called despised trades. Within these concentrations, trade guilds had grown up to regulate prices, to set working hours, and to

lend mutual aid in time of need. In some callings members agreed to open shop only every other day during periods when business was slow, presumably joining the common labor force on the off day.

Over the centuries, teachers of Jewish law had evolved an elaborate set of safeguards for the fair treatment of laborers. "You shall not oppress a hired servant who is poor and needy," Deuteronomy 24:14 enjoins, "whether he is one of your brethren or one of the sojourners who are in your land within your towns; you shall give him his hire on the day he earns it, before the sun goes down (for he is poor, and sets his heart upon it)." By Herod's time, the rules further defined a laborer's work hours; how he was to be fed, housed, and clothed; and how he was to be paid. Jews, for the most part, followed these precepts, and so did many of the foreign aristocracy in Judea. In the Hellenized cities of other areas, however, there was little regard for such rules.

Slavery was an ancient institution in Palestine. Though the slave market in Jerusalem dealt almost entirely in Gentiles (a healthy slave would fetch about 2,000 denarii), other cities had Jewish slaves. A free citizen might fall into slavery as a punishment for theft or for unpaid debts; a poor man might sell himself into servitude rather than let the family starve. According to Jewish law, he could be made to work no more than 10 hours a day, and never at night. He could not be made to work on the Sabbath. He would not be subjected to any humiliation or put to any task that would expose his position to

Both goldsmiths and silversmiths used ring molds of various sizes to shape ornate jewelry. Such jewelers were judged by some of the pious to be among the "despised trades," for their contact with women caused them to be suspected of immorality.

A wealthy merchant in Palestine could live in luxury in a multiroom villa. Most likely he could afford several wives and a dozen servants and indulge his taste by acquiring exotic goods from all corners of the Roman Empire. Here an importer of glass and his partners inspect goblets as an agent extolls the virtues of this new ware. The plastered stone walls of this fine house are decorated with imitation marble panels, just as in Herod's palaces. The walls are given an illusion of depth by painted columns that support seemingly projecting cornices.

the public, such as tailoring, barbering, or serving as a bath attendant. If he fled his master, he was not to be returned. If he was maimed or mistreated, the courts set him free. And if he was killed by his master, the master also was executed. Female slaves had somewhat fewer privileges than males did, but they too enjoyed the law's protection; and a comely young slave girl, kept as a concubine, could always

hope that the master would take her on as a wife.

These ancient laws of social welfare, rooted as they were in a tightly knit agricultural society, meant little to most urban slave owners. To them, as to the rest of the Mediterranean world, a slave was more an object than a person—a kind of tool endowed with speech, as one Roman had observed. Small wonder that in the cities, where such attitudes

in which David the shepherd had become king. Secure in their grand houses, tended by servants and slaves, and if they were extremely rich, catered to by several wives and concubines, they lived in the most sumptuous manner, consumed the best foods and wines, and draped their bodies in the rarest silks. Their gracious mansions of native limestone featured open courtyards, pools, gardens, arcades, Roman baths with hot running water, and in some cases even a form of central heating.

Their social life centered around the dinner table, where banquets were served. There were usually nine guests, seldom more, and most likely they would all be men. Early in the afternoon the guests would arrive on foot or in litters carried by slaves, and the host would greet them in the atrium, an open central court. A servant would wash the hands and feet of each new arrival and perhaps would crown him with a laurel wreath and anoint his head with oil or scent as gestures of hospitality. The assembled company would then move into the dining area.

Reclining on couches, the guests would converse in Greek, or possibly in Aramaic, the language of the streets—never in Hebrew, the language of the Temple, and seldom in Latin. The food would be served on plates of silver, bronze, rare wood, or *terra sigillata*—a fine red pottery imported from Italy. There would be goblets of blown glass, a technique that was just coming into fashion, and wine, sweetened with honey, would flow freely. The guests would pluck at their food with their fingers and sop up juices with bits of wheat bread; between courses the servants would circulate bowls of water and towels for washing and wiping the hands.

During the meal the guests might be soothed by musicians playing on flutes and drums, or diverted by singers or even dancing girls. In a highly cultivated household the host might call upon a poet to recite his latest odes or upon a noted orator to speak.

had invaded even the Jewish upper classes, there was an intense, growing thirst among the poor for someone—a messiah—who would drive out the Gentiles and restore the glory that had been Israel.

Feasts and fashion for the rich

No such thirst existed among the wealthy; the last thing they wanted was a return to the bucolic society

Painted ceramic bowls (above and on the stone serving table in the drawing) were local products of unique composition and style. None have been found outside Jerusalem. This so-called Jerusalem painted pottery was thin and delicate. The terra sigillata decanters (below and on an upper shelf in the drawing) were true luxury items, comparable to today's finest Wedgwood china or Waterford crystal. A complete set of this red, decorated pottery would have been the pride of any household in Jerusalem.

Then, as day faded and oil lamps were lit, and the diners settled back to sip their wine and enjoy their honey-soaked pastries and fruit, a troupe of acrobats and comedians might perform.

The diners would be clothed in the finest wool, linen, or imported silk—worth its weight in gold. Their style of dress was heavily influenced by Greek and Roman fashion. The basic garment was a tunic of white linen, held at the waist with a belt or sash. Over this would be draped a voluminous, often brightly hued mantle. Its cut and the way it hung about the shoulders were largely matters of personal taste; one distinctive version resembled a Roman toga.

The lyre, or kinnor (a replica is shown above), was the chief instrument of the Temple musicians and a favorite of the Jewish people. David the shepherd boy played the lyre to soothe Saul's rages.

Jewish tradition called for fringes at the bottom, and wealthy Jews made the most of the decorative opportunity. The most luxurious mantles were colored deep royal purple with a dye produced at Tyre (in modern Lebanon) from the secretions of the murex sea snail. Herod undoubtedly wore rich purple except on state occasions, when he would don elaborately embroidered robes, Asiatic in origin, with finely worked, multicolored fringes at the bottom. The feet of the wealthy would be encased in ankle-high boots of such expensive leather as hyena or jackal hide or perhaps in red-dyed shoes turned up at the toes. Sandals were common in all but the most Romanized circles, where they were deemed effeminate except for evening wear.

While Persian-type caps, Arab *kaffiyehs* (head-cloths), and shawls might be seen in the streets and bazaars, the up-to-date wealthy probably went bareheaded or sported brimmed straw hats against the sun. Beards were out of fashion; Gentiles and the cosmopolitan Jews probably were clean-shaven in the Roman manner. But ancient Jewish custom called for beards, so most Judean aristocrats may well have cultivated discreet facial hair, carefully clipped and perfumed. Wealthy households employed family barbers to keep everyone in trim.

Sculpted Roman hair styles—so familiar to us from Roman statuary—were popular: short and combed forward over the brow for men, elaborately coiffed for women. A great lady would sit patiently for hours while her servants plaited and curled her tresses into ever more fanciful shapes, perhaps adding nests of false hair for bulk. These creations would be secured with prickly arsenals of gold pins, ivory or tortoise-shell combs, jewel-studded headbands, and nets of gold thread or pearl. One especially eye-catching device, known as a "city of gold," was a diadem that resembled the fortifications of a town or city. Both men and women were known to dye or bleach their hair, often lending it the auburn tint of henna. Proud young bucks, out to dazzle, might sprinkle their hair with gold dust.

Traditional aristocracy

This princely way of life united the wealthy of Palestine, Jew and Gentile alike, with the upper classes of the rest of the Roman Empire, even as it separated them from their roots among the people. Herod's boundaries encompassed several very different regions, and his more than 2 million subjects included Jews, Arabs, Syrians, Phoenicians, Greeks, and various admixtures of each. Only some 4 or 5 percent of this varied population might have counted themselves aristocrats, and only a small percentage of these controlled nearly all the nation's wealth. Many owned large agricultural estates, others held lucrative positions in government, and some derived vast income from the Temple.

Judea's most tradition-bound aristocracy was a priestly caste of immense antiquity, which was especially centered on a few families that were closely linked with the high priesthood. Indeed, one of the proudest boasts a Judean could make was descent from the revered Zadok, high priest a thousand years earlier under David and Solomon. Members of the Zadokite clan had evidently formed the nucleus of the powerful and conservative Sadducee party (which derived its very name from that of the clan's founder) and, along with a few other Sadducee families, had for generations dominated Judea's traditional ruling council. Once known as the *gerousia,* or senate, this council had evolved by Herod's time into the 71-member Sanhedrin.

Second to the priests were the Levites, or descendants of Levi, who were charged with the maintenance of the Temple and with providing all Temple music. Although the Levites were forbidden to own land, they were not necessarily poor. Originally, the tithe that all Jews owed to the Temple was to be given to them, and they in turn were to give 10 percent of the proceeds to the Temple priests. In practice, the priests took the tithes themselves and made the division as they saw fit. But there was plenty to go around. In addition to the tithes, there was a constant flow of gifts and special assessments coming into the Temple. And because the priests were entitled by law to the hides of all sacrificial animals, there was a sizable income from the leather trades. Then too, the Levites were in charge of the highly profitable money changing that took place in the Temple court. Though they ranked below the priesthood in social standing, some Levites were wealthier than many priests.

An outsider could not achieve priesthood, nor could priesthood, when offered, be refused. The title, and the duties that went with it, were entirely hereditary. The priestly families were linked in intricate patterns of intermarriage, and great care was taken to keep track of lines of descent. Even so, centuries of procreation, complicated by repeated invasions and suppressions from outside forces, had diluted some priestly lineage and had brought about

These glass vessels date from about the first centuries B.C. *and* A.D.*: below, a bottle; at right, a measuring cup; below right, a bowl. Glassmaking was among Jerusalem's industries. In the refuse of a first-century* B.C. *glass factory, archeologists found shards of old-style molded glass alongside fragments of early blown glass, showing that the factory used both techniques.*

many offshoot clans. The men of these nonaristocratic clans were undeniably priests, and as such, were worthy of respect, but they had little share in the wealth and prestige that belonged to the great priestly families of Jerusalem. Thus, a tense thread of resentment already ran through the priestly caste when Herod came to power. His ascension did nothing to alleviate it. Rather, he increased the existing stresses and added several new ones.

The ornate hair styles that were fashionable among aristocrats required that a woman spend hours under the ministrations of servants, as shown in this first-century B.C. Roman relief. She could examine the result in mirrors of polished metal; a pair of mirrors is seen at left.

The new Herodian order

When, as one of his first acts after taking power, Herod had ordered the execution of the majority of the Sanhedrin, he had eliminated the heads of several influential families. The families still existed and were still wealthy, but they had to make way for a new elite of Herod's choosing. Sadducean priests still dominated the Sanhedrin under Herod, but that council had been rendered nearly powerless in affairs of state and was losing much of its domestic authority to the rising rabbinical tide of Pharisaic sages and scribes. Now some of the Pharisees who were on the crest of that tide began to assume the privileged aura of aristocracy and to take prominent places on the Sanhedrin—a fact that must have rankled many of the old-line Sadducees. More important from the king's point of view, the resultant internal tension rendered that council less likely to take a united stand in opposition to him.

Most of those who achieved power and prestige under Herod belonged to a few priestly families that had been gone from Judea since the Babylonian exile in the sixth century B.C. As the leaders among the far-flung communities of the Diaspora, they had mingled with the rich and powerful of the classical world and had absorbed cosmopolitan attitudes and tastes. Encouraged by Herod to return, or simply engulfed—as the king's own family had been—by Judea's spreading borders, they were more at home among the members of his court than they were with those who had maintained Judea's traditions over the centuries. Yet it was into their hands, during Herod's reign and the decades of direct Roman rule that followed, that the traditions of the Temple and the priesthood were to pass.

Outstanding among these families of the Diaspora was the house of Boethus, whose founder had already migrated back from Alexandria when Herod came to power. In 24 or 23 B.C. Herod appointed the highly respected Simon ben Boethus to the position of high priest and soon thereafter married his daughter, another Mariamne. Simon was to hold the post until the last, terrible year of Herod's life, when the king, suspecting the priest's daughter of plotting against him, divorced her and replaced her father. Before long, Simon's replacement lost the post, as did *his* replacement, who was followed in rapid succession by two of Simon's sons, Joezer and Eleazar. A third son, also named Simon, later held the high priesthood under direct Roman authority.

This rapid-fire replacement of high priests, first by Herod and then by the Romans, did much to dispel the position's inherent authority. At the same time, it sowed the seeds for a new elite within the priesthood, comprising all those who had ever been high priests, their immediate families, and their descendants. (It was probably this upper crust to whom the writers of the Gospels and the Apostle Paul were to refer when they wrote of "high priests.")

Although the Sanhedrin was the established council of the Jewish people, Herod seldom, if ever, conferred with it on issues of substance. Instead, he formed his own council, an inner circle of distinguished men who functioned both as advisers and as educators within the royal family. Herod was an insatiable collector of talent; himself an outsider, he reached outside Palestine for the skills he needed to implement his grandiose plans. Hence, the interests of this inner circle were—like his own—oriented less toward the concerns of the pious Jewish population, who formed the core of the kingdom, than toward the culture of the Greco-Roman world at large. Just as he had chosen his high priest from the Diaspora rather than from the local aristocracy, so his closest adviser and confidant, a man named Nicolaus, came not from his own realm but from the ancient, thoroughly Hellenized city of Damascus.

Nicolaus of Damascus was a man who had enjoyed a full Greek education in the arts and sciences and who followed the philosophy of Aristotle. A scholar

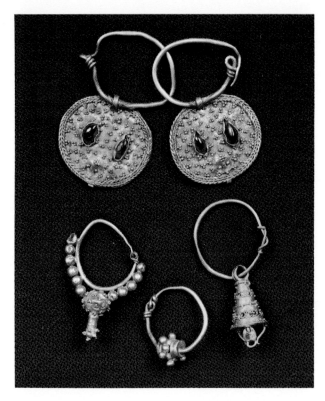

Jewelry was not only decorative but indicated a person's material worth. The gold earrings and nose rings at left were found in a Nabatean cemetery. Those who could afford it donned more elaborate ornaments, such as the one above, of gold and semiprecious stones. Bracelets, rings for the fingers and toes, and necklaces were also popular.

and philosopher of international reputation, he had been a tutor in the court of Antony and Cleopatra and after their deaths was transferred to Herod's employ. His principal literary work was a world history in 144 books, which culminated in a detailed account of Herod's reign. (It was from Nicolaus that Josephus drew most of the information for his description of Herod.) He also wrote philosophical and scientific essays, theatrical comedies and tragedies, musical compositions, an autobiography, and a biography of Augustus. He was tall, lanky, charming, and a fine diplomat. His influence grew as he came to be respected by both Herod and Augustus, and he seems to have been one of the few people who became genuinely close to Herod.

Colors and Scents

Many women wore makeup. Black eyeliner and mascara, made by mixing ground antimony with water or gum, highlighted the eyes as it protected them from the sun's glare. Rouge—used mostly by wealthy ladies—might come from mulberry juice or red ocher. Both sexes used body oils and perfumes. The poor had olive oil and homemade floral or herbal extracts; the rich imported nard (an ointment from the stems and root of a Himalayan plant) from India and scents from Alexandria, the center of the international perfume trade.

The glass cosmetic flask with snake-shaped handles shown above was discovered in Jerusalem, as was the bronze spatula resting in one of its twin compartments. The spatula was used for applying paint. Both items date from Roman times, but their basic design is strikingly similar to the implements being used by the Egyptian woman depicted in the ancient papyrus at the left. The Egyptian applicator would probably have been made of wood. The mixing of cosmetics from natural sources was a basic skill of ancient women.

All ranks and designations at court were Greek-inspired, from the most distinguished down to the special class of high-born youths called *syntrophoi*, who were official playmates for the royal children. Even the government's coins were inscribed in Greek rather than Hebrew, and Greek names were common among the Jewish upper classes—a tradition that had already begun at the time of the Hasmoneans.

The kingdom's chief financial minister, who had charge of the king's signet ring, was named Ptolemy. Little is known about him except that he organized the kingdom's administration along typical Hellenistic patterns. His was the task of supervising and gathering revenues from the royal lands, vast agricultural estates that may have embraced more than half the kingdom, as well as administering the funds that poured in from Herod's huge foreign holdings, from several state-owned commercial enterprises, and from taxes. Part of the collection of taxes was evidently carried out by Herod's own bureaucracy, while part was farmed out, in the Roman manner, to private individuals known as publicans. Such tax officials were notoriously corrupt, but as long as they turned in their quotas on time no one at court cared how much more they took from the people to line their own pockets.

The military, like most armies of the day, was composed largely of mercenaries. Like the government it defended, it was a blend of nationalities. It probably included a number of Roman advisers and some seasoned warriors from the king's own region of Idumea. Other swords for hire came from many parts of the world—even from Germany. Herod's personal guard was a company of Thracians, Germans, and Gauls, supplemented by 400 well-trained Galatians whom the emperor Augustus had given to Herod from the forces left behind by Cleopatra. There were also regiments of local Jewish conscripts and militiamen, whom Herod rewarded with grants of farmland or settled in military colonies along his borders; at one point he invited more than 500 disciplined cavalrymen from Babylonia, all crack shots with the bow, and installed them in their own new city in a key border province in the northeast. He made their land a tax-free zone, which in turn attracted other colonists.

For the most part, this impressive military aggregate served as a deterrent rather than as a fighting force. In Herod's Palestine, the strength of Hellenism confronted the strength of Judaism, and the confrontation was never far from explosive. And yet—despite occasional threats from outside and constant tensions within—Herod ruled over a kingdom that was largely at peace, both with itself and its neighbors. The lack of international conflict was due to the powerful presence of the Roman Empire and to Herod's good relationship with the emperor. The internal peace was his own achievement.

Family intrigues

Yet for all his political skill, Herod was never able to control his family, many of whom had egos as immense as his own. He had a total of 10 wives, and he sired numerous children, several of whom were possible successors to the throne. As he aged, and the question of succession became more urgent, the atmosphere of the court became poisoned by the competition among them. The struggle for succession divided his family into warring camps, as interested mothers and sons intrigued against the favorites of the moment.

When Herod had first come to power, a deadly family crisis arose from his attempt to secure the loyalty of the remaining Hasmonean nobility by taking the old ruler's granddaughter, Mariamne, in marriage. This astute maneuver was no sacrifice, for Mariamne was beautiful and the king was passionately in love with her. But when Mariamne's mother successfully conspired, through Antony and Cleopa-tra, to have Mariamne's 17-year-old brother appointed high priest in place of the priest whom Herod had appointed first, the king recognized a clear challenge to his rule. The tall, handsome youth cut a noble figure in his priestly regalia, and the crowds responded to him enthusiastically. Shortly after, while swimming with some young noblemen at the old Hasmonean palace in Jericho, the young priest was "accidentally" drowned, undoubtedly at Herod's direct orders.

This was the first of a series of family murders and executions. The other victims included Mariamne's grandfather, the old ruler Hyrcanus; Herod had ordered the old man strangled, probably before the crucial meeting with Augustus in 30 B.C., lest the new emperor consider restoring the crown to its previous owner. Herod also gave orders that, should he not return from the meeting with the emperor, his beloved Mariamne was herself to die. Learning of this order was the last straw for Mariamne. She insulted the king openly and refused him access to her bed. Then she found herself on trial for adultery and soon joined the list of dead Hasmoneans.

Herod grieved mightily for his lost beloved. According to Josephus, "he put aside the administration of the kingdom, and was so far overcome by his passion that he would actually order his servants to summon Mariamne as if she were still alive. . . ." He finally sank into such a deep delirium that "his life was despaired of." During this time of Herod's helplessness, Mariamne's mother—who had in fact been at the heart of many of the conspiracies—tried once more to take control of the kingdom. But she moved too slowly, and Herod, on the road to recovery, ordered her execution. With her death, the Hasmonean line was reduced to Herod's own sons by Mariamne, Alexander and Aristobulus. These two youths he had sent to Rome to be properly educated.

Bronze coins minted in Palestine by Herod the Great and his sons (except for Herod Philip) as well as by the Roman authorities who followed them, are inscribed in Greek with the names of the rulers who issued them. Some also include the dates of their issue. Most of the designs show ears of barley, lilies, vine leaves, palm fronds, cornucopias, canopies, and other symbols that do not break the Commandment against making graven images.

Herod's legacy

Herod was a uniquely textured individual, colored by all the cultural threads that came together in his land. He could play a dozen roles a day, and did; yet, for all his chameleon flexibility, he was no hypocrite. All the roles he played were integral to himself. He was at once a Jew, an Idumean, a Roman, a Greek; a ruthless conqueror, a benevolent tyrant, a faithful subject, and a canny competitor.

He proved himself capable of mass executions and cruel murder, yet he destroyed none of the powerful institutions that pulled against one another in his kingdom. Rather, he balanced each stress with another, creating a tense web with himself at the center, and by his political skill he maintained a coalition of sorts among disparate regions and disputant populations.

But the fine tuning that was the mark of his long reign became the curse of his legacy. No one else was capable of maintaining the balances he had struck in Judea—even Herod himself began to lose control in the closing years of his reign. And once the over-strained threads of his web began to snap, the entire construct was doomed.

When Herod died in Jericho, according to Josephus, "Archelaus saw to it that his father's burial should be most splendid, and he brought out all his ornaments to accompany the procession for the deceased. Herod was borne upon a golden bier studded with precious stones . . . and with a cover of purple over it. The dead man too was wrapped in purple robes and wore a diadem. . . ." Respecting custom, Archelaus hired a band of pipers and professional mourners. After the host of relatives, came his bodyguards, then the Thracians, Germans, and Gauls, "all equipped for battle. Right behind them came the whole army as if marching to war . . . followed by five hundred servants carrying spices." The body was conveyed to Herodium. "So ended Herod's reign."

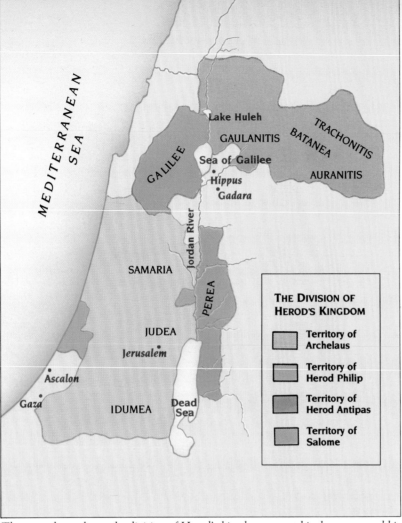

THE DIVISION OF HEROD'S KINGDOM

Territory of Archelaus

Territory of Herod Philip

Territory of Herod Antipas

Territory of Salome

The map above shows the division of Herod's kingdom among his three sons and his sister Salome, who also received the royal palace in Ascalon. The cities of Gaza, Hippus, and Gadara were placed under control of the Roman governor of Syria.

Struggle for succession

Later in Herod's reign, the two Hasmonean brothers, Alexander and Aristobulus, became the focus of murderous family warfare, along with Herod's first-born son, Antipater (by his first wife, Doris, a native of Jerusalem).

It was the emperor's right to bestow the kingship of a client state as he saw fit, but Augustus had given Herod the honor of naming his own successor. His first choices were Alexander and Aristobulus, who had become great favorites of Augustus during their years in Rome. But the two turned out to be arrogant and abusive, openly criticizing Herod and deriding the Idumean side of the royal family. Antipater, on the other hand, was sly and had a sharp, poisonous tongue; with the help and support of Herod's sister and brother, he saw to it that the king heard every complaint and slanderous rumor about the two. Herod was eventually persuaded to change his will, naming Antipater crown prince and demoting Alexander and Aristobulus to second and third in line.

Antipater was not satisfied and sought to be rid of the Hasmonean heirs altogether. Herod, in his mid-sixties, was falling ill in mind and body and was easy prey for the venom that was infesting the court. Suspicions were planted, and he saw enemies everywhere. He suffered hallucinations in which he saw Alexander coming at him with a sword.

Finally, a complex plot against Herod's life was uncovered in which both brothers were implicated. Alexander was charged not only with plotting to kill his father but also with seducing all three of Herod's favorite eunuchs. Investigations were held, and the palace torturers were kept busy extracting incriminating confessions from hapless underlings. Herod convened a court of noblemen, who declared both brothers guilty, and Herod ordered them strangled.

In his obsession with the intrigues of his wives and sons, Herod was beginning to lose control of his kingdom. A group of Pharisees, fined by Herod for refusing to take an oath of loyalty to Augustus, prophesied that the king would lose the throne, and that a palace eunuch named Bagaos would father the new ruler. The eunuch and some of the Pharisees were executed, but the damage had been done: discontent had flared, and other smoldering embers were now burning brighter.

Antipater now held sole and undisputed primacy. While his father lived, however, he could not be secure, and so he tried to rush Herod's death. When a servant revealed under torture that Antipater had ordered him to prepare a fatal drug for the king, Antipater was arrested and tried before the Roman governor of Syria. Herod flew into a violent rage at the trial. "No one shall escape who thirsts for my blood," he cried, "no, not though conviction should extend to all my children." Antipater was imprisoned.

The death of the king

Herod's illness was developing into a serious and painful malady, which it is not possible to diagnose exactly from Josephus' description. It was noised abroad in the most ghastly terms—including everything from gangrene and an infestation of worms in his private parts, to insatiable itching, severe convulsions, and ulcers in his bowels. His bewildered doctors could do nothing to help. The famed hot springs at Callirhoe, on the eastern shore of the Dead Sea, had no effect. When the king was lowered into a presumably soothing tub of heated oil, he fainted from the pain.

Meanwhile, discontent grew. In the spring of 4 B.C., a group of students, at the instigation of the two prominent Pharisees who were their teachers, hauled down a gilded eagle that Herod had placed over the Temple gate several years earlier and chopped it up with axes, on the grounds that it was a violation of the Commandment against graven images. They were immediately arrested and brought to Herod. Outraged by the insult to his generosity, he cited the sacrilege of defacing the Temple and ordered the ringleaders burned at the stake.

Herod, fearing that his imminent death would not be mourned, decided, in his burgeoning madness, to give the kingdom cause for sorrow. He commanded notable Jews from all parts of the land to come to him and had them shut up in the hippodrome. Then he gave orders that, upon his death, all of them were to be killed. It was his last executive command, save

one. Before he expired, the king told some of his bodyguards to kill Antipater. When Augustus was informed of the death sentence, he reportedly remarked, "It is better to be Herod's pig than his son."

Herod was buried with a pomp and splendor worthy of the emperor himself. Slowly the grand procession marched from Jericho across the Judean hills to Herodium. There, in the fortress that bore his name, King Herod the Great was laid to rest.

By Herod's final will, Archelaus, son of his fourth wife, Malthace of Samaria, was to reign as king over the bulk of the territory. The remainder of the kingdom was to be divided among two other surviving sons. Herod Philip, son of Herod's fifth wife (who was named Cleopatra), became ruler of the varied and difficult Transjordan lands of Batanea and Trachonitis; he was to rule them competently for many years. Herod Antipas, another son of Malthace of Samaria, became ruler of Galilee and Perea; an able and peace-loving man, he too governed well—although he was destined to be remembered as the man who ordered John the Baptist beheaded at the urging of his niece, Salome.

Augustus was unwilling to grant Archelaus the title of king, and so he was named ethnarch of the rich territories of Judea, Samaria, and Idumea. He was unable to control the flow of events in Jerusalem, and within a month the crowds that gathered in the city during Passover began to riot. Archelaus called in the army. In the ensuing massacre some 3,000 people lost their lives. The uprisings spread until the entire region was in revolt. The Roman governor of Syria moved in with a large army to restore order; before the crisis was past, part of Jerusalem's Temple was set afire and its treasury was looted. In A.D. 6, Augustus exiled Archelaus to Vienna and declared his inheritance an official province of Rome. From then on, it was administered by a series of military prefects, the most famous of whom was to be Pontius Pilate.

Chapter Four

Village Life

When Mary and Joseph returned from Egypt, they went home to Nazareth, where Jesus "grew and became strong," according to Luke. As a young boy, Jesus observed country ways, from which he drew many images for his later teachings.

In the first century A.D. the vast majority of people in Galilee lived in rural villages where farming determined virtually every aspect of their daily lives—their traditions and habits, their holy days and beliefs. Such a place was Nazareth, Jesus' boyhood home, high in a sheltered basin some 1,300 feet above sea level. The hills surrounding Nazareth are part of a limestone ridge that defined the southernmost border of Lower Galilee. From the summit above the village, the view west is to Mount Carmel on the Mediterranean coast, east to nearby Mount Tabor, and north to distant, snow-covered Mount Hermon. South of Nazareth stretches the fertile Plain of Esdraelon. Its gentle terrain and strategic location made it a battleground of conquerors and a crossroads of trade and travel from earliest times. The caravan route from Egypt, which hugged the flat coastline, was probably the one Mary and Joseph traveled with the young Jesus on their way home following the death of King Herod. After having spent much time on the road and hiding out in a foreign land, Mary and Joseph must have been eager to rejoin their family and friends and get back to the comfort of their home and carpenter's shop.

The hub of a typical village such as Nazareth was the marketplace and a street of shops where craftsmen made and sold their wares. The smith and the carpenter, whose combined skills were needed to make and repair farm implements—iron-tipped plows, sickles, cart wheels—were usually located near each other, side by side or opposite as shown. The villagers also depended on mat makers, potters, and basket weavers, who displayed their goods in the streets.

Nazareth was settled some 2,000 years before Jesus' birth. The first inhabitants were probably attracted to the sheltered hillside overlooking the fertile Jezreel Valley by a sweet abundant spring, known today as Mary's Well. Thirty miles from the Mediterranean and 15 from the Sea of Galilee, Nazareth was just a stone's throw from a caravan route to Egypt. The ancient village may have covered some six acres, not including the outlying farmlands. Today Nazareth is dominated by the Church of the Annunciation (center), reputedly the largest Christian church in the Middle East.

The lush countryside around Nazareth even today is very beautiful. The Jewish historian, Josephus, was inclined in his own time to wax rhapsodic: "The land is everywhere so rich in soil and pasturage and produces such variety of trees, that even the most indolent are tempted . . . to devote themselves to agriculture. In fact, every inch of the soil has been cultivated by the inhabitants." As was typical of Palestinian villagers of the time, Nazarenes divided their time between a central marketplace—an area crowded with houses and workshops—and the fields and vineyards that ringed the village.

The people of Lower Galilee

Though most residents of Galilee in Jesus' time were Jews, a number of Gentiles, both slave and free, lived among them. There were Syrians who had migrated from the north, Greeks who had moved in after the conquests of Alexander the Great, and

Romans, who had arrived about the middle of the first century B.C.

The Jews were fairly small in stature. Relatively light-skinned, they were nonetheless deeply tanned most of the year as a result of a lifetime spent out-of-doors. Their strong faces were almost always framed with dark brown or black hair, which was worn long by both men and women. Following tradition, most of the men wore beards.

The Galileans spoke an Aramaic dialect that sounded crude and uncultured to those with educations in Greek, and they were considered to be unsophisticated rustics by Jerusalemites. The stern religious leaders of Jerusalem distrusted the Jews from Galilee, suspecting them of being less than strict in their observance of the law.

Family life

Galilean social life centered on the family. Rural families tend to be large, cohesive, and extremely hardworking, and such was probably true of Jesus' kinsmen and neighbors. The husband was the spiritual and legal head of the household, and he was the final arbiter of all issues dealing with the welfare of his wife and children. A woman may well have called her husband *baal* ("lord") or *adon* ("master"). In return, of course, the husband bore the responsibility for feeding, protecting, and sheltering his family. Under the law, if his wife found "no favor in his eyes because he has found some indecency in her," a husband could give her a bill of divorcement. If the "indecency" stopped short of adultery, the marriage might simply be dissolved, with both parties becoming free to remarry. If a wife was suspected of adultery, however, a priest would conduct a trial by ordeal: A suspected woman was forced to drink a bitter potion. If she became sick, she was considered guilty and was stoned or otherwise put to death. If she showed no ill effects, she was presumed innocent and returned to her husband.

All village Jews were governed by the same stringent system of moral, religious, and social codes. Husbands had clearly established obligations to their wives and wives to their husbands; children were instructed early to honor their parents; parents knew with certainty what their duties to their children were. And every important event in a Nazarene's life, from birth to marriage to parenthood to death, had its proper time and its immutable rules and rituals, many of them involving prayer. For example, many Jews recited a blessing for nearly every occasion, including waking up, dressing, lacing their sandals, and washing their hands.

The family home

Parents, young children, unmarried adults, and married sons and their spouses might all live under one small roof, with little or no privacy and very few material comforts to ease their lives. While the better houses—especially in larger cities—were likely to be made of stone, encompassing several rooms in perhaps two stories, the typical village house was little more than a rude dwelling constructed of mud brick and consisting of just one or two all-purpose rooms.

Doorways were narrow and low, forcing a man to bend slightly when entering. The houses of the rich might have had locks with keys, but most houses had wooden doors hung on leather hinges, and if the doors were locked at all, it was probably with wooden bolts or iron bars that were simply pulled through sockets on the inside. As the animals were often kept in part of the house at night, interiors were often designed with two levels—the lower portion to shelter the animals and a raised portion, perhaps 18 inches higher, where the family ate and slept away from the domestic beasts.

Except in rich households, there was little in the way of furniture. Bedding was all but nonexistent. Family members usually stretched out on mats, cov-ering themselves with tunics or cloaks. Personal possessions, too, were scant. An entire family's total material wealth might fit in a single chest, so there was no need for many storage cabinets or closets. The "kitchen" consisted only of an oven, some pottery, a few utensils, and a stock of stored food. The only light in the house came from the dim glow of oil lamps, which were perched in wall niches or on shelves or stands. There was no bathroom; matters of personal toilet—washing, for example—were best done in the courtyard or in the street, where the discarded water could seep away without turning the dirt floor of the house into a bed of mud.

The roof of the house was generally flat. To make it, brushwood branches were woven together and laid on rafters and then covered with a thick layer of clay that filled the spaces between the branches and formed a smooth, hardened layer of plaster. To keep

Each day women gathered at the well to fetch drinking water, mingle with friends, and exchange news. This ancient well on a windswept plain must have supplied generations with clear, pure water as indicated by the deep grooves worn into the stone wall by the ropes used to pull up heavy buckets. Although some houses may have had cisterns for collecting rainwater, cistern water was not always safe to drink and so was used mostly for cleaning and washing.

the roof from washing away, the owner performed a number of maintenance chores that included rolling over the roof after a heavy rainstorm with a device very like the modern lawn roller, applying a fresh coat of clay plaster each fall before the start of the rainy season, and replacing the entire roof or sections of it, when needed. Fortunately, it was a fairly easy chore to cut away and replace sections of the roof. This is borne out in Mark 2:1–4. When Jesus was preaching in a house in Capernaum, the people crowded in so thickly that they blocked the door, and the friends of a paralytic could not bring the afflicted man before Jesus to be healed. Their practical solution was to cut away part of the roof and lower the sick man through the ceiling into the house.

The roof was generally made accessible by ladder or an outside staircase. On hot nights, people slept on the roofs, but they also used the roofs for meals,

meditation, private talks, shouting news to the neighbors, or dancing and other festivities. They dried fruits on the roofs and hung out wet clothes to dry in the sun. If the family grew too large for the house, an additional room may have been built on the roof. To make it relatively safe for all the activity that took place there, the roof was enclosed with a parapet, perhaps some 18 inches high. On this matter Deuteronomy 22:8 reads like a building code: "When you build a new house, you shall make a parapet for your roof, that you may not bring the guilt of blood upon your house, if anyone fall from it."

When the men and older boys left for the fields and shops, those women who weren't called upon to help with farming chores worked in and around the house, making daily trips to the well. Like every other member of the family, the wife—along with her daughters—worked hard and long, assuming the same arduous routines as her mother, grandmother, and generations of women before her. Proverbs 31:10–27 gives us a sense of what was expected of womankind in this hymn praising the virtuous wife:

> A good wife who can find? She is far
>   more precious than jewels.
> The heart of her husband trusts in
>   her . . .
> She does him good, and not harm, all
>   the days of her life.
> She seeks wool and flax, and works
>   with willing hands.
> She is like the ships of the merchant,
>   she brings her food from afar.
> She rises while it is yet night and pro-
>   vides food for her household. . . .
> Her lamp does not go out at night.
> She puts her hands to the distaff, and
>   her hands hold the spindle. . . .
> She looks well to the ways of her
>   household, and does not eat the
>   bread of idleness.

The simplest way to make flour was to place the handfuls of kernels in a hollowed-out stone mortar and grind them with another stone, or pestle.

Much of a woman's work was done in the busy courtyard where children played and animals were kept. Sheep and goats were raised for meat, milk, and wool; chickens for meat and eggs; and donkeys for carrying heavy loads. Here, too, was a large oven made of clay, mud brick, or stone for baking bread. The rotary mill, seen in the foregound, was more efficient than the grinding stone at top.

Making thread and yarn has changed little over centuries, as this contemporary scene of a young Palestinian woman spinning illustrates. To turn fibers into thread, the spinner attached the wool or flax to a distaff, or hooked rod, held in one hand, and drew them out in a continuous twist onto a spindle. The rod-shaped spindle was suspended and was spun by twirling the lengthening thread with the fingers of the free hand. The spindle generally had a stone or clay whorl—a perforated disc—at one end to weight it down and help maintain rotation. Because spinning was looked on as woman's work, the distaff became synonymous with womanhood.

Spinning and making clothes

When a good wife put her hand to the distaff and spindle, as the proverb states, she was beginning to carry out her duties as family clothing maker. She used the distaff and spindle to make yarn or thread from raw wool or flax (linen is made from flax). This done, she had to weave the yarn or thread into cloth. The typical loom in Jesus' time produced cloth about three feet wide, so to make most clothing, two lengths of woven material had to be joined side by side to gain the proper width. In Galilee, however, looms were often wider, so that an article of clothing could be woven in one piece. In John 19:23 we read that Jesus' tunic "was without seam, woven from top to bottom." Over his tunic Jesus and other men wore a loose-fitting outer garment, or mantle, with fringes bound by blue ribbon.

Galilee was known for its fields of sky-blue flax and for the sturdy linen cloth that was made from flax fibers.

The tunic or sometimes the outer garment would have been tied with a leather belt or cloth girdle about four inches wide. The girdle might have had a doubled section sewn into it to serve as a purse. A man wearing only his tunic was said to be naked, or stripped. Men sometimes dressed this way while working. And so, in John 21:7, when Peter is described as being "naked" (King James Version) or "stripped" (later translations) before leaping into the water upon recognizing Jesus, he was probably wearing only his tunic. If a man wore a girdle over his tunic it was called a loincloth. If he pulled his garment up between his legs and tucked it into his girdle to free his legs for easier movement, he was said to gird his loins. To complete his apparel, the Jewish man would have worn sandals and may have tied a white cloth over his head, letting it hang down to his shoulders.

The wife made her own clothes too. She wore the same type of tunic as the men, but her mantle was fuller, with enough fringe to cover her feet. While working, she might tuck the front of her mantle up over her girdle to form an apron for carrying small items. Most women wore head coverings. Both men and women wore sandals with soles of palm bark or wood and straps or laces of leather. They probably purchased their footwear from the local sandal maker.

Preparing the daily bread

As for her duties as provider of meals, a wife had to grind grain, bake bread, milk the goats, and make cheese and curds. These daily tasks began around daybreak. To grind the grain she used either a mortar and pestle or a hand mill, which consisted of two stones. The lower stone held the grain, and the upper stone was rubbed or rolled across the bed of grain to make flour. Next, she mixed the coarse meal with water, salt, and a little fermented dough saved from the previous day's bread making as a leavening agent. She kneaded the mixture into dough and let it rise for a few hours, and finally shaped the dough into flat loaves and baked them—generally in a clay oven in the courtyard. Jesus, who must have watched his mother make bread compared the Kingdom of God to leaven which transforms meal into risen dough.

While the bread baked, the woman of the house might have planned the day's meals. Most families ate two meals. Breakfasts were likely to be light and were carried to the fields or other places of work and eaten at mid-morning or midday. Suppers, by contrast, were substantial. Vegetables, eggs, cheese, bread, butter, wine, nuts, and fruit might all be served, and perhaps chicken or wild fowl. Fish was a common food, but red meat was a rarity, except on special occasions, when the fatted calf and the sacrificial lamb were presented with fanfare and ritual.

Certain meat and fish were forbidden as food on religious grounds. Pork and crustaceans, for example, were regarded as "unclean." So, too, was any animal that had not been slaughtered specifically for food and entirely bled, because, as stated in Deuteronomy 12:23, "The blood is the life," and should be regarded as sacred even in animals.

In warm weather cooking was done in the courtyard. On cold and rainy days, the cook brought her fire indoors to a portable clay stove fueled with charcoal or twigs. As there were no chimneys, the smoke and cooking smells permeated the house.

Most foods other than bread were boiled or stewed in a big pot and seasoned with salt and onions, garlic, mint, dill, cummin, coriander, rue, or mustard. Food was sweetened with wild honey or syrups made by boiling down dates and grapes.

Supper was a time of relaxation after a long day's work. Everyone was required to wash his hands before eating, as the food was generally served in a common bowl and eaten by dipping in with the fingers. In his later life Jesus was called down by a Pharisee for eating without first washing in the proper way, prompting him to point out how the Pharisees carried out the letter of the law while defeating its spirit.

Fun and games

Despite the long work day, the supper hour was probably not the only time a family had for relaxation. Although these times may have been rare,

Dyeing of thread and cloth was done at home or by the town dyer. A typical dyeing vat appears above.

To make cloth, lengths of yarn or thread (the warp) were hung from the cross beam of the loom and kept taut by attaching stone or clay weights to the free ends, as shown at left. A shed was formed with a heddle, or warping stick, to separate the warp into two series. Then other yarn or thread (the weft) was drawn through this shed and pushed up snugly against the fabric being formed. The fragment of first-century A.D. cloth shown below was found in the Judean desert.

Passover supper, or seder, commemorated the Hebrews' last meal in Egypt before the Exodus. The men and boys sat or reclined on straw mats around a low table while the women served. There may have been knives, but mostly people ate with their fingers. Passover foods included unleavened bread, lamb, bitter herbs (probably endives and chicory), wine, and fruit; other symbolic foods were added later. Some families may also have eaten biscuits made from ground locusts. The meal was punctuated by reciting from the Scriptures.

there must have been moments and occasionally whole days when members of the family—even the women—could relax. And in their spare time, both adults and children surely played and enjoyed one another's company. Children played ball games and what appear to have been hopscotch and jacks. Evidence of whistles, rattles, wheeled animals, hoops, and spinning tops have been found by archeologists. Older children and adults played various kinds of board games, including a form of checkers.

The Sabbath and holy days

The evening meal and scattered play were not enough to give hard workers sufficient rest. As part of the religious observances that touched almost every aspect of their daily lives, Jews were required to set aside one day of the week for the Lord. The Sabbath, the day of rest, which began at sundown on Fridays and ended at sundown on Saturdays, was so established and ritualized by Jesus' day that no farmer would have dreamed of going to his fields, no

Tableware was simple. The earthenware bowl, bronze jug, wooden dishes, and knife shown here were found in a cave where they had lain since the first century. The knife is a rare find in that its iron blade and wooden handle are both intact.

craftsmen to work at his trade, no woman to her housework, no merchant to the marketplace. Because no work was to be done on the Sabbath, Friday afternoon was an especially busy time. The men finished up their week's work and the women cleaned with special care, refilling lamps, preparing meals in advance, and laundering clothing.

Every Friday evening as the first evening stars appeared, the *hazzan*, a synagogue official, called the villagers to prayer with three sharp blasts of a ram's horn, and the faithful assembled at the synagogue. Friday's supper, which followed, was a joyful occasion for the family, notable for special foods and the the recitation of the Kiddush, a blessing said over the wine. The family went to the synagogue again on Saturday morning for more prayer and readings from Scripture before the Sabbath ended with another signal from the ram's horn.

While the Sabbath was celebrated every week, there were celebrations that occurred only once a year. The first day of the Jewish new year, Rosh Hashanah, came on the first day of Tishri (September–October). Ten days later came Yom Kippur, the Day of Atonement, on which Jews repented of their sins of the past year. Yom Kippur was not a day of celebration but one of total fasting and inner searching. Hanukkah, celebrated for eight days beginning on the 25th of Kislev (November–December) commemorated the rededication of the Temple in Jerusalem by Judas Maccabeus in 164 B.C. after its desecration by Antiochus IV Epiphanes. Purim, on the 14th and 15th of Adar (February–March), was the occasion of general merrymaking. Purim celebrated the deliverance of the Jews from their enemies as described in the Book of Esther, which was read in the synagogue as part of the celebration. There were also a number of feasts tied into the farming year and the week-long feast of Passover, which was to take on great significance in Jesus' life.

Passover observances represented the meshing of two ancient celebrations. On the one hand Passover commemorated the Jews' deliverance from the yoke of Egypt, probably in the 13th century B.C.; on the other hand the holiday had still more ancient origins, most likely as a festival associated with the spring migration of flocks. It began on the 15th day of Nisan (a date that fell somewhere in March or April), and Jews inaugurated the week-long festival with a special *seder*, or ritual feast, and the telling of the Passover story.

We are told in Luke 2:41 that Joseph and Mary went to Jerusalem to celebrate the Passover every year. Though it was a busy time for farmers, many of them too were able to make the pilgrimage to Jerusalem where their forebears had traditionally marked the start of the Passover. Otherwise, the farmers satisfied themselves by sharing the feast at home with friends and relatives.

During Passover, an early springtime holy day, dried fruits were served. Grapes were dried either on the vine, as shown at top, or spread out on the ground. Figs, a summer crop, were dried, strung together, and stored for later use. Some of the dried fruits might have been in the form of pressed cakes prepared during the harvest for use both on the table and as portable food for workers and travelers.

Land ownership

If the social life of the rural Jew was structured around the family, the life of the farming family was tied to the land, and daily activities were ruled by the demands of the farming year. Only God and family were more important to the rural Jew than his land, and the security of his family depended on the land he owned and worked. Precisely what legal arrangements regulated land ownership in Galilee are uncertain. But in some parts of Palestine, the best properties at this time were in the hands of a relatively few landowners—mainly Rome's rulers, the Herodian family, and the priestly aristocracy. In these places the farmers working the land might have been tenants or even slaves. In Galilee, it appears, the majority of Jewish farmers were either freeholders owning small plots of land or landless workers, in some cases related to the owners. In Maccabean times allotments of lands in Galilee were distributed and many small freeholds were handed down in families from those days.

Among the flowering trees cultivated in Palestine were the date palm (above), almond (above right), and olive (right). Date trees were grown for their fruit and for their leaves, which were woven into mats and baskets. Almond trees, the first to blossom and bear fruit each year, were heralds of the spring. Olive trees, grown for their fruit and oil, can live for 2,000 years, their magnificent gnarled trunks bearing witness to their age.

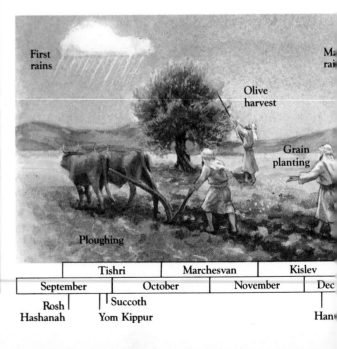

First rains

Ma rai

Olive harvest

Grain planting

Ploughing

	Tishri		Marchesvan		Kislev
September		October		November		Dec

Rosh Hashanah

Succoth

Yom Kippur

Han

Land ownership, by tradition, was a matter of family inheritance. In Scripture the tradition can be traced back more than 1,000 years to when Joshua distributed the lands of the newly conquered Canaan among the tribes of Israel according to God's plan. Ownership was supposed to pass in an unbroken line down through the generations, from father to sons, the eldest receiving double the share of any of his brothers. As the younger sons usually received shares too small to sustain independent farms, they had little choice but to sell their inheritance to the principal heir, who was thus able to keep the ancestral family farm intact. The then landless younger sons might remain in the village, taking up a trade or working as farm laborers for their brother, or they might leave the village to join the large numbers of migrant workers, who found casual labor where they could, or they might even resort to becoming brigands. If a landowner died, leaving no sons, the property went to his daughter or if he had no daughter to his brothers, uncles, or nearest living relative.

This tradition of family ownership reflects an ancient assumption, as can be seen in 1 Kings 21. Naboth, a farmer living in the ninth century B.C., had the misfortune to have a vineyard "beside the palace of Ahab king of Samaria." Ahab admired Naboth's vineyard, and wishing to annex it to his property, offered Naboth a better plot of land in trade, or if that was not sufficient, a sum of money. But Naboth said, "The Lord forbid that I should give you the inheritance of my fathers." The farmer was put to death on trumped-up charges, but the Bible makes clear that Naboth's resistance was righteous in the eyes of the Lord. The system of family ownership continued to be compromised by royal acquisition, however. Herod the Great, for example, had personally owned more than half the land in his realm.

Farm size and layout

Galilee rests on limestone bedrock, which could be readily hollowed out to make cisterns and grain storage vaults. Its fertile soil was composed mainly of

The farmer was tied to his land, and his work was determined by the seasons. In the farming calendar below the cycle of the agricultural year is illustrated by the months in which the activities generally occurred (the equivalent months of the Gregorian calendar are named below that). Major Jewish holy days, including those that celebrate the harvest, are named at the bottom.

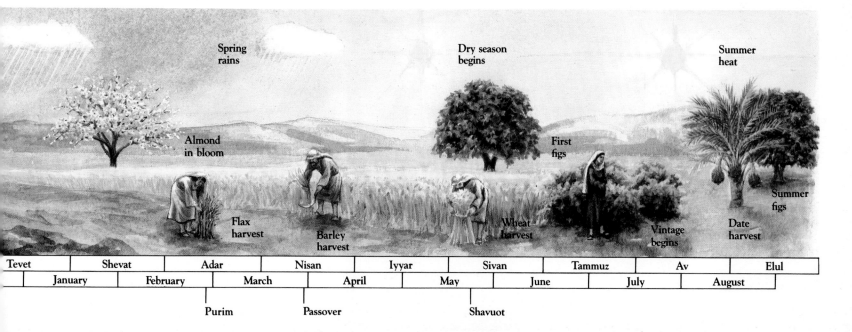

Spring rains

Dry season begins

Summer heat

Almond in bloom

First figs

Flax harvest

Barley harvest

Wheat harvest

Vintage begins

Date harvest

Summer figs

Tevet	Shevat	Adar	Nisan	Iyyar	Sivan	Tammuz	Av	Elul

January	February	March	April	May	June	July	August

Purim   Passover   Shavuot

Olives, an autumn crop, were harvested by shaking the trees with poles, as shown above. The many varieties were either marketed with other condiments, as at left, or pressed for oil. High-quality oils were made by bruising the olives in a mortar and hanging them in baskets to drip. A lower-grade "beaten oil" was made by pressing the pulp with weights. Cooking oil was made by crushing olives in a rotary mill like the one below.

terra rossa (residue from the dissolving limestone) and Mediterranean brown. As the soil and climate were generally favorable to mixed farming, most Galileans grew a variety of crops, making their families all but self-sufficient. Portions of each family's acreage were set aside for cereal grains, for garden crops, and for grapes and olives. Most families kept a goat or two to milk, a few sheep for wool, and one or two donkeys or oxen as draft animals. Chickens or other fowl probably pecked in the dusty courtyard, inspiring Jesus to speak of gathering the children of Jerusalem together "as a hen gathers her brood under her wings," in Matthew 23:37 and Luke 13:34.

The average Nazarene farmer supposedly owned the equivalent of from four to six modern acres. In Jesus' time a farmer might have described a field in terms of how many measures of seed it took to plant it, or reckoned its size in terms of the *zemed*, the amount of land a yoke of oxen could plow in a day. The Romans called this latter unit a *jugerum*; the modern equivalent of a *jugerum* is 28,800 square feet, or roughly two-thirds of an acre.

Rarely did a farmer enjoy the luxury of having all his land together. More often his grain fields were down on the flattest, most fertile land alongside those of his neighbors, his vineyard and olive orchards upon the hillside with other vineyards and orchards, and his vegetable gardens and grazing land somewhere else. Grain fields were not fenced, but their boundaries were marked with stones, whose permanence was protected by the full weight of the law. To remove such a landmark was considered a serious crime. Vineyards, however, were bounded by hedges or walls, not so much to define boundaries as to keep out animals and thieves.

Farm taxes and levies

Substantial taxes were exacted from the farmers by the royal government and by the Temple. There were secular taxes on the land and on certain goods, including slaves; the tax on land reportedly equalled roughly one-quarter or one-fifth of the produce of the land. A portion of these secular taxes was levied by tax collectors, called publicans, who customarily subcontracted the job in each village to a local official, who knew his neighbors and was therefore less likely to be deceived by wily tax evaders. Each collector was expected to turn over a specific sum to the imperial treasury, but just how he collected the monies and how much over and above that value he kept for himself was left to his discretion—or greed. Extortion and fraud seem to have been commonplace. Not surprisingly, villagers feared and distrusted the local tax collector and routinely denounced him as a thief and sinner.

Although the secular taxes were no heavier than those on other provinces of the Roman Empire, they became oppressive when combined with the Temple taxes, obligatory "gifts" gathered on the basis of a one-tenth, or "tithe," share of the farmers' harvest. Farmers also had to contribute the "first fruits" of harvest and the "firstborn" of livestock to the Temple as sacrificial offerings. Further, adult males were charged an annual Temple tax of one-half shekel. If all these taxes were paid by Jesus' neighbors in Nazareth, then surely what produce or profit was left to the farmer and his family must have been little more than what was needed for subsistence.

Planting season

The farmer's year was divided into three seasons—planting, harvesting, and vintage, although there was a measure of overlap to each of these activities. Planting began in the month of Tishri (September–October) or Marchesvan (October–November). The farmers waited until the sirocco—those strangely enervating desert winds—had come and gone and the west sea winds had taken their place. With the cooler winds came the first rains since April, and in just a few days they softened the hard, sun-baked fields enough to let the plowman prepare the earth for seeding. In the Book of Joel, 2:23–24, it says "Be glad . . . and rejoice in the Lord, your God; for he has given the early rain for your vindication. . . . The threshing floors shall be full of grain."

The work of readying the soil for planting was long and arduous. If the ground was very stony or if the land had lain fallow for several years, the farmer had to plow it over and over, stopping to dislodge rocks or pull up thistles with his mattock, a picklike digging tool. Usually, however, he plowed only twice. On the first pass he cut furrows the length of his field. After seeding, he plowed crosswise, gently turning the loosened topsoil to cover the seeds and protect them from being eaten by greedy birds or being blown away by gusts of wind. As a final step, he might rake the loose earth smooth with a branch.

The hardwood plow of Jesus' time looked like the forked digging sticks used by farmers for thousands of years except that it had an iron tip, or share, on its cutting prow and it was drawn by donkeys or oxen and not powered by the farmer. Today, some farmers in the Middle East still use this simple implement for turning the soil. The plowman walks behind, guiding the plow with one hand and wielding a goad for prodding the animals in the other.

The Nazarene farmer took his supply of seed from the previous harvest, and if he was clever, practiced a rudimentary sort of plant improvement, reserving only the seeds from the fattest, largest, most vigorous plants. In a typical year the skilled farmer could expect his wheat seed to yield fivefold (or five bushels of grain for every bushel of seed sown), which is very modest by modern standards.

The seeds of grain were not so much planted in the soil as broadcast over it. Walking the length and breadth of his fields, the sower carried the seeds in a basket or in a fold in his mantle and scattered fistfuls in all directions. According to the first century A.D. Roman historian Pliny the Elder, a wise farmer took care to match the sweep of his arm with the length of his stride in order to spread the seed evenly.

Growing up in Galilee, the boy Jesus must have watched neighbors sow their fields, for during his ministry he drew many images and parables from agricultural life. In Matthew 13:3–23 Jesus points out how different people react to the word of God when they hear it. In that parable some of a sower's seed fell on the path and was eaten by birds; some fell on rocky ground and sprang up quickly in shallow earth, but the tender seedlings were scorched by the sun; some fell into thorns and the plants were choked; but some seed fell onto good ground and "brought forth grain, some a hundred-fold, some sixty, some thirty." The good ground, of course, yielded far more than the farmer expected, and Jesus undoubtedly meant to show by this story that the word of God produces astounding results in the lives of those who accept it.

Except for certain vegetable crops, barley and wheat were the first seeds to go into the ground each fall, and their growth was anxiously watched through the unpredictable months of winter. Wheat claimed the largest and most fertile segments of the lowlands around Nazareth, constituting as much as half the food the farmer's family ate, much of that in the form of bread. Any surplus wheat served as a cash crop, with ready markets in the nearby city of Sepphoris.

In Galilee barley was second to wheat in the growing space allotted to it, but in the drier areas to the south it was more common than wheat. Though less tasty than wheat, barley had the distinct advantage of being resistant to drought and maturing more quickly in poor soil. Although it was used primarily as feed for the livestock, the farmer took comfort in knowing the barley could also be used as foodstuff if the wheat yield was meager. Flax, another major Galilean crop, was not a food but a source of fiber for making sturdy linen cloth.

Vegetables filled out the family's crop inventory and insured a measure of variety in the diet. Though the farmer might plow the garden once a year to turn over the soil, tending the garden from seed to harvest was usually left to the women. Cucumbers, melons, leeks, onions, garlic, and a variety of peas and beans thrived in the area and were prized as food in biblical times. Because most plants require a steady supply of water to grow, women were kept busy in very dry weather carrying water from the well or cistern to their vegetable gardens. The same garden plot might also have some fruit and nut trees, among them pomegranate, almond, pistachio, and date palm, but these of course were perennials and required little care until harvest time.

Once all the crops were planted, there was little the farmer could do except hope for favorable growing conditions. Too much or too little rain, wild fires, a plague of locusts, a searing wind that shriveled young growth, or any number of plant diseases could suddenly destroy a season's work and a year's sustenance. Meanwhile, he did his best to beat back the weeds, whose vigor often surpassed that of the cultivated plants. Particularly troublesome were the "weeds among the wheat," which Jesus alluded to in Matthew 13:24–30. In that parable, after a farmer sowed his fields, an enemy sowed weeds among the

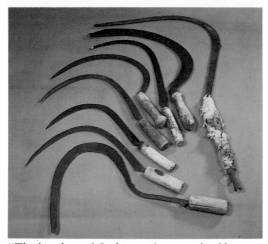

"The kingdom of God is as if a man should scatter seed. . . . The earth produces of itself, first the blade, then the ear, then the full grain in the ear. But when the grain is ripe, at once he puts in the sickle, because the harvest has come." Mark 4:26–29. Assorted sickles are shown above; modern laborers gathering in the sheaves are seen at right.

The threshing board, seen above, was a hardwood sledge studded underneath with jagged stones or bits of iron. An ox or donkey was hitched to the board, as seen at left, and the farmer and sometimes his children rode on it to give it weight. Driven in wide circles over the grain on the threshing floor, the board separated the kernels from the stalks.

Threshed grain had to be winnowed to get rid of the chaff. To do this the farmer needed a bit of breeze and considerable skill as he scooped up fork loads of the mixture, tossed them in the air, and watched the heavy grain drop at his feet, while the airborne straw fell nearby and the feather-light chaff floated farther still. The chaff was burned, but the straw was gathered and saved for compost, cattle feed, or making sun-dried bricks.

wheat. The farmer, however, ordered that the weeds be left to grow with the wheat rather than risk pulling up the wheat in an effort to root out the weeds. At harvest time he told the reapers, "Gather the weeds first and bind them in bundles to be burned, but gather the wheat into my barn." These weeds, or tares, a species of darnel grass, were almost indistinguishable from the young shoots of wheat. In the early stages of growth, the farmer in the parable could not help but let some weeds remain with the wheat prior to the harvest. However, if the tares were allowed to remain when the wheat matured and were unintentionally harvested with the grain, they could prove poisonous to anyone who had the bad fortune to eat them. A sharp hoe and a sharper eye were needed to keep the wheat free of tares.

Harvest season

The harvest season began in Adar (February–March) and continued, by stages, until well into autumn. Flax was probably the first crop to claim Nazareth's attention. Harvesters hoed up the individual shallow-rooted plants or pulled them out of the earth by hand, then carried off the stalks to be soaked, dried, and combed free of their valuable fibers. Families used flax for making various household items, including linen cloth, nets, and lamp wicks.

Bringing in the grain was a big job, which usually involved the whole family and possibly hired laborers, too. Timing was all important, for if the farmer waited too long and the cereal was overripe, the grains were apt to fall to the ground before they could be harvested. As the folk saying warns, better two days too early than two days too late.

When the moment was judged favorable, reapers young and old moved through the stands of waving grain, grabbing clumps of heavy-headed stalks with one hand and cutting them free with a sickle, a tool with a curved blade, in the other. Helpers followed, binding up the loose bundles into sheaves.

When the gatherers were finished, they signaled the gleaners, waiting expectantly at the field's edge to come and help themselves to the leftovers. By ancient and charitable custom, a share of the farmer's crop, usually the plants growing along the margins and in the corners of the field, was reserved for harvesting by the village's landless poor. Gleaners were forbidden to touch the sheaves, however; these were loaded onto donkeys or into wagons and transported to the communal threshing floor where the edible grains would be loosened from the stalks.

The threshing floor at harvest time buzzed with activity. A bountiful harvest was a joyous occasion, and the entire community gathered to watch and help with the work, probably shouting greetings to new arrivals and exchanging bits of news as they labored from dawn to dark. Nazareth's threshing floor was situated near the town on an elevated site, where it caught the prevailing west winds from the sea. Although the place itself was unimpressive (no more than a very large round court of pounded earth), it provided a good work surface.

There was more than one way to handle the threshing. Some threshers simply beat the grain loose with long, wooden sticks, pounding down on stalks piled about a foot deep, but most used the more efficient ox- or donkey-drawn threshing board or roller. The threshing board was a hardwood sledge with a jagged bottom. The threshing roller was a heavy ox-drawn conveyance that was rolled over the stalks on rows of movable iron discs; this early threshing machine even had a chair for the driver to sit in while he worked.

Everyone present had plenty to do. Some workers were kept busy bringing in the sheaves from the fields and unloading the donkeys or carts. Others busily spread the grain out in the path of the thresher. Perhaps the children had the most fun when a threshing board was used, as they would get to ride on it to increase the weight of the board and make it more effective.

The women would have brought food along, and around mid-day everyone took a little time out for food, prayer, and rest. The animals, for their part, were allowed to nibble as they trampled, for it was written in Deuteronomy 25:4, "You shall not muzzle an ox when it treads out the grain."

After wheat or barley had been threshed it had to be winnowed by tossing it into the air and letting the wind separate the grains from the chaff (husks and stubble) and straw (stalks). To rid the winnowed wheat or barley of any remaining unwanted matter, the grain was sifted through a sieve—a round wooden frame fitted with a fine mesh bottom made of woven leather thongs or sheep or goat gut. The heavier waste fell through the mesh and the lighter waste rose to the top and was removed.

The sifted grain was poured into large pottery jars, a portion was set aside for the tax collector, and the rest taken off for storage, probably at the family house in the village. The wealthier farmers, however, stored their grain in barns. During his ministry Jesus told of a wealthy landowner who spent his energy gathering riches for his later years, even tearing down his storage barns and building larger ones to hold his growing wealth. But, as told in Luke 12:16–21, the man soon died, still not believing in God, and never having had the use of his riches.

The Festival of Shavuot

To mark the end of the grain harvest, the farmers and their families celebrated Shavuot, or the Festival of Weeks (so called because it fell on the day following the completion of seven weeks after the start of Passover). Alternatively known as Pentecost (from the Greek word meaning 50th day) because it came precisely 50 days after the start of Passover, the feast also commemorated the revelation at Mount Sinai when, according to the Book of Exodus, God

For grinding large quantities of grain into flour, some families had mills consisting of a lower stone and an upper stone. The lower stone was hollowed out to hold the grain; the upper stone was rubbed or rolled over the grain in the hollow of the lower stone. In the mill shown here, a wooden handle was inserted into a protruding socket in the upper stone and used to turn it.

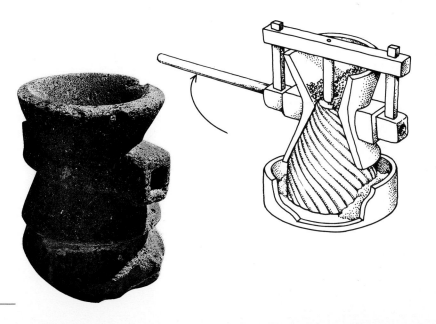

gave the Ten Commandments and other laws to Moses. Later, Christians celebrated a feast that is closely related to Shavuot. The Christian Pentecost, or Whitsunday, which comes 50 days after Easter, marks the beginnings of the church under the guidance of the Holy Spirit.

As Shavuot came at a time when work in the fields was ending and work in the vineyards was not yet in full swing, it is possible that many Nazarenes were able to travel to Jerusalem to make offerings at the Temple. They would have taken with them two loaves of leavened bread made with wheat from the newly harvested crop. Those who were forced to remain at home would have celebrated in similar manner, attending special prayer services at the village synagogue.

Vintage season

The third season of the year, vintage, began in Sivan (May–June), even as the last of the wheat was being brought in. The term *vintage* used in Leviticus applied loosely to the tending, harvesting, and processing of not only grapes but olives, figs, and some other fruits. Unlike cereal grains, these crops were the products of slow-growing perennials, which, once planted, became part of a man's patrimony.

Preferably, grapes were grown on the terraced slopes above the grain fields where the farmer could count on a heavy dewfall even in the dry summer months. The vines were planted in rows about eight feet apart, so that they had plenty of growing space and still left room for the workers to move through.

Once a vineyard was established, one of the farmer's principal jobs was spring pruning. In Isaiah 18:5,

"I am the vine, you are the branches. He who abides in me, and I in him, he it is that bears much fruit . . . ." John 15:5.

it says, "When the blossom is over, and the flower becomes a ripening grape, he will cut off the shoots with pruning hooks, and the spreading branches he will hew away." The farmer walked the rows, stopping at each vine in turn to cut away its less productive branches with a small, sharp knife. He then burned the discarded wood and propped up the fruit-bearing branches on forked sticks. Finally, he gently loosened the ground around the vines with a hoe to clear away any weeds and then watched and waited as the tiny clusters of fruit swelled and began to ripen under the hot midsummer sun.

As harvest time neared, the farmer built a shelter at the edge of the vineyard and moved in, the better to guard the ripening crop. For some it was enough to make a canopy of branches and stay beneath them day and night, but others probably welcomed this opportunity to leave their village houses and take refuge on the cooler slopes. Because the whole family might watch over a vineyard, the shelter could be a permanent one.

The most elaborate type of shelter was a round tower made of local stone with a storeroom on the ground level, rudimentary living quarters above, and an outer stairway to the roof. It may even have had a shade tree growing on its roof. Here the family worked, played, ate, and slept.

Jesus speaks of such a vineyard in Matthew 21:33–44, "There was a householder who planted a vineyard, and set a hedge around it, and dug a wine press in it, and built a tower, and let it out to tenants, and went into another country." In the parable the tenants first kill the owner's servants when they

A series of Byzantine mosaics at Beth-shan, a city at the juncture of the Jezreel and Jordan valleys, shows the steps in the vintage. From left to right, men are seen gathering the grapes, treading on them to release the juice, and finally putting the pulp through a press to extract the last of the liquid. In all likelihood, only the most prosperous vineyards would have had screw-type wine presses.

come to collect the master's fruit, and then his son, prefiguring Jesus' death. Although tenant farmers were not likely to have commonly mistreated the owner's servants and sons, it was probably not unusual for a farmer to let his lands out to tenant farmers if he had a lot of land or had to be away from it for a time.

Usually, however, the farmer and his family were not rich enough to depend on tenants and did the work themselves. The family activities in the vineyard shelter were the same as at home in the village. The mother probably even baked the family's daily bread using a simple oven. She placed flat stones in the live fire of a hearth, or fire pit, heating them to baking temperature, and then slapped loaves of dough onto the stones to cook them.

Everyone from small children to aged grandparents helped in the harvest, which began in Tammuz (June–July). Jesus told about a father who asked his sons to go work in his vineyard. The first son said no but afterward repented and went; the second son said yes but never went. Jesus used the parable to point out that sinners will go to heaven faster than the chief priests and elders because they all heard the word, but only the sinners heeded it. The parable describes the common experience that children were expected to work in their fathers' vineyards, although they did not always rush to the task.

When the crop was large, the farmer might hire day laborers to help with the harvest. Most of the grapes were destined to be pressed into wine, but workers were permitted to eat their fill as long as they took no grapes home. Another portion of the crop was set aside to make raisins, which were either left on the vine or spread out on the ground to sun dry. As with the wheat harvest, gleaners were invited to help themselves to what was left over.

In Jesus' time, wine was poured into goatskin bags or earthenware jars, the latter sealed with clay or beeswax, and stored in underground chambers to keep the wine away from the heat of the sun. One of these early forerunners of the modern wine cellar is shown here.

Succoth, or the Feast of Booths, commemorates the time Hebrews lived in the wilderness before entering Canaan. As part of the celebration, families built small huts, or booths, on the street and on the rooftops and shaded them with palm and willow branches and other greenery.

Pressing the grapes for wine began immediately. The press was typically an outcropping of limestone bedrock, hollowed out to hold the ripe fruit. Several people, standing in the soft pulp, trod the grapes with their bare feet as they sang and shouted. It was a messy business that turned the skin red, not to mention staining clothing.

The grape juice ran down into another bedrock vat, which may have been lined with a coat of plaster to seal its surface. The juice was left in the vat until the first stage of fermentation was over and the yeasts in the grapes had turned the sugars into alcohol. Then the liquid was drawn off into earthenware jugs and left to settle for a month or more. Finally, the wine was strained to remove sediment and stored in large jugs, sealed with pitch or wax, or in new goatskin bags. In Matthew 9:17, Jesus cautioned against putting "new wine into old wineskins." If you do, he said, "the skins burst, and the wine is spilled."

At the end of the summer the farmer turned his attention to the ripening dates and the fig crop.

Then just before the olives were ripe and the whole process of plowing, planting, and harvesting began once more, the farmers and their families took some time out to relax and celebrate the feast of Succoth.

The feast of Succoth

Succoth takes its name from the Hebrew word for "huts"—a reference to the rude shelters that farmers lived in during the annual grape and olive harvests. The festival of Succoth (also known as the Feast of Booths, Tabernacles, Tents, or Ingathering) came in fall in the month of Tishri, and was a celebration of the final harvest of the agricultural year. Part thanksgiving, perhaps part new year's festival, it was by all accounts the most joyous time of the year and generally included a trip to the Temple in Jerusalem. After arriving in Jerusalem, the whole family slept in booths and there was much dancing and parading in the streets. People carried braided switches, made up of a willow branch, a palm branch, and bits of myrtle, which they waved about as symbols of God's bounty and blessings.

In Jerusalem it was customary for the Temple priests to pour a pitcher of water over the altar on each day of Succoth. Whether its equivalent occurred at Nazareth's synagogue is unrecorded, but the villagers probably said a special prayer for the return of "the former rains," which would initiate yet another bountiful year in Nazareth and hundreds of other rural communities all over the land of Israel.

The life of a carpenter

Most villages, and Nazareth was no exception, supported a number of independent craftsmen, including carpenters, blacksmiths, potters, dyers, basket weavers and mat makers, and tanners and leather workers. These craftsmen often bartered their services for grain, oil, vegetables, and other foodstuffs. Among the most respected trades was carpentry. While virtually every village could support at least

According to Leviticus 23:39–40, for Succoth "you shall keep the feast of the Lord seven days. . . . And you shall take on the first day the fruit of goodly trees, branches of palm trees, and boughs of leafy trees, and willows of the brook; and you shall rejoice before the Lord your God seven days." Citrons (left) were probably the fruit referred to and myrtle (right) the leafy trees.

one carpenter, it is believed that Nazareth was known as a town of carpenters, and early in the first century A.D., Joseph must have been among them.

As with any craft, each artisan learned his trade from his father, grandfather, or another male relative. According to tradition, one of the chief duties of a father is to see that his son learns a useful trade. A young boy learned early by watching his elders work; then formal apprenticeship in a trade began when a boy was 15 years old. Jesus probably learned carpentry at Joseph's shop.

It seems likely that Joseph worked in his doorway or just outside of his house, which may have been one in a row of craftsmen's shops at the center of town, but he probably stored his tools and materials inside. Joseph must have owned a substantial kit of tools, some of which he accumulated in his own lifetime, some of which he inherited from his father. Basic carpenter's tools included an ax for chopping down trees, an adz for shaping wood, and a hatchet. Also essential were iron saws for cutting wood to precise sizes, a bow drill and bits for drilling holes through wood, a stone-headed hammer for driving nails, a wooden mallet for pounding chisels or hammering wooden surfaces together, iron chisels and files for shaping and carving, awls for putting small holes into wood or leather, and a supply of nails.

Joseph might even have owned one or more wood planes and a spoke shave, a recent innovation. Among his measuring tools were a rule, a compass or dividers, a chalk line, and of course, some pencil-like markers to score his patterns and to guide him in his cuts.

Part of any carpenter's skill revolves around knowing which kinds of wood and which section of a tree are most appropriate for the intended purpose, structural or decorative. In Joseph's Nazareth, the principal choices were sycamore, a porous but durable softwood from a species of fig tree (not to be confused with American sycamores, which are of the plane tree family); olive wood, a fine-grained amber-colored hardwood, which grew in abundance in the area; and possibly oak. Imported woods, such as cedar and cypress from Phoenicia, though used often in the big cities, were expensive and must have been uncommon in Nazareth and other small communities.

Given the fact that the carpenter worked in wood, a relatively perishable material, it is difficult to assess how skillful Joseph and his contemporaries may have been. But it is likely that the village artisan would have spent his time making farm tools, house construction parts, furniture, and kitchen implements. Farm tools ranged from wooden carts with wooden wheels to threshing boards, plows, winnowing forks, yokes, and handles for various metal tools. House parts included an assortment of posts and beams, doors, and door and window frames. Tables, chairs, and storage boxes were probably the most common wooden furniture.

The world of the potter

Of all the other craftsmen in rural areas, the potter was perhaps the most needed and the most artistic and creative. Scripture, especially the Old Testament, has many references to potters and pottery. In Isaiah 64:8, God himself is seen as a potter: "We are the clay, and thou art our potter." The numerous references to pottery in Scripture reflect its importance in daily life. The potter supplied the community with household ovens, oil lamps, and earthenware containers of every size and shape. These pots and jars were used for cooking and for storing all sorts of necessities, from drinking water to precious oils, from seed and grain to wine. On occasion, they were even used to store important documents. For

example, some of the Dead Sea Scrolls, a collection of biblical and theological texts, were stored in covered jars and hidden in caves near the shores of the Dead Sea, probably in the first century A.D.; when these priceless scrolls were discovered in the middle of the 20th century, they offered new insights into the Old Testament, Judaism, and the origins of Christianity.

The potter's basic tools were his wheel and his kiln. His basic material, clay, was readily available in the area, needing only be dug up, but rarely was clay fit for potting as it came out of the earth. Usually, the potter left the material in the sun for a time; when it had weathered sufficiently, he probably pounded out lumps with a mallet and picked out

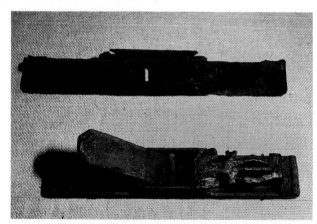

Many of the tools that Joseph and his helper may have used in their carpentry work were very much like the basic hand tools still used by carpenters. Like the planes of today, the ancient planes shown above have a single iron blade that can be adjusted for angle and depth.

A collection of tools and implements is shown at left. Some are replicas of those used in Jesus' time; they include a variety of carpenter's saws and handles that the carpenter might have shaped for winnowing forks.

any pebbles, twigs, or other debris. He then added water to the clay and mixed it thoroughly, treading the sticky substance with his feet to give it an even consistency. Once again he let the clay sit for several days, siphoning off any water that rose to the top. Finally, he folded and kneaded the clay to remove air pockets, often adding a binder as he did so.

When the potter was satisfied that his material handled as he liked, he took a proper quantity in his hands and began to give it shape. There were many ways to form a vessel. Some pieces were shaped entirely by hand; others were made by coiling up a rope of pliable clay; still others were made by pressing rolled-out sheets of clay into molds. Many pots were formed on a potter's wheel, a device used as long ago as the third millennium B.C. and still used by potters today.

The potter's wheel was actually two horizontal wheels, one at foot level and a second, higher one, joined to it by an axle. The potter worked his machine by kicking the bottom wheel with one foot as he pushed the clay down firmly onto the center of the top wheel. The pot began to take shape as the potter pressed his hands ever so gently against the spinning wet clay, inside and outside. If the pot was to have a long, narrow neck, or if the vessel was to be very large, the potter might have to make it in sections and join them later.

The shaped vessels were put aside to *set up,* or dry, then trimmed with a sharp knife to remove excess material. Sometimes the potter incised simple decorations into the damp clay. Sometimes he covered it with *slip,* a clay and water solution that made for a smoother surface. A still finer, lustrous surface was achieved by burnishing; the potter held a tool with a smooth, hard surface, such as a pebble, against the dried clay and polished it smooth.

Finally, the potter fired up his kiln, a two-story oven, and loaded it with a batch of pots. For at least three days the fires burned. First the potter raised the temperature just fast enough to allow the new clay to heat up safely; if he heated it too fast, any small pockets of water left in the clay would turn to steam and blow the pot apart. When the potter judged that he had reached the desired heat, he worked to maintain it at that level until the pottery reached the proper consistency; then, slowly, he brought the oven temperature down again. The finished pottery was traded for other goods or sold at the potter's shop or at the marketplace.

Getting married

Whatever a man did for a living he did it to support and care for his family, for it was ultimately the family on which his life was based. Most young people married, but their parents selected their partners. The process was started by the father of the bridegroom-to-be when his son reached 17 or 18 years of age. Selecting a suitable young woman from the village's unmarried 13- to 17-year-olds, he went to the father and negotiated a bride price that his

Weddings, like holy days, were times when families and friends got together. After the wedding ceremony, the young couple and their attendants led a joyful procession through the street to the accompaniment of music. At the wedding feast, which was hosted by the bride's or the bridegroom's family, God's blessings were given to the couple. Jesus must have attended many such weddings, and he was to perform his first miracle at a wedding feast in the town of Cana. According to John 2:1–11, when the bridegroom ran out of wine for his thirsty guests, Jesus turned water into fine wine at the request of his mother.

son was willing to pay in exchange for marrying her. (A young woman was regarded as an asset, and consequently the girl's father expected to be compensated for his loss.) The terms would be either written down or spoken before witnesses. Once this was done, a betrothal ceremony took place in front of witnesses.

For the next 12 months, the usual period of betrothal, the couple were considered practically married. A child born during that waiting period was considered legitimate. But it was not until the wedding ceremony that the bride left her father's house to move in with the bridegroom or his family.

The wedding day, which often came in the fall when the harvest was in, was eagerly anticipated by all the friends and families of the couple, for a wedding was an occasion for music, dancing, laughter, eating and drinking, and a general good time. Guests were expected to wear special clothes, and it was considered an insult to turn down an invitation to a wedding. In Jesus' parable of the King's Marriage Feast, reported in Matthew 22:1–14, when the invited guests refused to come, the king had people brought in from the streets, and when he discovered one guest without a wedding garment, he had him thrown out into the darkness. "For many are called, but few are chosen."

On her wedding day, the bride dressed in her own special wedding clothes (usually elaborately

The bride generally wore a headband of shiny coins to display her dowry, like this young Bedouin woman. Whatever she brought to the marriage remained hers.

The bride's attendants carried earthenware lamps during an evening procession. Oil was poured into the large opening; a wick protruded from the small one.

embroidered) and donned jewels, some of which may have been gifts from her betrothed. Then, surrounded by her female friends, who acted as attendants, the bride awaited the arrival of the bridegroom. To assure that the house would be brightly lighted when the bridegroom arrived, the bride's attendants often carried small clay oil lamps and swung small vials of extra oil on cords from their fingers, as acknowledged by Jesus in his parable of the Wise and Foolish Virgins. According to the parable, related in Matthew 25:1–13, the foolish virgins ran out of oil early in the evening and when the bridegroom arrived they were excluded from the festivities because they had not kept themselves ready.

The bridegroom left his own home with his male friends, who carried lighted torches. When he arrived at the young woman's door, he asked to see his future wife, and when she appeared, he lifted her veil and cried out in joy at the treasure he had found; his companions took up the cry, and the whole wedding party set out in a joyful procession through the streets. A feast at the bridegroom's house climaxed the happy occasion, with the new couple being blessed by their parents and friends. Sometimes wedding festivities went on for a week or two, but this was probably truer of the weddings of wealthy city dwellers than it was of those of poor villagers.

Raising children

To have a full family life, there must be children, and the more children there were in a family, the better, especially if they were sons. When children were born they were seen as God's gifts.

For the first few years of its life, the child was principally the concern of the mother. Children were nursed for as long as two to three years, but as soon as they were able to move about on their own and take instruction they were given family tasks to perform. Such education as there was for girls was left primarily to the mothers; boys also learned from their mothers, especially until the age of five.

Children were taught strict obedience to their parents, and most especially to their father, who was in every sense the head of household. As soon as they were old enough, sons were taught the family trade by their father or another male relative and were sent to study the Torah at school—usually in the local synagogue (see Chapter 6, "Life of the Mind"). The father also taught the entire family the precepts of the Jewish religion.

Once the children had learned their trade and grown to maturity, they too married, and in turn worked, raised families, grew old, and died. It was a process as natural as the seasons of the year, with spring giving way to summer, autumn, then winter. It was as natural as the farming cycle of planting, pruning and nurturing, harvesting, and turning over the earth by plowing.

"A *time to die*"

Death was marked by the family with great solemnity and ceremony. It set in motion a carefully prescribed set of activities, which began with the preparation of the body for burial. First the body was washed and rubbed with oil or sprinkled with perfume. It was then wrapped in special grave clothes, made of long strips of linen. Fragrant spices were packed between the cloth and the body to take away the smell of death, and the head was bound with a linen napkin.

Meanwhile, family and friends gathered round to lament with loud cries of sorrow. The intensity of their grieving may be reflected in Micah 1:8, "I will make lamentation like the jackals, and mourning like the ostriches." The mourners tore their clothes, usually of coarse sackcloth (a goat-hair fabric worn as testament to their discomfort), and they disfigured themselves with dust and ashes. Some may have even shaved their heads or beards, as was the custom in earlier times. If money permitted, professional mourners were hired to assist in the public expression of grief, although in a small town like Nazareth it is likely that most families would have been able to afford only one professional mourner. According to

Natural or man-made caves were often used as tombs. Sometimes they were sealed with a large cylindrical stone that was pushed across the opening and held tight by a wedge. Sometimes the front of the cave was faced with stone blocks.

a later ruling, a Jew was required to provide at least one professional woman mourner and two flute players for his wife's funeral, and this may have already been a custom at the time of Jesus.

Burials usually took place within 24 hours after death on account of the climate and the fact that Jews did not embalm or cremate their dead. Funerary societies helped to ensure this process. The body was carried through the town on a bier or stretcher, with people joining the mourners in the streets. The procession was often large and noisy and may have included flute players. At some stage of the procession, someone skilled at speech making probably gave a eulogy, praising the character and accomplishments of the deceased.

Jesus must have witnessed such scenes of mourning as he grew up, and he surely saw them in the years of his ministry. In Matthew 9:23, we are told that when Jesus went to the house of a synagogue leader whose daughter was reported dead, he "saw the flute players, and the crowd making a tumult."

The funeral procession ended at a grave site outside the village or in a hillside cave. These burial places were usually located on any side of town but the west, as the prevailing winds blew from that direction. Cave graves were generally simple rectangular openings in the rock containing ledges or niches where the bodies were laid with or without a coffin. Tombs of wealthier Jews might have had several chambers. The entrance of the cave was sealed with a large boulder or slab of rock to keep in the smells and to keep out the jackals and other carrion-eating animals, and the door of the tomb may have been whitewashed to warn people that there was a corrupting body inside. Jesus referred to this practice in Matthew 23:27, when he accused the scribes and Pharisees of being hypocrites, "like whitewashed tombs, which outwardly appear beautiful, but within they are full of dead men's bones and all uncleanness."

Anyone who touched a dead body was considered ritually unclean for seven days and had to perform a purification ceremony. This law may enter into the parable of the Good Samaritan. According to Luke 10:30–37, a man is attacked by robbers on the road from Jerusalem to Jericho and is left for dead. A priest and a Levite see him but pass him by, but a Samaritan—a member of a sect other Jews viewed with contempt—helps him.

Although it is not specifically stated in the parable, in such a situation a priest and a Levite (a hereditary caretaker of the Temple) would probably have feared that the victim was dead or would die in their care, and they would be forced to touch a dead man. This meant that they would have to undergo a rite of purification and would not be permitted to do their work for seven days. In considering the letter of the law and the inconvenience it would cause them to keep it, they neglected to act in the spirit of the law, which is love of God and neighbor. The Samaritan, on the other hand, less bound to purification laws, was free to help his neighbor in obedience to the great law.

The dead person's house was also considered unclean for a week after the body was removed from it: no food could be prepared there during that time. Neighbors brought food for the family to eat. In some places the bereaved stayed away from their labors for as much as a week after the funeral, but in rural areas such as Nazareth, where farming waited for no man, the period of bereavement was probably shorter—perhaps no more than a few days. The period of general mourning continued for a month or so from the date of death.

Death was seen as a part of life. After the appropriate period of mourning, the family went on as before. Children were born and grew up to do the work of those who had died. And early in the first century A.D., in the town of Nazareth, one of those children was Jesus.

Aloes, myrrh, and other aromatic plants were wrapped with a body in preparing it for burial. Myrrh was one of the gifts brought to the child Jesus by the Wise Men. Most probably aloes were oils extracted from the succulent leaves of the aloe plant shown here. The aloe has stiff, fleshy leaves edged with sharp teeth and produces reddish or yellow flowers every year. In John 19:39–40, we read that after Joseph of Arimathea claimed the body of Jesus, Nicodemus "came bringing a mixture of myrrh and aloes, about a hundred pounds' weight. They took the body of Jesus, and bound it in linen cloths with the spices, as is the burial custom of the Jews."

Chapter Five

Jerusalem, the Holy City

King David's hilltop stronghold, now dominated by Herod's magnificent Temple, had been the focal point of Judaism for about 1,000 years. When the 12-year-old Jesus accompanied his parents to the Passover feast, Roman troops watched over the crowds.

"Three times a year," Moses had commanded the children of Israel, "all your males shall appear before the Lord your God." And so, just before the year's three great religious feasts—Passover, Shavuot (the Festival of Weeks), and Succoth (the Feast of Tabernacles)—enormous numbers of Jews made their way to the Temple in Jerusalem. From all over Palestine they came, indeed from every corner of the Roman world, crowding the four major roads that led to Jerusalem and swelling the city's population several times over.

Jews who lived in Jerusalem and many who lived nearby were able to take part in all three feasts, observing the letter of the law exactly. In actual practice, however, an annual pilgrimage to the Temple was probably considered sufficient during Jesus' lifetime, and so those who lived at some distance from the holy city may have come regularly to the same feast each year. For the million or more Jews who dwelt in foreign lands, the festive opportunity to gather at the Temple and make sacrifice according to the ancient law was

"You shall take some of the first of all the fruit of the ground, which you harvest from your land that the Lord your God gives you, and you shall put it in a basket, and you shall go to the place which the Lord your God will choose, to make his name to dwell there." Deuteronomy 26:2. Following this command, villagers brought offerings of grapes, grain, figs, pomegranates, and other produce to the Temple in joyous procession. The first fruit offerings began at Shavuot, 50 days after Passover, and continued throughout the summer, until Succoth.

The aerial photograph at right, though distorted by the camera's wide-angle lens, shows Jerusalem's Old City as it appears today. On the opposite page is a map of the city Jesus knew. Both views are from the north—the direction from which Jesus and his family would have approached the city at the end of their journey from Galilee. The Kidron Valley, on the east (left in the illustration), separates the Old City from the Mount of Olives. The Hinnom Valley, on the west, curves around to join the Kidron at the Old City's southern tip. The Tyropoeon Valley, which divided the city from north to south, is now only a shallow depression. Herod the Great had a viaduct built across it, connecting his palace and the elite Upper City with the Temple Mount. Today, the Temple Mount is dominated by the golden Dome of the Rock, Islam's third most sacred shrine, after Mecca and Medina.

probably less an obligation than a goal someday to be achieved; the trek into the heart of Judea was for most of them a once-in-a-lifetime experience, the last leg of a long overland journey or ocean voyage that had been undertaken at great expense.

The Passover pilgrimage

In Jesus' time, the springtime feast of Passover was the most popular and crowded of the pilgrim festivals. The rainy season had ended and the roads were no longer ribbons of thick mud. Most pilgrims came in groups or caravans—the natives of a town or district banding together for safety, foreign pilgrims allying with others from the same ports of call. Some rode donkeys or even camels, but the majority came on foot. They carried their provisions with them, and some from nearby towns and villages probably brought lambs for the Passover sacrifice. Those who did not stop at caravansaries may have set up informal camps at night, taking turns at standing guard against brigands and highwaymen.

Passover began with an evening feast shortly after sunset—the start of the 15th day of the month of Nisan according to the Jewish calendar, in which days ran from sunset to sunset. The principal food at the feast was a lamb that had been sacrificed at the Temple as an important part of the Passover observance. This sacrifice had to take place during the afternoon of the 14th day, so most pilgrims probably tried to arrive in Jerusalem a day or two early in order to make arrangements.

Traveling on the road from Galilee, among the contingent from the village of Nazareth, were Mary, Joseph, and—on the threshold of manhood—their

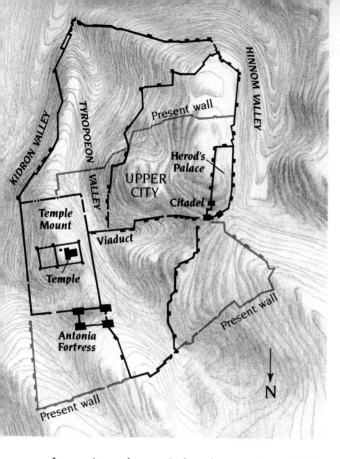

sions instead of quenching them. In A.D. 6 the emperor had removed him and had installed a Roman prefect in his place. Once again, the heart of world Jewry was under the direct rule of a foreign power. Roman troops were everywhere, a strong and ominous presence.

Passover, commemorating the Jews' delivery from ancient slavery, took its name from God's promise in Exodus 12:13: "I will pass over you, and no plague shall fall upon you to destroy you, when I smite the land of Egypt." It was both a solemn and a festive occasion, and in this time of Roman military occupation it took on an added, electric significance. During the seven days of the Passover observance, the air of Jerusalem was fraught with the hope and promise of liberation. The Passover crowd was potentially dangerous; but had Rome tried to deprive the Jews of this religious observance, the troops would surely have met with massive resistance.

Approaching the city

As Jesus and his family crested the nearest of the ridges of hills that helped to protect Jerusalem on the north, the rural lad would have seen spread before him, perhaps for the first time since his infancy, one of the major cities of the age—one that would be described by Pliny as "by far the most famous city, not only of Judea, but of the whole East."

At home in Nazareth, during the regular Friday evening Sabbath services, Jesus, like all other boys, would have heard about the wisdom and history of the Jews. As part of this religious upbringing, he would have learned that the city was a source of deep pride and religious significance—the fulcrum of the Jewish nation's troubled and precarious existence. But his training could hardly have prepared him for the reality he would encounter in this seat of political power, religious fervor, and Jewish culture.

Over the past several decades, thanks to the ambitions and tastes of Herod the Great, Jerusalem had

son, Jesus. According to Luke, the couple made the Passover journey every year, and Jesus accompanied them when he was 12 years old. Luke does not tell us that this was the boy's first such pilgrimage, but it may well have been. At 13 he would have been considered a man, and in the year preceding this watershed age, some families tried to accustom their sons to the religious obligations of adulthood, including a pilgrimage to the holy city.

Things had changed significantly in Jerusalem in a few short years. After the death of Herod the Great, during the reign of his son Archelaus as ethnarch of Judea, Samaria, and Idumea, the land had been torn by a decade of civil and religious strife. Archelaus, possessed of all of his father's viciousness and none of his political skill, had dealt with his subjects in a clumsy and brutal manner, inflaming rebellious pas-

As in Jesus' time, Old Jerusalem is surrounded by walls, and entry to the city is through a number of gates. Shown here (clockwise from upper right): the Jaffa Gate near the Citadel; the Lion's Gate, also called St. Stephen's Gate, in the eastern wall; the Golden Gate, also on the east facing the Mount of Olives (the gravestones belong to a Muslim cemetery); and the Damascus Gate in the north. All but the Golden Gate were the work of Suleiman the Magnificent, the 16th-century Ottoman sultan. The Golden Gate, built around the Byzantine era, has been sealed for nearly 1,000 years. The arch seen beneath the Damascus Gate is part of an older gate built by the second-century emperor Hadrian.

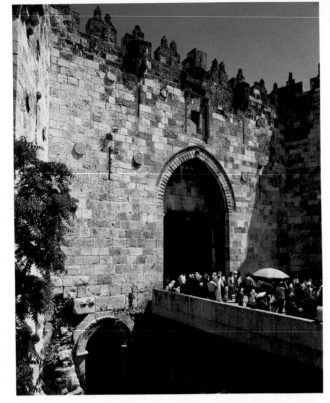

been transformed into an astonishing showcase of architectural magnificence. Shining palaces, noble public buildings, strong defensive walls, and the great Temple plazas stood side by side with the busy swarm of ancient marketplaces, narrow streets, and clustered homes that were the city's historic legacy. Near the great city gates, as though squeezed out by the pressure of festival crowds within, were sprawls of tradesmen, their booths and stands adorned with goods to catch the eyes of passersby. On open plains near the city, and on such hillsides as the Mount of Olives, groups of tents were springing up, encampments where many pilgrims would live among their own townsfolk during their short stay.

Above it all stood the Temple—the jewel and heart of Jerusalem and of the Jewish nation. Testament to nearly a thousand years of revered tradition (as well as to King Herod's extraordinary financial power), the sanctuary was an awesome, thrilling sight. Radiant on the Temple Mount, it stood isolated from the city by a courtyard large enough to hold about 20 football fields. Its walls gleamed like snow on a mountaintop, according to Josephus, and so much gold covered its sides that, had the sun been shining brightly, the boy's eyes might have smarted from the glare.

Cosmopolitan crowds

The traveling group from Nazareth may well have split up outside the city gates, some going to set up camp while others made their way through the city to visit the Temple. Some authorities believe that the Nazarene encampment would have been in the same area every year, probably on the Mount of Olives to the east of the city. Assuming that this Passover pilgrimage was indeed Jesus' introduction to the holy city, it seems likely that Mary and Joseph would have taken him to see the Temple immediately, perhaps to make a personal offering on this, the last day of normal Temple activities before the

special rituals of Passover week were due to begin.

Amid a polyglot babble of accents and foreign tongues, and under the alert, watchful eyes of Roman soldiers, the road-weary family was funneled through one of the city gates to be swallowed up by the crowd. The passage into the sacred city must have been impressive to the thoughtful boy from Galilee. Raised among plain-spoken village people, he was now thrust into a cosmopolitan throng, beset on every side by raucous, aggressive hawkers and professional beggars.

Streets and markets

Jerusalem was a buzzing hive of activity on a normal day; on this day its steep, hilly streets were choked with pilgrims, as well as with the usual complement of workmen, tradesmen, slaves, and high-ranking citizens with their attendants. Its marketplaces were hardly less hectic and probably even more crowded than those outside the gates.

The path to the Temple may have led Jesus and his family through the traditional market situated in the city's lowest ravine, the Tyropoeon Valley, or Valley of the Cheesemakers. Here, their view of the religious center would have been blocked by massive stone walls looming formidably to the east. Rebuilt by Herod, the Temple walls were in themselves impressive; single stones have been found that weigh as much as 100 tons.

Nothing in Jesus' experience would have prepared him for the busyness of business here—the haggling over prices, the shouting and teasing, the furious single-mindedness of buyers and sellers alike. Laid out on tables or held up to view was a kaleidoscopic display of souvenir trinkets and fine goods (scores of different types of luxury items were available in the city's marketplaces). Slaves and servants were buying food and provisions for their masters; farmers were offering fresh fruits and vegetables, probably at appalling prices. The streets were thronged with

123

domestic animals, including those being brought to the Temple for sacrifice and those being offered for sale to pilgrims. Such villagers as Jesus' family, with their rustic clothing and accents, probably drew the attention of many desperate peddlers, beggars, and thieves. People without work tended to migrate to the cities, and such unemployed poor were a constant problem in Jerusalem, where many were forced to live by their wits.

As his parents pushed on through the hurly-burly toward Jerusalem's focal point, the Temple, Jesus would have caught glimpses of some of Herod's other architectural legacies. The family's path would probably not have led through the Upper City—the isolated section of Jerusalem where the wealthy lived in splendid mansions—but they might have seen the towers of the Citadel adjoining Herod's palace there (part of one tower survives today, as the base of the structure known as David's Tower). Near the Temple Mount they would have seen the towers of the Antonia, the huge fortress named in honor of Mark Antony, Herod's early patron, and now the headquarters of the Roman garrison in Jerusalem.

Ancient inhabitants

Jewish history had become linked forever with Jerusalem when King David, the most beloved of all the nation's leaders, conquered the site about 1000 B.C. But a pre-Israelite city had existed here by at least the 19th century B.C., when "Rushalimum" was mentioned in Egyptian texts. Later, "Urusalim" appeared in the court records of the Pharaoh Akhenaten and his wife, Nefertiti.

Scholars continue to debate the original meaning of the city's name; most agree that it probably honored Shalim, a Canaanite deity whose name also came to be associated with the Hebrew word *shalom*, meaning "peace." When, in the 13th century B.C., Joshua led the Hebrews across the Jordan River and into the land of Canaan, the city was called Jebus

and its occupants Jebusites, ruled by Adonizedek. Although Joshua conquered the countryside, he did not occupy the city.

Apart from its naturally protected position, the area offered few other advantages. It was not near any of the well-traveled caravan routes; little of its soil was suitable for growing food; water was available only from the spring called Gihon in the Bible (also known as the Virgin's Fount and St. Mary's Spring today). Since the spring lay outside the defensive walls, a tunnel had been dug so that water could be obtained when the city was under siege.

The city of David

Centuries after Joshua, internal politics led David to take Jerusalem from the Jebusites. Hungry for national unity, the northern tribes of Israel wanted to join with David's kingdom of Judah in the south. Recognizing that Hebron, his capital, was too strongly associated with Judah's power, David wisely and diplomatically chose Jerusalem, on the border between north and south, to be his new seat of government. Not only was it politically well situated, but its hilltop position made it easily defensible.

So defensible was the city, in fact, that the Jebusites laughed at David's threat, saying that the blind and the lame could defend the city's walls. David had his own brand of humor. According to 2 Samuel 5:8, he told his men, "Whoever would smite the Jebusites, let him get up the water shaft to attack the lame and the blind." Chronicles tells us that Joab, who was to become the general of all David's armies as a reward for the feat, led a contingent of soldiers up the limestone tunnel from Gihon and surprised the complacent defenders. Jebus fell and Jerusalem became the political and religious capital of the newly united Jewish nation. It belonged neither to Judah nor to Israel, but was the king's personal possession. "And David dwelt in the stronghold," says 2 Samuel, "and called it the city of David."

Watering an Arid City

During most of its long history, Jerusalem's main water source was the sporadic Gihon spring in the west wall of the Kidron Valley. Its waters flow only once or twice a day in the dry season, and so from earliest times the city's people have built storage pools and cisterns to catch rainwater. In order to reach the spring when under attack, the ancient Jebusites sunk a shaft inside the city walls and tunneled to it from the spring; it was through this shaft that Joab, David's military leader, entered the city. In the eighth century B.C. King Hezekiah, under threat of an invasion, had a deeper tunnel cut through the limestone, channeling the spring's water 1,765 feet into the Pool of Siloam. By Jesus' time, the city had several other pools and may have had more cisterns than houses. The Romans built a 42-mile aqueduct from other springs, near Hebron.

The Pool of Siloam, fed by the ancient spring called Gihon, has been a water source since about 700 B.C., when King Hezekiah had a new tunnel dug through the limestone bedrock beneath the city.

The Pool of Towers, also known as Hezekiah's Pool, was one of several such reservoirs in which water was stored for public use. It was just north of the Citadel, which was connected to Herod's palace.

The carving above, found in the ruins of a second- or third-century A.D. synagogue in Capernaum, on the northwest coast of the Sea of Galilee, depicts a wheeled Ark of the Covenant. The Ark, said to hold the tablets of the Ten Commandments, was of supreme importance to the ancient Jews. During the wanderings in the wilderness, Moses assigned the Levites to guard and transport it. They continued to perform this function throughout the conquest and settlement of Israel. According to 1 Samuel, the Ark once fell into the hands of the Philistines, who put it in the temple of their god, Dagon. Within seven months, Dagon's statue had fallen on its face and broken and two cities had been devastated by a plague, and so the Philistines returned the Ark.

The city of God

Later in David's reign, when the kingdom was beset by a plague, the prophet Gad told him to build an altar to the Lord on a threshing floor belonging to a man named Araunah the Jebusite. Araunah offered to donate the land, along with the oxen for a burnt offering. David replied, "No, but I will buy it of you for a price; I will not offer burnt offerings to the Lord my God which cost me nothing." According to 2 Samuel, David paid the modest sum of 50 silver shekels for the land; according to 1 Chronicles (in which Araunah is called Ornan) the price was set at 600 gold shekels, a small fortune. Both accounts agree, however, that the sacrifice was made and the plague ended, and that David dedicated the threshing floor as a permanent altar. He installed the Ark of the Covenant, a chestlike, portable shrine that was supposed to contain the two tablets of the Ten Commandments. The Ark, in David's time, was believed to be the place where the Lord was manifested; facing it, one stood before God. And so it was that Jerusalem came to be acknowledged in the Bible as "the city which the Lord had chosen out of all the tribes of Israel, to put his name there."

The priesthood

David appointed two priests, Zadok and Abiathar, to watch over the Ark. In so doing, he planted the seed of a new institution, a centralized priesthood, which would one day grow into the ruling power of the land. Earlier, sanctuaries had existed throughout the land, and many of these had had hereditary families of priests. These priests had been part of a larger group, called Levites, or descendants of Levi, who had been charged with the care and—in the earlier nomadic society—the transporting of the sanctuary. One of the primary duties of the priests (who were, by tradition, descended from the Levite Aaron, the brother of Moses) had been to act as oracles in determining God's will. They would cast two objects, the Urim and the Thummim, to find the answer to a simple yes-or-no question. With the establishment of a permanent sanctuary in which the Ark of the Covenant itself was kept, David also ensured the establishment of an elite priesthood connected to that sanctuary. And by centering that sanctuary on an altar devoted to burnt offerings, he gave these priests a unique ritual function.

Solomon's Temple

David had intended to build a temple on the site, but it was his son Solomon who actually did so, starting about 960 B.C. No architectural fragment of Solomon's Temple has ever been found. The most detailed description comes from 1 Kings; it tells us that the main building was about 90 feet long, 30 feet wide, and 45 feet high. It gives few other dimensions that are useful in trying to recreate the whole complex, but the resplendent image it evokes is firmly embedded in the imagination of the world—huge bronze columns ingeniously decorated with the forms of pomegranates and lilies; great galleries around the main building; massive walls of the stately cedars of Lebanon, all ashimmer with gold. The knot-free cedar, insect-repellent and rot-resistant, is frequently mentioned in the Old Testament as the best wood for construction.

This great edifice—the first temple of a nomadic people who had made the transition to a settled way of life—necessarily reflected the architectural skills of peoples more experienced in construction than the Jews were. Phoenician woodcarvers, the most accomplished of the era, were hired to execute decorative highlights; an expert from the city of Tyre saw to the casting of bronze objects. The unprecedented undertaking required seven years to complete and, in addition to the skilled craftsmen, involved the forced labor of at least 30,000 Israelites.

Solomon's Temple was tangible proof that the kingdom and its supreme deity were forces to be reckoned with. It resembled other temples of the region in many details; various characteristics of the structure could be found throughout the Middle East, from Egypt to Syria. Solomon had striven to rival the most majestic of these other buildings in richness of materials rather than originality of design. The lamps, incense holders, tongs, fire pans, and other implements of animal sacrifice were of gold. Elaborate bronze lavers were used for ritual purification and included a mysterious "sea" that held 10,000 gallons of water and weighed about 30 tons. Inside the Holy of Holies, which could be entered only one day a year and only by the chief priest, two enormous winged cherubim, carved from olive wood and decorated with gold, stood watch over the Ark of the Covenant.

To believers, the richness of the Temple's materials was less a testimony to earthly glories than

The two cherubim in the Holy of Holies in Solomon's Temple may have resembled this Phoenician ivory carving, done in the ninth century B.C. The winged creatures, with leonine bodies and human heads, were familiar figures of ancient myth.

a supreme attempt to build a house worthy of the presence of God, the Creator, who had brought his chosen people into the promised land and had helped them defeat their enemies. Never mind that some critics suspected that Solomon had been more interested in demonstrating his own might.

Just as the splendor of Solomon's Temple brought new prestige to the kingdom, so did it increase the power and standing of the priests who attended it. Only one of David's two appointments—Zadok—remained as chief priest under Solomon. (David's other priest, Abiathar, had supported another of David's sons, Adonijah, to succeed David; when Solomon had taken the throne instead, Abiathar had been banished from Jerusalem.) For about eight centuries, the direct descendants of Zadok were to hold the chief priesthood, which later would be formalized as the high priesthood, in an almost unbroken succession, each serving for life.

Sadly, the glorious Temple became a lightning rod for divisive and destructive forces. From time to time, the Temple treasury was plundered or drawn upon to pay tribute to potential invaders. Gold was stripped from the doors for the same purpose. One king even desecrated the holy precincts by setting up altars to heathen deities. Finally, in 587 B.C., the Babylonian king Nebuchadnezzar looted and razed the Temple. The following year he took the Jews into captivity.

The Second Temple

Solomon's Temple had endured for about four centuries. Its apparently more modest successor, built by the Jews who returned to

The pomegranate's scarlet flowers (above) are followed by juicy fruits about the size of oranges. They were among the favorite symbols of God's blessings, depicted on the columns of Solomon's Temple and used to ornament the hem of the high priest's robes. They also decorate the bronze tripod stand shown above right, found in western Syria. The work of a Phoenician craftsman, it dates from the 15th or 14th century B.C. and is probably similar to the 10 bronze, wheeled stands that supported lavers in Solomon's Temple.

Jerusalem from Babylonia under the amnesty of the Persian king Cyrus the Great, lasted about 500 years. This Second Temple was finished by 515 B.C. It is sometimes called the Temple of Zerubbabel, in honor of the first leader of the postexilic community in Jerusalem. Its construction may have been subsidized by the Persians, whose state policy allowed local religious customs to be observed by subject peoples so long as they remained loyal to the empire.

Little is known about the physical characteristics of the Second Temple. It may have been smaller than Solomon's Temple, and it was certainly less lavish, both in concept and in execution. There is no doubt, however, about the fundamental role it played in the spiritual life of the Jewish people. We know that Temple services were splendid occasions, led by an officiating priest in gorgeous attire; and we know that—because the Ark of the Covenant had presumably been destroyed by the Babylonian conquerors—the innermost chamber, the Holy of Holies, was and would remain empty.

During the time of the Second Temple, the basic

rituals grew more complex. The Temple staff grew in number, and a system of social stratification developed, based on Temple function. The chief priest became more commonly known as the high priest; after the return from Babylonian captivity, he had become the acknowledged leader of the Jewish community. No longer subordinate to a king, he had civil, as well as religious, authority.

His elevation was accompanied by the elevation of the entire priesthood to an elite class, highly respected because they were responsible for all Temple ritual. The Levites, a class that earlier had not been clearly distinguished from priests, now became a distinct, subordinate group of Temple functionaries. This group was itself divided into several occupations, each hereditary in nature. Foremost among the Levites were the singers and instrumentalists, who provided music for Temple services. Farther down the scale were the doorkeepers, who opened and closed the gates and guarded against intrusion by unqualified people. Other Levites cleaned and maintained the Temple grounds, served as Temple police, helped the priests on and off with their vestments, and performed other such essential tasks.

A *revered memory*

Jesus would have learned about the Second Temple from the study of the Scripture, and he would have heard legends and stories of how important it had been as a political sanctuary. In times of struggle with outside enemies, as well as during such internal strife as the civil war between the Hasmoneans Hyrcanus II and Aristobulus II, which began in 67 B.C., the sacred building was sometimes used as a last refuge by whatever faction was defending Jerusalem. It had been strongly fortified early in the second century B.C. under the direction of the high priest Simon II. Only once, so far as is known, did any conquering adversary ever dare to enter the Holy of Holies: that was the Roman general Pompey, in 63 B.C. (see Chapter 2). Remarkably, the Second Temple was a relatively unscarred survivor of many a fierce battle for control of the city when Herod began to dismantle it about 20 B.C. in order to build a larger, more impressive building.

Herod's Temple

It was toward this new Temple that Jesus and his family made their way through the Passover crowds. Older friends and relatives might have seen the Second Temple in their youth, and some no doubt remembered it with a nostalgia burnished by religious zeal. But hardly a stone remained in place.

When Herod had begun his grand project, the priesthood, suspicious that this cosmopolitan king intended to destroy the Temple and build no replacement—or worse, erect some profanation in its place—had resisted his plans. To prove that his intentions were honorable, Herod hired 10,000 laborers and ordered 1,000 wagons built for hauling stone. Moreover, to allay their fears that the most sacred areas of the new Temple might be profaned by nonpriestly hands, he had 1,000 priests trained as masons and carpenters. (About 80 years later, during the reign of Nero in Rome, some of the work that these inexpert craftsmen had done was to collapse and need replacement.)

Unfortunately, although we know more about the dimensions and functions of Herod's Temple than we do of its predecessors, we must guess at much of what Jesus must have seen as he entered the holy precincts. Nowhere in the Scriptures is there a detailed or systematic description of it, and—as is so often true in Jerusalem—archeology has yielded little information because the Temple Mount remains a hallowed site to Muslims, Christians, and Jews alike. We have some idea of the glories of Herod's Temple, however, principally from Josephus, who, as a young man, lived among the priests in Jerusalem before the Temple was destroyed.

Outdoing Solomon

From the writings of Josephus we learn that Herod wanted to rival the opulence and size of Solomon's Temple, and that he assumed it to have been twice as high as the existing Second Temple. And we know that, in order to accommodate the huge Court of the Gentiles around the Temple, he, in effect, enlarged the Temple Mount by building supporting structures into the deep valleys that border it. The

Continued on page 132

The cedar of Lebanon can attain a height of 125 feet and a girth of up to 50 feet, and can live longer than 1,000 years. The fragrant conifers, which once forested the snowy mountain ranges north of Israel, were cut by the hundreds for Solomon's Temple. They continued to be cut over the centuries and are no longer common.

129

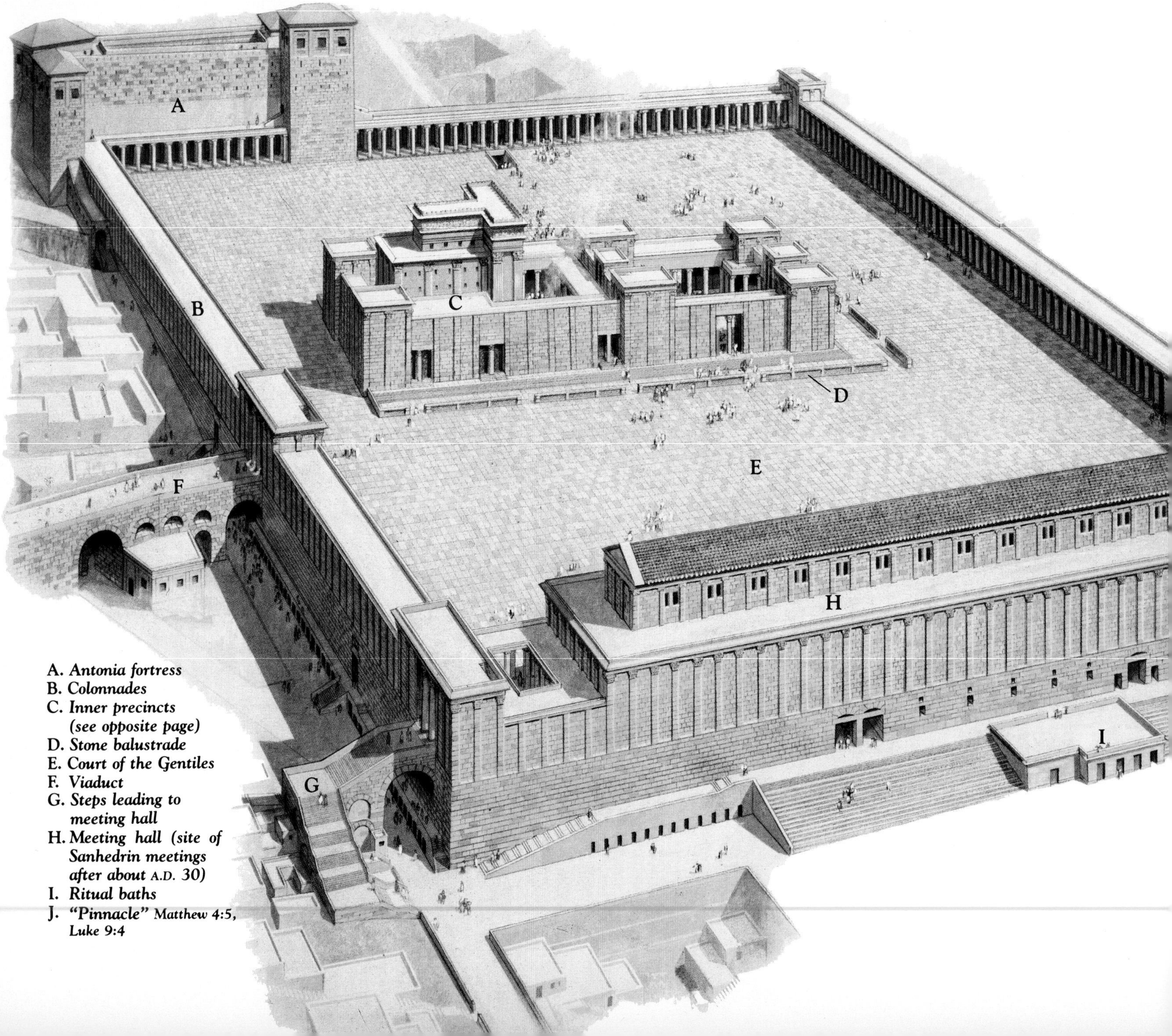

A. Antonia fortress
B. Colonnades
C. Inner precincts
   (see opposite page)
D. Stone balustrade
E. Court of the Gentiles
F. Viaduct
G. Steps leading to
   meeting hall
H. Meeting hall (site of
   Sanhedrin meetings
   after about A.D. 30)
I. Ritual baths
J. "Pinnacle" Matthew 4:5,
   Luke 9:4

King Herod's Magnificent Temple—the Heart of Judaism

Although scholars and historians include it in the Second Temple Period, the Temple built by Herod the Great was actually the third—and by all accounts, the largest—to occupy the Temple Mount. Herod, seeking to reconcile his Jewish subjects to the rule of an Idumean monarch who reigned at the pleasure of the Roman emperor, had tried to rival the fabled grandeur of Solomon's original Temple. In fact, since he was competing with a legend, he probably outdid the First Temple in most respects.

The First Temple had been envisioned by King David, when, according to 2 Samuel 7:2, he said to Nathan the prophet, "See now, I dwell in a house of cedar, but the ark of God dwells in a tent." But his son Solomon had actually built the Temple, and it stood for about 400 years. In the month of Av in 587 B.C., it was destroyed by the armies of the Babylonian king Nebuchadnezzar.

The Second Temple was built with the support of the Persian king Cyrus the Great, who had defeated the Babylonians and, in 538 B.C., had allowed the Jews to return to their homeland. It stood for nearly 500 years until it was destroyed, not by a conquering force, but by King Herod, in order to replace it.

No precise description of Herod's Temple exists, so some details shown on these pages are speculation. The ground plan below shows the likely arrangement of the inner precincts. During the Temple's construction, which began about 20 B.C., not a day of sacrificial offerings was missed. The sanctuary was finished in about a year and a half, but work continued on the Temple Mount until at least A.D. 63, only seven years before the Temple was destroyed by the Romans—also in the month of Av.

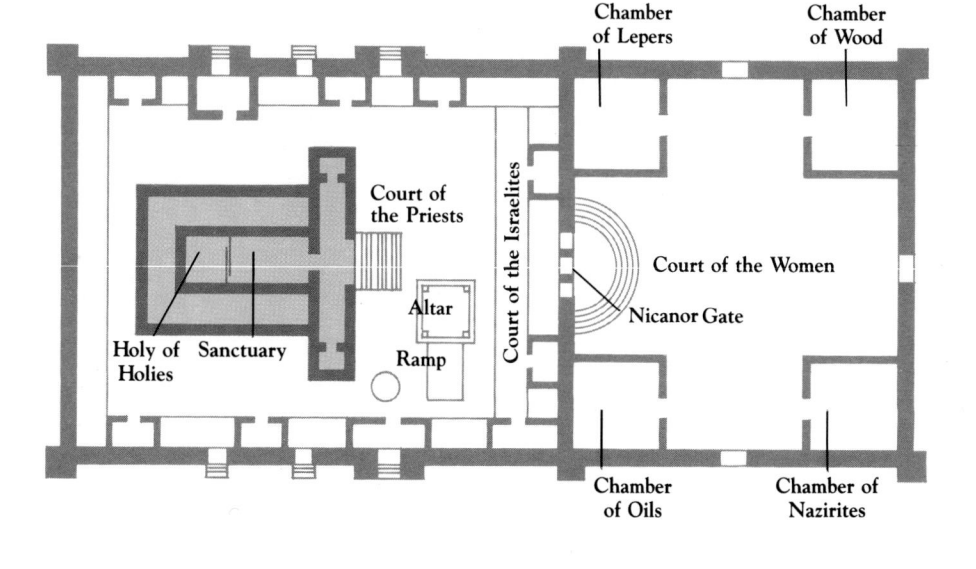

Court of the Priests

Court of the Israelites

Chamber of Lepers

Chamber of Wood

Court of the Women

Nicanor Gate

Altar

Ramp

Holy of Holies   Sanctuary

Chamber of Oils

Chamber of Nazirites

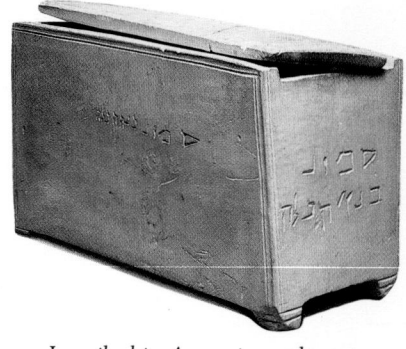

Inscribed in Aramaic on the ossuary shown above is the identification, "Simon, builder of the Sanctuary." It probably holds the bones of an architect or master builder who contributed to the king's mighty project.

entire complex—bounded by a wall that has been estimated at 840 feet long on the south, 945 feet long on the north, 1,410 feet long on the east, and 1,455 feet long on the west—covered almost 30 acres. The vast undertaking was not completed in Herod's lifetime (nor, indeed, for many decades after his death), but the Temple structure itself had been built in about a year and a half, faithful to the traditional Solomonic design in the arrangement of its rooms.

The walls and the double doors of the two-story sanctuary were covered in gold and topped with golden vines and clusters of golden grapes that were, according to Josephus, "as tall as a man." Suspended before the doors was a spectacular tapestry that had been woven in Babylon; its multicolored design was a panorama of the universe. Within the building was an altar for incense, a golden menorah (a seven-branched lamp stand), and a table for the holy bread, or shewbread. Each Sabbath, 12 loaves of unleavened bread were laid out in rows upon this table, along with fragrant frankincense, and were consecrated as an offering to God. The entrance to the innermost room of the Temple, the Holy of Holies, was always kept covered by a double veil, and into this empty, windowless room—an exact cube of 30 feet—daylight was never allowed to enter.

The Court of the Gentiles

Neither Jesus nor his family were ever to see inside the Temple; it was reserved for priests, as usually was the area immediately surrounding it, called the Court of the Priests. When the family first entered upon the Temple Mount, after having immersed themselves in a ritual bath, or *mikveh*, they would have found themselves in the broad Court of the Gentiles. Here, even non-Jews were allowed to bring offerings to be sacrificed by priests at the great altar. Josephus reports that Marcus Agrippa, lieutenant to the emperor Augustus, once sacrificed 100

A portion of a stone inscribed in Greek, which warned Gentiles not to enter the inner courts of the Temple on pain of death. The letters were painted red, and much of the paint remained when the stone was found outside the Lion's Gate in 1935.

oxen as a burnt offering during a visit to Jerusalem. The Temple was a tourist attraction; foreign kings, merchants, and servants alike visited the Court of the Gentiles and gazed in wonder at the building about which the Talmud, the book of Jewish law and commentary, was later to say: "He who has not seen the Temple of Herod has never in his life seen a beautiful building."

On a normal day the construction of the Temple complex, at which great numbers of workers were still employed, would have added the noises of labor, the crackle of disagreements, and the drone of ancient work chants to the babble and hubbub. During and just before the Passover Festival, because of the onslaught of thousands of pilgrims, work was probably stopped. In the colonnaded portico around the Court of the Gentiles, money changers would have been changing foreign and local currency into Tyrian shekels, the only acceptable coins for Temple offerings. Animals and birds would have been offered for sale to sacrificers. People might have been anxiously searching for relatives lost in the crush. All voices would necessarily have been raised over the general din, and the cacophony of languages would have reminded many a devout Jew of the story of the Tower of Babel. While Hebrew was used in Temple services, and Aramaic was the language of the streets, many traders, scholars, scribes, and aristocrats would have been speaking Greek, and other pilgrims from the Diaspora may have been using the tongues of their home countries.

The family from Nazareth would probably not have spent much time in this crowded and hectic area, but would have pushed their way toward the low stone wall that surrounded the inner courts of the Temple. Inscriptions on the wall warned visitors in Greek and Latin that "No foreigner may enter within the balustrade and enclosure around the Temple area. Anyone caught doing so will bear the responsibility for his own ensuing death." The Ro-

mans respected this prohibition and allowed even Roman citizens who offended it to be executed.

The Court of the Women

Having passed through the stone balustrade, the family would have climbed a low flight of steps that stretched around the Temple precincts, and would have entered one of the three gates that opened onto the Court of the Women—so named because women were allowed to go no closer to the sanctuary and its altar. Here they would immediately have found companionship; the area was well known as a social gathering place, in many ways the heart of the Jewish community. Voices would be raised in greeting and in laughter as friends met friends; and today many families and traveling groups, having been separated among the crowds in the Court of the Gentiles, would be searching one another out.

Preachers and would-be prophets came here to exhort believers with their personal visions of truth. Scribes and scholars met here to discuss religious issues and debate points of religious law while students—even children—listened, learned, and perhaps asked questions. And here Jews could speak openly of their hopes and longings for the Messiah, the promised one, who was expected by many to deliver them from the Romans, whose soldiers stood nervous guard outside.

The Temple treasury

Adding to the activity in the Court of the Women were the 13 chests of the Temple treasury, each shaped like a shofar, or ram's-horn trumpet, open to receive the various offerings given to defray the costs of sacrifice. The money would be transferred to one of the numerous treasury chambers built into the inner forecourt of the Temple, each for a distinct purpose. The Shekel Chamber held an enormous, constantly growing treasure—the half-shekel annual dues imposed upon all Jewish men. In the Chamber

of Utensils was a great store of gold and silver vessels for use in the worship services. Funds in the Chamber of Secrets were secretly handed out to "the poor of good family." Private individuals, too, could bring their money to the treasury for safekeeping. The operation of this remarkable enterprise required competent, detailed administration. Its preservation must have required the watchful eyes of many Levite guards. But its ultimate protection was the sanctity of the Temple itself.

In each of the four corners of the Court of the Women was a separate walled enclosure that served a special purpose. One was for storage and inspection of wood, for no wormy wood was to be used in the altar fire. A second held oil and wine for use in the services. A third was reserved for lepers who believed themselves cured; here they were inspected by priests, and if they were found to be cured, they

Tyrian silver shekels, such as that shown above, were the only acceptable coins for the payment of Temple taxes. "Bankers," or money changers, performed a valuable—and profitable—service for worshipers who lacked the proper coins. The Roman relief at the top of the page shows a banker at work.

The shofar, or ram's horn, is one of the earliest musical instruments still in use today and is the only one from ancient times still used in synagogues. It was the shofar that sounded at Joshua's siege of Jericho, as the Hebrews circled the city seven times, and it is the shofar that is blown in modern Israel on various ceremonial occasions. Capable of producing only two or three notes but a wide range of expressive intonations, it has never served to play melodies. Rather, its reverberating sound has historically been a call to worship or to battle.

would purify themselves in a *mikveh*. Then, to complete the process of purification, they would make a burnt offering in atonement for the time that they had spent outside God's service. The fourth enclosure was set aside for Nazirites, the "dedicated" or "consecrated" ones, who were forbidden to drink wine, cut their hair, or approach a dead body.

Approaching the altar

Mary might have accompanied Joseph and Jesus to the foot of the 15 curved steps that led up to the magnificent Nicanor Gate in the west wall of the Court of the Women, but there they would have left her. As Jewish men, they alone were allowed to enter the third court, the Court of the Israelites. From this long and comparatively narrow strip of stone pavement that preceded the Court of the Priests, they could see the high altar, an isolated structure made of unfinished stone that had never been touched by metal tools, each of its four corners decorated with a horn-shaped projection. Beyond it was the facade of the magnificent Temple itself. Tradition had it that nearby, perhaps beneath the inner sanctum of the sanctuary, was the sacred rock upon which Abraham, at God's command, had prepared to sacrifice his son Isaac.

Reverent awe surely filled their souls as they came into this place, although the atmosphere was hardly cathedrallike. They stood amid a crowded mass of men, some of whom would have been chanting prayers, while others were excitedly conversing. Some would have brought lambs, rams, goats, doves, pigeons, or even cattle to be sacrificed, and the bleatings and other animal noises would have punctuated the chorus of human voices. The air would have been heavy with the mixed odors of blood, incense, and charred animal fat—a smell that had been growing in intensity as the family had made their way across the Temple Mount.

Flies were not a problem, however—apparently

because of the dry air and the frequent breezes. Birds of prey and scavengers, which could be problems at sacrificial altars from Egypt to Greece because they swooped down to snatch up the slaughtered meat, did not interfere with the rites in Jerusalem. This was all the more surprising because kites and ravens were abundant in the region. Some believers of the day felt that their absence in the holy precincts was a miracle, an indication of the true holiness of the site. A more secular explanation was that the golden spikes on the Temple roof prevented birds from nesting or gaining a foothold. Similar spikes may have been set up near the sacrificial altar as well.

The rites of sacrifice

Animal sacrifice was central to the rituals of the Temple. On a normal day, the Temple priests' public duties began at dawn with the burnt offering of a lamb and ended 8½ hours later with the sacrifice of another. Each animal's throat was cut and its blood was ceremonially splashed against the altar. Both animals were butchered and the parts were burned in the altar fire in such a way as to maintain a continuous offering to God.

In addition, on every day except the Sabbath, there was a steady flow of private sacrifices, ranging from bulls to pigeons. Many were guilt or sin offerings, meant to remove an impurity or to atone for a misdeed; these were generally burnt offerings, in which the animal's flesh was reduced to ashes on the altar. Other sacrifices were peace offerings, made on such occasions as a family reunion, the recovery from an illness, the sealing of a private pact, or the harvesting of first fruits. In these, only parts of the animal—the entrails, some fatty tissue, and perhaps the kidneys—were burned, and the remainder of the meat was later eaten by the priests and by the offerer. In all offerings, the animal's blood (said to contain the essence of its life) belonged to God and had to be smeared on the horns of the altar or dashed

against its sides or base, depending on the nature of the offering. The skins of sacrificial animals were the property of the priests. Although no private offerings were made on the Sabbath, the priests sacrificed two additional lambs as community offerings.

The institution of animal sacrifice had been a part of Judaism since the earliest times, an acknowledgment that all life belonged to God. It would not have shocked or revolted Jesus or his family. In ancient times the patriarch of a family had per-

formed the sacrifices himself, often upon a "high place," such as a raised platform or an altar constructed on a mountaintop. (Although animal sacrifice was a common religious tradition throughout most of the ancient world, only two Semitic peoples, the Canaanites and the Israelites, burned their offerings on an altar, as did the Greeks to the west.) Even after David and Solomon had centered religious activity in Jerusalem, sacrifices were still being made in many of the high places. It was not until after the

In today's Jerusalem, Christians and Jews observe different occasions with palm branches. The annual Palm Sunday procession (above) marks Jesus' entry into the city before his crucifixion. At the left, Jews pray during Succoth at the Western Wall, the bottom stones of which are the only remnant of Herod's Temple.

Priests were distinguished by their dress when serving at the Temple. The garments worn by an ordinary priest are shown on the left. Over white linen underclothing, he wore an ankle-length, seamless tunic of white linen, bound at the waist by a long girdle. On his head was a white linen hat. The high priest, depicted at the right, wore a blue headdress, and over the priest's white tunic he wore a blue robe fringed with golden bells and pomegranates. Upon his shoulders was a vestlike ephod, embroidered with bands of gold, purple, scarlet, and blue. On his chest was a gold purse inset with 12 gemstones, representing the tribes. In an earlier day, the Urim and the Thummim—two ceremonial objects that were used to divine God's will—were kept in such purses. All priests went barefoot in the Temple.

return from the Babylonian Captivity that the rituals of sacrifice became the province of the Temple.

Only domestic animals that were raised for food were acceptable for sacrifice—cattle, goats, sheep, pigeons, and doves—and they had to be free from blemish, injury, disfigurement, and disease. For private offerings, the believer's rank and wealth were important in determining which animal was acceptable; where a high priest would have to offer a young bull to atone for a sin or impurity, a king would offer a ram, a merchant or landowner a goat or a lamb, and a poor person a pair of birds—as Mary herself had done, according to Luke 2:24. A very poor man might offer only a small measure of fine flour. Most animal sacrifices were accompanied by cereal offerings, consisting of cakes made from wheat flour, and drink offerings of wine. From the cereal offerings, too, the priests received a portion for their own use.

A team of priests, each with a precisely assigned role, was in charge of the entire sacrificial process. The roles were chosen by casting lots; one priest would be assigned as the slaughterer, another would sprinkle blood on the altar, another would clear away the ashes, and so on. In most sacrifices, the worshiper simply laid his hand on the offering and perhaps announced the reason for the sacrifice before the animal was taken by a Levite to be slaughtered by a priest at a spot near the north side of the high altar. If the sacrifice was in atonement for a civil wrong, such as fraud, robbery, or other infringement of property rights, a confession of the crime and full restitution (plus a 20 percent fine) had to precede the offering of a burnt sacrifice. If the victim was no longer alive, the prescribed payment had to be made to the Temple priests. No one had to pay for the privilege of making a sacrifice, as did worshipers in most other temples of the day. The right to sacrifice at the Temple in Jerusalem was basic; wood for the altar was supplied free.

Community sacrifices, such as the daily burnt

offerings of lambs, followed Old Testament prescriptions. On the day of the new moon that began each month, two young bulls, a ram, a goat, and seven lambs were sacrificed. The same numbers were sacrificed for Shavuot and on each day of Passover week. During the eight days of Succoth, a total of 71 young bulls, 15 rams, 8 goats, and 105 lambs were sacrificed upon the altar. Other days that called for special offerings included the first day of the New Year and the Day of Atonement. Community offerings had also been made in the past to observe such momentous events as the consecration of an altar, the celebration of a military victory, or the atonement by the community for a collective misdeed.

The blood of the lamb

In many ways, the most important of the sacrifices that took place during Passover was the one made on the afternoon preceding the Passover feast, or *seder*. This was the group offering of the paschal lambs, which would be eaten simultaneously by many thousands of Jews who were in Jerusalem. It would have been to take part in this ceremony that Jesus and his father might have returned to the Temple after their first, introductory excursion. If they had done so, they would have been acting as the representatives of 10 or more people who would share the feast, and they would have carried with them an unblemished lamb that was at least eight days and no more than one year old. Perhaps they or one of their companions had brought the lamb from Nazareth; more likely the group had shared the cost of buying a lamb in the city.

The offering of the paschal lambs differed from all other community sacrifices in several ways. It was a group offering in which each sacrificer killed his own animal. The sacrifice was prepared for the meal to follow; only small portions of the fat and internal organs were removed and burned on the altar. The blood of the sacrifice was dashed against the base of the altar in lieu of the ancient practice of sprinkling it on doorposts of houses. (This practice had itself been a ritual remembrance of the original Passover, when the Hebrews had marked their doors with the blood of the lamb in order that their firstborn would not be taken along with those of the Egyptians.)

The preparations on the Temple Mount would be different for Passover than for any other day. The normal day's rituals would finish an hour early, and the remainder of the afternoon would be given over to the orderly slaughter of thousands of lambs. The Temple precincts would be crowded with pilgrims holding lambs, waiting for the gates to reopen after the final burnt offering had been made. Then about a third of the multitude would be admitted, and—to the sharp, piercing sound of a shofar—the gate would be closed behind them. The sacrificers would confront a long row of priests, each holding a bowl of gold or silver; behind each of these priests would be more priests, forming a line to the altar. When a worshiper reached one of the front rank of priests, he would use a sharp knife to open the carotid artery in the neck of the lamb he held and would drain the blood into the priest's bowl. The bowl would then be passed back to another priest, who would replace it with an empty bowl of the same precious metal and

Bronze incense shovels like the one at left may have been used in Temple ceremonies. Blazing coals were placed in the shovels, and incense was kept in the two small dishes above them to be sprinkled on the coals as needed.

pass the full bowl on until it reached the altar. There the blood would be splashed on the base of the altar, and the empty bowl would begin its return journey through the hands of the same priests to be refilled.

When all of this group's lambs had been killed and flayed, the gates would be reopened and a second wave of sacrificers would enter to repeat the process. The third and final wave would include all the pilgrims still waiting in the courts. Throughout the long ritual, the voices of Levite singers would be raised, singing from the Psalms to the accompaniment of reed pipes and other instruments.

The sacrificers would return with the prepared lambs to their families—or perhaps to groups of friends or fellow travelers—and there the lambs would be roasted and eaten, along with unleavened bread and bitter herbs. In the course of the meal, the story of the Exodus would be retold. (It was such a Passover *seder*, shared by Jesus and his disciples, that history was to remember as the Last Supper.)

The remaining days of Passover week—known as the Feast of Unleavened Bread—were linked not only to the story of the Exodus but also to an agricultural festival that traditionally marked the beginning of the grain harvest. During this solemn week, no leavened bread (nor anything else that contained yeast) could be eaten.

Other pilgrimage festivals

Shavuot, or the Feast of Weeks, 50 days after Passover, remained essentially an agricultural festival, as it had been for centuries. By that date, the wheat harvest was complete, and it was time to offer the first fruits to God in thanksgiving. In Jesus' time this was done in a ritual fashion, by offering two large loaves of leavened bread at the Temple.

Succoth, the autumn Festival of Tabernacles, was the most joyous occasion of the year, and it was the festival during which the most sacrifices took place. It, too, was rooted in a harvest festival of thanksgiving, this time for the great harvest of grapes, olives, and all remaining summer grain. Solomon's Temple had been dedicated during this feast, and every seven years the Torah was read publicly on this occasion. Among the regular observances were the morning water libations, when a procession of priests carried a pitcher of water from the Pool of Siloam to the Temple and poured it on the altar. This was one of the rare occasions when the people were allowed to approach the altar; in a joyous procession, the adult male populace circled it seven times. From the first night of the festival, there was dancing by the light of bonfires as the Levites played their instruments. The festivities, which might feature respected scholars dancing or juggling lighted torches for the crowd, would continue until dawn. The characteristic joyousness of Succoth and the symbolic importance of the city of David can be seen in the farewell salutation from Psalm 128 offered by pilgrims as they departed for home: "The Lord bless you from Zion! May you see the prosperity of Jerusalem all the days of your life! May you see your children's children! Peace be upon Israel!"

The Day of Atonement

The most solemn day of the year was the fast of Yom Kippur, the Day of Atonement, when the high priest himself administered all Temple services and went before the Lord to offer atonement for the sins of the nation. Although it was not one of the ordained pilgrim festivals, Yom Kippur preceded Succoth by only five days, and so many Jews assembled in Jerusalem for both the fast and the feast.

For this critically important service, the high priest had to prepare with great care. To avoid the possibility of ritual impurity, he would leave his home and enter a special apartment in the Temple seven days before the Day of Atonement. During this week, every step of the prescribed ritual would be studied and reviewed in detail, for it was of

When, on the Day of Atonement, the high priest entered the Holy of Holies for the first time, it was a dramatic moment. After passing between the two curtains that covered the entrance, he heaped incense on the coals he carried, and the room filled with smoke. Before presenting himself to the people, he prayed. "But he did not prolong his prayer," says the Mishnah, the book of law, "lest he put Israel in terror."

utmost importance that no mistake be made. On the night before the service, he would maintain a vigil in the company of several other priests, who would read Scripture with him and help him to stay awake. Meanwhile, in case anything should happen to him, another priest was also being made ready to take his place.

The high priest wore special vestments for Yom Kippur, and in the course of the long day of ritual he would change them several times, bathing 5 times and washing his hands and feet 10 times. Early in the ritual, he would ceremoniously cast lots to choose between two goats—one to be offered as a burnt sacrifice, the other to be driven into the fearsome Judean Wilderness to die as a "scapegoat." He would confess that he himself had committed sins and would sacrifice a young bull as an offering for those sins and for the collective sins of all priests.

Then, as the people followed his movements in apprehensive silence, fearful that he and they would be met with divine wrath, he would make his annual entrance into the Holy of Holies, there—in the name of all Israel and on their behalf—to offer atonement in the presence of God. Three times the high priest would go into the empty room, wherein, it was believed, God's presence would be made manifest, and at each reemergence, the people would breathe a collective sigh of relief. The first time, he would make an offering of incense, filling the room with aromatic smoke. The second time, he would sprinkle the chamber with some of the blood

of the young bull he had sacrificed earlier. Before his third and final entry he would sacrifice the goat that had been chosen for the purpose, and then he would sprinkle the chamber with some of the goat's blood.

Returning to the altar, the high priest would then lay his hands on the scapegoat and make confession for all the people, transferring their sins onto the animal. At the end of each confession, he would speak the Lord's name aloud—the only time the hallowed word could properly be spoken. Then the people formed a pathway through which another priest led the scapegoat toward the desert. It was taken to a deep ravine some 12 miles from Jerusalem, and there pushed over a steep cliff. The news of the animal's death was relayed by signals back to the high priest, and after he had performed a few final ceremonies, the day was concluded with great rejoicing. Atonement had been made for the year; it was time to go back home and try with renewed faith and determination to live truly by the laws of God.

Priests and Levites

The rituals performed by the priesthood were its reason for being, but the actual day-to-day work of the Temple required veritable armies of administrators, security forces, priests, and Levites assigned to a variety of essential functions. The Temple hierarchy was an extraordinary and complex engine, indeed. At a feast such as Passover in Jesus' day, some 17,000 priests and Levites would probably have been in working attendance at the Temple. Besides the high priest and some 200 chief priests, there would have been about 7,200 ordinary priests and 9,600 Levites. The vast majority of these would have come to Jerusalem for the occasion, as did the pilgrims themselves, from various parts of the land.

Jesus had certainly seen priests in Galilee and had probably known some. But until he came to Jerusalem he had probably not seen them in their ritual attire—a close-fitting tunic of white linen and a simple linen cap. Here at the Temple they carried an unmistakable aura of authority. They could be seen at the high altar slaughtering the sacrificial animals, burning incense, and giving blessings to the assembled people. At key points of the ritual, they signaled for singing to begin by sounding the Temple's sacred silver trumpets.

Food, including a share of sacrificed meats and grains and the loaves of shewbread that were placed each Sabbath on a table in the sanctuary, was available to the officiating priests, but most of it had to be eaten in the Temple court. Animal skins, which were divided among the priests, could be taken home and were often sold to leather tradesmen.

Only during the great pilgrim festivals did all the priests gather in Jerusalem. The ordinary priesthood was divided into 24 groups known as courses, or clans, each of which served at the Temple for a week at a time; the changeover came on the Sabbath, before the afternoon sacrifices. Each course may have been centered in a given region of the country, where its members lived. The courses were further divided into families, or houses, each of which served one day of the designated week.

The Levites, too, were divided into 24 courses, but they may not have been subdivided into families in the same way. It is likely that all members of each course of Levites served for an entire week, their family divisions specifying which duties they performed. Musician Levites played harps, lyres, cymbals, and other instruments during services in accompaniment of singing Levites; but only priests could blow the silver trumpets or the shofar. While priests guarded the inner precincts of the Temple at night, Levites were posted at the outer gates. Some 200 doorkeeper Levites were required daily to open and close the Temple doors. Although Levites were responsible for keeping the Temple Mount clean, the priests themselves saw to the cleaning of the sanctuary and the Court of the Priests.

Administration of the Temple complex was tightly controlled by a permanent staff of Temple officers, who supervised all operations, including the training and ongoing evaluation of the priests who held services. We do not have a complete accounting of these executives and their assigned functions, but some examples have survived, including a list that tells us that, sometime before the final destruction of Herod's Temple in A.D. 70, "Johanan b. Phineas was over the seals, Ahijah was over the drink offerings, Mattithiah b. Samuel was over the lots, Petahiah was over the bird-offerings. . . . Ben Ahijah was over bowel sickness, Nehunyah was the trench digger, Gabini was the herald, Ben Geber was over the shutting of the gates, Ben Bebai was over the knout, Ben Arza was over the cymbal, Hygros b. Levi was over the singing, the House of Garmu was over the preparation of the shewbread, the House of Abtinas was over the preparation of the incense, Eleazar was over the hangings, and Phineas was over the vestments." Clearly, the proper functioning of this holy place required discipline, specialization, and attention to detail.

The high priest

Of all these Temple servants, it was the high priest who carried the most authority. By definition he was a leader of the people and by law he was the head of the Sanhedrin, the council of authorities empowered to make judgments in Jewish religious and legal disputes. He was not required to officiate at daily Temple services, but he had the exclusive right and duty to perform certain services, such as that which took place on the Day of Atonement. He was generally preferred for such others as Passover, Succoth, and the burning of the red heifer.

This last sacrifice took place on the Mount of Olives, near a mikveh built especially to purify the high priest for the ceremony. The ashes from the ritual were collected and kept in a repository. As

Spiritual Cleansing

The purpose of immersion in a *mikveh*, or watertight ritual bath, was to cleanse the spirit, not the body. A *mikveh* could not be portable—many were cut from living rock—and had to contain some free-running water, usually spring water or rainwater. The Temple had several *mikvehs* for priests, including at least two reserved for the high priest. Public *mikvehs* also existed near the Temple Mount; worshipers had to be cleansed before entering holy ground.

A mikveh found at Masada (below) was built according to strict ritual requirements. At the right is the way it would have looked in use. An open conduit (1) leads to a pool for collecting rainwater (2). The water reaches the bath (3) through an underground pipe. The shallow pool (4) is for washing the hands and feet before entering the mikveh.

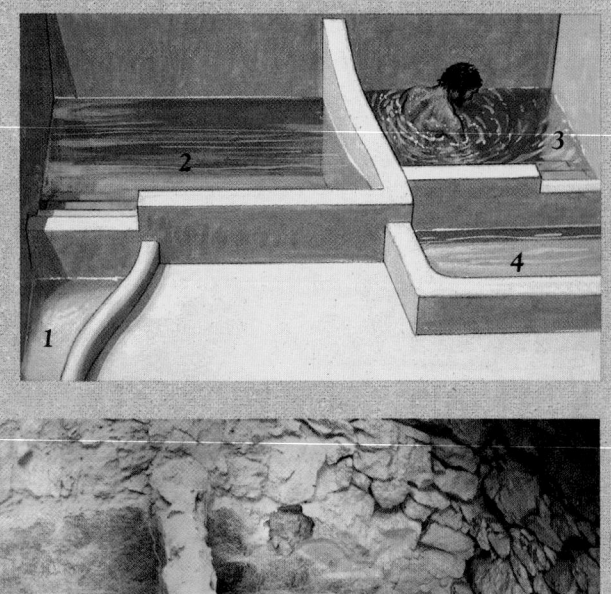

needed, ashes would be added to spring water to make lustral water, which was used in the ritual purification of someone, usually a priest, who had been contaminated by contact with a dead body. Priests took great care to avoid such contamination, and so lustral water was rarely needed; moreover, only a small amount of ash was required to make it. Hence, the burning of the red heifer occurred infrequently—some authorities say only seven times in the history of the Jews.

The high priesthood was no longer a lifetime post, nor was its holder a member of the Zadokite clan.

The last legitimate Zadokite, Onias III, had been replaced by his own brother in 175 B.C. at the order of the Seleucid ruler Antiochus IV. Three years later, the brother had been replaced by a non-Zadokite, Menelaus. About 20 years of turmoil and confusion had followed, in the course of which the next rightful Zadokite heir, Onias IV, had fled to Egypt and there, under the sponsorship of the Egyptian ruler, had built his own temple. Finally, during Succoth in 152 B.C., the Hasmonean ruler Jonathan—of a priestly but non-Zadokite family—had assumed the high priesthood himself, thus combin-

Archeologists face a formidable task in uncovering Jerusalem's past. Not only have areas of the city been destroyed and rebuilt several times—the builders often using materials left from earlier ruins—but many historical sites are occupied by homes or by shrines sacred to Jews, Christians, or Muslims. The Citadel, at right, once connected to Herod's palace, was saved by the Romans for their own use when they razed the city in A.D. 70. Since then, it has been frequently rebuilt or restored as a defensive fortification. The present structures are largely the work of Crusaders, Turks, and Mamelukes, but beneath the surface have been found the remains of the Hasmonean city wall (foreground), including additions that were probably made by order of King Herod.

The above mosaic, the earliest known map of Jerusalem, dates from about A.D. 560. It came from a ruined Byzantine church at Madaba, east of the Dead Sea. Inside the northern gate (left) is the pillar from which distances were measured. Roman-style columns, shown at right, supported a portico along the colonnaded central thoroughfare.

ing the secular and religious authorities of the land in his own person. The Hasmoneans had continued to hold both offices until the dynasty was destroyed by Herod the Great, who instituted the practice of appointing high priests as he saw fit. After his death the Roman authorities continued to appoint new high priests at frequent intervals, choosing from among a few aristocratic families.

Jesus, attending his first Passover, would probably have seen Annas officiating in this role. A wealthy and powerful politician, he was to be succeeded in office by five of his sons and then by his son-in-law, Caiaphas, who would hold the high priesthood at the time of Jesus' crucifixion. Although the office had lost its political authority and much of its singularity as a result of Herod's innovation, the high priesthood was still viewed with the greatest respect by the people. Moreover, the ever-growing number of ex-high priests formed an influential circle that could, because of the respect they retained, wield considerable political power.

Among the teachers

As Jesus returned with his family to the Temple Mount during the week of Passover to witness other sacrificial offerings and perhaps even to make an offering of his own, his lively and intelligent mind was drawn to the debates and discussions about interpretations of sacred texts that went on in the inner courts. He would have heard angry arguments as well as patient lectures, the excitement of intellectual discovery as well as the calm pronouncements of well-established views. There must have been many debates about the precise meaning of prophecy, about the time and place and manner of the Messiah's expected coming. Surely the thirst for delivery from Roman domination was on the minds of many of the students who gathered about the great teachers, listening, asking questions, learning.

Few of these exchanges would have involved the Temple priests, concerned as they were with the performance of the rites. But many would have been dominated by the learned men known as scribes.

Their designation, which in Hebrew comes from the words "to cipher" or "to write," indicated that they could read and write, and it was for this ability that they had been singled out centuries before. Their position had grown into that of law interpreters, roughly analogous to today's attorneys. They knew, interpreted, and taught Jewish religious law, which included the traditional civil and criminal law as well. They were, in short, the learned men of the day. To Jesus, they would have presented the opportunity to come in contact with Jewish knowledge and theory at its height.

There also would have been representatives from the many synagogues that existed in Jerusalem. And among the pilgrims from around the world would have been scribes, scholars, teachers, and intellectual leaders of far-flung communities. The festivals gave them the chance to exchange views. Here, amid the the buzz and roar of human activity, they met with one another and with their counterparts in Jerusalem to debate, to teach, and to learn. From the exchanges there continually emerged, if not agreement, an ongoing awareness of the vital multiplicity of the Jewish faith.

Hence, the gathering of world Jewry that took place at the pilgrim festivals was more than an observance of ancient sacrificial rituals, more even than a reaffirmation of faith. It was an important element in maintaining the powerful continuity at the heart of Judaism. It served the common people in a similar way. Here Jews saw how other Jews were faring throughout the known world—still pious and devoted to their spiritual home, though speaking different languages and displaying the clothing and behavior of many lands. The pilgrims took home with them the tales of what they had seen; and the fact that a Jew might be a middle-class Babylonian, a prosperous Greek trader, or a landowning Egyptian did much to widen the horizons of those who lived in the cities, towns, and villages of Palestine.

"My Father's business"

The departure of the pilgrims from Jerusalem at the end of the festival was at least as hectic as the arrival. Once again, the roads were crowded with caravans and groups of travelers, all leaving at once. We can gain an idea of the turmoil that must have been involved when we read, in the second chapter of the Gospel According to Luke, that Joseph and Mary left their son behind and traveled an entire day before they discovered that he was not among their party. They returned to Jerusalem and searched for three days before they found Jesus "in the Temple, sitting among the teachers, listening to them and asking them questions."

This may well have occurred in the Court of the Women, where much of the intellectual exchange went on, for Mary was there when Jesus was found. To whom was he listening for all those days? What questions did he ask? What answers did he receive? What did he say in response? We do not know. Luke tells us only that "all who heard him were amazed at his understanding and his answers." In other words, not only did the teachers answer his questions, as they did with many young men in the Temple precincts, but they asked him questions in return. Simple rote answers, no matter how complete and accurate, would not have been astonishing from a boy on the verge of manhood. Surely, if scribes and teachers from around the world were interested in the views of this rural lad, it was because they had met in him an intellectual acumen and depth of understanding that approached their own.

Mary's reaction to the situation was quite understandable. One can imagine any mother at any period of history, including our own, ignoring the exalted company in which she had found her lost child and scolding him: "Son, why have you treated us so? Behold, your father and I have been looking for you anxiously."

Jesus did not apologize or make excuses. Instead

he replied, perhaps being understood no more profoundly by his parents than by the teachers who were listening, "How is it that you sought me? Did you not know that I must be in my father's house?" (According to the King James translation of the Bible, Jesus' words were, "I must be about my Father's business." The difference between this and the Revised Standard Version's "in my father's house" is not as great as it appears: each is a valid interpretation of a Greek phrase that means, literally, "in the things of my father.")

With mixed emotions and some confusion, then, Jesus and his family were reunited in the Temple. It was an unusual conclusion to the Feast of Passover.

The boy who had been brought from Nazareth to see the wonders of Jerusalem and to learn more about the wellsprings of his faith had ended the week discussing religious concepts at a level that intrigued and amazed learned men.

Mary, we are told by Luke, did not share the story with anyone, but "kept all these things in her heart." Presumably, the incident was not noised abroad, and Jesus returned to the normal life of a village boy in ancient Palestine. He certainly, again according to Luke, was "obedient" to his parents. The time had not yet come for him to take up the mission that would lead him from his earthly parents in pursuit of the will of his heavenly father.

Today, all three of the world's great monotheistic religions regard Jerusalem as the Holy City. Jews worship at the Wailing Wall. Muslims revere the Dome of the Rock, on the Temple Mount, as the spot from which Muhammed is said to have ascended to heaven. Christians retrace Jesus' steps and visit the Church of the Holy Sepulchre, built by the Empress Helena and her son, Constantine the Great, over the supposed site of Jesus' tomb.

Chapter Six

The Life of the Mind

For the Jews, the Torah was the source of all learning—religion, history, and ethics. The synagogue was not only a place of worship but a place of instruction for all ages. Living as they did in a Hellenistic world, the Jews also absorbed some of the Greco-Roman culture that surrounded them.

Every Jewish child in Palestine became aware early in life of belonging to a people for whom religion was a passion. Even toddlers must have felt the excitement in the air on a Sabbath morning, especially in a small place like Nazareth, when all the Jews of the town gathered in early daylight in the building that served as their synagogue. Men, women, and children arranged themselves on benches lined up along three of the stone walls or sat or stood on the stone floor. In front of the fourth wall—the one that faced toward Jerusalem—pinpoints of flame danced in a seven-branched lamp stand set near a reading desk on a raised platform. Upon this dais stood the prayer leader for that morning. He was not a priest, like those in the Temple, nor was he necessarily an elder of the congregation or the *hazzan*—the official who was in charge of the service and whose powerful blasts on the ram's horn announced the arrival of the Sabbath. The prayer leader could be any adult male member of the congregation, someone who was known to the villagers during the week as a carpenter, potter, or farmer, but who was transformed and honored on this special day appointed by God for rest.

A group of young men, their heads covered with prayer shawls, congregate in a room in the synagogue used for study groups. The aged teacher, seated behind a desk brightly illuminated by oil lamps, has brought out a parchment scroll containing one of the books of the Torah for their discussion. Such exchanges were common in the life of first-century Jewish students.

In Jesus' time the Torah was copied on lengths of parchment stitched together and wrapped around staves called "trees of life." When not being read, a scroll was covered with a linen mantle. Over the centuries, mantles became more ornate. In the one shown above, the staves are adorned with a decorative crown and a shield indicating the days on which the scroll is to be read.

This fragment of a Torah scroll was found in a synagogue at Peki'in in Galilee. The centuries-old scroll was in the possession of a Jewish family whose ancestors had eluded the Romans during the siege of Jerusalem in the first century A.D.

Whoever the prayer leader was, his voice rang out in the opening blessings and praises to God, the eternal and mighty, who had established his covenant with Abraham, Isaac, and Jacob and who would bring a redeemer and grant peace to his people, Israel. "Amen!" shouted the worshipers. Then, together, young and old, men and women, united as one, all chanted the bedrock statement of their faith: "Hear, O Israel: The Lord our God is one Lord."

Then the *hazzan* brought forward the Ark, a wooden chest he had placed in the back of the synagogue at the start of the service. Opening the chest, he withdrew a Torah scroll, swathed in fine linen. Removing the linen and unrolling the staves, he held the scroll up so that all could see the columns of bold, black letters marching across the tan parchment. This was one of the first five books of the Bible, containing the record of the law given to Moses by God. It was the duty and the joy of congregations of Jews everywhere to read the Torah aloud every Sabbath, festival, and new moon, and on Mondays and Thursdays (market days) as well.

The Sabbath lesson

The Torah scroll was laid on the reading desk. The lesson was divided into three or more portions, depending on the occasion. The prayer leader uttered a blessing of gratitude for the gift of the Torah, then called on a different man of the congregation to come forward and read aloud each portion in turn, and probably proclaimed a blessing after each portion. But in the Palestine of Jesus' childhood the classical Hebrew of the sacred text was already centuries old and no longer commonly in use as a spoken tongue. So after a reader had recited three verses, he paused as a translator spoke the passage in Aramaic, the language of everyday life in Palestine.

When the reading of Scripture was completed, the scroll was reverently replaced in the Ark, while another exultant blessing rose from the gathering. Then a speaker walked to the reader's desk and delivered a sermon, a commentary on the text. He might be an official of the congregation, but he could also be any one of its members who was invited or who volunteered to give an interpretation of the lesson. If he was an able preacher, interweaving quotations from Scripture and illustrating his points by poetic and lively images, the audience leaned forward attentively, their faces knit in concentration or relaxed in appreciative smiles in the warm glow of the oil lamps. The Scripture lesson was, for hardworking fishermen, craftsmen, farmers, and mothers, a chance to take their minds off their daily round of toil.

The concluding portion of the Sabbath morning service would be the haftarah, a reading by one man from one of the prophetic books of the Bible. In Luke 4:16–30 we are shown—up to a point—how this reading might have gone.

Early in his ministry, Jesus went to the synagogue in Nazareth on the Sabbath. "And he stood up to read; and there was given to him the book of the prophet Isaiah." Jesus opened the book and read a passage about the works of a prophet anointed by the Lord. "And he closed the book, and gave it back to the attendant, and sat down; and the eyes of all in the synagogue were fixed on him. And he began to say to them, 'Today this scripture has been fulfilled in your hearing.' And all spoke well of him, and wondered at the gracious words which proceeded out of his mouth; and they said, 'Is not this Joseph's son?' " Then, however, Jesus told the congregation things they did not want to hear, and they turned against him. Normally, the synagogue service would have ended with a final benediction and exchange of Sabbath good wishes.

In the modern custom of the bar mitzvah, the haftarah is often read by a boy who has just reached his 13th birthday and therefore has come of age as a worshiper. There is no evidence that this was the practice in Jesus' time, but as the congregation streamed out into the sunshine after a Sabbath service, all the boys present must have looked forward to the day when they too might stand before their friends and neighbors and read the sacred words of Scripture. Regular community worship, so engrained in the fabric of life, was one of the most powerful educational forces at work on the young from their earliest childhood.

The Torah

Although the Temple stood at the core of Jewish religion, the essence of Jewish life was becoming centered more and more in the synagogues. Ordinary Jews most likely drew more inspiration from what they and their fellows did in the synagogue each week than from the pomp and grandeur of the Temple. And at the very heart of the synagogue ritual was the reading of the Torah.

The Hebrew term *torah*, although commonly translated as "law," actually comes from a root word meaning "instruction" or "guidance." Whereas the word *Torah* can be used to include the sum of all Jewish beliefs, it generally refers specifically to the scrolls containing the Pentateuch, the first five books of the Bible: Genesis, Exodus, Leviticus, Numbers, and Deuteronomy. Together, these tell the story that is at the heart of Jewish belief—how God made a covenant with the Patriarchs, brought their descendants out of Egyptian slavery, gave them

In Exodus 25:31–40, God ordered Moses to make a seven-branched lamp stand, or menorah, to light the sanctuary. Menorahs, like the one represented in the third-century stone carving above, have been used by the Jews ever since. The shape of the menorah is found in nature in Salvia judaica, *a species of sage with seven distinct branches. Another species, Salvia palaestina, shown at left, has a stem and eight branches, resembling the eight-branched menorah used at Hanukkah.*

the law, including the Ten Commandments, and led them to the promised land.

It was long held by tradition that each of the five books of the Torah was written by Moses himself. Modern biblical criticism suggests a more complex authorship. Scholars generally agree that in the period of the independent Jewish kingdoms of Israel and Judah (922–587 B.C.) there were circulating among the Hebrews various oral and written versions of the events—and even the commandments—described in the present-day Torah. This literature mixed together the traditions, folktales, poetry, ritual instructions, laws, chronicles, prayers, and prophecies that had accumulated over the centuries.

As related in 2 Kings 22, during the reign of King Josiah of Judah (640–609 B.C.), while the Temple in Jerusalem was under repair, a "book of the law" was found and brought to the king. This is believed to have been the Book of Deuteronomy. Scholars are divided over its origin. Some maintain that it was compiled by a party of reformers who were anxious to standardize, purify, and restore the faith after a period of backsliding. Others believe that it had been part of the literature of the kingdom of Israel to the north and was brought to Jerusalem after the Assyrians destroyed Israel in 721 B.C.

At any rate, Josiah did mend his ways, crack down on idolatry, and promise to obey the rediscovered sacred writings. Meanwhile, the reformers and their successors worked to establish a compilation of the ancient tradition of Judaism by collecting the various documents that were being used in Israel. These constituted the additional four books of the Torah, which were joined to the one known to Josiah. The work continued over a turbulent period of several generations during which the kingdom was overthrown by the Babylonians and the Jews were forced into exile but were later allowed to return and rebuild their destroyed Temple.

By the middle of the fifth century B.C. the five books had become the accepted Torah. The Torah, Jews believed, was more than a history of the world and a rule book for their lives. Each word in it came from God. It was the foundation of all morality. Together with the sacred books of wisdom, chronicle, and prophecy, which were added subsequently, it made up the Jewish Scripture (the Old Testament of the Christians) and contained all the knowledge necessary for life on earth for all time. Therefore, to study it and to obey its laws was to grow spiritually. Studying the Torah was also a form of worship, and a lifelong obligation. Hillel, a great Jewish teacher of

It was customary for male Jews to strap phylacteries, or tefillin, to their foreheads and left arms for morning prayer, except on the Sabbath and festivals. The small black leather boxes held folded slips of parchment containing four passages from the Bible, including the Ten Commandments. At right, a Jewish boy of today is shown wearing phylacteries in Jerusalem while celebrating his bar mitzvah, or passage into religious maturity. The phylactery shown below was found at the Qumran Caves in the Dead Sea area and is the only known surviving head phylactery from the time of Jesus.

the time of Jesus, declared: "An ignorant man cannot be pious."

Early education

Training in the Torah began at the earliest possible age, even before formal schooling, for it was the obligation of the father to teach his children by both word and example. A child could observe the father binding on his arm and on his forehead the phylacteries, or *tefillin,* small boxes containing verses of the Torah. To the natural question of "What are you doing?" the parent could answer, in the words of Deuteronomy 6:5–8, that it was everyone's duty to "love the Lord your God with all your heart, and with all your soul, and with all your might," and that he himself was further commanded: "And these words . . . shall be upon your heart; and you shall teach them diligently to your children. . . . And you shall bind them as a sign upon your hand, and they shall be as frontlets between your eyes." Moreover, each year at Passover, the father was required, according to instructions in Exodus 13:6–8, to tell his son that they were eating unleavened bread and feasting " 'because of what the Lord did for me when I came out of Egypt.' " In the same fashion most customs—such as building outdoor booths for the Feast of Tabernacles—could be traced to their roots in God's covenant. Each act of life, however small, had holy meaning. Home, school, and synagogue supported each other in this lesson.

Starting to school

Formal schooling began—for boys—usually at the age of five, with enrollment in an elementary *bet hasefer,* or "house of the book." There a boy would spend at least half a day, six days a week, for the next five years. "A child ought to be fattened with the Torah," said one sage, "as an ox is fattened in the stall." Mothers or fathers brought the youngest children at daybreak and came to guide them back home about the "sixth hour," or midday. (When a boy was not at school he was generally learning a trade, be it farming or one of the crafts.) In a small town, the teacher was apt to be the *hazzan* of the synagogue, which also served as the schoolroom. In larger villages, where there might be as many as 25 students, an extra teacher might be appointed.

The children literally sat at the feet of the teacher, who began by tracing out the 22 letters of the Hebrew alphabet for them. After that, the children were introduced to individual words and then whole phrases from the Torah, their only "reading" material. But because Hebrew at that time was written without vowels, they could learn the sounds of the words only by listening to the teacher and repeating aloud after him. Memorization became an important skill, and those boys who could commit many passages to memory could become outstanding scholars. This was all the more true because it was not considered proper, except for teaching and liturgical purposes, to copy the words of the Torah. The whole style of teaching was geared to a culture in which the spoken word was passed down through generations. So the schoolroom and the narrow streets around it resounded each day with the rhythmic chanting of little boys committing their lessons to memory.

In later centuries, this method of learning came to be seen as essential for the preservation of Jewish life. According to one story, some of Israel's enemies asked a wise man how the Jews might best be destroyed. "Go round to their synagogues and schools," he said, "and if you find there children with voices uplifted you cannot subjugate them; if not, you can." With some exaggeration but also with confidence the first-century Jewish historian Josephus could boast, "Should anyone of our nation be questioned about the laws, he would repeat them all more readily than his own name. The result then of our thorough grounding in the laws from the first dawn of intelligence is that we have them, as it were, engraven on our souls."

Advanced classes

At 10 a boy like Jesus would go on to the next step of his education, the "advanced" class, or the *bet talmud,* "the house of learning." It might be held under the same teacher in the same place, but the subject was not simply the Torah itself, the "written law," but the more complex "oral law," which was later written down as the Mishnah. This was the body of interpretation of the Torah's commandments as generation after generation of Israel's spiritual leaders had sought to explain and clarify the principles of the Torah and to adapt them to specific problems and changing times. It was hard work. Both morning and evening sessions were probably held and inattentive students may have received corporal punishment.

Education was entirely concentrated on the Torah and its accompanying traditions. Little place was given to the physical training, mathematics, music, art, rhetoric, and philosophy in which the students in the gymnasiums of the Hellenistic cities spent their time.

Once again, memorization, tested and strengthened by chanting aloud, was the starting point, for the oral law and commentaries on it were not put into the written form that we know today as the Talmud until several centuries after Jesus' time.

Seated on his bench, the teacher would raise a question of law. "Are there any kinds of work permitted on the Sabbath?" he might ask. Then he would repeat the verses that applied and follow them with a description of how this sage and that had answered in case after case; each of his comments sought for new definitions of the very words *permit,* and *work,* and *sabbath,* and each rested on the authority of other verses from the sacred text. The students gathered around the teacher would repeat the lesson, together or one by one as he called on them, until the general outline, and ultimately the exact wording, was imprinted firmly on their minds.

Delving into the law

Such discussions were often strictly concerned with technical legal obligations, but the oral law also dealt with the general questions of philosophy and morality that underlie all law. What are our duties to God, family, society, and government? How may we be ethically responsible people in the daily world? What is God's plan for us? How do we prepare our children and ourselves for the world to come?

One method of study was to analyze the text closely, with the precision of judges or lawyers. But some Jewish scholars also used legends, folktales, animal fables, imaginary stories, and other illustrative devices to draw meaning from the Torah. Such commentaries were collectively known as Midrash.

One important type of exposition was the parable, a form that was to be used effectively by Jesus in his teaching. Parables were told in ancient times by diverse peoples. Both Plato and Aristotle discuss them in their writings, and a number of parables are found in the Old Testament, including the one in 2 Samuel 12. When the prophet Nathan learned that David had committed adultery with Bathsheba and then arranged it so that her husband would be killed in battle, freeing her to marry, Nathan told David about two men, one rich and the other poor. The rich man had many flocks, but the poor man had only one little ewe lamb. When the rich man needed a lamb to provide food for a visitor, he was unwilling to part with one of his own, so he killed and cooked the poor man's ewe. When David expressed anger over the rich man in Nathan's account, the prophet told him, "You are the man."

A parable is a story that has at least two interrelated levels of meaning, a literal meaning and a figurative one. In this example, the parable is a simple allegory. On the literal level the two men are rich and poor shepherds and the ewe is simply an animal. On the figurative level, however, the rich man is David, the poor man Uriah, and the ewe is Bathsheba. The purpose of a parable is to make the hearer or reader think about the issues under discussion and change in some way as a result. And so the parable of the ewe made David aware of the gravity of his act

Teacher and students sometimes moved outdoors. Under the trees they learned the alphabet and chanted passages from the Torah. Older students delved into the oral law, thrilling to parables, and engaging in animated question-and-answer sessions.

Music was played for all festivals and festivities, often as an accompaniment to singing or dancing. As a part of their education some Jewish children were taught to play one or more musical instruments, including the cymbals, flute, and lyre.

and his need to change his ways. During his ministry, Jesus was to use many types of parable to great effect, but it was probably in the course of his studies that he first became acquainted with them.

Although much of the instruction at this higher level consisted of passing on information, the students were also taught to reason and argue in response to questions. For example, a teacher might discuss the dietary laws that forbade the eating of "unclean" animals, such as the pig, and the use of earthenware pots that have held the meat of unclean animals. He might then launch into a question-and-answer period like the following.

"Eliezer," asks the *hazzan*, "must a pot contaminated by an unclean animal's touch be destroyed?"

Quickly Eliezer answers, "yes," and quotes Leviticus 11:33 to support his answer, " 'And if any of them falls into any earthen vessel, all that is in it shall be unclean, and you shall break it.' "

"Ah," says the teacher. "But Simon, tell us, is this true in every case?"

Simon thinks, then responds with a quotation from the oral law that distinguishes among pots made of different materials.

"Good," answers the teacher. "Now, Joshua and Elihu, let's go to another subject. We know that work is forbidden on the Sabbath, but is this true in all cases?" Hands wave, more verses and commentary are cited. Sometimes it is necessary to break the law to save a life. Would that principle apply in all cases? The tempo increases as the answer is tracked down, point by point. The excitement mounts as the boys learn to test wits, reason by analogy, and sift and weigh examples and arguments.

The language used by the teacher and student was what later came to be known as Mishnaic Hebrew. Although it was a later style of Hebrew than that of the Scriptures, it was strongly influenced by the vivid images and poetic parallelisms of such biblical passages as: "Day to day pours forth speech, and

night to night declares knowledge" (Psalms 19:2). "Go to the ant, O sluggard; consider her ways, and be wise" (Proverbs 6:6). "Where were you when I laid the foundation of the earth? . . . when the morning stars sang together, and all the sons of God shouted for joy?" (Job 38:4–7).

Truly gifted teachers and scholars are rare in any age, and so many of the days passed in the three years of the *bet talmud* must have been filled with droning repetition, drowsiness in the Palestinian heat, the buzz of insects, the shuffling of feet, the shifting of bodies, an occasional shouted reprimand. Most of the boys probably forgot the memorized verses once they had escaped the discipline of the schoolroom and graduated into manhood. But they never forgot the fundamental lesson that they were God's people, who must never lose sight of the teachings of his lawgivers, leaders, and prophets.

Their studying of the Jewish Scripture not only taught them specific skills in interpreting their laws but also gave them a comprehensive view of history from Creation to their own time and taught them that the events of history were to be evaluated primarily in ethical terms. It gave them heroes to emulate and examples of moral failure to avoid. It taught them to value freedom and to recognize no human authority as absolute but only the authority of one God. It led them through the literary heights of Hebrew poetry in the Psalms and Prophets. Even as they were taught of their special covenant with God, their Scriptures reminded them of their repeated human failures. Their textbook led them through the struggle with the problem of evil in the world and gave them advice for everyday life in its wisdom books. They were taught their obligation to the weak in society—to the poor, the orphaned, the homeless, the stranger. They were taught to look for the will of God in all things and that the future was in God's hands. In short, this Scripture-based curriculum was weak in sciences and creative arts, but strong in law, ethics, and history. It sought to create decent human beings who had a profound sense of moral values.

Education of girls

In a traditional Jewish village, girls were not given regular schooling, but they were not left in ignorance of their duties. A girl's mother taught her what she needed to know to fulfill her role as wife and mother in accordance with Jewish law and tradition.

Among the most important lessons were the rules that marked out the family's devotion to God in all the rhythm and activities of everyday life. For example, the dietary laws made the most ordinary routine of each day into an expression of identity with one's people and obedience to God. As spelled out in the Torah, these regulations prohibited the eating of unclean animals or of clean animals that had not been killed and bled in the ritual manner and the cooking of the meat of any animal in its mother's milk. Over the years this latter law would come to be interpreted to mean that separate pots and utensils had to be used for meat and dairy dishes.

A mother taught her daughters all the intricacies of the dietary laws as they were practiced in her time. The laws were specific. For example, a pot coming into contact with unclean meat must be broken. The girls were taught the practical side of the very laws the boys were studying in their synagogue schools.

Most likely, neither the boys nor the girls inquired into the explanations for the dietary or other purity laws. They simply believed that these laws were given by God. It was only in much later times that rabbis conjectured that the laws came into being to discourage cruelty, pagan ritual (heathens may have boiled kids in their mothers' milk), or ill health (certain animals harbor parasites and spread disease).

A girl also learned how to set the table and to decorate and purify both table and home for the Sabbath and special holidays, such as Passover and Succoth. In learning to make these preparations, she also came to know the customs and history that lay behind them, and one day she would be able to pass this heritage on to her own daughters and to her sons in their very earliest years when they were still being taught at home. It was through practical training that a girl became familiar with the many parts of the Torah that related to daily life within a family. The belief was that she needed no more in the way of schooling.

Training as chief homemaker was not taken lightly. Even an "uneducated" young girl came to master a variety of skills, including spinning and weaving, treating illnesses with herbal remedies, and helping with the delivery of babies. In addition, a girl would probably have learned to sing and dance, and to play on an instrument like the flute, the harp, or an ancient version of the harp called a psaltery, and the timbrel, a kind of small tambourine. Music was permitted and even encouraged, provided that it was connected with religious festivities.

The house of assembly

By the age of 18 or so, Jewish boys and girls of a place like Nazareth had completed their formal training for life. A kind of education would go on for them throughout their days, however, in the synagogue. For the synagogue was more than just a house of worship; it was also a gathering place for Jews, as its name implies—both the Greek word *synagogue* and the Hebrew equivalent, *bet haknesset*, mean "house of assembly." *Continued on page 158*

The flute, or pipe, was the most popular biblical wind instrument. A primitive version of the modern clarinet, it must have been capable of sad wailing tones as well as joyous ones, for it was played at funerals as well as on happy occasions. This bronze statue shows a musician playing a flute (missing).

The Synagogue

The ancient synagogue was not only a house of Jewish worship, it was a focus of community activity—school, religious center, meeting hall, and courtroom. A synagogue did not replace or imitate the high holy functions of the Temple at Jerusalem; there were no priests, and sacrifice was not practiced. Early synagogues probably consisted of a simple room, where 10 or more men of the Jewish community would gather to offer prayers and debate scriptural concepts. Later, communities erected a special building, generally the tallest building in the community. Architectural designs varied over the years, although some of the features were common to all synagogues. Apparently, windows were always considered essential because the Torah should be read in full light. The facade had three doors, approached by way of a porch, or vestibule, as the worshiper was expected to take a moment to compose himself before entering. Inside, benches were placed in rows on three sides, facing the dais where the speaker stood. In some cases, the building was aligned so that the congregation would be facing in the direction of both the Ark, where the scrolls of the Torah were kept, and the Temple in Jerusalem. Certain benches were probably reserved for community elders. Most floors were flagstone, but wealthier communities installed decorative mosaics. The cutaway at right shows a synagogue based on one built in the third century A.D. at Kafr Bar'am in northern Galilee, where such structures tended to have richly detailed facades. The schoolroom annex, left, is modeled on the one found at the third-century A.D. synagogue at Capernaum, also in Galilee. The interior columns of the synagogue supported a gallery, as they do in many synagogues today. The corner columns, which look heart shaped to the modern eye, were actually designed to withstand stress.

The mosaic floor of the sixth-century A.D. synagogue at Beth-shan illustrates some of the ritual objects used in worship: the Ark (at center) that houses the Torah, menorahs, ram's horns, and incense shovels.

The second-century A.D. synagogue at Capernaum is a monument to Jewish workmanship, as can be seen in these fragments from its excavated ruins. The elaborate capital at right is carved with a date palm. The frieze shown below is richly ornamented with rosettes, pomegranates, and a six-pointed star of David.

In Jesus' time scribes made copies of the Torah for the synagogues on scrolls of parchment, writing in ink with a split reed, not with a goose quill as this modern Torah scribe is doing. The quill was not used as a writing tool until the fourth century A.D.

Scribes wrote on parchment made from the treated skins of sheep or goats or any clean animal. One parchment scroll was used for each book of the Torah—Genesis, Exodus, Leviticus, Numbers, and Deuteronomy. The ink, a mixture of lampblack and gum, had to be diluted. The pen was a reed that was split at the end to form a nib, much like that of modern fountain pens. Metal pens in the shape of split reeds were also used. The first-century A.D. Roman pen and ink pot at right were excavated from the Tiber River.

In a village where the population was almost entirely Jewish, the synagogue was public property, and its president and other officials were also the chief civic officers. In larger cities the civil and synagogue authorities were separate, and there might be numerous synagogues. In Jerusalem itself there were probably many synagogues even while the Temple stood. Synagogues existed throughout the ancient world, from Rome to Parthia, in North Africa, and throughout Asia Minor, in great cities and small, or wherever Jews were found.

It is clear that the purpose of the synagogue was to assemble Jews in small groups for lifelong teaching through Scripture readings, sermons, and discussion groups that sometimes met for further study of the law. There had to be at least 10 men present at a synagogue before public prayers could take place.

The synagogue was also a community center where local affairs were discussed, announcements were made, donations for charity and support of the synagogue were collected, and trials were sometimes held before community elders, who served as judges. There is even evidence that the synagogue in small places may have served as a public dining hall and lodging place for travelers. But, above all, the synagogue was a center of education.

Within the walls of the synagogue there was a kind of democracy—at least for the men of the community. There were no special qualifications for president of the body. Any man over the age of 13 could be asked to lead in prayer or could be invited or could request permission to speak. If there were members present who belonged to the clans of priests or Levites, so important in the Temple service, they had no special role, except that priests might recite the benediction formulated in Numbers 6:24–27: "The Lord bless you and keep you: The Lord make his face to shine upon you, and be gracious to you: The Lord lift up his countenance upon you, and give you peace."

Even "God fearers," non-Jews who followed many precepts of the Torah, might come to the synagogue if they wished to learn the ways and beliefs of the Jews. When Jesus began to preach and later when his disciples carried on his message, it was easy for them to find ready audiences in the synagogues.

The role of the scribe

Although all Jews went to the synagogue to learn, there were always some boys who were clearly more gifted than the rest. These special students might go further with formal training, aiming to become scribes, or doctors of the law, two terms that had become loosely interchangeable by the time of Jesus.

Hundreds of years before the birth of Jesus, during the reigns of David and Solomon, the scribes had been public officials, just as they were in other ancient Middle Eastern lands. At that time, scribes were among the few who were thoroughly and professionally skilled in the art of writing, and they were known by the writing tablets and pen cases that hung from the belts of their robes. These early scribes drew up contracts of marriage and divorce, bills of sale, and other legal documents. They recorded royal decrees and decisions. They kept the accounts of taxes collected and money spent, and they drafted the diplomatic letters that messengers carried by foot and horse between rulers of countries. And of course it was the responsibility of the scribes to make copies of holy writings and whatever was connected with the work of the priests in the Temple. Many of the early scribes probably came from the tribe of Levi.

After the return from the Babylonian exile, however, the scribes became more exclusively involved with purely religious matters, and they were entrusted with making copies of the Torah for the scattered Jewish communities. That task alone was considered a sacred responsibility to be delegated only to men who were specially trained. Over the centuries the scribes also transcribed the words of the prophets and the "wisdom literature," including the Proverbs, Ecclesiastes, and the Book of Job.

During the century of Ptolemaic rule in Palestine, when the Torah functioned as the body of civic as well as religious law for Israel, the scribes became not only the copiers but also the guardians and interpreters of the law. They were the ones who created the many commentaries, searching deeper and deeper into the familiar words for new shades of meaning, while the priests continued to be responsible for the details of worship and sacrifice in the Temple. During the Maccabean revolt the scribes took a leading role in the struggle to restore the legal authority of the Torah. By the time of Jesus their political power had been undercut by Herodian and Roman rule, but their religious authority as interpreters of the Torah was firmly established.

On becoming a scribe

The first step on the path of advanced education, or becoming a scribe, was enrollment in an advanced school called the *bet midrash,* the "house of study." This was not necessarily a building or a place but a group of teachers, who in addition to working with students might also give scholarly judgments in a variety of settings. Each group was dominated by a particularly powerful teacher.

The young men who came to the *bet midrash* began by sitting in small groups with one or more teachers, with whom they went much more deeply into the matters they had learned as boys. Although once again the beginning emphasis was on memorization and chanting aloud, there must also have been more writing exercises to prepare future scribes. Certainly the curriculum was more demanding and the questions, commentaries, and responses to the commentaries more intricate and detailed. And, as always, all answers had to be based upon the authority of Scripture and tradition alone.

There was some study of related subjects, too. Students learned enough astronomy to calculate the times of holidays by going out into the velvet-black night with their masters to memorize the different positions of the heavenly bodies in the changing seasons. They studied enough mathematics to help in determining the Jewish religious calendar. They learned enough natural science to interpret the laws pertaining to the various kinds of edible plants and animals that were permitted or forbidden by the Torah. There was also some simple geography, which put the Holy Land at the center of the earth, washed by seven "seas." But no study was encouraged merely for its own sake or to make any inquiry into knowledge not dealt with in the Bible.

There was no fixed time for completing studies in a *bet midrash*. When a master believed that a student could, on his own, make a correct decision on a difficult matter of law, he would then declare that the young man was an ordained scholar, who could himself be called a teacher (rabbi).

Wisdom of the sages

Ordination as a scholar was still not the end of the road for a truly devoted seeker of wisdom. A scholar could go to a great teacher whose entire life was devoted to meditation and teaching and continue to study with him as a disciple. A small group of disciples would live with such a sage, no longer learning in formal classes but in discussions held while sage and disciples carried on the duties and responsibilities of daily life together.

There was an emphasis on doing deeds of service, with the teacher setting the example. Together with their teacher, the young men might take money collected for charity at the synagogue, buy food and clothes, and actually bring them to poor people who were too sick or too ashamed to come forward and ask for help. They might water the animals of a crippled widow, conduct a burial service for a family in need, or ask from house to house for someone to take in an orphaned child. Before and after performing such works, the sage might gather his disciples around him to discuss which commandments they were following and what biblical verses were brought to mind by what they saw.

The disciples joined the sage in prayer and also at meals, where, traditionally, someone asked a question that would lead to a lively discussion. The meals were prepared in turn by different members of the group; they were paid for out of a fund to which each contributed as he was able.

Money came from different sources. Some sages, as well as their disciples, spent part of their time working at a craft. Work was considered dignified. Sometimes an able student was supported by his family, since it was a good deed to support a scholar.

In ancient times, many medicines were extracted from plants. Jesus' contemporaries sometimes eased severe pain with opium made from a species of poppy, right, that is native to the Holy Land. They used oil extracted from the mustard plant, above, in remedies for bodily aches.

160

In some instances the sage and disciples traveled from town to town, staying at the homes of families who were honored to put them up and conducting a study session for the townsfolk. Sessions were held in the synagogue or perhaps outdoors in the market square, where the sage sat on a chair or pillow and addressed his listeners. If the sage was hard of hearing or if he had a weak voice, one of his disciples might stand at his side to repeat questions from the audience or relay back the answers. Eventually, some of the disciples might write down their teacher's words of wisdom. Or when a disciple felt ready to leave his master's side and take pupils himself, he would tell stories of his old master, which might also—long after the master's death—find their way into written form. That is partially how the Gospels came into existence.

Studying medicine and the arts

Able young Jews who did not want to become teachers, farmers, or craftsmen found their choices limited. The Jewish kingdom was part of the Roman Empire, which provided its own soldiers, builders, and administrators. Those Jews whom the Romans allowed to work with them, such as the children of high Jewish officials, were sent to Rome for training.

If a young Jewish man wished to apprentice himself to a doctor, however, there were some Jewish healers with whom he could study. From early times it had been the duty of the priests to recognize the symptoms of the dreadful disease of leprosy and to make sure that its victims, who were thought to be unclean, did not contaminate others. (The diseases referred to as leprosy in the Bible included not only the disorder we recognize as leprosy—or Hansen's disease—today, but any number of acute skin diseases characterized by inflammation.) While studying leprosy, the priests learned to identify other ailments that caused swellings or eruptions and blemishes of the skin and flesh and to discover, by trial and error,

different kinds of baths, ointments, and poultices made from herbs and oils. It is likely that they passed on such knowledge to nonpriestly families.

Jewish healers probably also administered medicines made from powdered roots or potions made by steeping leaves or berries in water. These were supposed to help expel poisons from the body by inducing sweating or by other means. Surgery was also practiced, but studies of anatomy could not advance very far scientifically because Jews were forbidden to dissect dead bodies.

Was there a future for a Jewish boy with a strong artistic talent? That depended on the talent. Although music was encouraged, someone gifted in the

Surgical procedures included cataract removal, tracheotomies, and amputations. Among the Roman medical tools shown here are a speculum, a cup for bleeding, a box for medicines, a hook for excising tissue, a scalpel, a spoon for warming salves, and several probes. The forked instrument is a retractor for removing arrowheads. The evangelist Luke may have used such instruments in his work as a physician.

visual arts would have had a far harder time finding a master under whom he could develop. Jews were bound by strict observance of God's Commandment, as given in Exodus 20:4: "You shall not make for yourself a graven image, or any likeness of anything that is in heaven above, or that is in the earth beneath, or that is in the water under the earth." It was possible to take this prohibition simply to mean that no one should worship or pay tribute to such images, but the prevailing interpretation among the Jews of the first century was that any representation of humans or animals—especially animals that were commonly used as objects of pagan worship—was forbidden. There was, therefore, practically no Jewish representational sculpture, drawing, or painting. Artists decorated such everyday objects as pottery with relatively simple designs, perhaps of leafy scrolls or rosettes. In architecture, periods of extensive building provided considerable scope for the talented architect and craftsman. Although King Herod had tried to win the favor of his devout subjects by lavishly decorating the Temple, he had been careful to make sure that his artists included no figure of man, bird, beast, or fish anywhere within its walls. When once he failed to do so and had an eagle mounted on the Temple gate, a riot ensued, which ended in its removal.

Boys who had a gift for poetry would have been encouraged to exercise it in the composition of religious verse. Perhaps even girls were not forbidden to do so, because Israel had known prophetesses and singers such as Deborah in Judges 5 and Miriam, Moses' and Aaron's sister, who sang triumphantly after the Egyptians were drowned in the Red Sea, as recounted in Exodus 15:20–21. Unfortunately, little such poetry was preserved in written form.

Greek education and the Jews

In the towns and regions of Judea and Galilee where the Jewish population was clearly dominant, an education system centered on synagogue and Torah could often function almost untouched by Hellenistic culture. It effectively preserved the distinct ethnic identity of the Jewish people and produced professional scribes and sages who could interpret the unified body of law and literature that was the center of both the curriculum and the culture. The surrounding Greek-speaking culture certainly had some limited influence on that education, but the barrier of language blocked much of its power, since the education system was based on Aramaic and Hebrew.

A substantial percentage of Jews, however, did not live in areas where Aramaic was the dominant language. In the many Greek cities and towns of Palestine itself, large communities of Jews lived in municipalities dominated by non-Jewish majorities. In the influential port city of Caesarea, for example, a body of some 20,000 Jews lived in almost continuous tension with the larger population of non-Jews. Repeated disputes over the civic rights of the two populations eventually led to the spark that set off the revolt against Rome in A.D. 66. In spite of its location in Judea and its large number of Jews, the municipal institutions and public religious life of Caesarea were clearly marked by a Hellenistic, non-Jewish orientation, symbolized by the grand temple to Augustus that stood at the heart of the city.

Sports were an important aspect of Greek education as a means of developing the body. The Greeks held the beauty of the human body in high esteem, and so their athletes generally stripped off all their clothing and rubbed themselves down with oil while competing in sports such as wrestling, shown in this marble relief from the sixth century B.C.

Athletic competitions were staged in large stadiums and participants endured strenuous diets and worked hard to prepare for a contest. These mosaics from Roman Gaul (France) show a runner and a discus thrower. In 1 Corinthians 9:24–27 Paul refers to the rigorous training athletes undergo and points out that although all the runners in a race compete, only one wins the prize. He exhorts his readers to run to win, since they have more at stake than the runners. "They do it to receive a perishable wreath, but we an imperishable."

Similarly, in such western-oriented cities as Ptolemais, Ascalon, Scythopolis, Hippus, Gadara, and others, Jews were in a minority. This minority position was even more pronounced outside the Palestine area in the numerous Jewish communities of the Diaspora. In cities such as Alexandria in Egypt, Miletus in Asia Minor, or Antioch in Syria, the principal language not only of the general population but also of the Jewish community itself was Greek, and the Jews were of necessity in daily contact with non-Jews.

The closer contact with Hellenistic culture often gave the Jews in these cities a perception of Hellenism different from that of the Aramaic-speaking Jews of Judea and Galilee. If, for example, Jews in Hellenistic municipalities wished to be involved in any way in governing the cities of which they were lifelong residents, they had to become part of the citizen class. That meant that at some point Jewish parents had to try to give their sons a Greek education, since only those who had received an education in the "gymnasium" system of a city could ordinarily become participating citizens with full civic rights. The choice was often painful for families that in some spheres had achieved considerable importance in city life. They could either live in permanent exclusion from the city government or strive to make some accommodation to Greek education and culture without compromising basic principles.

Most Jews chose one or the other of these alternatives. There were a few Jews, however, who chose to leave their ties to Judaism altogether and to become fully merged into Hellenistic culture. In several cases records survive of Jews striving to obtain admission to city gymnasium education in the face of stiff opposition from non-Jews, who demanded that they worship the gods of the city if they were to share in its privileges and governance.

The Hellenistic gymnasium

What was this gymnasium education that they sought? It was many things. In the Greco-Roman world at large it was an instrument of Hellenization, the means by which non-Greeks could be steeped in Greek values and a Greek style of living and thus "become" Greek. It was the training ground of municipal aristocracy; in most cases it was the province of the upper classes of a city. It was an athletic education centered around competition in sporting events and extending that competitive spirit even into literature and the arts.

In spite of all the criticisms that were directed against its superficiality by the intellectuals of the society, gymnasium education was the pride of those who shared in or aspired to Hellenistic culture. Although there was much local variation in the curriculum, gymnasium education remained nearly constant in its basic character throughout the Greco-Roman period. It aimed to shape the ideal Greek man, a gentleman of noble character who could function with credibility in the economic, political, and social life of the municipality.

Perhaps the most striking characteristic of gymnasium education was its emphasis on physical training. A typical gymnasium consisted of a large area of open ground for exercise and competition surrounded by colonnades and rooms of various sizes that could be used for storing equipment or for reading, lectures, or discussions. The very name "gymnasium" derives from *gymnos*, the Greek word for "nude," referring to the fact that the boys were given their physical training in the nude.

When a gymnasium was established in Jerusalem in the years before the Maccabean revolt, the sensibilities of many Jews were scandalized. In contrast, the positive values of the gymnasium could be seen by a Jew like the philosopher Philo, who lived in Alexandria. Philo praised parents who nurtured their children's bodies "by means of the gymnasium and the training there given, through which the body gains muscular vigor and good condition and

The Greek system of education, which stressed the development of both mind and body, was common throughout the Roman Empire. While pursuing the intellectual side of the program, the teacher sat in a chair with his students grouped around him in chairs or on benches or stools. The students had no desks. They held their writing tablets on their laps. In this relief from a third-century A.D. German tomb, a bearded teacher is seen flanked by two seated students holding scrolls, with a third student coming in late and addressing the teacher—possibly offering an excuse for his tardiness.

the power to bear itself and move with an ease marked by gracefulness and elegance."

In a large city several gymnasiums would be built, often to accommodate varying age groups. Boys were usually divided into three groupings: children (age 7 to 14); secondary pupils, or ephebes (15 to 17); and youths (18 to 20). In some cities, such as Teos in Asia Minor, provisions were also made for girls to participate fully in gymnasium education.

The honorary director of the gymnasium was often one of the most important dignitaries of the city, a wealthy citizen who could financially underwrite portions of the gymnasium's expenses in return for the honor of being "gymnasiarch." The actual management and teaching in the schools was in the hands of lower functionaries.

A man holds a papyrus scroll and his wife holds a waxed writing tablet and a stylus in this first-century A.D. *painting from a house in Pompeii.*

Elementary Greek education

Most elementary education was left to private teachers, who were supported by fees paid by the parents of the students. Generally, the state was not directly involved in financing education. Sometimes, however, an official supervisor of elementary education was appointed by the city.

However the system was set up, the education of youngsters began in the same systematic way. Children were first taught the letters of the Greek alphabet, then the combination of letters into syllables, finally the formation of words and sentences. After that the children began to read aloud and memorize short passages from Homer, Euripides, and other classical authors selected from anthologies. Training in syllables and oral reading was important because the written language was not divided into words or provided with punctuation but was written as a continuous stream of letters that the reader had to separate into words. Basic arithmetic was similarly taught: counting, addition, multiplication, and fractions used in measurement.

Secondary Greek education

At the age of 14 or 15 a boy became an ephebe and entered the period of education to which the gymnasium was especially devoted. The regimen concentrated on physical education with continual intramural competition in running, jumping, throwing the discus and javelin, wrestling, and boxing. Such training had originated as military preparation, but during the Hellenistic period it became more simply athletic and sporting.

Some emphasis was also given to the arts, especially music. Training on the lyre and flute was common as well as training in choral singing and the dancing that often went with choral song. Less emphasis was given to graphic arts, such as drawing or painting.

On the literary side, the centerpiece of all gymnasium education was the study of Homer. The *Iliad* and the *Odyssey* not only provided a text for continuous literary analysis, they gave youths their images of valor, competition, companionship, chivalry, and nobility. They implanted the mythic images of the anthropomorphic Greek gods deep in the minds of those who shared in that education.

Alongside Homer certain other classical authors were extensively studied. It was during the Hellenistic period that selections were made for school use from the extensive writings of earlier Greek poets, playwrights, and orators. It is often those Hellenistic collections of "selected works" that survive today. Hellenistic scholars were very conscious that they were transmitting a rich tradition of literary classics, and they devoted substantial effort to identifying what they considered best in that tradition. Time in the gymnasium was given to the poetry of Hesiod, with its retelling of traditional myths; the stark, powerful tragedies of Aeschylus and Sophocles and the rollicking comedies of Aristophanes, which were still sometimes performed in local theaters centuries after they were first written; the orations and letters of Isocrates, which were used as models for speaking and writing; and other works. In each major area of literature, however, one author was held supreme. In epic poetry it was, of course, Homer and especially the *Iliad*. Of the tragic playwrights, Euripides was valued above all, possibly because his characters, although still great heroes, were less lofty and more down to earth than those in the purer tragedies of Aeschylus and Sophocles. For comedies, Menander received more attention than even the great Aristophanes. Menander's "new comedy" was more refined and graceful and less virulent and ribald than the "old comedy" of his predecessor. Among orators Demosthenes was the standard.

The Romans helped foster Greek culture throughout their empire, even in such ancient cities as Beth-shan, called Scythopolis by the Romans. Situated between the Jezreel and Jordan valleys, the city's history extended back more than 1,500 years before Jesus' birth. One of the imprints of its occupation by the Romans is the theater seen at right, which may have seated as many as 8,000 spectators. In typical Greco-Roman style, the audience sat in an incomplete circle that was cut by a scene building with a protruding porch, or stage. The scene building consisted of two stories connected by spiral staircases and contained doors and balconies for the actors' use. The ground area between the stage and the seats was used by the chorus. The bone token at top is believed to be a Roman theater ticket.

Higher Greek education

The study of classical literature combined with artistic and especially athletic training provided what was considered the ideal moral preparation for citizenship in a Hellenistic city. Beyond their years as ephebes, students (who in modern times would be in their college years) could often continue their education for as much as two more years, sometimes in their own gymnasiums, sometimes as upper classmen in the same facility used by the ephebes. Those who continued in this manner usually came from the wealthiest families of a city and spent their time gaining a fuller introduction to the adult life of civic affairs and high society. They also pursued literary and philosophical training but usually without much rigor.

To pursue the study of philosophy, medicine, or some other such subject, a student would go to a prominent university town, such as Athens, Pergamum, or Alexandria. There he might hear lectures by some of the greatest scholars of the ancient world. In the early Hellenistic period, a famous scholar, such as Theophrastus, successor of Aristotle in Athens, could have lectured to crowds of 2,000 students.

Alexandria's library and Museum

In Alexandria the student would have found a large research library and an institution called the Museum—literally the sanctuary of the Muses. The Museum was an institute for advanced research, a community of international scholars working together. It enjoyed extensive royal patronage during the period of Ptolemaic rule beginning in the third century B.C. and supported both literary study and scientific research across a broad spectrum of mathematics, astronomy, geography, physiology, physics, and engineering. During its heyday advances were made in science that were not to be matched again until modern times. Euclid systematized geometry. Aristarchus of Samos proposed that the sun was the center of the universe. Eratosthenes of Cyrene mea-

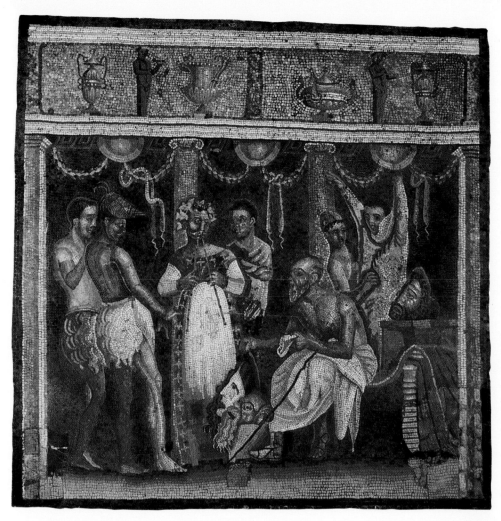

sured the circumference of the earth. Herophilus of Chalcedon made major advances in anatomy by using dissection and vivisection.

Poets, playwrights, and philosophers as well as scientists found support for their work under the umbrella of the Museum. In fact, as striking as the scientific discoveries of that day are to modern perceptions, in its own time Alexandria was probably more influential through its literature and its literary research than through its science.

Actors rehearse a Greek satyr play in this mosaic from the ruins of Pompeii. A satyr play was a comedy performed after a trilogy of tragedies, usually burlesquing the tragedies and employing a chorus of satyrs. Jews would have found these lewd plays especially distasteful.

The Alexandria Library

The library in Alexandria, Egypt, was the most famous in all antiquity and one of the greatest of all time. It was intended to house nearly every work in the Greek language—from the epics of Homer to the most recent writings of fact and fiction—and Greek translations of foreign works, including the Torah. The library was founded early in the third century B.C. by Ptolemy I Soter, ruler of Egypt upon the death of Alexander the Great. To build the collection, Ptolemy II ordered his soldiers to seize books from all the ships that docked in Alexandria, then had them copied for inclusion in the library. Eventually, the library spilled out into a complex of buildings containing study rooms, lecture halls, and offices as well as manuscript rooms. By 250 B.C. the library contained about half a million

A man reading a scroll in a Pompeiian fresco.

volumes. It suffered damage and decline at the beginning of the first century B.C. as a result of wars and civil unrest, but continued into the Christian era until it was finally destroyed in the late fourth century A.D.

Books in the Alexandria library were written on rolls of papyrus, a paperlike substance made from strips of pith taken from the stalks of the papyrus plant. Long works were divided into *tomes* (from the Greek word for "cut"), carefully labeled, and stored in buckets. The collection of manuscripts at Alexandria was the largest in history to that time.

Alexandria suffered severe setbacks during the political turmoil of the last centuries B.C. The worst occurred when Julius Caesar captured the city in 47 B.C. and its famous library was partly burned. But Mark Antony took 200,000 manuscripts from the library at Pergamum and gave them to Cleopatra to help compensate for the loss. This helped revive the library, and the Alexandria Museum and library remained a dominant force in Hellenistic culture and education throughout antiquity.

Hellenistic Jewish literature

It is not hard to imagine the fascination that Hellenistic education and culture had for many intellectually active Jews who grew up surrounded by it. No statistics survive to indicate how many Jews in various regions actually went through a full gymnasium education or some part of it, but clearly many were strongly influenced in their outlook by the cultural atmosphere in which they lived. In few cases, however, did their fascination with Hellenism suggest to Jews the abandonment of their own traditions. Quite the contrary, the extensive fragments of Hellenistic Jewish literature that survive demonstrate a wide range of efforts to support the traditions of Judaism using the cultural tools of Hellenism.

When the Jewish Scripture was translated into Greek beginning in the third century B.C., it was a rare cultural event in the Hellenistic world, since very little other non-Greek literature was translated. The translation of the Scripture, called the Septuagint, was celebrated as practically miraculous in Greek-speaking Jewish communities. A long literary work known as the "Letter of Aristeas" was composed in the second century B.C. to present the excellence of Judaism to the Greek-speaking world by telling the story of the translation. The letter presents the translators, who had come to Alexandria from Jerusalem, as profound philosophers and sages who amaze King Ptolemy II of Egypt by their acumen. Judaism is presented as in most points identical with Greek philosophy except that the Jews recognize that there is only one God.

In the first century of our era it was the Jewish philosopher Philo of Alexandria who was carrying out precisely the enterprise envisioned by the "Letter of Aristeas." He was a member of a very wealthy family with deep roots in Alexandria. He was a thoroughly educated philosopher, well trained in Greek literature and history as well as in the traditions of Judaism. As a philosopher he was imbued with the Platonic teachings of his time; as a Jew he was convinced of the divine truth of the Jewish Scripture (in the Greek translation). He was confident, therefore, that these two streams of truth must agree. From the extensive remains of his prodigious literary output, it is clear that Philo undertook, as one of his major, lifelong tasks, to demonstrate by allegorical interpretation the profound philosophical meaning that lies within the stories and laws of the Jewish Scripture. He wrote defenses of Judaism, philosophical commentaries on the Scripture, and biographies of the Jewish Patriarchs that showed them as ideals of virtue and the philosophic life. In this endeavor Philo stood in succession to other Jewish philosophers from whom much less survives and was followed in the next century by Christian philosophical teachers.

It was not only through philosophy, however, that Jews strove to see the links between their traditions and Hellenism. Some of the more curious products of Hellenistic Judaism derive from the attempts to link the stories of Genesis and Exodus to the legends of the Greek and Egyptian past. The Patriarchs and Moses were often seen as great heroes of the culture who had made major contributions to the education and advancement of the human race. One writer named Artapanus went so far as to identify Moses with Musaeus, the teacher of Orpheus in Greek mythology. He asserts that Moses was the one who invented ships, devices for drawing water and for fighting, and philosophy. He was responsible for the organized divisions of Egypt, for their priestly writings, and even for their local deities. The Greeks had had a long tradition of attributing to the gods such feats of invention; Artapanus appropriates that tradition in order to elevate the traditions of Israel. Again, Artapanus was only one of many who rewrote the story of the Jews, though he was more free-wheeling than most in his revisions.

The impact of Greek epic poetry led a Jewish poet named Philo (not the philosopher) to compose an erudite epic called *Jerusalem*. In this work, the poet attempts to retell biblical history in the revered garb of Homeric verse. Another poem in Greek epic verse called *The Jews* was written by a man named Theodotus and is striking for its emphasis on rigorous observance of the Jewish law and its rejection of all intermarriage with non-Jews.

Greek tragedy also made an impact on the Jews. In the theater of Miletus in Asia Minor an inscription has been found that reserves certain seats for the Jews. But some Jews not only attended Greek plays, they wrote them. Several extensive fragments of a Greek play entitled *The Exodus* have survived. These were written in the third or second century B.C. by a tragedian named Ezekiel, who tells the biblical story with some elaboration. It is not known whether the play was ever staged, but since it has a speaking part for God, it may have been intended more for reading than for performance.

Such writings are only a glimpse of the extensive productions of Jews living within the Greek cities. But these samples and the education they imply were clearly a long way from Jewish life in the villages of Galilee, which were largely insulated from the Hellenistic world. Both, however, were part of the variegated tapestry of Judaism in the first century B.C. Both contributed to the the cultural atmosphere in which Jesus grew up and taught.

Chapter Seven

Trade and Travel

The peace and firm administration that Rome bestowed on its territories in the first century A.D. gave rise to a rigorous flow of trade and travel. The lands on the east shore of the Mediterranean prospered from their role in the caravan trade, receiving goods from the East and forwarding them westward.

One of the best-known travelers of the first century A.D. was the Apostle Paul, who after Jesus' death spread his message throughout Asia Minor and northeastern Greece. When the Roman authorities agreed to send Paul to Rome to face trial sometime around A.D. 60, he was taken to Caesarea, the port that served Jerusalem, and with other prisoners put aboard a "ship of Adramyttium." The vessel had obviously arrived with cargo from its home town on the northwest coast of Asia Minor and was heading back there; it would bring the group at least part of the way toward their destination. En route, at Myra on the southern coast, they came upon a big grain freighter that was sailing directly to Rome; so Paul and the other prisoners were transferred to the larger vessel.

Paul's experience was typical for the times. There was a constant stream of trading vessels plying between the ports that studded the coasts of the Mediterranean. Rome's strong hand had unified the surrounding lands and given them a measure of peace. Its navy had effectively stamped out piracy on

Caesarea Maritima, ancient Palestine's man-made seaport and Herod's engineering masterpiece, was a cosmopolitan gateway for trade between the East and Rome. At left, stevedores handle bales of wool and amphorae, or large clay storage jars used for wine or dried fruit. Along the quay travelers wait while the vessel's master checks cargo being loaded on board the merchantman. Two giant towers in the background mark the harbor's entrance.

The chief exporter of grain was its neighbor, Egypt. Indeed, the Levant had few things to offer for sale: Syria manufactured excellent glassware, Palestine's famed balsam was much in demand, and Lebanon shipped out timber from its fine stands of cedar. But all this did not amount to very much. The Levant's commercial importance lay in its position as a transit point for the exotic products that arrived by caravan from the East, from as far as China.

Desert caravans

Caravans were not haphazard collections of men and beasts. Each was an organized group under a leader, who determined the order of march, the stopping places, and other such matters crucial to survival. Proof of how vital a good leader was to the success of a caravan is evidenced by a monument erected in honor of one by the people he had led. It reads: "For Neses . . . , caravan-commander, [set up by] the merchants who made the journey with him from Forat and Vologesias [to Palmyra], in honor of and gratitude to him." The journey was from Babylonia to Palmyra, a key caravan route.

Camels were the preferred pack animal for crossing tracts of desert. No one caravan went the whole of a route from beginning to end. The trek was made in a series of relays, each caravan going through a given territory and then transferring its goods to another. When passing through remote, uncivilized areas, caravans bedded down for the night as best they could. In more accommodating regions they spent the nights in caravansaries, or inns, generally located on the outskirts of a town, that were designed to take care of their special needs (a reconstruction of a typical inn appears on page 20). They were large complexes in the shape of a square: the open center was an ample courtyard for the unloading, feeding, and stabling of the animals, while the quadrangular structure surrounding it contained a continuous series of small chambers.

Camels were ideally suited to travel on the long arid caravan routes of the ancient Middle East. Carrying 400 pounds and a rider, they easily cover more than 20 miles a day, and they can survive longer than two weeks and lose a quarter of their body weight to dehydration before they must drink. Their nostrils close for protection in a sandstorm, and their broad, padded feet give stable footing in the burning sands. Since at least the 12th century B.C., man has benefited from the camel's milk, meat, and heavy coat of hair.

the sea, and its army and miscellaneous police forces had made at least most of the major land routes safe from brigands. Conditions were good for travel and trade, both local and international. Throughout ancient history, trade was what most interested the businessman. Today investors willing to take risks turn to the stock market; in ancient times they turned to trading ventures. Some, to be sure, chose manufacturing, but mostly it tended to be small-scale, carried on by individual artisans and offering scant promise of quick and large profits. It gained scale when merchants bought up quantities of the artisans' products to sell in out-of-town markets.

Of all the goods traded in ancient times, grain bulked the largest; it was to the shippers of those days what oil is to shippers today. The Levant (another name for the eastern shores of the Mediterranean) had only enough to feed its own people.

In the barren waste east of the Dead Sea the imposing ruins of such a building still stand. The exterior measures about 150 feet square and the inner court about 100 feet square. The chambers are generous in size, averaging some 20 by 13 feet or better, and there are even some two-room suites. Other ancient caravansaries may have been more elaborate, boasting the features to be found in those of later ages: a two-story arrangement with the ground floor given over to rooms for storage and the upper to chambers for sleeping, and a continuous covered arcade along the sides facing the court to supply welcome shade. The court was entered by a single gateway just wide enough for a loaded camel to pass through. At night the entry was easily and effectively closed by heavy doors, thus freeing the weary sleepers inside from worry about thieves or attackers slipping in unnoticed.

Routes from the East

There were three main caravan routes that ended at ports along the coast of the Levant. One was the route from Arabia to Palestine. Along it traveled caravans loaded with Arabia's frankincense and myrrh; fragrant frankincense smoked on altars the length and breadth of the Mediterranean world, and myrrh was a key ingredient in ointments and salves. Various tracks led from southern Arabia, where these products were grown, across northern Arabia to Petra, capital of the powerful Nabatean kingdom, which still ruled this region in the days of Jesus and efficiently ensured the caravans a well-policed passage. At Petra one main track turned west to Gaza, while another continued north to Hebron and Jerusalem to end at Caesarea.

A second caravan route started in Babylonia at the top of the Persian Gulf and went, either all by land or partly by land and partly on the Euphrates River, north to Palmyra; there it turned west to end at Antioch and its port of Seleucia. The kingdom of Palmyra played the same role for this route as the Nabatean kingdom did for the Arabian route. The caravans traversing it brought not only the fine rugs and embroideries of Babylonia but also products that had come by sea from India to the head of the Persian Gulf and there had been taken out of the ships' hold and loaded on pack animals. These cargoes included spices—especially pepper, a boon to people who lived in a warm climate and had no

Continued on page 177

Petra, a major northern Arabian caravan stop on the route from India to the Mediterranean, was hidden at the end of a mile-long, 1,000-foot-deep gorge, the Siq. A weary traveler entering the city through this awesome corridor, left, was greeted by the Corinthian columns of the Khazneh, a tomb cut into the rose-red sandstone of the surrounding cliffs. At the height of its prosperity, during the time of Jesus, this Nabatean capital's strategic location gave it immense power in East-West trade. The Romans added the prosperous Nabatean kingdom to their empire, conquering it in A.D. 106. Although its influence was greatly reduced, Petra remained an important center for 200 years, before gradually declining into obscurity.

The Vigor and Variety of Trade

In Jesus' time the Roman world reached from Britain to the Red Sea, changing what had once been small warring kingdoms into the greatest trade cooperative the world had ever seen. Industry, agriculture, and invention flourished as efficient roads were built and Mediterranean sea lanes were cleared of pirates. Burgeoning trade routes carried not only an enormous variety of material goods but also new ideas—among the most revolutionary, the idea of Christianity. Listed below are trade items of the period.

Grain
Mainly barley and wheat, primarily from Egypt and North Africa. Also from Sicily, Sardinia, Palestine, Gaul, and Spain.
Wheat was used for bread and as a Temple offering. Barley was mainly used for fodder, but the Hebrew poor made bread from barley, and it was also brewed to make a beerlike drink.

Wine
A major Italian export, enjoyed from Britain to India. Fine vintages from Gaul, Spain, Greece, Asia Minor, Syria, and also Palestine.
Wine was drunk at meals, used in religious rituals, and mixed with gall, myrrh, or oil as a medicine. Traditionally, the vine was a symbol of prosperity.

Oil
Pressed from olives in Italy, Spain, Gaul, North Africa, Palestine, Asia Minor, and Greece.
A staple in food preparation, oil was also used in cosmetics, internal medicines, salves for wounds, and as a lamp fuel. The body was anointed with oil after bathing to moisturize the skin. Oil was prominent in religious rituals, especially those of purification. It was a traditional symbol of gladness and comfort.

Fancy foods
Artichokes and pickled fish from Spain; hams and pickled meats from Gaul; carrots from Germany; goat cheese and honey from Sicily; onions, cheese, shellfish, and tuna from Asia Minor; plums and figs from Palestine and Africa; truffles from Jerusalem; dates from Jericho. Flocks of Belgian geese were driven all the way to Rome; their livers were a delicacy.

Balm, perfumes, and spices
Balm is native to Somaliland and Arabia. According to legend, this resinous, desert shrub was brought by the Queen of Sheba to King Solomon as a gift. The export of balm's fragrant sap was nearly a Judean monopoly. Among other perfumes, frankincense and myrrh from southern Arabia and nard from India. Pepper was an important Indian export.
Balm resin was used in holy oil, an ointment for wounds, and an antidote to snake bite and scorpion stings. Mixed with oil, it made a costly perfume. The resins from frankincense and myrrh trees were burned as incense and used in medicinal ointments and perfumes. Pepper flavored and preserved food.

Papyrus
Writing paper made from this water plant of the Nile Delta was an Egyptian monopoly.
To make a sheet of paper, the cores of stems from papyrus plants were cut into thin strips. These were then arranged in two layers, the strips of one layer at right angles to the strips of the other, and beaten or pressed into a single sheet. Generally, 20 sheets formed a roll.

Cloth
Flax from Egypt, Syria, Asia Minor, Greece, Gaul, and Spain; wool from Palestine, Asia Minor, Gaul, and Spain; cotton from India; silk from China. Magnificent rugs were exported from Asia Minor.
Fiber extracted from flax stalks by soaking and beating them was woven into linen, which was used for clothing by the wealthy and for shrouds for the dead. Jesus' body was wrapped in a linen shroud. White Indian cotton was a luxury fabric, as was Chinese silk. Wool was abundant in many areas and commonly used for clothing.

Purple dye
From the Levantine coast, especially around Tyre. Originally a Syrian monopoly, owing to the secret method of manufacture.
Extracted from glandular secretions of two species of Murex sea snails, the dye was costly to produce and ranged in color from reddish to true purple. Cloth dyed this color was extremely expensive and was worn only by the rich.

Bitumen
Petroleum tar primarily from Mesopotamia. It also welled up naturally at the Dead Sea.
Bitumen was used in caulking ships to make them watertight, as a cement, and in Egypt to embalm the dead.

Glass
Major export centers in Egypt, Syria, and Italy.
Glass was originally valuable and scarce when vessels were made by winding strands of molten glass around a metal core. The invention of glass-blowing, probably in Syria toward the end of the first century B.C., made glass much cheaper and increased the types of vessels that were made.

Metals
Gold, silver, copper, tin, iron, and lead. Mining centers were found in Britain, Gaul, Spain, the Danube Valley, Italy, Asia Minor, and Africa.
Gold was used mostly for jewelry and ornaments. Silver was the primary coinage. When Judas betrayed Jesus for 30 pieces of silver he probably took the money in Jewish shekels—the equivalent of 120 days' wages. Copper was mined in huge quantities in Cyprus, from which the English word copper is derived. Mixed with tin to make bronze, it was used in implements, jewelry, and ornaments. It was also minted for coins of small value. Iron, because of its strength, was used for weapons and heavy tools. Lead does not corrode; it was used to encase the bottoms of ships.

Timber
Especially from Asia Minor, Macedonia, and Mauritania.
Wood was used for shipbuilding and other construction, as well as for fuel. Macedonian pine was prized. Citron from Mauritania and boxwood from Asia Minor were valued for fine furniture.

Ivory
From Africa and India.
Expensive, ivory was a sign of wealth. It was used for figurines, plaques, and furniture ornamentation.

As the map below shows, at the heart of the Roman world (the area in orange) was the Mediterranean Sea, a 2,300-mile-long basin uniting the ports of Europe and Africa with caravan and sea routes that stretched from the Middle East all the way to China (inset). Roman control of the Mediterranean ensured peace and gave rise to a new prosperity. Silk came from China, pepper from India, and ivory from Africa. But trade was not limited to such luxuries. One of the most important routes ran between Rome and Alexandria and carried grain to feed the Roman masses.

An aerial view of Caesarea, right, shows traces of the ancient seaport, built by Herod the Great on the sandy Mediterranean shore some 70 miles by road from Jerusalem. The reconstruction below of the busy trading center as it looked in Jesus' day shows its 50-acre basin sheltered by a massive breakwater about 2,500 feet in circumference, designed not only to protect vessels from the rough seas but also to prevent the harbor from silting up with sand carried by the prevailing southern current. Famed for its beauty, the city became the seat of Roman procurators and served as the occupation capital for six centuries.

means of refrigeration—drugs, ivory, and silks that had come to India from China.

The third and longest route was the one along which silks came from China itself. It began at Loyang or Sian. Chinese caravans brought loads of silk garments, cloth, and yarn as far as Kashgar near the modern border between China and the Soviet Union; there the goods were taken over by central Asians and Indians. The Indians carried their share south to their homeland to send it farther west by sea; the central Asians carried theirs on into Persia to turn it over at some point to Syrians, who brought it by way of Palmyra to the coast. Although the whole journey took more than a year and the risks were great, the compensation was the generous profits to be reaped at the end.

Role of the Levant

Some of the goods that the caravans delivered to the Levant, such as frankincense or silk cloth or rugs, could be shipped right out to more distant ports along the Mediterranean. But some arrived as raw material to be finished locally before being exported. The yarn that came from China along with the silk cloth or garments was woven in the shops of Tyre and Sidon and other towns. The myrrh from Arabia was made into perfumes and salves by skilled craftsmen; there were so many ointment mixers in Jerusalem, for example, that a street lined with their shops was named after them.

The merchants of the Levant played a vital role in the Mediterranean trade. It was they who forwarded these valuable goods to the West, especially to the great capital at Rome. Rome was the ultimate market for much of the merchandise, and what Rome did not consume, its merchants sent farther westward, to the ports of Carthage in northern Africa, of Marseilles in France, or of Cadiz in Spain. For economic reasons the forwarding was not in a few massive shipments but in multitudinous small ones.

The world of business

Dealing in trade requires capital, and the ancient world did not have the mechanisms such as mighty banks and worldwide shipping concerns for accumulating large amounts of it. Ancient commerce by and large was in the hands of either individuals or groups of partners, who for the most part borrowed the funds they needed, enough to finance a small cargo or a portion of a large one. There were exceptions, to be sure, a few who were able to operate on a larger scale. The story was told of a Syrian in the silk trade whose interests were so grand that he dispatched his own agents all the way to the Chinese border to look after them. There was a manufacturer and shipper of glass in Sidon who maintained his own branch office in Rome. For the ordinary merchant, however, the Italian side of things was attended to by fellow countrymen who had set up in business there. At Puteoli (just west of Naples), which in the time of Jesus was Italy's foremost port, a resident association of merchants from Tyre and another from what is today Beirut, handled the shipments of their counterparts back home.

Some merchants were also shipowners and thus needed to borrow only enough money to cover the cost of the cargo. Most were not, however, and they had to seek much larger loans to pay for both the cargo and chartering space aboard a freighter. Both obtained their funds from moneylenders, who charged exorbitant interest, as much as a third of the amount loaned. There was good reason for the high cost of doing business. All the risk was on the lender's account—and there was no such thing as insurance to cushion it. The high interest compensated for this lack since it served as inducement for a lender to chance losing his whole investment if a ship failed to come in. To be sure, a borrower had also to put up collateral for his loans: he could pledge the cargo or, if he also happened to be a shipowner, his vessel. But neither was of much consolation to

Weights and Measures

Before standardized coinage, weights were used to check out the claimed value of money. Often, however, the weights themselves were suspect. Sometimes they were dishonestly lightened by chiseling, which may be the source of the modern word *chiseler* to refer to a cheat, and many biblical passages, such as Micah 6:11, condemn unscrupulous merchants who carry "a bag of deceitful weights." Some weight makers inscribed their weights with a figure of the goddess of justice—a pointed reminder to give true value. Customers were usually safe with "king's weights" certified by government authorities.

This heavy, bronze lion-weight from ancient Assyria, left, was probably used for large transactions. The humbler stone weights and weighing pans, left above, were used to measure the small change of daily Judean commerce. The value of each round weight is inscribed in Hebrew on its top. Merchants often carried beam balances like the one pictured on the German relief above.

the lender if the ship went down, cargo and all.

There were also bankers in the ancient world, and their chief service was exchange. They accepted whatever currency clients offered them and paid the equivalent in whatever currency clients desired. It was an absolutely essential service, since coins of every type circulated in the Middle East—imperial Roman coins, coins minted locally by the Roman government, and coins issued by certain Levantine cities, by the Jewish states, and so on. Like today's exchange counters in airports and business districts, the bankers of antiquity set up their tables at harbors, bazaars, and other places of business.

The banker would first test each coin to make sure it was genuine, and then he would weigh it to be certain it was up to standard. He charged a sizable fee for this service, as much as 5 percent. Bankers also occasionally kept money on deposit for clients, but this service was more often provided by the temples, which offered not only deposit but safe deposit; they accepted custody of valuables as well as money. The Temple at Jerusalem did this for Jews, the pagan temples for non-Jews.

Sailing ships

Ships of all sizes and types plied the waters of the Mediterranean. The merchants of the Levant not only carried on long-distance commerce with Rome and lands farther west, they also engaged in short-distance trade up and down the Mediterranean coast, south to Egypt and north to Asia Minor. Although the ships used on the short and long runs differed in

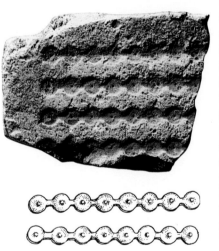

Ancient coins were sometimes produced by pouring molten precious metals into stone molds, above; once hardened, the connected coins were cut apart. Molds were also used to produce blanks of a precise weight; the blanks were then heated and struck with a design punch on an anvil to inscribe the coin's surface.

size, their design and rig were basically the same.

Roman freighters were square-riggers, whose chief drive was furnished by a large, square mainsail set amidships. Far forward in the bow was a much smaller sail, whose function was to aid the steering of the vessel rather than to supply drive. These two sails were the essential features of all rigs and satisfied the needs of the smaller vessels that worked the coastal routes. The larger craft employed in overseas transport added a triangular topsail above the mainsail, while the very largest, such as the grain carriers that plied between Alexandria and Rome, were fitted with a mizzen on the afterdeck. But even these derived most of their drive from the mainsail. The mizzen was always a relatively small piece of canvas.

The sails on all ships, big or small, were fitted with a special arrangement for reefing (shortening sail), which was more efficient and considerably safer for the crew to handle than the system traditional in the square-riggers of later ages. On these later ships the crew had to go aloft—usually in the teeth of the wind, the only time when reefing was required—and balance precariously along the yard (the spar from which a square sail hangs down) while they bunched up a part of the sail and tied it round with a series of short ropes. The ancient system consisted of a series of lines, which, made fast at fixed intervals along the foot of the sail, traveled from there up the front surface to the yard and passed over the yard down to the deck aft. To shorten sail, all the hands had to do was to pull on the lines; and this action bunched

Carved reliefs are often richly informative about ancient shipping. On the relief above, a square-rigged cargo vessel entering Rome's harbor, Portus, has its sails trimmed by ropes attached to the canvas. On the stern, three people, perhaps the captain and his family, celebrate their safe return with a sacrifice.

the sail upward much the way a venetian blind is raised. Since a number of the lines could be grouped together, just a few men were required for the job, each handling a group. And it all could be done from the deck; nobody had to go aloft. (That was required only when a vessel entered harbor, at which time the crew climbed up the mast and crawled along the yard to furl the sail to it.) What is more, any part of the sail could be shortened any desired amount simply by pulling less or more on certain of the lines. In short, the rig the ancients favored had a scanty spread of canvas and was consequently slow, but, in compensation, it was safe and in emergencies permitted quick and easy shortening with minimal danger to those handling the sails.

Hull construction

Not only was the rig safe but so too was the hull. Today most wooden vessels are made by erecting a skeleton of keel and ribs—or frames—and then fastening to it a skin of planks. The Greeks and Romans did it precisely the other way around. They laid a keel, to be sure, but then built up from it a shell of planks, fastening these to one another in a way that more resembles cabinet work than ship's carpentry. They set the planks edge to edge and linked the edges by close-set mortise-and-tenon joints. On a well-built hull the joints could be as close as a finger's distance apart. The number of such joints on even a small craft ran into the thousands. As an extra precaution, each joint was transfixed by a dowel to ensure that it would not come apart. Lastly, the shipwrights inserted a complete set of frames into this tightly knit shell as stiffening. The result was a hull of surpassing strength and durability, one that required a minimum of caulking.

The ship that was carrying Paul and other prisoners to Rome was, unquestionably, put together this way. Its rugged hull withstood two weeks of battering storm and, after running aground at Malta, stayed together long enough to allow everyone on board to escape to safety. Hulls built in this manner were able to stand up to years of hard use. The wreck of a Greek ship that went down toward the end of the fourth century B.C. in the waters north of Cyprus has been found and carefully studied; the indications are that it was a venerable 80 years old at the time it came to grief.

Time-tested designs

In addition to lethal storms, there were other dangers affecting sea travel. In the warm waters of the Mediterranean, the marine borer is a constant menace. To prevent its ravages, Greek and Roman shipwrights covered the underwater surface of the hull on many of their vessels with a skin of lead sheathing. After the second century A.D. the practice fell into disuse and eventually was so totally forgotten that it had to be reinvented some 16 centuries later, but substituting copper for lead.

Ancient ships of all sizes, from little skiffs to huge freighters, were steered with two side rudders, not, as a ship of today is, by a single rudder at the stern. They had two oversized oars, one on each side of the after part of the vessel, with a tiller socketed horizontally into the upper part of the shaft. The helmsman grasped one tiller in each hand and, by pulling them toward him or pushing them away, was able to pivot the shafts, thus angling the blades to the hull and changing the ship's direction. The side rudder lasted until the Middle Ages, when it was replaced by the single stern rudder.

On the average, freighters of Greek and Roman times were not very big. A common size seems to have been some 100 tons in capacity, and there is reason to believe that the smallest size considered suitable for carrying on overseas trade was 70 to 80 tons. But there were plenty larger than that. Excavators off the coast of southern France near Toulon found the completely preserved hull of an ancient

Like fine cabinetwork, the hull of a Roman craft, shown in a cutaway at right, was a tightly joined shell of cedar, pine, or fir. Tenons were precisely fitted into mortises and secured with dowels. Into the shell, framing was then inserted and made fast to it with wooden pegs, or treenails. The outside of the hull was smeared with pitch to preserve the wood. Finally, to protect the vessel from marine borers, wormlike creatures that burrow into submerged wood, ancient shipwrights covered the hull's exterior up to the waterline with a layer of tar-impregnated fabric; over it they nailed a thin sheathing of lead.

freighter of the first century B.C.; with a length of 135 feet and a beam of 30, it could carry more than 400 tons. Then there were the Alexandria-Rome freighters. The city of Rome annually imported from Egypt some 135,000 tons of grain. To haul this huge amount, it employed a fleet of carriers, which, running some 180 feet in length and 45 in beam, could each accommodate about 1,300 tons of grain in their capacious holds.

Once, sometime in the second century A.D., one of these mighty craft was blown off course and ended up in the port of Athens, which, by that time, had become a sleepy backwater no longer participating in international trade. The ship's arrival created a sensation as people rushed down to the waterfront to get a look at the unexpected sight. One of the awed spectators described it as follows: "What a size the ship was! 180 feet in length, the ship's carpenter told me, the beam more than a quarter of that, and 44 feet from the deck to the lowest point in the hold. And the height of the mast, and what a yard it carried, and what a forestay held it up! And the way the stern rose up in a gradual curve ending in a gilded goosehead, matched at the other end by the forward, more flattened, sweep of the prow with its figure of Isis, the goddess the ship was named after, on each side! Everything was incredible: the rest of the decoration, the paintings, the red topsail, even more, the anchors with their capstans and winches, and the cabins aft. The crew was like an army. They told me she carried enough grain to feed Athens for a year. And it all depended for its safety on one little old man who turns those great steering oars with a tiller that's no more than a stick!" After the fall of Rome, great merchantmen like these did not sail the seas again until the end of the 18th and the beginning of the 19th century, when East Indiamen finally achieved such impressive dimensions.

The most striking proof of the size and capacity of the vessels in the Roman merchant marine are the obelisks that now stand in the city of Rome, each having been brought by ship from Egypt. One of the largest, the obelisk in front of St. Peter's Basilica, together with its base weighs close to 400 tons. The vessel that carried it, we are told, in order to counterbalance such a ponderous load on its deck, took aboard some 800 to 900 tons of lentils as ballast.

At the opposite end of the scale from the great sailing merchantmen was the merchant galley. The word *galley* generally conjures up thoughts of a man-of-war, since ancient warships were all galleys, slender vessels powered by a long line of oars pulled by crack crews. On larger vessels, the equivalent of modern cruisers and battleships, these crews could number in the hundreds. But there were also humble, workaday galleys, which were used for the peaceable purpose of hauling cargo and passengers; some were no bigger than rowboats, while others were large enough so that, in emergencies, they could be pressed into service as auxiliary war craft. Their great virtue was that, when there was no wind or when the wind was contrary, they could run out the oars and keep moving. They were chiefly used for short hauls, carrying miscellaneous goods and passengers along the coasts or between islands. Some of the short voyages made by Paul along the coast may well have been in merchant galleys.

Grain, wine, olive oil

Throughout ancient times three commodities in particular made up the bulk of overseas trade. The most important, already mentioned, was grain. The other

Sacks of beans and seeds, below, recall the lively agricultural trade of the ancient Mediterranean. Egypt, for example, was a major exporter of grain. Amphorae, tall clay jars shown at right, held up to seven gallons of wine or oil. To retard seepage, resin was smeared on the inside and the cork was sealed with clay or cement. The pointed ends made it possible to sink the amphorae deep in sand and keep the contents cool.

two were wine and olive oil. In the days when Jesus lived, Italy shipped to various ports of the Mediterranean thousands of gallons of its wine and olive oil. In the next century the fortunes of trade turned, and France began its long career as a leading figure in the export of wine, while Spain became the major supplier of olive oil.

The transport of grain was a simple matter. The grain was poured into sacks, which were lowered into the vessel's hold, or it was poured directly into bins in the hold. The one precaution shippers had to take was to keep the grain dry. On arrival, grain shipped loose was put into sacks and the sacks were loaded on donkeys or mules or in carts for delivery to the dockside warehouses.

Wine and olive oil were much more troublesome since they had to be shipped in containers. The standard container of the ancient world, the equivalent of the barrel of later ages and the steel drum of modern times, was the amphora, a long and heavy jar made of coarse clay. Each region produced its own distinctive shape, which varied in minor ways over the years, but one feature remained constant: all amphorae came to a point at the bottom. On an average, they stood some three feet high and held in the neighborhood of five to seven gallons; when empty they weighed about 50 pounds, when full, double that. Since clay was porous, the jars had to be made leak-proof, which was done by smearing the insides with resin. After the contents were poured in, each was stoppered with a cork and sealed with clay or cement. Often shippers, by way of labeling their jars, would impress their name and insignia on the soft sealing material.

The first challenge in shipping amphorae was stowage. They had to be packed aboard so that they would stay rigidly in place and at the same time not be smashed, no matter how violent the movements of the ship. They were stowed in tiers, standing on their pointed ends with dunnage—generally pieces

of pliant branches—stuffed between them as cushioning. In a big ship the tiers in the hull could rise five high, and sometimes a deck load of amphorae was taken on as well.

The second was the handling of the jars. A stevedore could carry only one at a time, balancing it on his shoulder and back. Since a ship of average size carried some 3,000 jars, and a large vessel as many as 10,000, every ancient harbor of any importance must have had ready a veritable army of stevedores when a shipload of wine arrived. We can picture them in endless, ever-moving lines striding up one gangplank and, bent under the weight of a jar, descending cautiously down another, in a constant shuttle between the vessel and the warehouses that lined the docks.

From the warehouses some of the jars would be transported on beasts of burden or in carts to their ultimate destination. But many would be first decanted into skins, since this reduced by half the

Working on a barge, as indicated by the towrope on the right of the above relief, packers protected a cargo of wine by wrapping the jars in plaited straw, a practice that may be the forerunner of modern straw-encased wine bottles. Roman wine producers did not successfully challenge Greek vintners until the first century B.C., but soon they were exporting more than half a million gallons a year and earning an annual return of 18 percent on their investment. Their entrepreneurial zeal converted the beer-drinking Gauls into wine lovers, sparking the esteemed French viticulture.

weight to be carried. And this procedure, in turn, created yet another problem: what to do with the empties? They could not be shipped back for refilling since it was cheaper to turn out new ones. Some of the empties no doubt were given away, or even sold, for miscellaneous uses. They were very convenient for storage of all sorts of things, from water to scrap metal. One shipwreck has yielded a reused amphora that was filled to the brim with scrap bronze—old nails, tools and kitchen utensils, old bracelets and fragments of bracelets, random chunks, and so on, all intended for melting down and recasting. Discarded amphorae even served as tombstones: the poor, unable to afford anything better, would mark a grave by setting a broken amphora top over it. But all such uses still left a huge number to dispose of. One way, it seems, was simply to crush them and toss the fragments into a rubbish heap. Near the docks at Rome, for example, there stands a hill, about 1,000 yards in circumference and 115 feet high, called appropriately Monte Testaccio, "Mount Potsherd," since it is made up, from top to bottom, of pieces of broken amphorae. It was the result of centuries of smashing unwanted containers and dumping the fragments in one heap.

Travel by land

Merchants, merchandise, and money circulated freely all around the Mediterranean, thanks to the peace and policing provided by the Roman imperial government. Indeed, in the first century A.D. travel there was probably safer and easier than it was to be for many centuries after the fall of Rome. The Acts of the Apostles describes the journey Paul took from Syria through various parts of what is today Turkey in Asia, across to Macedonia, and thence on to Greece as far as Athens and Corinth. There is no indication whatsoever that there was anything unusual about such an undertaking, nor is there mention of any untoward happenings.

Pyramids at Giza

Tourist Attractions

Although trade and government affairs were the primary reasons for travel, other, more personal motives also prompted journeys. There were people traveling for their health, heading for the great healing sanctuaries, such as those of Asclepius, the healing god, at Pergamum in Asia Minor or at Epidaurus in Greece; thousands made the pilgrimage to these spots yearly in order to beseech the god for cures. There were people heading for the great oracles, such as those of Apollo, the fortune-telling god, at Delphi in Greece and at Claros and Didyma in Asia Minor, where supplicants asked the god what the future held in store. And there were the

Hanging Gardens of Babylon

Sanctuary of Asclepius at Epidaurus

Acropolis at Athens

people who flocked to see the great international games, such as the Olympics in honor of Zeus. It drew crowds relatively as great as its modern version does today. Finally, there were the fortunate few with the leisure and money to go about taking in tourist sights, such as the acropolis at Athens and the battlefield at Troy, or the pyramids of Egypt, the Colossus of Rhodes, the lighthouse at Alexandria, and the rest of the Seven Wonders of the Ancient World. And there were, of course, the Jews who traveled to Jerusalem from the various settlements of the Diaspora to take part in the three great pilgrimage festivals dictated by the Scripture.

Lighthouse at Alexandria

Rome's navy controlled the Mediterranean from the second century B.C. to the third century A.D. Fast warships, their speed and maneuverability increased by banks of rowers, cleared the seas of pirates. Though most warships had a single sail, some coastal vessels carried two sails, as shown at right.

Heavy, slow-moving cargo vessels, below, were sturdy enough to sail year-round, though most avoided winter. As many as 100 were in transit at a given time. Average capacity was 100 tons, but huge Egyptian grain ships held 1,300 tons. Some vessels could accommodate 600 passengers.

Paul was on the road to carry out a religious mission, but a variety of reasons brought out throngs of other travelers. Rome's multifarious government personnel was responsible for the greatest number as they moved about in the course of their assignments—couriers carrying official dispatches; proconsuls and procurators and other administrators, along with their staffs, setting out to take office or returning from office; tax collectors; circuit judges; the units of Rome's ubiquitous armed forces shuttling about. Then there were also traders, or their agents, accompanying their goods to where these were to be sold. The tourists, on the road purely to take in the sights, were always but a handful.

Travel by sea

The Mediterranean lay at the center of the Roman Empire, its broad expanse offering the shortest and most comfortable way of getting from any point on its coast to another. Thus, for all journeys, but especially those to distant places, a ship was the preferred mode of travel. When Paul, having completed his missionary tasks, was ready to return home, he boarded a vessel at Corinth, which brought him straight across the water to Ephesus, and from there another carried him down the coast to Caesarea. For the moving of heavy and bulky goods, such as the massive amounts of grain that Egypt exported to Rome, water transport was the only feasible means. Had the grain been moved overland, it would have required the services of a monumental aggregation of donkeys and carts.

Navigation

There were, to be sure, some disadvantages to travel by sea. To begin with, it was not always available. The best time was from the late spring to the early fall, but the rest of the year most vessels went into hibernation, drawn up on beaches or snugged down in inner harbors. Since the mariner's compass had not yet been invented, Roman skippers had to rely on prominent landmarks or the sun to plot their courses by day and on the stars at night; for this navigation they needed clear skies, and one could simply not count on getting enough of them during winter months. Then, too, the winter offered a greater danger of running into bad weather. The storm that ended Paul's voyage to Rome in shipwreck off Malta happened after the close of the sailing season.

A second disadvantage was that sailing vessels, which handled the bulk of ancient water transport, certainly all heavy transport, are at the mercy of the wind. If there is none, they do not move, of course; if there is wind but from the wrong direction—blowing from the direction of the desired destination or from a point on either side of it—they either do not move or move very slowly. One of the most busy sea lanes was that between Alexandria in Egypt and Rome. The voyage from Rome was easy and quick since the winds are prevailingly northwesterly, a matter of only two to three weeks. In the other direction, however, it was a fight against foul winds all the way, and the voyage could take months. The same, of course, was true of the passage between Rome and the Levant.

The best way to go from Rome to the Levant was aboard one of the great grain freighters. Even passengers who wanted to reach Jerusalem went by ship, though doing so involved a considerable detour, landing at Alexandria in Egypt and backtracking northward through Sinai to Palestine. It was the way the emperor Caligula advised the Jewish prince Agrippa to go when the latter was planning to leave Rome for Palestine in A.D. 38 "The ships," Caligula told him, "are crack sailing craft and their skippers the most experienced there are; they drive their vessels like race horses on an unswerving course that goes straight as a die."

Booking passage

People traveled on these grain ships or on one or another of the myriad cargo vessels because they had no alternative. Passenger vessels did not exist in ancient times. When Paul, for example, crossed from Troas in Asia Minor to Neapolis, the port of Philippi, he undoubtedly made the trip in some freighter that worked that route. He must have come upon it as all who sought a passage did in those days, by tramping up and down the waterfront and inquiring of the ships in port until they came upon one that was scheduled to leave either for their exact destination or for some point en route. Cargo vessels, since they carried passengers only as a sideline, offered no services of any sort beyond furnishing drinking water. Voyagers took deck passage and came aboard accompanied by their servants loaded down with bedding and other supplies, including enough food and wine to last until the first stop, or if there were to be no stops, for the whole trip. When night fell, the servants prepared a bed on deck, either in the open or under a tentlike shelter. There was usually a galley on board, and, when the crew was finished with it, the servants took turns preparing their masters' meals.

Once a traveler had arranged for passage, he collected his baggage and had his servants haul it to a waterfront inn or the house of some friend who lived near the harbor. There he stood by with his ears cocked for the cry of a herald making the rounds to announce the departure of his vessel. For departures never took place on a fixed schedule, since they had to await not only the right winds but also the right omens. The first century A.D. was a superstitious age in general, and seamen are a particularly superstitious lot. On many days of the year, the religious calendar forbade business of any sort, including the business of putting a ship out to sea. Then there were days, like our Friday the 13th, which were thought to be ill omened. No Roman skipper would shove off on August 24, October 5, or November 8, and the end of every month in general was considered no time to be found on the water.

Sailors' superstitions

On a day that had no taint about it and during which a favorable wind was blowing, the ship's authorities proceeded to make a presailing sacrifice. If this did not come off well, then the departure had to be delayed until it did. Even if it did come off, there was still a battery of bad omens to worry about: if someone sneezed while going up the gangplank, that was bad; so too was a crow or magpie sitting and croaking in the rigging, a glimpse of wreckage on shore, or the uttering of certain words or expressions. A departure could be held up by dreams, if the ship's officers took them seriously, and most people did. To dream of turbid waters or an anchor was an unmistakable omen forbidding a sea voyage. To

Rough seas were a menace to ancient mariners, as shown in the carving at right, which decorates the sarcophagus of a boy who drowned at the tip of Rome's harbor. In sight of the sea wall, he was washed from his little rowboat by choppy waves. As he reaches for the sprit-rigged ship racing out from shore, it must suddenly swerve to avoid smashing into the square-rigger on the right, which is entering the harbor from the sea. The second rescue ship will arrive too late. Though unsuccessful in saving the boy, the sailors demonstrate remarkable seamanship in the strong winds.

dream of goats presaged big waves and a storm, of black goats terribly big waves. To dream of wild boars meant violent storms in the offing, so too did a dream of bulls—and if they gored somebody, it meant shipwreck. Owls and other night birds meant storm or attack by pirates, gulls and other sea birds meant danger, although danger short of death. Dreaming of flying on one's back or walking on water were good omens—of which there seem to have been few compared with the opposite kind.

And then there were omens to watch out for when under way. Birds settling in the rigging during a voyage was a good omen—and, indeed it was, since it was a sure indication that land was near. During good weather no one aboard was to clip nails or hair; if the weather turned bad, nail clippings and shorn hair could be tossed to the waves as an appeasement offering. No blasphemies were allowed; they were bad even if merely contained in a letter

received on board. There was to be no dancing. And, if anyone died en route, the body was immediately cast into the sea, since death aboard a ship was the worst omen of all.

During a crossing, passengers were free to amuse themselves as best they could. However, if the vessel ran into danger, they joined the crew in meeting the emergency. When a storm hit Paul's ship, he and all the other passengers helped throw overboard useless tackle. When the situation grew worse, everyone pitched in to lighten the ship more by dumping the cargo of grain.

Storms and shipwrecks

One very good reason why passengers at such moments were so ready to help out is that the ship was their sole hope, for there was practically no lifesaving equipment aboard. Some pieces of cork were kept on deck to be tossed to someone who had fallen overboard, but that was all. If a ship had to be abandoned, passengers and crew leaped into the sea and clutched whatever could help keep them afloat—broken spars, pieces of planking, or anything that came to hand. Nor were there lifeboats. Every vessel, to be sure, had a ship's boat, which was towed behind when under way, but it was for ship's work such as setting out anchors, checking the sides of the hull, going ashore from a mooring off a beach, and the like. Of course it could be pressed into service during an emergency, but it would accommodate a mere handful.

In one of the few novels that has survived from Roman times, there is a vivid account of a shipwreck. On the storm-battered vessel, manifestly headed for disaster, passengers and crew fought one another to the death for places on the ship's boat. In the course of the bloody melee the boat went down, leaving everybody in the heaving waters. A similar confrontation could well have taken place on the ship carrying Paul to Rome, save for his authority

Ancient lighthouses were used only to mark harbor entrances, not to warn of dangerously rocky areas. Italy's largest lighthouse was at Portus, Rome's port near Ostia at the mouth of the Tiber River. This stepped, four-story beacon was topped by a blaze probably of resinous wood soaked in flammable liquids. Lighthouses often appear in detailed pavement mosaics, such as the one above, set in front of shipowners' offices at Ostia. The mosaics were advertisements identifying ports to which an owner's vessels sailed.

189

and good sense. As it was being thrust nearer and nearer to the rocky coast of Malta, members of the crew started to lower the ship's boat into the sea—it had been giving trouble under tow shortly after the storm broke out and so had been drawn up on deck—glibly explaining that they were lowering it just in order to set out some additional anchors. Paul explained to the officer escorting him that the only way anyone could survive was by staying with the ship. Orders were issued to abandon the boat.

That Paul had a say in the operation of a ship on which he was merely a passenger illustrates one of the great differences in maritime ways between Roman times and the present. Today the captain of a ship is an autocrat. Though he may hold some consultations, he alone makes all decisions and his word is final. In ancient times, a captain was required to consult and give heed to others aboard,

notably the merchants who were acompanying their goods. Paul's ship ran into trouble because it risked a run along the coast of Crete after the sailing season had ended. The decision to do so had been taken by a majority vote. The captain and owner were for going on, Paul for staying where they were. They took a vote, the ship shoved off, and forthwith ran into the tempestuous wind that eventually drove it to destruction. This curious system of running a ship by committee lasted up to the Middle Ages.

When Paul's vessel was felt to be in serious danger, all aboard cooperated in carrying out a measure that is still standard under such circumstances, heaving part of the cargo overboard to lighten ship, known as jettisoning. Such a situation is described in the Roman novel mentioned earlier. "The waves roared, the wind shrieked, the women moaned, the men cried out, orders were shouted to the sailors—

Romans enjoyed the finest products of their vast dominions. At far left a Roman woman decants precious perfume into an alabastron. Mold-blown glass, left, reduced the price and increased the variety of glass vessels. A purplish dye made from the murex sea snail, above, was a guarded Phoenician monopoly. Exotic beasts, right, were imported from Africa for Roman circuses.

everywhere there was wailing and lamenting. And the captain gave the command to jettison the cargo. There was no distinction made between gold or silver as against cheap things; all of it, indiscriminately, we hurled out of the vessel. Even many of the merchants, seizing their goods with their own hands—goods in which they had all their hopes—hurried to shove them overboard. The ship by now was stripped of whatever was movable—but the storm did not abate."

Jettison is the subject of numerous complicated rulings in Roman law caused by situations when the ship was saved but not all the cargo had been tossed over, just enough to avoid total disaster. Knotty questions arose as to who was to be reimbursed and to what extent. Merchandise that may have been swept overboard by the smashing of the waves or any other act of nature did not count, only what had

been deliberately sacrificed by the people aboard. Those whose goods happened to have been spared were liable to pay a proper proportion of the losses suffered by those whose goods had been sacrificed, and so on. The arrival in port of a storm-battered ship meant work not only for shipwrights and riggers but sea lawyers as well.

At the mercy of the winds

When a voyager boarded a vessel for a destination that lay over open water, he was well aware that the crossing would take time, for ancient sailing craft were slow. With their conservative square rig, under the best possible breeze they could do no more than six knots. And working against the wind, they crawled along at two or even less. And for most of the travel in the eastern basin of the Mediterranean, conditions were such that one was bound to sail against the wind either coming or going.

Greek legend tells how King Agamemnon, when ready to lead the Greek fleet across the Aegean to the shores of Troy, was held up for endless days by contrary winds. The legend has a solid meteorological basis. From the starting point in Greece the course to Troy was northeast, and the prevailing summer winds in the Aegean—the Etesian, or "yearly," winds as the Greeks called them, the Meltem of today—are northerly. South of the Aegean, over the waters from the Levant westward to a line beyond the west coast of Greece, they are prevailingly northwesterly. This meant that for sailing vessels the outbound voyage from the Levant was slow and hard but the return home quick and easy. Ancient records reveal that the trip from Gaza to Constantinople took 20 days but the return only 10, exactly half as long. From Caesarea to Rhodes was 10 days, and from there to Athens another 5 or 6; the return could be done in a third of the time. Thus, from the Levant to Rome might take months, but from Rome to the Levant was a matter of weeks.

Roman Roads

Although Roman roads were fundamental to the energetic commerce of Jesus' times, they were built primarily by and for the Roman army and its engineering corps for military purposes. Rome went to the great expense of paving the most important highways, to make them passable in all weather. Traffic and terrain determined construction techniques. In soft soil a trench was filled with stones and clay to make the roadbed. Heavy traffic demanded massive paving stones, often 18 inches across and 8 inches thick, usually quarried from a local source. The road surface was sloped for proper drainage. Roman road-building methods were unsurpassed until the invention of macadam in the 19th century.

Along Roman highways, milestones, like the one above, gave distances and honored the emperor. The roads were ramrod straight, often 12 feet wide, and in heavily traveled areas were paved with thick slabs of durable igneous rock, right.

If the course lay along a coast, speed was dictated not only by the wind but also by the stops the ship had to make to take on or leave off cargo. Paul's return from Greece to Palestine is a case in point. He went overland to Philippi in Macedonia. From there he crossed by boat in five days to Troas on the northwestern coast of Asia Minor. At Troas he boarded a vessel that inched its way along the coast, spending practically every night in some port. It took him well nigh two weeks to sail to Caesarea.

Network of roads

The Assyrians, Persians, and the other great powers that ruled the Middle East before the coming of the Romans had created a network of good roads, but they were content to leave them unpaved. Rome insisted on all-weather roads, at least along the main routes, and perfected a technique for building them. The homeland of Italy was the first to acquire highways so finely surfaced, but, by the first and second centuries A.D., they were also to be found in well-trafficked areas throughout the empire. East of Antioch one can still walk upon long stretches of the impressive paved road that went from Antioch to the Euphrates River, a region not very far from the farthest limit of Rome's control. When Rome fell, most of the lands it ruled had to wait until the 19th century or so before they once again enjoyed the use of such roads.

The principal purpose of Rome's great road network was to serve the army and the *cursus publicus*, the government post; for the one it permitted the quick and efficient movement of troops, and, for the other, the quick and efficient delivery of dispatches from the capital to every corner of the far-flung empire. Inevitably the local populations took advantage of the roads for their own purposes. The road links between the towns of Asia Minor, for example, enabled Paul without any hardship to reach the various communities he wished to see.

Ordinary travelers, the likes of Paul and his companions, went on foot. People who could afford it used carriages, either their own or hired from the livery stables conveniently located at town gates for just this purpose. The usual passenger vehicle was a light, two-wheeled cart, but for going over rough roads, or for carrying goods, there were heavy, four-wheeled wagons. Both types were drawn by a pair of draft animals, carts by horses or mules, wagons by these beasts and by oxen. Livery stables as a rule furnished plain, open vehicles. Privately owned vehicles reflected the owners' wealth, ranging from the simple versions to fancy models fitted with a roof and curtains to close in the sides and hide the passengers from view. There was even a "dormitory carriage" for journeys through areas where there were no overnight accommodations available. This roomy, four-wheeled vehicle, closed in by an arched canopy of leather or cloth, looked somewhat like the American Conestoga wagon that carried settlers west. Since ancient vehicles lacked springs—this invention lay far in the future—they offered an uncomfortable trip. Wealthy travelers who wanted to avoid hours of jouncing had the alternative of going by litter; these, too, were available for hire. The rider reclined at his ease as six or eight muscular bearers strode stolidly along balancing it on their shoulders. For long journeys the men could be replaced by a pair of mules harnessed to the carrying poles, one ahead and one behind.

Some travelers went on muleback, with their servants trudging behind. Only a few ever used saddle horses. These were not only expensive, but, for long distances, wearisome to ride: stirrups were unknown (they did not come into common use until the 9th century), and saddles were rudimentary, often consisting of little more than a cloth on the horse's back. Even most government couriers, except in emergencies or momentous occasions, eschewed horseback and preferred to go by carriage.

The couriers, enjoying regular change of the teams that pulled their vehicles, could average 5 miles an hour for a total of 50 in a normal day's traveling. Private people went more slowly, averaging about 25 to 30 miles in a day; 40 even 45 was possible for them, but it meant a long, hard, exhausting day's ride. People on foot averaged only slightly less distance, from 15 to 20 miles. The reason for the small difference is that carriages were deliberately driven slowly. It was standard practice for a carriage to be preceded by a *cursor*, or "runner," a man who walked along at the bridle holding the animals to his pace.

Roadside inns

There was little choice in lodgings in ancient times. There were only modest inns, at best workaday, no-nonsense places designed to supply overnight shelter and a simple meal to the rank-and-file traveler and at worst lowly hostelries catering to sailors and carters and slaves. The owners of such establishments were the subject of special legislation in the Roman law, since a guest was completely at their mercy and the law was aware that, as a group, they were hardly noted for scrupulous honesty. Anyone who could, stayed away from public lodgings, even the best kind. Wealthy travelers put up at the homes of friends or people to whom they had been given introductions; government officials or important personages stayed at the homes of mayors or other town magistrates.

In the open country, inns were strategically located a day's travel apart. Along roads that had light traffic but that were used by government couriers, the Roman administration saw to it that inns were available. Near towns a traveler would have a choice, since numbers of inns lined the roads leading to the gates. Roadside inns provided not only rooms for sleeping but a courtyard for handling vehicles and stables for the animals. There were also inns in

Wealthy travelers might cover as much as 45 miles a day in horse-drawn, four-wheeled passenger wagons like those shown above, but the absence of springs made for a bumpy journey. At the center of the scene a toddler braces himself on walking wheels. The coin below, honoring Emperor Augustus's wife, Livia, depicts a carpentum, a two-wheeled cart popular with upper-class ladies.

town, but these catered only to travelers on foot, since they lacked courtyard or stable space.

Whether an inn was outside of town or inside, guests could count on no more than a small room, which usually had to be shared with as many fellow guests as the innkeeper could cram in. The furniture was minimal: bedstead, sleeping mat, oil lamp or candleholder, and chamber pot. Experienced travelers would look the mat over carefully since bedbugs were so common they were known as "the summertime creatures of the inns." The apocryphal Acts of John tells a story of how the apostle dealt with these nuisances during a trip from Laodicea to Ephesus in Asia Minor. He and his companions spent the night at an abandoned inn—abandoned, it turned out, by all but the bedbugs, since John, who had been given the only bed, was heard to cry out during the night, "Oh bugs, behave yourselves, one and all, and leave your abode for this one night." Afterward the Apostle slept in peace, and in the morning the bugs were found all dutifully lined up outside the front door.

More likely than not, the room a traveler was ushered into would bear mementos of previous guests

in the form of graffiti. We know about these through the excavations at Pompeii, where a number of ancient inns have been found in so good a state of preservation that the walls still stand and still bear the messages scratched on them by their occupants. Some travelers were content merely to scrawl their names; others gave vent to emotion. One romantic graffito reads, "Vibius Restitutus slept alone here and yearned for his Urbana"; she may have been his wife—or his mistress. Another records irascible dissatisfaction with the room. "Innkeeper," it reads, "I deliberately wet the bed. Want to know why? There was no chamber pot!"

A roadside inn had an outhouse, and washing up was done at the inn well. An inn in town generally had a single latrine, tucked away in a corner of the building, which served the entire establishment. For washing up, guests repaired to the public baths, which in this age were a regular feature of towns of any size; they found there the range of facilities offered by modern Turkish baths.

Inns in town thus offered a fuller range of services, but they had one disadvantage: they were noisy.

And in some towns, the noise did not diminish at night, since the authorities, to keep the streets from getting hopelessly clogged with traffic, banned nearly all wheeled vehicles from them during daylight hours. Heavy transport had to take place between dusk and dawn—and this meant that a weary guest had to fall asleep amid the creaking of cart wheels, cracking of whips, and swearing of muleteers. And if he had chosen an inn near a public bath, tempted by the convenient proximity, he paid for it in yet another variety of noise, as an eloquent description from one who made that mistake attests: "I live right over a public bath. Just imagine every kind of human sound to make us hate our ears! When the muscular types work out and toss the lead weights, when they strain (or make believe they're straining), I hear the grunting, and whenever they let out the breath they've been holding in, there's the whistling and wheezing at maximum pitch. If it's a lazy type I'm up against, someone satisfied with the cheap massage given here, I have to hear the crack of the hand as it hits the shoulder, one sound when it's the flat of the hand, another when it's the cupped hand. But if a ballplayer arrives on the scene and begins to count shots, then I'm done for. Add the toughs looking for a fight, the thieves caught in the act, and the people who enjoy hearing themselves sing in the bathtub. . . ."

Eating out

One solid advantage of staying in town was a choice of where to eat. A guest could avail himself of the inn dining room—or merely of the inn kitchen by having food sent up to his room. Or he could send his servant out to bring in a meal. A standard feature of most towns was snack shops, which not only served customers at a street-side counter but had food ready to be taken out. Or he could sally forth to a restaurant. These tended to cluster around the town gates, the main square, the theatre, and the public baths. An ordinary restaurant would have a counter facing the street but also a kitchen with a charcoal fire for cooking and a dining room with tables and chairs. A deluxe restaurant would have several dining rooms, a few private rooms for dalliance as well as eating, and latrines.

Even at country inns, travelers were not strictly limited to the inn dining room: they could also eat in their own rooms, dining on provisions that their servants had purchased from markets they had passed en route. We have some idea of what such shopping was like, thanks to the survival of a series of accounts kept by a high Roman official during a trip he made along the coast road through Palestine and Phoenicia. He traveled, as was customary, with a sizable entourage. Each day supplies were purchased for the whole party. These consisted of, for the servants, cheap wine, cheap bread, and local vegetables and fruit; for the master, fine wine, fine bread, the same vegetables and fruit, and, in addition, a variety of meats—usually beef or veal, on occasion lamb or pork or goat's meat. Only once did they have fresh fish, despite the fact that they were making their way right along the sea.

Saga of a bad trip

We have a good idea of the dim view that travelers—at least those of the upper classes—took of the ordinary inn from an account left by Aristides, a well-known public lecturer and writer of the second century A.D. He fell ill during the summer of A.D. 165 and left his bed at Smyrna to go for help, as so many other sufferers did, to the famous healing sanctuary of Asclepius at Pergamum; it lay a little less than 60 miles to the north. Since he was going to be away for some time, he had a good deal of baggage. On the morning of the day set for departure, he had it loaded on carts or wagons, with instructions to his servants to push on as far as Myrina, one of the more important towns on the way, and await him there. But, by the time the baggage was launched, it was already noon, the sun was in full blaze, and Aristides elected to delay until the heat had abated. About half-past three in the afternoon, he finally set off. By seven the party had covered some 14 miles and reached an inn. The inn was not at all inviting, there was no sign of or word about his baggage, and, as dusk descended, they decided to push on. After 10 more miles, they came to a town with an inn, but this was just as bad.

By midnight they arrived at yet another town, but it was so late that everything was tight shut. They had by now covered 35 miles; all the others in the party were dropping with fatigue, but Aristides refused to stop. About four in the morning they clattered wearily into Myrina—and there, sitting in front of one of the inns, were the servants with the baggage. But it was still all packed up; they had arrived so late they found the whole town closed up for the night. Finally Aristides led his party to a friend's house, but, just as they were ready to settle down and start a fire to warm themselves, dawn broke. Aristides could not abide spending good daylight hours in sleep; he grimly drove everybody back to the road, and they finally bedded down for the night—their second on the road—at a town 12 miles beyond Myrina. The following day they did the last 16 miles into Pergamum.

Cards and letters home

Besides lodging and food, another basic traveler's need is some means of communication. This was no simple matter in an age whose postal service was solely for government use. Roman officials, though it was against the rules, often slipped their personal correspondence into the couriers' pouches and even extended this privilege to favored friends. The very rich had their own couriers: their household staff included a number of slaves whose main duty was to serve as letter carriers. Those who were neither officials nor very rich had but one recourse: to find some traveler going in the right direction who would be willing to take and deliver a letter. "Finding somebody going your way from Cyrene," writes a young Greek en route to Rome from Egypt, "I felt I had to let you know I was safe and sound." "I was delighted to receive your letter," writes a Greek living in Egypt, "which was given to me by the sword maker; the one you say you sent with Platon, the dancer's son, I haven't got yet." This sort of notice occurs in letter after letter. Since there were no such things as envelopes, correspondents inscribed their message on one side of a sheet, rolled it or folded it with the writing on the inside, addressed it, tied it about, and, by way of sealing it, fixed a blob of wax or clay to the tie and impressed on this their private seal. The address was minimal, for example, "To Apollinarius from his brother Irenaeus"; there was no need for anything more, since the person making delivery was headed for the proper town and would be told by the sender what street and house to go to.

The travelers' letters that have survived were all addressed to recipients in Egypt because it is the one place where, thanks to the bone-dry climate, even fragile materials can last for centuries without decomposing. The letters were written on a form of paper made from strips of the papyrus reed, which, like modern paper, cannot resist damp. But in parts of Egypt there is no damp at all. People there would toss the letters they received into the rubbish, and there they lay, gradually becoming covered over by a protective blanket of sand, until in the last century archeologists and other diggers began to unearth them. Unquestionably, similar letters were sent to recipients in Syria and Palestine and elsewhere, but the rainfall there caused their destruction.

Many letters were sent for the very same reason travelers write home today, to report safe arrival. "Having arrived on Italian soil," runs one, "I felt it

essential to let you know that I and all with me are fine. We had a slow voyage but not an unpleasant one." Others tell of the difficulties encountered en route. Here, for example, is one addressed to a mother by a daughter, who, between missing connections and running out of funds, never arrived at all: "Dear Mother, First and foremost, I pray to God to find you in good health. I want you to know that on Tybi 13 [January 8] I went to Tyrannis but I found no way I could get to you, since the camel drivers didn't want to go to Oxyrhynchus [the town where her mother lived]. Not only that, I also went up to Antinoe to take a boat, but didn't find any. So now I've thought it best to forward the baggage to Antinoe and wait there until I find a boat and can sail. Please give the bearers of this letter two talents and 300 drachmas in compensation for what I asked and received from them in Tyrannis to pay for transportation. Don't delay them even an hour. . . . If you know you don't have it on hand, borrow it . . . and pay them, since they can't wait around

even an hour. See to it that you don't fail me and hold up these people who have been so nice to me. My regards to [and here follows a series of names]."

And some ancient travelers could not get matters at home out of their minds, could not resist sending back a stream of instructions. Here is part of a letter written by an official who had docked at the port of Sidon on the Levant coast to an associate back in Egypt: "Please take care of yourself and write me if you want anything done that I can do for you. Would you please buy in time for my arrival three jars of the best honey, 600 bushels of barley for the animals . . . and take care of the house . . . so that it has its roof on when I arrive. Try to keep an eye as best you can on the oxen, pigs, geese, and the rest of the stock. . . . And see to it that you somehow get the crops harvested, and, if there are any expenses to meet, don't hesitate to take care of them."

It was an extraordinary time. After the fall of Rome, such a volume of trade and such ease of travel were not to reappear for more than 13 centuries.

Chapter Eight

Religious Conflict

*Rome permitted freedom of religion but not of political action
in the empire. In Palestine, where politics and
religion were inseparable, ancient schisms intensified.
Some Jews took up arms in the name of God; others awaited the
Messiah in desert sanctuaries.*

Winding and twisting southward, the muddy, often rushing waters of the
Jordan River must travel nearly 200 miles to cover the 65-mile stretch,
as the crow flies, from the Sea of Galilee to the Dead Sea. The drop in
elevation from the earth's lowest freshwater lake to the lowest point on the
surface of the earth is about 600 feet, and so, even in its quieter stretches, the
Jordan is rarely sedate. In spring, fed by runoff from winter rains and melting
snow from the north, the river often overflows its serpentine banks to
inundate the broad, ribbonlike floodplain through which it winds, and when
the seasonal flood is over, its channel may have changed in places. Except in
the lower reaches, where the soil is too salty to sustain much vegetation, the
floodplain is green, its dense thickets of tamarisk, willow, poplar, cane, and
oleander entwined with vines and spiked with brambles to form a lush,
junglelike tangle under the blazing sun.

Several fords exist—shallow spots where the river can be waded—but

*From a bluff overlooking the west bank of the Jordan River, a group of Sadducee
priests and Levites observe and discuss the activities of John the Baptist.
The fiery, charismatic preacher, whose doctrine of baptism and repentance for
the forgiveness of sins attracted large crowds, represented one of many divergent
aspects of Judaism. He and his followers were of concern not only to the
religious authorities in Jerusalem but to the Romans as well.*

the crossing is not always easy. In many places the gritty, tumbling waters strive to capsize the wader and carry him along, as they carry logs and branches and silt. Yet there are shallows, where the water swirls and eddies gently and one can wade at least partway into the river without much danger.

John the Baptist

It was probably at such spots that, sometime around A.D. 28, a mysterious new prophet began preaching to huge crowds. Such men were not rare, to be sure. Numbers of them traveled the land in those days, preaching a variety of doctrines. But John the Baptist was different.

It was not entirely his appearance, striking though it must have been—his body lean and hardened by solitary desert life, his single garment of roughly woven camel's hair bound with a leather belt, his hair and beard wild and unkempt. Nor was it an aura of age and wisdom; he was not much more than 30 years old. No, what held the attention of his many listeners, and what drew more listeners by the day, was John's urgent message and the passionate conviction with which he delivered it: "Repent, for the kingdom of heaven is at hand."

The voice resonated with the fervor of the ancient Hebrew prophets of God's judgment—men such as Amos, Elijah, or Isaiah. Here in the wilderness, with all its associations of God's original covenant with Moses and the Hebrew people, many responded to his call for repentance and renewal. The day of God's judgment was coming, he told them, and he described it in terms each listener understood. "Even now the axe is laid to the root of the trees," he cried, and "every tree therefore that does not bear good fruit is cut down and thrown into the fire." The image would have sent knowing shivers along the spines of his audience, most of whom worked as farmers or rural laborers and knew what it was ruthlessly to weed out unproductive plants.

Moved by the power and eloquence of his call, members of the crowd would wade with John out into the Jordan, and he would baptize them in the muddy flow.

Washings of purification were extensively practiced in Judaism for a variety of reasons. Some groups, the Essenes among them, performed a daily round of repeated purifications. But John's washing was different enough that he came to be called "the immerser," "the baptizer." For John, this baptism was not one washing in a series of ongoing purifications, but a unique seal that marked those who repented as belonging to the renewed people of God, prepared for God's intervention in the world. Many of his hearers wondered whether he might not be a deliverer, the Messiah.

And so, we are told in the Gospel According to John, a group of priests and Levites came from Jerusalem to question John the Baptist. In some ways they were coming to see one of their own, for John too bore the hereditary rights of the priesthood— his father, Zechariah, had long served as a priest in the Temple in Jerusalem.

Strictly speaking, nothing that John was doing went against the precepts of the Torah, nor would it even have been illegal for him to claim to be the Messiah. Still, experience and Scripture cautioned against the ever-present danger of false prophecy and of trusting false claims. It was reported that Herod Antipas, ruler of Galilee and Perea east of the Jordan, was increasingly upset by John's popularity, fearing that such influence over the people might lead to an uprising.

Having made their way down to the river, through the tangle of greenery shrouding its banks, the priests and Levites confronted John the Baptist. The Gospel of John reports the following exchange.

"Who are you?" they demanded.

"I am not the Christ," John responded.

"What then? Are you Elijah?"

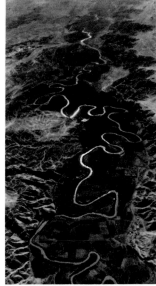

The precise location where John baptized Jesus has never been determined, but one likely spot may be the Hajlah Ford on the lower Jordan as shown on the map below. Another tradition places his activities at Aenon, a ferry crossing in Samaria.

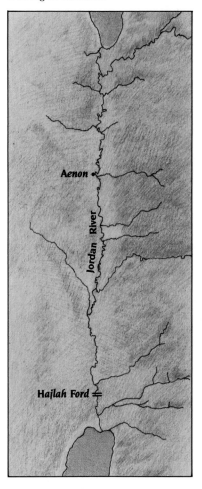

South of Galilee the Jordan meanders in tortuous curves through a low-lying floodplain (above). Today, the upper Jordan is flanked by neat plots of farmland. The lower section is so choked with thornbush and tamarisk—and was once so dangerously alive with lions, wolves, and other beasts—that the prophet Jeremiah called it "the jungle of the Jordan."

At left, the waters of the Jordan River, linked in Scripture to God's deliverance of Israel and to miracles of the prophets Elijah and Elisha, swirl between grassy banks near the Sea of Galilee. Here the river, descending from its headwaters in Mount Hermon, runs cold and swift.

201

Ruler of the Mediterranean world and beyond, the emperor Tiberius, shown above, took power in Rome in A.D. 14, after the death of his stepfather, Caesar Augustus, and held sway for the next 23 years. His domain included Judea, wracked by age-old tensions of religion and politics. In A.D. 26 Tiberius named a new prefect of Judea, his countryman Pontius Pilate. Pilate had little sympathy for his Jewish subjects and soon provoked their hatred. But he did know how to curry favor with the emperor. He erected a building, possibly a temple, honoring Tiberius in Caesarea, the Roman capital of Palestine, and inscribed both the emperor's name and his own on one of its stones (right).

"I am not."

"Are you the prophet?"

"No."

"Who are you? Let us have an answer for those who sent us. What do you say about yourself?"

"I am the voice of one crying in the wilderness, 'Make straight the way of the Lord,' as the prophet Isaiah said."

Such remarkable questions! Why nothing about his hometown, his family, his political and religious affiliations or aspirations? Elijah had lived centuries earlier. Why even ask if he was Elijah? Who was "the prophet"? But for both John and his questioners, no one needed to explain these allusions to the Hebrew Bible. The ancient Scriptures spoke of their own times, and all present were familiar with the expectations aroused by those words. (When John

responded that he was not Christ, certainly his listeners knew he meant one anointed by God: in Hebrew, the Messiah; in Greek, the Christ. The question about Elijah was a shorthand reference to God's promise reported at the end of the prophecies of Malachi 4: "Behold, I will send you Elijah the prophet before the great and terrible day of the Lord comes." As for "the prophet," the questioners were alluding to God's promise to Moses in Deuteronomy 18, "I will raise up for them a prophet like you from among their brethren; and I will put my words in his mouth, and he shall speak to them all that I command him." John's final response was a paraphrase of yet another passage of Scripture, one from the prophecies of Isaiah 40 that says, "A voice cries: 'In the wilderness prepare the way of the Lord, make straight in the desert a highway for our God.' ")

All four Gospel writers tell us something of John the Baptist, though only Matthew and Mark give a physical description. All, however, agree that he was a prophetic figure whose clarion voice struck a resonant chord in the hearts of multitudes. According to Matthew, even Pharisees and Sadducees, the two most powerful factions in Judea, came to be baptized by him.

"You brood of vipers!" he thundered at them. "Who warned you to flee from the wrath to come? Bear fruit that befits repentance, and do not presume to say to yourselves, 'We have Abraham as our father'. . . ." Neither their birthright as Jews, nor their piety, nor their important positions would serve them if they did not open their hearts in true repentance. "I baptize you with water for repentance," he told them, "but he who is coming after me is mightier than I, whose sandals I am not worthy to carry; he will baptize you with the Holy Spirit and with fire. His winnowing fork is in his hand, and he will clear his threshing floor and gather his wheat into the granary, but the chaff he will burn with unquenchable fire."

Messianic hopes

It was no wonder that John the Baptist's passionate message attracted a large following. Men's fears and furies ran high throughout the land in those days. And, as frequently happens when matters of politics and faith are inextricably intertwined, civic unhappiness took the form of a growing religious ferment.

About two decades earlier—after more than 30 years of uneasy peace and comparative prosperity under the rule of Herod the Great—there had followed a decade of civil disruption under his brutal and incompetent son Archelaus. In A.D. 6 Rome deposed Archelaus and made Judea (including Samaria and Idumea) a province of Rome. The Jews had never truly accepted the idea of Roman rule in the first place, but the situation became much worse in A.D. 26 when Pontius Pilate was named prefect of Judea. A reckless and insensitive administrator, he did nothing to win the hearts of the people he governed.

Many Jews recognized themselves and their times when they read or heard the words of the prophets of old, such as Isaiah:

"Therefore justice is far from us,
    and righteousness does not overtake us;
we look for light, and behold, darkness,
    and for brightness, but we walk in gloom.
We grope for the wall like the blind,
    we grope like those who have no eyes;
we stumble at noon as in the twilight,
    among those in full vigor we are like dead men."

Isaiah was describing a vision of the end of an age, the true nadir in the fortunes of the Jewish people. But he went on to proclaim that such a moment should not be a time of despair but of hope, for it heralded the coming of a new age:

"For behold, the Lord will come in fire,
    and his chariots like the stormwind,
to render his anger in fury,
    and his rebuke with flames of fire."

Throughout the land people were gripped by a messianic longing, a hope that, before very long, an unnamed hero would be sent by God to transform their lives. Some expected a great military leader who would free them from Roman servitude. Others looked for a holy priest who would restore the faith of Moses in all its original purity. Still others awaited the intervention of God himself—without any human intermediary—who would sweep away the world's corruption and bring about a new order of universal justice and peace.

Roman religious tolerance

Roman rule, though deeply resented in Palestine, allowed much leeway in private matters. Merchants were free to trade and prosper, landowners to administer their estates, local fishermen and farmers to conduct their affairs as they saw fit—provided they stayed out of trouble and paid their share of taxes. Most important, the Judeans and their neighbors enjoyed freedom of worship and belief.

Such freedom was generally the rule throughout the empire. It was good policy to allow any religion to be practiced in its land of origin. Some religions, including Judaism, were allowed to expand to other parts of the empire. Only when a sect challenged Rome's political power, threatened to disturb public order, or indulged in outright criminality did the authorities intrude. For example, they suppressed the criminal rites of the Druids, who practiced human sacrifice, and they eradicated similar rites of a Phoenician sect who cast children into the fire.

Although the Sadducees and Pharisees were at constant loggerheads with each other, they presented no threat to the Romans. Each strove to promote its influence in civic matters and to establish its religious views as the true standard of devout Judaism, but neither sought to spearhead a revolt. At the same time, other sects proliferated, ranging from those who withdrew into solitary asceticism devoted to spiritual life on one extreme to those who were committed to violent action on behalf of their beliefs on the other.

The abominable census

Periodically, the Romans conducted a census of the male population to determine their status with regard to citizenship, rank, and taxable property. Such a tally also served to drive home the point that everyone in the land belonged to Rome.

The census was a blow to Jewish self-esteem and for many an unbearable denial of their position as a people belonging to God. The Scripture told of the pestilence that befell the land when even King David carried out a census, since such an action implied his ownership of the people. What made the Roman census even worse was that it was ordered by the Roman emperor Augustus, who was also worshiped as a god in temples in Caesarea and Sebaste and in other Hellenized towns. For many Jews, the census came to be seen as enslavement to a mere man claiming to be divine and imposing his rights in place of the rights of the God of Israel. And so, when the census takers tried to start work in A.D. 6, trouble erupted, sparked by a rebel named Judas of Galilee.

This Judas was perhaps the same as a Judas the son of Ezekias who had led one of several popular uprisings a decade earlier, after the death of Herod the Great. In the power vacuum that had existed before Rome confirmed the authority of Herod's sons, there had been a flurry of rebels—popular "kings" and generals who had rallied the people against Herod's

Few acts of Rome earned such deep resentment in Palestine as the census, where Jews were forced to line up under the watchful eyes of foreign soldiers and officials, as in the frieze at right, to have their names entered into the books. To the Jews, paying taxes to Rome was tantamount to paying tribute to a pagan overlord.

heirs. Varus, the Roman governor of Syria who had been called upon to put things right, swept through the land with more than two legions of troops. He easily suppressed the rebels and ultimately crucified about 2,000 captives. This demonstration of raw power had a great impact; one Jewish apocalyptic work even saw it as a sign of the end of the world.

In his writings the historian Josephus expressed contempt for these rebel leaders, whom he called "brigands." Indeed, some may well have been upstart men of the sword who sensed an opportunity and tried to take advantage of it. Judas, however, was a clear exception. He was a man of action who was also a spiritual leader, heir to a long tradition of patriotic fervor combined with deep religious conviction. It had been his father who had led a partisan revolt against the last Hasmoneans and their Roman sponsors when the young Herod was serving as Galilee's administrator. Herod had put down the uprising with such severity that he himself was brought to trial before the Sanhedrin. Now the sons of Herod faced the sons of the rebels.

"The fourth philosophy"

Spurred by the Roman census, Judas joined with a Pharisee named Zadok to form a group that Josephus calls "the fourth philosophy"—following the Pharisees, the Sadducees, and the Essenes. Adherents of this new philosophy resembled Pharisees in most ways, but, Josephus reports, "they have a passion for liberty that is almost unconquerable, since they are convinced that God alone is their leader and master." (Today the term *Zealot* is commonly applied to all Jewish rebels of the period, but there were actually many different groups. The Zealots did not come into being until later in the first century A.D. Their roots, like those of rival rebel movements, reach back to Judas and his followers.)

Both Judas and Zadok were teachers of the Torah as well as popular leaders. They developed the ratio-

nale for resistance to the Romans that came to be shared by most of the Jewish revolutionary groups of the time. According to them, paying taxes to Rome was slavery to foreign overlords. Thus they organized a boycott of the census, which they tried to impose by force of arms. They believed that though they were responsible for their actions, God was on their side and would ultimately grant them victory. This conviction gave them the courage to face overwhelming odds and even death unafraid.

Theirs was also a fight to preserve the integrity of the faith, and they especially liked to invoke the memory of the priest Phinehas, the grandson of Aaron (Moses' brother). In a time of crisis, when Phinehas saw Zimri, a lapsed Israelite, brazenly take a Midianite woman to his tent, he followed them inside and plunged a spear through both of them. This display of zeal had so pleased God, Scripture recounts, that he stopped a plague.

In spirit, the men of "the fourth philosophy" also harked back to the Maccabees, whose successful revolt against the Seleucid kings, begun in 167 B.C., had achieved nearly a century of Judean independence. "Let everyone who is zealous for the law and supports the covenant come out with me," Mattathias, the Maccabean patriarch, had cried. Farmers and traders and priests and laborers had flocked to him in the hills to join in the fight.

The lesson of history was clear for Judas. Like slavery in Egypt or subservience to the Seleucids, collaboration with the Romans was intolerable. Insofar as the Romans ruled in the land of Israel they were God's enemies—as was anyone who was willing to accommodate them. The census was a snare, seemingly harmless, ultimately deadly.

The rebel cause

Although the high priest in Jerusalem, a political realist, had told the people to submit to the Roman requirement, Judas and his followers called upon

In a cave high up in the lime-stone cliffs overlooking the Dead Sea, a group of brigands (later called the Zealots) waits in ambush for a company of Roman soldiers winding its way along the canyon far below. When the sect's founder, Judas of Galilee, was killed, probably in the revolt of A.D. 6, the surviving members retreated to natural bastions such as this one. From there they waged a stubborn guerrilla campaign for Jewish independence, probably with homemade weapons, such as clubs and bows and arrows.

them to resist. Their movement spread rapidly in Judea, particularly among the young. Hiding out in caves and ravines in the eastern mountains, the patriots would swoop down on traveling officials and small detachments of soldiers. Wealthy Jewish collaborators lived in terror that their homes would be ransacked and their lives put in jeopardy.

Eventually Judas was killed—the circumstances are unknown—and history does not record Zadok's fate. But the movement continued underground, led by two of Judas' sons. Its members lived their lives according to a strict interpretation of the Torah. They observed the Sabbath without compromise. They immersed themselves in ritual baths. And they insisted that to acknowledge anyone but God as king or lord of Israel was to break the Commandment "You shall have no other gods before me."

Little is known about the followers of "the fourth philosophy" for four decades after the census. It was

evidently a time of considerable disorganization in which systematic action against the Romans was rare. Sporadic attacks were carried out by guerrilla groups living in the hills. When they were caught, the Romans dealt with them as thieves and bandits. It is conceivable that Barabbas, who was under arrest at the same time as Jesus, was a member of this group. He is described in Mark and Luke as a rebel who was trying to stir up insurrection and thus was probably such a guerrilla fighter. Similarly, the unnamed "thieves" or "robbers" who were crucified beside Jesus would be more accurately described as "bandits" or even "insurrectionists."

The Maccabean legacy

"The fourth philosophy" was by no means the only viable political-religious point of view in Jesus' time. It did, however, represent one branch, one particular viewpoint of a much larger understanding of God, of the world, and of man's role in it. Other groups such as the Pharisees and Essenes—and later even the Christians—turned the same framework of thought in sharply different directions. Only the Sadducees stood apart.

The roots of this shared understanding of the world reach all the way back to the time of the Babylonian exile in the sixth century B.C., but like much else in Judaism of the period, the Maccabean revolt had brought it to flower. Among the Maccabees' staunchest allies at that time had been a party called the Hasidim, literally, "the pious ones." (This ancient group should not be confused with Hasidic Jews of modern times.)

The Hasidim were primarily teachers and interpreters of the Torah before they allied themselves with Judas Maccabeus and his rebels in the struggle to restore the Torah after it had been outlawed by the Seleucid king. The First Book of Maccabees, possibly written in the second century B.C., describes them as "mighty warriors of Israel, every one who offered himself willingly for the law."

But for all their readiness with the sword, there was a profound spirituality and trust in God that underlay their commitment. This dual aspect of their character is exemplified in the Book of Daniel, one of the surviving documents from this troubled period, which scholars attribute to the Hasidim. The story is set in the time of the Babylonian exile. It tells of the hero, Daniel, steadfast in his faith, careful in his obedience to dietary laws, persistent in his prayers to God alone.

In face of inescapable dangers brought upon him by pagan enemies, who threw him into a den of lions, God delivers him. His faithful compatriots, similarly persecuted, are saved from a fiery furnace. The lesson was clear: keep faith, even under the cruel persecutions of conquerors.

But the book is more than a collection of inspiring stories. It also contains visions that interpret the course of history up to the time of the Hasidim. In spite of all of Daniel's excellence and deep faith, power still lay with his pagan persecutors. Daniel and his compatriots are still in exile, still under the domination of pagan powers—but eventually, the story reveals, God will intervene at his own chosen moment and reclaim the course of history and bring blessings to those who have been faithful. The final vision of the book describes a day when "many of those who sleep in the dust of the earth shall awake, some to everlasting life, and some to shame and everlasting contempt. And those who are wise shall shine like the brightness of the firmament."

In spite of the fact that to many modern ears such visions might seem strange, they were expressions of that understanding of God and the world that led the Maccabees and the Hasidim into battle, that fired the zeal of Judas the Galilean against the Romans, that called the Essenes out into the desert, and that inspired John the Baptist to cry, "Repent, for the kingdom of heaven is at hand."

The assurance that the sufferings of the present are temporary and that what is of absolute importance is the struggle to be true to God's covenant, even against overwhelming odds, burned in the heart of the Maccabean martyrs, as it did in so many of their spiritual descendants.

The hereditary priesthood

This widely held belief did not, however, settle all religious and political differences among the Jews, not even for those who shared the belief. The fact that there was great concern not only for the preservation of the law but also for its complete implementation meant that many details of observance were important. Just as in modern times, when everyone in a nation may share a common constitution and legal system yet follow sharply different political and legal philosophies that affect their interpretation of their laws, so in that time, also, the areas for disagreement were vast.

One point of shattering dissension focused on the office of the high priest. In the period before the Maccabean revolt the high priest had been head of state, combining the chief governmental and religious functions in a single individual. By ancient hereditary right and scriptural precedent, the position belonged to a direct descendant of Zadok, who had been chief priest in Solomon's time. Indeed the whole priesthood in the Jerusalem Temple belonged to the family of Zadok. When the Seleucids placed in the office of high priest a man not of the Zadokite family, a major spark was struck for the Maccabean revolt and for the involvement of the Hasidim. In the wake of their victory, when the triumphant Maccabees claimed the title for themselves, some of the Hasidim and their followers felt betrayed—their erstwhile allies were breaking an honored and binding tradition and thus becoming usurpers of a holy office. The name *Zadok* and all that it implied became a divisive religious and political issue that remained for decades.

One can imagine the disgust of the older priestly nobility at seeing their noble office of high priest taken over by the Hasmoneans (as the descendants of Mattathias were called), upstart people allied with the Hasidim and their interpretations of the Torah. In spite of their setbacks as aristocrats caught in the backwash of a people's revolution, however, these wealthy priestly families remained in place. They were pragmatists above all and gradually moved to consolidate their political and religious position so as to regain the preeminence they believed was rightfully theirs.

The outcome of all the religious renewal and ferment caused by the Maccabean revolt was the growth of three major religious and political parties in Judaism. The Hasidim split into two groups over the issues of the high priesthood. One group emphasized priestly leadership and demanded the restoration of a pure Zadokite priesthood in Jerusalem—these became the Essenes. The group of primarily nonpriestly Hasidim that remained loyal to the early Hasmoneans became the Pharisees. In spite of their differences, both groups shared the Hasidim's legacy of emphasis on renewal of the Torah and adaptation and expansion of the laws by the interpretation of Scripture. Against these two groups arose the aristocratic party, the Sadducees, who evidently took their very name from Zadok and thus indicated their own claim to priestly tradition.

The Sadducees

The Sadducees refused to accept the authority of the legal rulings of the scholars of the Hasidim. The elaborate oral tradition of case law, precedent, and interpretation of the Scripture that the Pharisees came to uphold placed far too great a limitation on their own judicial and doctrinal authority as priests. In the party of the Sadducees the interests and beliefs of the aristocracy were consolidated into a relatively consistent legal, religious, and philosophical stance that could be effective even in the new situation in which they could not presume political dominance but had to struggle for it.

As the Hasmonean rulers themselves became more aristocratic and Hellenized, an opportunity for the Sadducees arose. When the high priest John Hyrcanus, Simon's successor, came to an irreconcilable breach with his Pharisaic advisers, he turned away from them and their regulations and toward the Sadducees as his counselors. As members of powerful families, Sadducees no doubt already had seats in the senate under Hyrcanus, but now they returned to a position of dominance in both political and religious affairs. With few interruptions, they remained in control of the senate, or Sanhedrin, until the destruction of Jerusalem in A.D. 70.

The 71-member Sanhedrin was an important base for the Sadducees. It was a combination of supreme court and legislature, which even the Romans al-

The "Bad" Samaritans

On Mount Gerizim, the most sacred spot on earth for Samaritans, the ruins of Hadrian's temple (above) are thought to rest on the ancient Samaritan temple built around the fourth century B.C. as the center of their faith. (The Samaritans rejected the Temple at Jerusalem because they believed that the Scriptures proclaimed Mount Gerizim as God's chosen place.) Though the army of John Hyrcanus destroyed the sanctuary in 128 B.C., the sect survived. A number of the 500 or so adherents still gather near the mountain's summit each year during Passover (above, right) to sacrifice paschal lambs.

It has been said that neighbors and kinfolk make the deadliest enemies. Certainly the long enmity between Judeans and Samaritans is a case in point. It began after Solomon's death, when his kingdom was divided into the two rival states of Israel and Judah, and deepened through centuries of warfare. It hardened when, in 128 B.C., John Hyrcanus razed the main Samaritan shrine on Mount Gerizim. In Jesus' day, travelers between Galilee and Jerusalem were in danger of Samaritan attack, and as the Gospel of John notes, "Jews have no dealings with Samaritans."

Although Roman authorities paid little heed to the seemingly minor religious variations between Samaritans and Judeans, the differences were vital from the believers' viewpoints. To the Samaritans, Mount Gerizim was the "navel of the world," the site God had explicitly chosen for his temple. It had existed before creation, had escaped the flood, and would survive Doomsday. Adam was made from its dust. Abraham went there to sacrifice Isaac.

The Torah, to the Samaritans, was the only law, its every word written by Moses himself. They revered Moses even more than Judeans did. The "light of the world," he would return to establish God's covenant among all people. On this day of "vengeance and recompense," angels would erect scales on which to weigh the deeds of men. The good would go to Eden and the wicked to a fiery underworld.

lowed to operate with great freedom. All matters that could not be dealt with on a local level or were not under direct Roman control fell to the Sanhedrin. Later Jewish tradition often looked back on the Sanhedrin as a council of Torah scholars, but the descriptions of it in Josephus and the New Testament show that the leadership in the time of the Herods and the Roman governors was firmly in the hands of the high priest and his clan and the party of the Sadducees. The legal jurisdiction of the Sanhedrin was limited to Judea, though its moral authority extended wherever Jewish communities chose to yield to its rulings. The great powers that later tradition attributed to it—to declare war, to judge cities and tribes—were largely theoretical, since such matters were kept in the hands of the kings and governors. Still, its influence was great, and its powers, though limited, were very real.

Pragmatic in politics and aristocratic to the tips of their manicured fingernails, the Sadducees included not only the priestly upper classes but also a substantial number of nonpriestly nobility. Far more than the Pharisees, their power was localized in Jerusalem. In spite of their Hellenizing tendencies, they were deeply conservative in outlook and, perhaps not surprisingly, attributed the greatest religious significance to the elements of Judaism in which they were dominant—the Temple and its sacrificial worship. They had no interest, however, in spreading the standards of purity of the Temple worship to all aspects of ordinary life.

The Sadducees strove to maintain their position against the arguments of the Pharisees through what might be called a "strict constructionist" reading of the Torah. First of all, only the first five books of the Hebrew Scriptures, the "books of Moses," were to be used for legal ruling. While the other Old Testament books of prophecy or wisdom were certainly accepted by them, they were not regarded as law. Whereas an Essene or Pharisee might "interpret" or expand a ruling of the law in the light of a prophecy by Isaiah, for example, the Sadducees would not have done so.

Second, the Pharisees' delight in developing binding oral tradition handed down from master to disciple was foreign to the Sadducees. When "tradition" was being used to bring about change in the application of the law, the Sadducees set themselves firmly against it. Josephus reports that they counted it a virtue to dispute their own teachers.

Their strict orientation to the law as well as their positions of power and wealth meant that Sadducees and the aristocracy in general had experienced little of those struggles of faith that had led the Hasidim to develop the belief that the world is somehow under evil domination and that God must intervene. Nor did they share the Hasidim's concerns for the world to come and the resurrection of the dead.

For the Sadducees, life was to be lived in the here and now. Any son of Abraham was free to follow God's instructions, as carefully spelled out in the Torah, and to conduct his affairs with honor and prudence as he saw fit. If he did so, he would find his reward here on earth, in a ripe and prosperous old age, and his afterlife in the honor and prestige that his name would lend to future generations.

The Pharisees

It was among the Sadducees' rivals, the Pharisees, however, that the seeds for the future of Judaism lay. Time after time the ancient sources present the two groups in opposition to each other, so it is easy to forget that, in contrast to the rest of the world, they agreed far more than they disagreed. Still, in most of the points of their disagreement, the Pharisees represented a position that would continue to characterize much of later Judaism, while the position of the Sadducees hardly survived the destruction of the Temple later in the first century A.D.

The opposition of Pharisees and Sadducees lay deep in their very identities. In contrast to the

Judaism's highest tribunal was the Sanhedrin, a body of 71 leading priests, scribes, and prominent laymen, which wielded final authority on religious matters. As shown in the diagram below, the members sat in a semicircle, with the president in the middle; facing them were two scribes and rows of students. With its own police force, the Sanhedrin could order arrests on both civil and criminal charges, and it could mete out a roster of chastisements, including 39 lashes for grievous wrongdoing; the scene at right depicts a typical trial. Only the death penalty probably fell outside its scope, requiring a ruling by the Roman administrator.

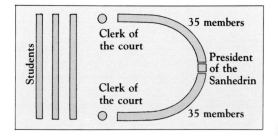

aristocratic power base of the Sadducees, the Pharisees derived their standing from their learning and the rigor of their devotion to the Torah. They were heirs of the scribes and Hasidim in their scholarship and piety.

Although numerous priests were Pharisees, the majority of Pharisees were not of priestly descent. That fact, however, by no means suggests that the Pharisees were somehow against the Temple. The Temple regulations were, after all, a part of the Torah, and the Pharisees would yield to no one in the absolute fulfillment of all tithes and offerings to the Temple, the priests, and the Levites as specified in God's law. If they erred at all, it was on the side of generosity in the payment of those dues. The Temple was not what determined their own identity, however, as it was for the Sadducees.

The name *Pharisee* may mean "separatist," and it probably indicated that the Pharisees took seriously the fact that the observance of the rigorous purity of the laws required their separation from many people who were not so observant. Their own designation for themselves was, in Hebrew, *haverim*, "companions," pointing to the mutually supportive communities formed by the Pharisees.

In their separatist stance, however, the Pharisees remained within society and did not withdraw into a desert monastery, as did many of the Essenes. Thus, in spite of their separation in communities of "companions," the Pharisees remained present among the people as teachers and interpreters of the law and were able to become genuine religious leaders in the period of religious renewal that continued long after the Maccabean revolt.

The Pharisees envisioned the creation of an ideal Jewish society, described in Exodus as "a kingdom of priests and a holy nation." Such an ideal could be reached only if each member of society was so familiar with the Torah that it guided every aspect of his daily conduct.

The two Torahs

Intimately connected with this process of applying the Torah to every moment of life was the development of the "oral law" alongside the written Torah. It was the life's work of the scholarly Pharisees to transmit and develop this vast body of applied law— legal arguments, rulings, and precedents, all the "traditions of the elders"—to succeeding generations of interpreters of the Torah. As the oral law grew, its importance grew. It came to be attributed to Moses himself, and indeed Moses was thought to have received it from God. It had simply been handed down from those ancient times and was as venerable and as binding as the written law.

To the modern eye these traditions appear as adaptations and transformations of ancient laws for very new situations. To the Pharisees all was ancient. Their interpretations simply drew forth what was already there. Either way the effect of the oral law was revolutionary. Rather than allowing the Torah to become a rigid fossil of centuries past, the oral law made it a living, flexible, growing reality. Only at the end of the second century A.D. was a body of this tradition reduced to writing in the form of the Mishnah. It continued to grow, however, and the following centuries produced the Babylonian and Jerusalem Talmuds and lengthy commentaries.

An example of the interpretative challenges faced by the champions of the oral law was application of the laws of the sabbatical year. Several passages of the written Torah (especially Exodus and Leviticus) provide that every seventh year all land is to go uncultivated, all Hebrew slaves are to be freed, and all debts are to be canceled—an event that would have caused havoc in Jerusalem's marketplaces.

In ancient times, the cancellation of debts served to keep money lending from becoming a business, maintaining it as an act of aid from one person to another. In the increasingly money-based economy of the Roman Empire, however, the effect was to dry up credit sources as the sabbatical year approached. If debts were to be canceled, a banker simply would not lend. And so, according to the Mishnah, the great rabbi Hillel instituted a new form of contract in which debtor and creditor could agree before judges that a particular debt secured by real property would not be canceled by the sabbatical year. The new practice changed the effect of the law so that those who needed credit were not punished by an ancient institution that was intended to aid them. A system was devised whereby any debt could be signed over to the law courts, thus allowing the creditor to stay within the rules and still obtain his money.

It was the kind of solution in which the Pharisees took delight. Their goal was to apply the Torah's rules to every aspect of human existence, down to its smallest detail. If this involved considerable legal ingenuity, that only made the process more challenging. They would "make a fence for the law," they declared, by erecting a barricade of cautionary arguments and decisions that would keep anyone from straying off God's intended pathways. Though laymen, they would become as holy as priests.

Pharisees as prophets

Not only were the Pharisees heirs of the scholarly scribes as interpreters of Scripture, they were also beneficiaries of the theological revolution of the Hasidim and their apocalyptic understanding of the world. Although the Pharisees do not appear in the ancient sources to have had any great interest in visions and historical allegories, they did hold to a fundamental belief that there would be a resurrection of the dead and a world to come. To them the supernatural powers of angels and demons surround human life and struggle over the fate of human beings. Although the situation of a person's life is

The very image of self-satisfied piety, a Pharisee looks haughtily over his shoulder in this 17th-century drawing by Rembrandt. Though most Pharisees were sincere in their beliefs, the sect acquired a lasting reputation for stressing religion's outer forms at the expense of its inner meaning because of the accusations against them in the New Testament. "They do all their deeds to be seen by men," Jesus charged in Matthew 23; "for they make their phylacteries broad and their fringes long"—a reference first to the passages of Scripture that they wore strapped to their foreheads and arms and second to the tassles that adorned their prayer shawls. The fringed ends of a modern prayer shawl are shown above.

greatly influenced by divine providence, the ultimate decision whether to follow God's law is a matter of free choice. Life with all its hardships and injustices is a transitory state, and the true rewards of a good and pious man will come in the hereafter, as will punishments for evildoers. Though men's bodies die, their souls are immortal, and after death comes resurrection. A day of reckoning will arrive, and a messianic figure will appear to usher in a new reign of God on earth. At that supreme moment, the righteous will awaken to eternal bliss as charter members of the new order. All others will be consigned to everlasting punishment.

Implicit in this scheme was the thought that each individual should prepare himself for the life to come. And, while no one could really control his basic circumstances—a man might be born rich or poor, handsome or hideous, as determined in advance by the Almighty—each person could nonetheless choose to follow the path of righteousness. Beyond that choice, his fate was up to God. "Everything is in the hands of God but the fear of God," the Pharisees declared.

Synagogues: Centers of influence

Although the Pharisees never wished to denigrate the Temple but celebrated it as a place of divine worship, their own work was more concentrated in a newer institution, the synagogue, which they placed beside it. They held the synagogue to be a valid and important sanctuary of study, prayer, and reflection. Nearly every town had one, serving as a combination meeting house, school, and place of worship. The Pharisees would quite naturally assemble there to conduct their disputations and to instruct the people in the ways of proper piety. In doing so, they began to undercut the authority of the priestly aristocracy. Indeed, in their close attention to such matters as ritual purity and devout conduct—so many days of fasting, so many strictures for observing the Sabbath—they began, in effect, to behave like priests themselves.

It was only through such a local institution as the synagogue, where ordinary folk, who could never in their lives hope to own or actually to read a copy of the Torah, could hear it read and discussed week by week, that the Pharisaic vision of a "kingdom of priests" could be realized.

Hillel and Shammai: Two great teachers

As the Pharisees grew in strength, their version of Judaism came to be the most respected among the mass of devout Jews. More and more, they moved away from the actively political role that they had played under the Hasmoneans and toward the role as the religious guides of the whole people. Rivalries developed between teachers, however. The most notable of these took place between the great conservative scholar Shammai, who tended to take a rigid approach to the interpretation of Scripture, and the more liberal Hillel.

The two rabbis became the centers of two opposing schools of Pharisaic thought, and their debates left a deep imprint on Pharisaic teaching. Most of the discussions between their followers centered on the minor applications of Jewish law that Pharisees had always loved to argue about—how best to observe the Sabbath, precisely how the Temple tithes should be differentiated from priestly dues, in what manner prayers should be said, and the like. There are some 300 known points of disagreement between them. But in the final analysis, the most significant contrast between the two schools had to do with Hillel's attitude and personality.

Hillel's disciples often repeated a favorite story to illustrate their master's uniquely personal approach to the law and its interpretation. It seems that a Gentile once approached Shammai with a bizarre request. He would, he said, convert to Judaism if, during the brief time that he was able to stand on one leg, the sage could teach him the Torah. Shammai, who did not suffer fools gladly, whacked his interrogator with a ruler and sent him packing.

The Gentile then went to Hillel with the same proposition. Hillel did not hesitate in answering: "What is hateful to you, do not do it unto your neighbor; that is the whole of the Torah, all else is commentary." It was Hillel's philosophy in essence, and he would repeat it time and again—and it was to be echoed by Jesus in the Golden Rule.

Hillel had little concern for apocalyptic visions. Like other Pharisees he believed that the means to salvation lay in the here and now, in leading a humane and law-observant existence. "He who has acquired for himself the words of the Torah," he maintained, "has acquired life in the coming world."

"O ye hypocrites"

By the time of Jesus, the Pharisee party numbered at least 6,000 members, and their influence was often dominant in the Sanhedrin. When questions arose on points of Temple ritual, it was usually the Pharisees, with their superior knowledge of the law, who provided the rulings that even Sadducees had to

follow. As the group gained more and more respect, certain of its members seemed to display a conspicuous pride in their own piety, halting at street corners to recite their prayers, taking the most prominent seats in the synagogue, wearing oversized phylacteries (leather pouches containing Scripture quotations) on their arms and foreheads, and otherwise calling attention to themselves. Scrupulous in following the law, many of them were quick to condemn anyone whom they deemed improperly attentive to it.

This detail from a bronze menorah dramatizes the encounter between the Jewish teacher Hillel and a Gentile who challenged the rabbi to teach him the entire Torah while standing on one foot. Hillel countered by citing a version of the Golden Rule, which was probably a popular expression of the time.

The Essenes built their Qumran monastery in one of Palestine's most desolate regions. This cluster of buildings—the ruins can be seen at top in the photo at right—covered nearly two acres and included workrooms, storage chambers, and a scriptorium. Devotees lived in tents or in caves like the ones in the foregound cliffs. To the east lies the Dead Sea with the cliffs of Moab in the distance, as seen below.

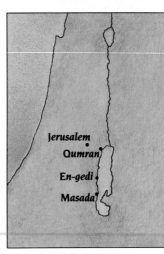

Jerusalem
Qumran
En-gedi
Masada

Enmeshed in these tangles of argument and practice, often disdainful of those who did not follow them, such Pharisees seemed to have lost their way. They became the objects of severe criticism from the Sadducees and Essenes as well as from other teachers including both John the Baptist and Jesus.

The Essenes

Even as the Pharisees were out instructing the people, other factions were seeking God by removing themselves from everyday society. The most prestigious of these monastic groups were the Essenes, many of whom lived in the wilderness at Qumran on the shore of the Dead Sea.

It is difficult to imagine any sect taking the demands of piety with more utter, uncompromising seriousness than did the Essenes. They were true holy men of the desert, "a solitary race," wrote the Roman historian Pliny, "and strange above all others in the entire world."

Self-denying, often celibate, the Essenes subjected themselves to a discipline as rigorous as any soldier's. All goods were held in common. Every moment was accounted for. They combined two basic elements in their identity. First, the priests among them were the true "sons of Zadok," excluded from the Temple by the renegade priesthood that held control. Second, they were deeply committed to an apocalyptic vision of the world.

The world, as they saw it, is divided into two innately hostile camps—the Sons of Light, representing the forces of truth and righteousness, and the Sons of Darkness. Each of these camps is controlled by a heavenly being appointed by God. There is a Prince of Light and an Angel of Darkness, and war continuously rages between these two powers at every level, from the sphere of the angels down to the innermost chambers of the human soul. Every man and woman belongs to one of the two groups, and no one has much choice over which camp he or she is in, for the enrollments are predestined by God. Even so, the Angel of Darkness keeps trying to ensnare the souls of the righteous, who must constantly battle against him.

The struggle is predestined to conclude with the victory of God. On Judgment Day, the Sons of Light will prevail. Not just one messianic figure will appear, but three: a prophet as foretold by Moses, a kingly messiah descended from David, and a priestly messiah, who is the most important of all. At their arrival, the Lord's angelic armies will give forth a great shout, the earth's foundations will shake, "and a war of the mighty ones of the heavens will spread throughout the world." The devastation will be fearsome, consuming all creation, but at its finish a

new order will prevail with all evil abolished and "righteousness revealed as the sun." As in the apocalyptic scenarios of other visionaries, the elect will live in eternal peace and happiness, while the wicked will fall to perdition.

Thus it was that the Essenes went forth into the wilderness, to prepare in the desert "the way of the Lord." The great day might occur at any moment. They would be ready for it, their souls purified, their bodies hardened, fully prepared to take their places as soldiers in God's heavenly host.

God's army

The Essenes, like the Pharisees, apparently originated from the Hasidim; indeed their name is often interpreted as the Aramaic form of *Hasidim,* "pious ones," though it may be more closely related to the word meaning "healers." Many scholars believe that the decisive event for the emergence of the Essenes as a distinct group was the moment when, in 152 B.C., Jonathan the Hasmonean received for himself the office of high priest from the hand of a pretender to the Seleucid throne. For these wholly committed Zadokites such betrayal meant that the Temple in Jerusalem was defiled and no longer a place where those who were true to God's law could worship. The leader of the group, who, remarkably enough, is known in the Essene literature only as "the Teacher of Righteousness," denounced the authority of the high priest, the Jerusalem Temple, and all its priestly establishment. Declaring its rites and sacrifices invalid—even its calendar was in error, he had said, and so it celebrated the great Jewish festivals on the wrong dates—he had moved out to Qumran with a band of dissidents.

A high Temple official had hurried to Qumran after them, apparently intent on humiliating or even killing the Teacher of Righteousness. It may have been Jonathan himself; Essene documents refer simply to a visit from "the Wicked Priest." But, digging their heels into the desert hardpack, the Essenes had refused be intimidated. They had then set about shaping the future of their new monastic order.

The result was a sect as strictly organized as any Roman legion, with a fixed hierarchy of leaders and ranks. Seeing themselves as soldiers of God, the Essenes spent their days strengthening their bodies and souls in anticipation of the battle that was to come. The monastery itself was designed as a model of God's perfect kingdom, which would come to be after the battle had been won. Totally self-sufficient, it had a bastionlike headquarters containing a scriptorium, workshops and meeting rooms, and an irrigation system that provided water to the surrounding fields where the Essenes grew their food.

Each day began at sunrise with a prayer. Before its recital, no other word might be spoken. Then the members went to their appointed jobs—some to the grain fields; some to the kitchens; some to the pottery kilns; some to looms, where they wove the white linen robes that the order wore; others to the scriptorium, where they pored over documents and diligently copied out sacred texts.

It was the manuscripts produced by this last group that have become known in modern times as the Dead Sea Scrolls. After the sect had been in existence for more than 200 years, it was virtually wiped out by the Roman armies that overran Jerusalem in A.D. 70. It is believed that as the enemy army approached, the Essenes carefully packed their precious scrolls in pottery jars and hid them in caves in the cliffs that overlook the Dead Sea.

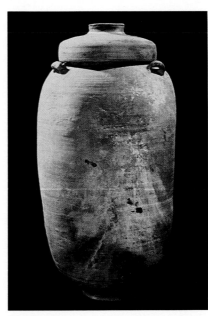

To store their sacred documents—the so-called Dead Sea Scrolls—the Essenes used pottery jars such as the one above. Protected in this way and buried in caves, hundreds of scrolls have survived.

There they remained until 1947, when some were accidentally discovered by an Arab shepherd boy searching for a lost goat. The parchment and papyrus documents number in the hundreds, and it is largely from them that we know details of the sect's organization, its laws and practices, and its intense and sweeping vision of apocalypse. Included also were Hebrew texts of Old Testament works and psalm books of praise and thanksgiving.

At the fifth hour of the day, all Essenes assembled for a ritual bath in cold water and a simple communal meal in a large refectory. The afternoon's schedule repeated the morning's: a return to labor and a communal evening repast of utmost sobriety. Then the membership retired to barrackslike quarters, either in tents or in caves in the surrounding hills.

So life went, six days a week. On the Sabbath, as with pious Jews everywhere, all activity ceased—but the Essenes were even more scrupulous than the most pious Pharisee about observing the day of rest. Meals were cold, having been prepared the day before. And no Essene would undertake to relieve himself, lest his waste profane God's holy day. Failure to observe the Sabbath as prescribed was punishable by exclusion from full membership in the sect for seven years.

Woven into the routine of life were two daily practices whose natures set the Essenes apart from other sects—the extensive ritual washings and the common meals. By long tradition, all pious Jews washed their hands before eating or praying, and they immersed themselves in *mikvehs*, or ritual baths. But the Essenes gave the practice a greater spiritual weight and made it more important in their lives, immersing their bodies daily before meals and requiring each new member to bathe himself in flowing water, a ritual of initiation that presaged John the Baptist's rite of baptism.

Eating together was perhaps an even more important rite. Meals began in silence, until an officiating priest had invoked God's blessing. A fine decorum prevailed, with the diners refraining from idle chatter. "No clamor or disturbance ever pollutes their dwelling," one commentator marveled; "they speak in turn, each making way for his neighbor. To persons outside, the silence of those within appears like some awful mystery."

Not only did the meals commemorate the unity of the brotherhood and its removal from the world's wicked ways, but they were eaten in joyful anticipa-

The two earthenware inkwells at left may have been the property of scribes. The common type of ink used on the Dead Sea Scrolls was made from powdered charcoal. It is still legible even after 2,000 years.

tion of the messianic banquets that would surely occur in the world to come. The fare might be meager and the mood austere. No matter. The breaking of common bread was a holy act, seen in much the same light as the early Christians would look upon the sharing of bread and wine as a celebration of Jesus' Last Supper with his disciples.

A new member of the order underwent a lengthy period of testing and indoctrination to prove his

The basic tenets of Essene belief are set down in a six-foot-long parchment scroll known as the Manual of Discipline, *which dates from around 100 B.C. Despite the time-ravaged edges, as revealed in the segment at left, the scroll gives a remarkably complete account of the sect's laws and ideology, including some of its rituals and community activities. It also spells out the punishments for such infractions as lying, blaspheming, laughing too loudly, and spitting during meetings.*

worthiness. After the first year he received his habit—loincloth, white linen robe, and small ax. (This instrument was both a token of membership and a sanitary device; before relieving himself an Essene would cut a foot-deep trench with the ax, and when he finished he would fill in the hole with the excavated earth.) The neophyte spent another two years as a junior member, taking part in the round of work and daily bathing but not yet participating in the celebratory meals. At some point, he made over all his worldly possessions to the order.

The pure of heart

Once his apprenticeship had ended, each member took a lifelong oath: to practice piety toward God, to act justly toward all men and to hate the unjust, to injure no one, never to lie or steal, to keep no secrets from his brethren, and never to reveal the secrets of the order to outsiders. Above all, he must shun evil and turn his mind toward whatever is holy and good.

It was a deeply serious commitment. It enrolled him in a life far more rigorous than that of either the Sadducees or the Pharisees. Neither ritual purity nor ethical conduct by itself was good enough for the Essenes. What mattered was the member's innermost state of mind—the piety and grace of his soul. As Essene texts admonished, "It is by an upright and humble spirit that sin can be atoned."

To ensure the membership's spiritual welfare, each initiate would undergo periodic examination by his elders. At certain times the whole community would meet to confess their sins and openly receive a blessing from the priests. The assembly would be reminded that ablutions, unless performed with true sincerity, were but empty and profitless ceremonies.

And woe to the erring brother. He would be demoted in rank or perhaps even exiled from the brotherhood. Such expulsion was a fearful punishment, for every member had taken a vow to eat no food that was grown by people outside the community. As long as he lived in exile and did not renounce his oath, he was compelled to live by foraging for wild foods—as an outcast of the community, he probably could not even eat food that he had grown himself—and in that desert land, he might easily starve to death.

Not all Essenes remained within the Qumran

The god-hero Mithras, originally a Persian deity, makes ready to strike down the bull—the key mythical act in an ancient mystery religion. This Roman marble statue dates from the second century A.D.

monastery. The sect flourished and expanded until, by the time of Jesus, its members numbered perhaps 4,000, most of them in tightly knit religious cells in villages and towns. Out in the world they continued to follow the ideals of the sect—avoiding luxury, obeying their elders, helping the needy, eating their communal meals, and practicing their rites of purification. Some even married and raised families, though these were a minority; most were celibate.

Josephus, who may have spent some time studying with the Essenes, gave them his unstinting admiration if not his participation. "Holding righteous indignation in reserve, they are masters of their temper," he wrote, "champions of fidelity, the very ministers of peace."

One of the most important effects of the discovery of the Dead Sea Scrolls for modern scholars has been the direct insight they have provided into a previ-

Worshiping Other Gods

Pagan cults flourished throughout the Mediterranean world during the Hellenistic and Roman periods, not only in Rome and Greece but also in Egypt, Asia Minor, Syria, and other eastern regions. Slaves, soldiers, and merchants—who tended to move from place to place—took their deities with them. Thus, even in Palestine people were devoted to Jupiter, Minerva, and others of the Greco-Roman pantheon and raised statues in their honor. Foreigners may also have erected shrines to Cybele, mother goddess of Asia Minor, and her young lover Attis, who according to legend had been born, like Christ, from a virgin.

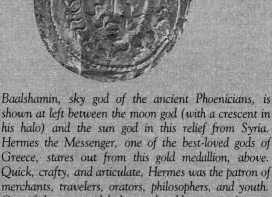

Baalshamin, sky god of the ancient Phoenicians, is shown at left between the moon god (with a crescent in his halo) and the sun god in this relief from Syria. Hermes the Messenger, one of the best-loved gods of Greece, stares out from this gold medallion, above. Quick, crafty, and articulate, Hermes was the patron of merchants, travelers, orators, philosophers, and youth. One of the most widely honored goddesses was Artemis of Ephesus, at right. She was not the virgin huntress of Greek mythology but a more ancient, many-breasted fertility goddess, whose cult spread from Asia to Gaul.

The beanlike pods of the carob tree—known also as the locust tree—were the possible mainstay of John the Baptist's wilderness diet. Sharply sour when green, the pods as they ripen in spring fill with a dark, nutritious, honeylike syrup that is used today in making sweets. In biblical times, the dried pods were fed to cattle and pigs; only the very poor ate them. (One likely carob consumer was the Prodigal Son in Jesus' parable, who, the Bible says, "would gladly have fed on the pods that the swine ate.") For John as well, the fruit would have provided a ready source of nourishment—a notion reflected in one popular name for it—Saint John's bread.

ously mysterious group within ancient Judaism. They have revealed how profound was the intellectual and spiritual ferment within Judaism during the first century. Laid open to our eyes is a group that was at once completely Jewish and at the same time alienated from both the Temple and its sacrifices and from the Pharisaic teachers, whom the Essenes disparaged as "seekers of smooth things," who would not make the hard commitment to the discipline of the desert.

Yet no matter how vehemently Judea's religious factions differed from one another, all were agreed on the importance of maintaining Judaism in the purest form possible. Palestine was rife with foreigners and pagans, from Roman soldiers and administrators to ordinary citizens of other races, religions, and cultures. Most God-fearing Jews looked upon the alien religions with shuddering abhorrence. Devoted to a single God, they shared none of the ancient world's tolerance toward gods of others. Yet for all the differences between Jewish and pagan beliefs, a surprising number of parallels existed, and it seemed that a subtle cross-fertilization of religious ideas was taking place.

John's message

From the Hasidim to the Pharisees and Essenes, to "the fourth philosophy" and the Zealots, to the Sadducees, to the numerous solitary prophets and teachers, the religious landscape of Judaism in the period of Jesus was colorful and changing. It is little wonder then, in this time of ferment, that the appearance of a charismatic figure such as John the Baptist was both familiar and disturbing. In many ways John fit right into the variegated landscape. In other ways, the leaders of society, from Herod to the Sadducees, were well aware of the threatening power that such a prophetic figure could wield among the people. Their positions, their fortunes, indeed, their very lives might depend on preventing the kind of mass religious movements that the Romans could perceive as

threatening. And this voice that spoke with such vehemence and hope of the coming of the mightier one in judgment was not a force for moderation.

John himself came from a devout and simple background. Son of an elderly village priest, he had been born during the reign of Herod, about six months before Jesus, to whom he was related—his mother, Elizabeth, was Mary's kin, possibly her cousin. Little is known of his formative years. Presumably, as a child of a pious household, he had received the normal synagogue instruction. But at some point he had become infused by religious ardor that had sent him off alone into the desert, where he lived on locusts and wild honey.

Some scholars believe that he may have joined the Essenes at Qumran for a time. His teachings resembled theirs in some ways; but unlike them, he reached out to the public at large, challenging people to repent and be baptized without taking the order's vows of exclusivity. Certainly his diet of locusts and wild honey, mentioned by both Matthew and Mark, would have been similar to that of an outcast Essene.

Draping himself in his camel-hair coat—the garb of ancient prophets—John had begun baptizing in the Jordan. The ethical teaching that accompanied his call to repentance, as given in the Gospel According to Luke, was straightforward and humane. "He who has two coats, let him share with him who has none; and he who has food, let him do likewise." Tax collectors might keep their jobs, he said, provided they did not cheat the public; and soldiers might continue to soldier, provided they did not rob or falsely accuse the people.

But John's overriding message was that the moment of God's intervention in the world was near. The one "who comes after me" was at hand, and all Israel should prepare. As Christian tradition remembered him, John was the great forerunner of the Messiah.

The baptism of Jesus

One day—the Gospel According to John says that it was the day after his interrogation by the priests and Levites—as John was preaching, he saw a figure approaching and stopped.

"This is he," John cried, "of whom I said, 'After me comes a man who ranks before me, for he was before me.' "

Matthew says that when Jesus asked to be baptized John was astonished. "I need to be baptized by you, and do you come to me?" he asked in wonder.

"Let it be so now," Jesus insisted. "For thus it is fitting for us to fulfill all righteousness."

And so John performed the rite. When Jesus emerged from the water, as the Gospel of Mark relates, "he saw the heavens opened and the Spirit descending upon him like a dove; and a voice came from heaven, 'Thou art my beloved Son; with thee I am well pleased.' "

The moment for Jesus had arrived.

In the rite of baptism performed by John in the Jordan River, the penitent would probably have knelt down in the shallows to confess his sins, while John, standing beside him, would extend God's forgiveness. The Bible does not give details about how the act of baptism was carried out; it says simply that John baptized with water.

Thompson

Chapter Nine

The Mission of the Messiah

In word and deed, Jesus challenged many of the accepted traditions in the land and thus attracted the attention of his countrymen. Some saw him as a gifted teacher. To others he was a welcome leader who symbolized their opposition to Rome. But in the eyes of a growing minority, he was the Redeemer sent by God.

Not far from the cooling waters of the Jordan rise the bone-dry ridges of awesome desert mountains. In this hostile Wilderness of Judea Jesus prayed and fasted for 40 days, the same number of days Moses had spent on the mountain in Sinai where he received the Ten Commandments from God. Perhaps Jesus, too, was contemplating a new interpretation of God's will. Traditionally Jews fasted as a rite of repentance; but Jesus went without food the entire six weeks as a means of denying the body in order to strengthen the spirit. The austere setting reflected an ancient belief that God's voice is heard most clearly in the mountains. According to another ancient belief, however, evil spirits also frequented the desert wastes. Indeed, at the end of 40 days, according to the Gospel of Matthew, Satan came to tempt the famished, exhausted young man. The scene of the temptation may have been the slopes of the 1,200-foot mountain of dull-white chalk called Jebel Quruntul, northwest of Jericho. There, the barren ground was littered with rough blocks of brownish stone resembling loaves. But Jesus resisted the temptation to change the rocks

"Again he began to teach beside the sea. And a very large crowd gathered about him, so that he got into a boat and sat in it on the sea; and the whole crowd was beside the sea on the land. And he taught them many things. . . ." Mark 4:1–2. From his vantage point in the boat, Jesus could address the multitude and be heard by all who had come to this cove on the Sea of Galilee.

The traditional site of Jesus' temptation, Jebel Quruntul climbs in barren solitude from the desolate hills of the Judean Wilderness. So many religious ascetics spent time in this region that it became known as the "nursery of souls." Jebel Quruntul's name, from the Latin for "forty," refers to the 40 days Jesus fasted there.

into bread; instead, he countered with his own version of Deuteronomy 8:3, "Man shall not live by bread alone, but by every word that proceeds from the mouth of God." Then, Jesus found himself on the so-called pinnacle of the Temple in Jerusalem. According to Josephus, one could not look down from there to the ravine of the Kidron Valley below without feeling dizzy. Were Jesus to leap, suggested the Tempter, God's angels would bring him safely to earth. But Jesus again put temptation behind him, recalling the injunction in Deuteronomy 6:16 not to test God. Once more back in the wilderness, the devil took Jesus to "a very high mountain"—possibly again Jebel Quruntul—and "showed him all the kingdoms of the world" and offered him the opportunity to rule them like a caesar. "All these I will give you, if you will fall down and worship me," said the Tempter. But Jesus replied, "Begone, Satan!"

In retelling the story of the temptations or any other event in Jesus' life, we are following the accounts left to us in the four Gospels. These Gospels, written in the later decades of the first century A.D., are proclamations of Jesus as the Messiah and Son of God. The Gospels differ from one another in many ways, and thus the early Christian church was unwilling that any one of them be used alone without the others. For example, each Gospel has its distinctive approach to reporting the temptations in the wilderness. Mark's Gospel tells of them in a single verse. The Gospels of Matthew and Luke tell the story in detail, but reverse the order of the second and third temptations. The Gospel of John does not mention them at all.

The Gospel writers demonstrated Jesus' faithfulness to the commands of God as given in the Old Testament. They demonstrated Jesus' power to confront the demonic forces of the world and overcome them. They proclaimed that Jesus' ministry was not to be one of political or miraculous self-glorification, but rather of trust in God and submission to God's will.

After the temptations, Jesus did not remain in the wilderness, calling the people to come forth and purify themselves for the coming judgment as did John the Baptist. Instead, he went into the villages and cities to spread his message among the people.

Early ministry

According to Luke, Jesus was about 30 years old when he began his ministry. Aside from that, we have no report on what Jesus looked like. Since the Jews believed that it was wrong to represent the human form in painting or sculpture, no contemporary likeness of Jesus has come down to us. The earliest attempts to describe him date from the third century A.D., when Church Fathers decided that Jesus was unattractive and even ugly, based on Isaiah 53:2, which says that the servant of God "had no form or comeliness that we should look at him, and no beauty that we should desire him." But in the fourth century, Christian writers, influenced by idealized Greek and Roman art, held that Jesus was beautiful, citing Psalm 45:2: "You are the fairest of the sons of men. . . ." Of course, there is no evidence to support either view. All we know is that Jesus was a Galilean Jew, and we may assume that he looked like other Galilean Jews of his day, bearded, and dressed in tunic, mantle, and sandals.

It is not clear what Jesus did for some weeks at the start of his ministry, for the Gospels differ in their accounts. The Gospel of John reports that while he was east of the Jordan, where he had been baptized, Jesus called his first disciples, an unnamed person (possibly John) and the fisherman Andrew, who had also come down from Galilee to hear the preaching of John the Baptist. (The term *disciple* means students, apprentices, or followers.) These first two disciples quickly fell in with Jesus, sensing his spiritual uniqueness. When Andrew brought his brother Simon, Jesus instantly took his measure and renamed him Peter, meaning "rock." To the Jews of

Jesus lived in the wilderness "with the wild beasts," according to Mark's Gospel, and for all its bleakness the Judean Wilderness was inhabited with wildlife, especially in the rainy season. There were birds and serpents, along with such grazing animals as the gazelle (top left), the ibex (top right), and flocks of goats (above), which fed off shrubs and scattered tufts of desert grass.

227

The Sea of Galilee figured in much of Jesus' early ministry. Along its shores he called disciples, taught, and worked miracles. One night, he even walked on the water to reach his disciples, who were in a boat far from shore. Afterwards, the boat crossed the lake and landed at Gennesaret. The above photograph was taken at Gennesaret on the northwestern shore.

Palestine, this special sign of giving someone a new name—as in Genesis God had changed the name *Abram* to Abraham and *Jacob* to Israel—indicated that the person was chosen for a divine mission. Once again, Jesus harked back to Old Testament tradition even as he inaugurated his revolutionary movement of spiritual renewal.

After the meeting with Peter, the Gospel of John reports, Jesus decided to go to Galilee, and he inspired Philip, who was from Simon Peter's town of Bethsaida, and Nathanael, who hailed from Cana, to join him.

The Gospel of Luke, however, tells us that Jesus began his ministry by teaching in the synagogues of Galilee, "being glorified by all." But he did not remain in the synagogues. He went out and mixed with the people. From some he asked a deeper commitment than listening to his word, and perhaps it was at this time that he told his fishermen disciples to follow him and become "fishers of men." They did so promptly. James and John responded in such haste that they left their father, Zebedee, in the boat

with the hired servants. These fishermen gave up their livelihood to serve Jesus, though they probably had been used to a comfortable income—ordinary considerations faded before their conviction that indeed "the kingdom of heaven is at hand."

In and around Capernaum

The headquarters for the new ministry was Capernaum, a principally Jewish lakeside town of about 5,000 or 6,000 souls. Located on a major trade route between Damascus and Alexandria and probably a border station just south of the line between Herod Philip's territories to the east and the lands ruled by Herod Antipas, the town was surely more cosmopolitan than Nazareth. Possibly Jesus made his second home in Peter's house.

Certainly, Jesus would have taught often in the local synagogues, and in this way he must have begun to make his reputation as an unusual teacher. According to Mark 1:22, the common people "were astonished at his teaching, for he taught them as one who had authority, and not as the scribes."

For some months, Jesus may have continued his teaching in synagogues in and around Capernaum. But another characteristic of his ministry—his power to heal the sick and demon-possessed—caused his fame to spread. It was probably his reputation as a healer that attracted the crowds described in the Gospels.

Jesus did not seek out the sick—he did not have to. His readiness to help those who were in despair in a society that had few effective medical resources was advertisement enough. The people flocked to hear him. At times the multitudes became so large that Jesus was forced to put out to sea in a boat in order to avoid being crushed. For Jesus, this ministry was the demonstration of God's love.

While in Cana, John tells us, Jesus was found by a frantic military officer, whose son was dying in Capernaum. With calm authority, Jesus said, "Go; your son will live." When the officer arrived at home the

Continued on page 232

Fishing in the bountiful waters of the Sea of Galilee

The Sea of Galilee is stocked with a wide variety of edible fish, one of the tastiest of which is the *Tilapia galilea*, or Saint Peter's fish. According to Matthew 17:27, Jesus told Peter to take a coin from the mouth of a fish to pay the Temple tax; legend has it that the fish was a *Tilapia galilea* and that Peter left his fingerprints as markings that identify the species today.

Various types of nets were used for fishing. A small circular net was cast into the water from the shore or from shallow water and hauled in with its catch. Peter and Andrew were casting from shore when Jesus called them. A dragnet was drawn between two boats or between one boat on the water and fishermen walking along the shore. Since Luke tells us that James and John were Peter's partners and had their own boat, they may have used a dragnet on occasion.

Later the fishermen sorted their catch, discarded fish that were forbidden by Jewish dietary laws, cleaned and sold the rest, and mended their nets. James and John were mending their nets when Jesus called them.

"The kingdom of heaven is like a net which was thrown into the sea and gathered fish of every kind; when it was full, men drew it ashore and sat down and sorted the good into vessels but threw away the bad." Matthew 13:47–48. Fishing boats on the Sea of Galilee are shown above; a fisherman gathering in a cast net and a catch of Saint Peter's fish are shown at right.

First-century House

A fisherman's house at Capernaum, like the one the Apostle Peter lived in, probably looked much like the dwelling shown at right. It was made of stone without mortar, and the outside was plastered with clay and lime. The house was relatively secure against the heat of summer and the cold rains of winter. A roof of reeds and sticks coated with thick clay kept off rain but needed constant maintenance. A door from the unpaved street led directly to the inside courtyard, where there was an oven for cooking and baking. To the left of the gate was the entrance to the living, sleeping, and dining areas. The open front door and a few small windows set high up under the eaves were the pincipal sources of light. Furnishings were simple, and the people slept on the floor on straw mats.

Another outside door from the street opened to the fish shop, where the catch of the day was sold at the going price. Other rooms served as storage and work areas. In the open courtyard at the rear, donkeys, sheep, and goats were kept. The sheep and goats were the source of dairy products, and their wool and hair was used to make clothing and rugs.

The excavations at Capernaum have revealed an orderly town arranged in blocks of private houses with interspersed public buildings. At the far left stand the remains of an fifth-century octagonal church that covered the first-century house shown above. At the right is a fourth-century synagogue built of white limestone. Beneath the synagogue were found the remains of a public building of the first century, apparently the earliest synagogue in Capernaum.

The limestone pillars of a third- or fourth-century A.D. synagogue rise above the excavated ruins of Capernaum, the Galilean fishing town that Jesus made his headquarters for a time. Several earlier buildings had occupied this site, and archeologists digging among the ruins have found the paving stones of an earlier synagogue, perhaps the very one in which Jesus preached on the Sabbath and "astonished" the crowd with his eloquence and power.

next day, he discovered that the boy's fever had broken at the very hour Jesus had spoken.

Another time, according to Luke 4:33–36, in the synagogue in Capernaum, where Jesus was teaching, a demon-possessed man shrieked aloud, "What have you to do with us, Jesus of Nazareth? Have you come to destroy us?" Taking this acknowledgement of his divine mission as the taunt of a demonic voice, Jesus commanded, "Be silent, and come out of him!" The man's seizure ended, and he was unharmed by the incident. To onlookers, this was proof of Jesus' authority over the powers of darkness.

Later in that same astonishing day, Jesus was about to have supper at Simon Peter's house when he was told that his host's mother-in-law was suffering from a fever. According to Luke, when Jesus took the woman by the hand, the fever vanished, and, in a homely touch, she got up and took charge of serving the Sabbath meal to her guests.

Such acts of healing were not unknown in Jesus' day. In both the Jewish and Hellenistic circles, godly and divinely inspired men were believed to have the power to perform miraculous cures. Also, many Jews may have been especially receptive to such practices, since they believed that the approach of national salvation would be heralded by miraculous acts.

The accounts of Jesus' healing are remarkable in several respects, however. No one else was known to cure such a variety of problems, including blindness, paralysis, leprosy, and a severed ear. The Gospels tell of three occasions on which Jesus brought a human being back from the dead. But Jesus did not use magical formulas or obscure rituals as other healers reportedly did. Rather than recite prayers and openly ask for healing power, Jesus often stressed the faith of the afflicted or of those who brought them to him. Nor did Jesus heal for pay.

Choosing the Twelve Apostles

The day after the miracles at Capernaum, Jesus sought solitude, slipping away before daybreak to a lonely place. According to Mark, when Simon Peter and some friends found him and suggested to him that the crowds wanted him back, Jesus refused. "Let us go on to the next towns, that I may preach there also;" he explained, "for that is why I came out."

As that remark suggests, it was time for Jesus to gather a core of followers. Concentrating on the province of Galilee, where barely 300,000 people lived in an area of about 1,500 square miles, Jesus decided to choose 12 of his disciples to be Apostles, whom he could send out as principal emissaries of his work. (The word *Apostle* is from the Greek meaning "to send.") The number of the Apostles corresponded to the number of the tribes of Israel, perhaps emphasizing that the mission was directed first toward a renewal of the people of Israel.

On the whole, the Apostles were of Jesus' social class—poor compared to the upper classes of society but not impoverished, being skilled at some trade or craft. These men committed themselves to Jesus as other men had traditionally decided to follow other Jewish teachers. Students of a respected teacher were expected to learn as much from his actions as from his words, but they were also expected to retain his teachings as completely "as a lime-washed cistern, which does not let one drop of water escape."

There were at least two major differences, however, between following Jesus and becoming apprenticed to a traditional teacher. First of all, the Apostles were themselves *chosen*, unlike students of other teachers, who had been enjoined by the Torah to "choose a teacher." Second, Jesus did not base his teaching upon rigorous explication of the Torah or gain his position from formal education with an expert in the study of Jewish Scripture. Rather, he believed his authority derived from his ability to interpret God's will directly. This was a fundamental difference, and it was, to many traditional believers, the most troubling.

But the task before the Twelve Apostles was not merely theoretical. These men would have to put aside the pleasures of the world, giving second place

to their livelihood, family ties, marriage, and personal possessions. In the end they would share the dangers, privation, and humiliation that resulted from their loyalty to Jesus.

At the time the Twelve were chosen by Jesus, there was a sense of joy and impending victory in the air. The enthusiastic crowds grew, seeking out Jesus wherever he went. Jesus had many disciples in addition to his specially chosen Twelve, and surprisingly, given the customs of the times, a considerable number of them were women. Luke 8:2–3 states that the financial support for the travels of Jesus and his Twelve Apostles came from a group of women that included Joanna, who was the wife of Herod Antipas' steward; Susanna; and Mary Magdalene, from whom Jesus had cast out seven demons. (Although tradition holds that Mary Magdalene was the sinner who washed Jesus' feet with her tears and dried them with her hair, there is no evidence to support this; they may have been two different women.) In Mark 15:40–41 we are told that a group of women followed Jesus throughout Galilee and later accompanied him to Jerusalem. Mark names Mary Magdalene, Mary the mother of James the younger and of Joses, and Salome. For a teacher of the time to have women followers was unheard of, and it points to the distinctive character of Jesus' ministry.

Visit to Nazareth

At some point in his Galilean ministry (the Gospels place it at different times), Jesus visited Nazareth, where he had been brought up. Fame had surely preceded him, for we know that the rumor mills of Palestine were tireless and efficient instruments, and

A shaded pool fed by a strong spring elicits an atmosphere of peace and serenity in the fishing village of Bethsaida. The Apostles Philip, Andrew, and Peter came from Bethsaida, and Jesus taught and performed miracles there.

The Twelve Apostles

"In these days he went out to the mountain to pray; and all night he continued in prayer to God. And when it was day, he called his disciples, and chose from them twelve, whom he named apostles" (Luke 6:12–13). Although a diverse group, the Twelve were strongly united in their love of Jesus and, ultimately (except for Judas Iscariot), in their dedication to carrying his message to all mankind. They were as follows:

Peter. Simon, the Galilean fisherman, received the name *Peter*, "the Rock," from Jesus. In spite of that name, the Gospels seem to stress his impulsiveness. He was quick to declare his faith in Jesus, but during Jesus' trial he denied knowing him three times. In the new church, Peter worked particularly among the Jews while Paul worked with the Gentiles. According to tradition, Peter was crucified upside down in Nero's Rome.

Andrew. Peter's brother Andrew was also a fisherman. The brothers came from the town of Bethsaida. Tradition holds that Andrew preached in Scythia, and was put to death on an X-shaped (Saint Andrew's) cross.

James the son of Zebedee. A fisherman, James left his trade with his brother John to follow Jesus. When some Samaritan villagers refused Jesus hospitality, James and John asked Jesus if they could call down fire from heaven upon the village. According to Mark 3:17, Jesus named them "sons of thunder." Along with Peter, James and John were Jesus' closest disciples. James was probably the first Apostle to die for his faith; he was beheaded by Herod Agrippa about A.D. 44.

John. James's brother John may be the disciple "whom Jesus loved," according to the Gospel of John, and the one to whom the crucified Jesus entrusted the care of his mother. Paul called John one of the "pillars" of the church in Jerusalem, and he was probably the author of or the source for the Gospel and the Epistles of John, but he probably did not write Revelation, as was long supposed. According to some traditions, he lived to a very old age.

Philip. Like Peter and Andrew, Philip was from the town of Bethsaida. At the Last Supper he asked Jesus to "show us the Father," to which Jesus replied, "He who has seen me has seen the Father." According to tradition, in his later life Philip preached in various parts of the world.

Bartholomew. The Apostle named Bartholomew in Matthew, Mark, and Luke may be the same as Nathanael in the Gospel of John. Some scholars believe that Bartholomew ("son of Thalmai") was Nathanael's surname. According to John, Philip told Nathanael that Jesus was the one about whom Moses and the prophets had written. Nathanael responded, "Can anything good come out of Nazareth?" According to one tradition, Bartholomew brought the Gospel to India and to Greater Armenia, where he was flayed alive and beheaded.

Matthew. The tax collector Matthew left his work when Jesus passed by his office at Capernaum one day and said, "Follow me." Like other Jews who collected taxes for the Romans, Matthew probably earned the contempt of his fellows. An alternate name, Levi, is given for this Apostle in the Gospels of Mark and Luke. While feasting in his house, Jesus was criticized for associating with "tax collectors and sinners," but responded with "I came not to call the righteous, but sinners." Matthew is traditionally thought to be writer of the Gospel bearing his name.

Thomas. Called the Twin in the Gospel of John, Thomas was eager to follow Jesus to Judea even if he had to die with him, but he believed that Jesus had risen from the dead only after seeing him in person. According to tradition, Thomas brought the gospel to India, where he was martyred.

James the son of Alphaeus. This James may be James the younger of Mark 15:40, to distinguish him from the brother of John. A rather dubious tradition identifies him with "James the Lord's brother" (Galatians 1:19), who succeeded Peter as leader of the Christians in Jerusalem and was stoned to death in A.D. 62.

Simon the Zealot. Nothing is said of Simon in Scripture other than that he was one of the Twelve. The epithet after Simon's name indicates that he was zealous for the Jewish law. He may even have been a member of a Zealot band of Jews, who fought Roman rule. In Matthew and Mark he is called Simon the Cananaean, from the Aramaic word meaning "Zealot."

Judas the son of James. This Judas (sometimes called Jude) is probably the Thaddaeus of the Gospels of Matthew and Mark, which may have used the Apostle's surname to avoid confusing him with Judas Iscariot. In the Gospel of John, Judas asked Jesus at the Last Supper, why he did not manifest himself to the rest of the world as he had to his disciples. He is closely linked to Simon the Zealot in tradition, and both supposedly went to Persia to preach and were martyred there.

Judas Iscariot. The surname of Judas the traitor may mean "man of Kerioth," which would indicate that he was probably the only non-Galilean Apostle (Kerioth is in Judea). Judas was the treasurer for the group and, according to the Gospel of John, a dishonest one. He betrayed Jesus for money with a kiss. According to Matthew, when it was too late, Judas tried to get Jesus released, then in despair hanged himself. According to Acts 1:18, Judas bought a field with his blood money, "and falling headlong he burst open in the middle and all his bowels gushed out."

apparently the tales about the local boy had aroused astonishment and skepticism born of familiarity. Even as he spoke at the local synagogue, Matthew 13:55–56 relates, some citizens grumbled to one other: "Is not this the carpenter's son? Is not his mother called Mary? And are not his brothers James and Joseph and Simon and Judas? And are not all his sisters with us? Where then did this man get all this?" Their very astonishment at the teachings of one they thought they knew so well generated ill will among the villagers and ultimately resulted in their taking offense. Jesus departed, marveling at their unbelief. In Luke's version of this incident, the townspeople were so filled with wrath that they rose up in a mob and tried to cast him off a cliff at the edge of town. (The story is perhaps reminiscent of how a priest cast the scapegoat over a cliff each Yom Kippur in atonement for the sins committed by the people during the year.)

Jesus was never again to return to the dusty streets and byways of his childhood. Nazareth was to become an object lesson, a warning to all men—forever associated with Jesus' poignant remark, "A prophet is not without honor, except in his own country, and among his own kin, and in his own house."

Jesus' family

And what of his own house? Mary is scarcely mentioned in the accounts of Jesus' ministry. Tradition assumes that Joseph died before it began. The "brothers" and "sisters" mentioned by the Nazarenes in the synagogue are not discussed at length in the narrative. Some believe that Mary remained a virgin all her life and that these were cousins or more distant relatives. There was no separate word in Hebrew to distinguish between siblings and other family members, they point out. Others believe that Jesus indeed had younger siblings. Was there conflict between Jesus and at least some members of his family? It is possible that his family joined others who tried to stop Jesus' work because, as Mark reports, he was "beside himself." In spite of such brief glimpses of Jesus' family, the emphasis of the Gospels is so completely on Jesus himself that we simply do not know, for example, what role Mary played in these years until she is glimpsed again at her son's death.

Sermon on the Mount

Jesus continued to teach, leaving his work only to make pilgrimages to Jerusalem and to visit Tyre and Sidon and Caesarea Philippi—possibly to rest from the Galilean heat or retreat temporarily in the face of opposition to his ministry. For Jesus' message frightened the authorities as much as it found favor with the common people. Why? As events were to prove, neither adherents nor detractors could agree on what Jesus was teaching. The debate continues to this day.

The profound and searching sayings that make up the Sermon on the Mount show both the power and the problematic character of Jesus' teaching. Few scholars, however, believe that these sayings constituted one specific sermon to the people at large. Matthew indicates that they were directed primarily to the disciples. Certainly, the passages collected by Matthew, nearly four times longer than those in Luke's account (referred to as the Sermon on the Plain), would have been all but overpowering at first hearing for members of a huge crowd assembled in the open air.

Whatever the actual historical setting, which some associate with a prominent hill overlooking the Sea of Galilee, the Sermon on the Mount is thought to sum up Jesus' teaching. New interpretations have arisen in generation after generation of Christians, but usually emphasis falls on at least three sections, which awaken and strengthen the individual conscience and suggest an example that requires faith and spiritual determination to follow.

First come the Beatitudes, those brief blessings that seem so paradoxical when first encountered in Luke. "Blessed are you poor, for yours is the kingdom of God.

Jesus said to his disciples: "And why are you anxious about clothing? Consider the lilies of the field, how they grow; they neither toil nor spin; yet I tell you, even Solomon in all his glory was not arrayed like one of these. But if God so clothes the grass of the field, which today is alive and tomorrow is thrown into the oven, will he not much more clothe you, O men of little faith?" Matthew 6:28–30. Here "lilies" may refer to the crown anemones (third from left) that carpeted Palestine's hillsides each spring. In the course of his teaching, Jesus also mentioned various other plants of the area, ranging from the humble thistle (above) to such aromatic herbs as dill (next in line) and the colorful rue (far right), used in medicine and cookery.

Blessed are you that hunger now, for you shall be satisfied" (Luke 6:20–21). Equally emphatic are the maledictions: "Woe to you that are full now, for you shall hunger. Woe to you that laugh now, for you shall mourn and weep" (Luke 6:25). As set down by Matthew, the Beatitudes could be seen as more obviously open to spiritual interpretation than in Luke's version—for example, "Blessed are the poor in spirit. . . . Blessed are the meek, for they shall inherit the earth" (Matthew 5:3, 5). But each Gospel has retained the spirit of paradox: the kingdom of God, as explained by Jesus, is the reverse of the world as it appears to the average person. The Beatitudes point to the mind and spirit as they will become when a person fully accepts God's will in his life.

Lest this provocative message be misinterpreted, Jesus immediately adds that he is fulfilling God's law: "Think not that I have come to abolish the law and the prophets; I have come not to abolish them but to fulfil them." His interpretation is at once penetrating and demanding; it brings thoughts under the same rigorous scrutiny that the law had applied to actions. Yes, the law forbade killing, but Jesus also warned against the kind of anger that was murder of the heart. The law punished adultery; Jesus judged lustful thoughts to be equally sinful.

The sayings of Jesus forced those who took him seriously to rethink their most basic reactions. These sayings are more than advice for specific situations. They are little lightning bolts that break up comfortable patterns of thought and behavior: "But if any one strikes you on the right cheek, turn to him the other also." And "Love your enemies and pray for those who persecute you." The goal of discipleship—perhaps strictly unattainable in the human sphere but always to be diligently pursued—was to "be perfect, as your heavenly Father is perfect."

Nor was a person to boast about spiritual accomplishment or crave public approval for decent actions. Even prayer required the proper attitude of humility, as can be seen in the model Jesus provided, known today as the Lord's Prayer.

Jesus also warned his listeners against devoting their lives to accumulating material goods rather than the authentic treasures of service and justice. "You cannot serve God and mammon," he warned; the Semitic word *mammon* means "riches." It is better to trust in the bounty of God, who gives us what we need: "Look at the birds of the air: they neither sow nor reap nor gather into barns, and yet your heavenly Father feeds them. Are you not of more value than they? And which of you by being anxious can add one cubit to his span of life?" (Matthew 6:26–27). Jesus urged his listeners to attend rather to the tasks of God's kingdom and of justice, "and all these things shall be yours as well."

The Sermon on the Mount goes on to give injunctions that define godly action. The most famous is the Golden Rule: "So whatever you wish that men would do to you, do so to them" (Matthew 7:12). Salvation, Jesus makes clear, will be granted only to those who do the will of his Father in heaven.

Jesus ended with a parable. Those who heed his words will be like a man wise enough to build his house on a foundation of solid rock. It will survive a severe storm. But those who hear his words yet fail to act upon them are like a man foolish enough to build his house on sand. It will collapse in a tempest.

Jesus' use of parables

Throughout his ministry, Jesus often spoke to his audiences in parables that were much like the ones used in the synagogue schools to explore the deeper meanings of Scripture. Jesus' parables include a wide range of metaphors and comparisons that vary from a few words to extended stories. For many listeners, no doubt, the stories were merely stories, but for those in Jesus' circle they became revelations that pushed them to examine their understanding of God and themselves.

One can perhaps discern the importance of the parables for Jesus by thinking of his treatment of so basic a theme as the "kingdom of God." So far as the Gospels reveal, Jesus never said in a simple statement exactly what he meant by that all-important phrase. Rather he trusted in a variety of parables to bring his followers to a grasp of what the "kingdom" was and was to be, including the parables recounted in Matthew 13:44–46. "The kingdom of heaven is like treasure hidden in a field, which a man found and covered up; then in his joy he goes and sells all that he has and buys that field. Again, the kingdom of heaven is like a merchant in search of fine pearls, who, on finding one pearl of great value, went and sold all that he had and bought it." It is of course beside the point to ask whether the discoverer of the treasure should have notified the owners of its exis-

The loaves and fishes on which Jesus fed the multitudes were staples of the Galilean diet. Fields of rippling barley (left)—the poor man's wheat—were a common sight; the Sea of Galilee supplied ample quantities of many types of freshwater fish. The miracle of the loaves and fishes may have taken place at Tabgha, near Capernaum, where a sixth-century A.D. mosaic of two fish and a bread basket (above) celebrated the event.

tence. Jesus is not really talking about fields and pearls but of finding a supreme value in life that reverses the past (he sells all) and sets the person on a new course (he buys with joy).

Death of John the Baptist

During the early part of Jesus' ministry, John the Baptist had been arrested by Herod Antipas, who saw him as a threat, and lay moldering in a prison at the fortress of Machaerus east of the Dead Sea. At one point, the imprisoned man's faith seemed to waver, or perhaps he had been listening to his followers, who felt that Jesus' actions were questionable. (Jesus did not require his disciples to fast, for example, as John did.) We don't really know John's motives, but he was able, even from his prison cell, to send two of his followers to find Jesus in Galilee and confront him with the sharp query, "Are you he who is to come, or shall we look for another?"

The question may have arisen from the fundamentally different character of Jesus' ministry from that of John the Baptist. John was a fiercely ascetic figure of great eloquence, who called people into the wilderness to be baptized as a sign of the coming of God's judgment. He was neither "a reed shaken by the wind" nor "a man clothed in soft clothing," to use Jesus' words, but a prophet "and more than a prophet."

Although Jesus saw his own ministry as intimately connected with John's, he also knew that he had chosen a different way to carry out that ministry. In Luke 7:33–35, he is reported as saying, "John the Baptist has come eating no bread and drinking no wine; and you say, 'He has a demon.' The Son of man has come eating and drinking; and you say, 'Behold, a glutton and a drunkard, a friend of tax collectors and sinners!' Yet wisdom is justified by all her children." Rather than calling people into the wilderness to attain ascetic purity, Jesus took his place in the cities and towns and mixed with people who by no stretch of the imagination could be counted as keepers of God's law—with all those who were outcast, in need, and uncared for. It took considerable vision for anyone to imagine Jesus as the one "who is to come."

As reported in Luke 7:22–23, Jesus returned a mild answer to John the Baptist's question: "Go and tell John what you have seen and heard," he said; "the blind receive their sight, the lame walk, lepers are cleansed, and the deaf hear, the dead are raised up, the poor have good news preached to them. And blessed is he who takes no offense at me."

John suffered imprisonment for 10 months. Then, according to Josephus, Herod Antipas had him killed, claiming he was a rebel leader. Jesus might have come under similar suspicion, as his extraordinary popularity might seem to put him as well as John into a position of rebelling against Herod's authority.

The Gospels of Matthew and Mark, however, tell a more vivid and gripping tale of John the Baptist. In these versions, Herod's wife Herodias loathed John for denouncing her as an adulteress. During a banquet, her beautiful daughter, Salome, danced before Herod. Tradition holds that the young woman executed one of the exotic dances long associated with the nomadic cultures of the Middle East, giving a performance of agility and grace bathed in subtle eroticism. Charmed, Herod swore an oath to give her anything she liked. At her mother's urging, according to Matthew 14:8, Salome replied, "Give me the head of John the Baptist here on a platter." Remorsefully, Herod kept to his oath.

Certainly, the death of John the Baptist was a shock. The news may even have caused Jesus to seek refuge briefly in Herod Philip's territory.

Miracle of the loaves and fishes

It is after John's death that Matthew, Luke, and Mark place Jesus' miracle of the loaves and fishes. The Gospel of John locates it shortly before Pass-

In Jesus' footsteps

During his lifetime, Jesus traveled throughout Palestine. The specific places often associated with his life are shown on the accompanying map.

Galilee. Region where Jesus grew up and did much of the work of his ministry.

Sea of Galilee. Where Jesus called Peter and others to become "fishers of men." He also taught from a boat anchored offshore, calmed a storm, and walked on water. After his resurrection, Jesus appeared to the Apostles who were fishing on the lake.

Bethsaida. A prosperous fishing village, home of Peter, Andrew, and Philip, where Jesus cured a blind man.

Capernaum. Center of Jesus' Galilean ministry. He also healed many people here, including Peter's mother-in-law, the centurion's servant, and a paralytic.

Gennesaret. Place where after feeding the 5,000 and walking on water, Jesus came and the people brought their sick to be healed.

Cana. Site of the first miracle, when Jesus turned water into wine.

Nazareth. Jesus' boyhood home. He was rejected by the people when he returned to teach in a synagogue.

Mount Tabor. Possibly the "high mountain apart," site of Jesus' transfiguration.

Nain. Place where Jesus raised a widow's son from the dead.

Decapolis. Region through which Jesus passed, teaching and healing.

Samaria. Region where the people of one town refused Jesus hospitality.

Sychar. Where Jesus met the Samaritan woman at the well.

Jordan River. Traditional site of Jesus' baptism.

Perea. Region where Jesus retreated just before Lazarus' death.

Judea. Region including the great city of Jerusalem. Jesus ended his time on earth here.

Jericho. Desert town where the rich tax collector Zacchaeus met Jesus and repented. Nearby, Jesus cured the beggar Bartimaeus of blindness.

Emmaus. Place where, after his resurrection, Jesus stopped with two disciples and revealed his identity to them.

Jerusalem. The scene of many events in Jesus' life. He was presented at the Temple here in infancy, he impressed the teachers in the Temple at the age of 12, he taught here, worked miracles, parried with his enemies, and was condemned to death and crucified. A separate map of the events of his final day appears on page 258.

Mount of Olives. Where Jesus spoke privately to his disciples of his Second Coming. Also, site of the ascension.

Bethany. Home of Lazarus, Martha, and Mary. After Lazarus' death, Jesus returned and brought his friend back to life. Jesus was anointed at the house of Simon the leper.

Bethlehem. Jesus' birthplace. As far as we know, Jesus never returned here.

over. Jesus had sought respite from the constant pressure of the crowds in Capernaum by joining some disciples in a boat and sailing off to a lonely place. As the craft approached the shore, however, the people were already waiting.

The day started like so many others with Jesus teaching and healing the sick. We can surmise that the day was vitally engrossing for all, because evening drew near before anyone recognized that there was a problem. Thousands of people who had surged out into the countryside to hear Jesus were hungry and the only provisions were a paltry five barley loaves and two fish. This hardly seemed sufficient, but Jesus told the Twelve to seat all the people. Then, he blessed the food and broke the loaves before he passed them along to the hungry. Some 5,000 people were fed and the leftovers filled 12 baskets. This astonishing story has been considered by some to be a parable that demonstrates that God, having created all varieties of creatures in the world, continues to sustain them.

Sending out the disciples

The miracle of the loaves and fishes also suggests that the disciples had been learning the practical tasks of their role, including the ability to handle crowds. For soon they were assigned more challenging duties. Jesus ordered them to set out in pairs across the land to spread the word that all should repent because the kingdom of God was at hand. Granted the power to heal the sick and exorcise demons, these followers were being given a kind of training.

Jesus was very precise in one aspect of his instructions. Usually, a traveler on the road in those days took along changes of clothes and sandals, a staff,

Sandals have been worn in the Holy Land since time immemorial, and those worn by Jesus' disciples were probably similar to the leather one shown above. Only people in mourning and the very poor went barefoot.

food, and money. But, according to Mark, Jesus' disciples were enjoined from taking anything at all but a walking staff and the sandals and tunic they were wearing. In Matthew's account, even the staff and sandals are excluded; they were to travel with no resources except the message they preached. They were to accept the first hospitality offered when they arrived in a new town, and if they were rejected, they were to move on, and "when you leave that town shake off the dust from your feet as a testimony against them."

We do not know how this mission was received, but we can infer that it made a mark because of Herod Antipas' increasing concern about Jesus, whom he had never heard speak or met. Apparently, Herod heard rumors that this increasingly popular leader was John the Baptist, risen from the dead to taunt him. At the very least, it was the same problem all over again. Though very different from John the Baptist in many ways, both Jesus and his disciples, like John, called Israel to repentance and pointed to the demands of living as part of God's kingdom rather than Herod's tetrarchy. Herod knew well the political impact that such a message could have, since practically every political movement in Israel had religious roots. The image of the just and powerful rule of God carried with it an inevitable criticism of the inept and often ruthless patterns of human rule that the Galileans knew.

Jesus as Messiah

As time went on, Jesus began to turn his attention more to his inner circle since they, as well as his enemies, had difficulty in accepting his challenge to their common values. He may even have doubted his success with those closest to him. Did they really know who he was? Several times he had rejected or ignored their eagerness to hail him as the Messiah. Would they remain loyal when no earthly kingdom was established, no caesar or Herod deposed? Were they prepared for the suffering and humiliation to come?

In one of the most moving episodes of the New Testament, Jesus took his disciples apart for a private discussion outside of Galilee in the district of Caesarea Philippi. Perhaps it was one of their first encounters after the Apostles' mission, for the conversation begins in the nature of a progress report. According to Matthew 16:13, Jesus asked, "Who do men say that the Son of man is?" (In Mark 8:27, he asks more pointedly, "Who do men say that I am?") Oddly, considering the expectations of the people and the beliefs on the part of some of the disciples that he was the deliverer, no one was calling Jesus the Messiah. It was rumored that he was John the Baptist, Elijah, Jeremiah, or one of the other prophets. Evidently, most of his followers recognized his teaching within the prophetic tradition.

At Capernaum Jesus most likely lived in the rough stone house of his disciple Peter, where his closest followers would meet, as here, to share meals and take instruction. Peter, known for his impulsiveness, sits at the far left in this imaginary rendering, with his brother Andrew beside him. John and his brother James recline near the dinner bowl, while the highly dedicated but occasionally skeptical Thomas sits at Jesus' right hand.

The domelike, 1,930-foot summit of Mount Tabor has long been identified as the place where Jesus' disciples witnessed his astonishing transfiguration. Even though the Gospels do not name the site, the description of it as a "high mountain apart" suggested Mount Tabor to early pilgrims. By the sixth century A.D. three churches had been built here, one for each of the booths Peter wished to build. Today a Franciscan church marks the traditional spot of the transfiguration.

Then Jesus focused on the views of the Apostles themselves: "But who do you say that I am?" According to Matthew 16:16, Peter spoke up immediately, making a brief yet eloquent confession of faith in Jesus. "You are the Christ, the Son of the living God," he answered. (The title *Christ* is derived from the Greek for "anointed one" and is a synonym for the Hebrew designation "Messiah.") Jesus called Peter "blessed" in knowing this truth, for it could only have been revealed by God. Then playing upon the meaning of the name *Peter* ("rock"), Jesus continued, "And I tell you, you are Peter, and on this rock I will build my church, and the powers of death shall not prevail against it. I will give you the keys of the kingdom of heaven, and whatever you bind on earth shall be bound in heaven, and whatever you loose on earth shall be loosed in heaven." Jesus then told the disciples to keep his identity secret for the time being.

What was lacking in Peter's confession is revealed in the following words of the Gospel: "From that time Jesus began to show his disciples that he must go to Jerusalem and suffer . . . and be killed, and on the third day be raised" (Matthew 16:21). Associating the idea of the Messiah with suffering and death was foreign to the disciples, and Peter forthrightly rebuked Jesus for suggesting such a link. Jesus, however, saw Peter's rebuke as a temptation to elude his mission. "Get behind me, Satan!" he commanded, in a phrase reminiscent of the temptations in the desert. Jesus then told his disciples, "If any man would come after me, let him deny himself and take up his cross and follow me."

Transfiguration of Jesus

About a week later, Matthew tells us, an even more select group experienced a sign that bolstered the faith that Peter had already expressed, perhaps for all. On that occasion, Jesus led Peter, James, and John up a "high mountain apart." As Jesus stood before them and prayed, Matthew reports, his physical aspect underwent an astonishing transformation. His face shone like the sun; his clothing became as white as light. Suddenly, Matthew, Mark, and Luke all tell us, the three disciples discerned two figures talking to Jesus—Moses, who had brought God's law to the Hebrews, and Elijah, the archetypal Old Testament prophet.

Impetuous Peter offered to build booths for the three—he may have been thinking of the temporary rooftop shelters built during the Festival of Succoth. But, while he was still talking, according to Matthew 17:5, "a bright cloud overshadowed them, and a voice from the cloud said, 'This is my beloved Son, with whom I am well pleased; listen to him.' " The cloud passed, the vision dissipated. Again Jesus told the Apostles to keep the event secret, but this time "until the Son of man is raised from the dead." The disciples had no idea what he could possibly mean.

Traveling to Jerusalem

Soon afterward, Jesus left the Galilean region for good. It had been the scene of his greatest sermons and most remarkable miracles, but it was almost time for a new and final confrontation. So purposely, according to Luke, "he set his face to go to Jerusalem," for he believed that a prophet must "perish" only there. From the bountiful Galilee he led his disciples to rocky Judea, where the hearts of those who opposed him would prove to be as stonily unyielding as the inhospitable land. We catch a glimpse of the drama of the journey in Mark 10:32: "And they were on the road, going up to Jerusalem, and Jesus was walking ahead of them; and they were amazed, and those who followed were afraid." Palpable fear was in the air, but Jesus' decisive stride carried the tense band forward—into danger.

Along the road, however, Jesus continued to teach, as crowds gathered wherever he appeared. At one point some children were brought up so that Jesus might touch them. When the disciples tried to intervene, Jesus was indignant, according to Mark, and said to them, "Let the children come to me, do not hinder them; for to such belongs the kingdom of God. Truly, I say to you, whoever does not receive the kingdom of God like a child shall not enter it." And Jesus picked up the children and blessed them.

Before Jesus could move on, a young man ran up to him and fell on his knees, asking what he must do to gain eternal life. According to Mark, when Jesus told him to keep the Commandments, the man said that he always had. "And Jesus looking upon him loved him, and said to him, 'You lack one thing; go, sell what you have, and give to the poor, and you will have treasure in heaven; and come, follow me.' " But the young man went away sorrowful, for he had many possessions. Jesus looked about him and said to his disciples, "It is easier for a camel to go through the eye of a needle than for a rich man to enter the kingdom of God."

When they heard this, Jesus' disciples were distressed and asked their teacher, who then could be saved. Jesus assured them, "With men it is impossible, but not with God; for all things are possible with God." Upon being reminded by Peter that his disciples had given up everything and followed him, Jesus answered that "there is no one who has left house or brothers or sisters or mother or father or children or lands, for my sake and for the gospel, who will not receive a hundredfold now in this time, houses and brothers and sisters and mothers and children and lands, with persecutions, and in the age to come eternal life. But many that are first will be last, and the last first."

Jesus in Jerusalem

It may be that, as John suggests, Jesus arrived in Jerusalem just before the Feast of Succoth, in the autumn; or if we follow the chronology of the other Gospels, in the spring, shortly before Passover. In any event, he made himself highly visible and came into open conflict with the Pharisees and Sadducees.

Jesus' triumphal Palm Sunday entry into Jerusalem may have taken him through the Golden Gate in the city's east wall. It appears in the foreground above, overlooking the Kidron Valley and the Tomb of Absalom at the valley's base. The gate's twin arches are shown in close-up at right.

It was a period of contention, John tells us. People asked, "How is it that this man has learning, when he has never studied?" (Jesus seems never to have attached himself to a great teacher, or sage, the usual path to becoming a sage oneself.) They wanted a clear answer: "If you are the Christ, tell us plainly." And Jesus' impact alarmed the authorities, as we see in a comment reported by John: "Is not this the man whom they seek to kill? And here he is, speaking openly, and they say nothing to him! Can it be that the authorities really know that this is the Christ?" Apparently, on one occasion, Temple guards sent by the chief priests and Pharisees to arrest Jesus came back empty-handed—even they had been swayed by his words.

A *woman taken in adultery and a blind man*

Many times the Pharisees and scribes tried to trick Jesus into self-condemning statements or into betraying ignorance of ancient law. Not only did they never succeed, according to the Gospels, but Jesus was always able to turn the debate into a positive lesson. Nor did he ever forget the human dimension, as is demonstrated in the story, told in John 8:1–11, of a woman taken in adultery.

One day, while Jesus was teaching in the Temple, some scribes and Pharisees brought a woman to him. To trap Jesus, they challenged him: "Teacher, this woman has been caught in the act of adultery. Now in the law Moses commanded us to stone such. What do you say about her?" Jesus was known as one who befriended such sinners, but if he recommended the woman be set free, he would be defying the law.

Silently Jesus turned aside, bent down, and began writing on the ground with his finger. (Some later texts explain that he wrote on the ground "the sins of each of them.") Finally, Jesus stood up, directed his gaze toward them, and answered, "Let him who is without sin among you be the first to throw a stone at her." Unable to reply, one by one the accusers

and hangers-on slipped away. It was an ingenious reply; it was, moreover, the reply of a man who could interpret the principles of law with compassion for the individual offender. When Jesus looked up from his writing, he saw the woman standing alone, no doubt stunned by this unexpected rescue from a painful death.

"Woman, where are they?" Jesus asked. "Has no one condemned you?"

"No one, Lord."

"Neither do I condemn you," he told her, "go, and do not sin again."

On such occasions, Jesus' detractors had no case against him. But there were other opportunities, often centering on Jesus' refusal to keep the rest ordained for the Sabbath day by the Ten Commandments as applied by the scribes and Pharisees. One Sabbath day, Jesus passed a beggar who had been blind from birth. Jesus spat on the ground, made a paste of the spit and the clay, smoothed the mixture over the beggar's eyes, and told him to wash it off in the Pool of Siloam. Following Jesus' instructions, the beggar found his sight restored and rushed to spread the joy of his cure. Word soon reached the Pharisees, who hounded the bewildered man. To them, a cure that was the result of a violation of God's command could not be accepted—Jesus had worked on the holy day. For the Gospel of John, the contrast between the demands of tradition and concern for real human need could hardly be more stark. The Pharisees saw the cure as an act of defiance, not as reinterpretation of the law; they considered Jesus a heretic, not a healer with a divine mission.

Apparently, these were days of conflicting views of Jesus. Some learned men were willing to discuss ideas with him, while others hatched plots against him. Many people were drawn to him, but others were angered by him. Some accused him of being possessed by the devil; otherwise, they thought, he would not be able to perform the miracles. Others denounced him to Herod Antipas, hoping the ruler would intervene. At least once, according to John, Jesus' words in the Temple caused some listeners to pick up stones to throw at him.

Yet all during this tumultuous year Jesus continued to teach, until, for the last time, he felt the need to take a spiritual retreat. For some time, according to John, he crossed over the Jordan and stayed in Perea, the district east of Jerusalem.

Raising of Lazarus

Then, John reports, news came that his friend Lazarus, the brother of Martha and Mary, was ill, and two days later Jesus said to his disciples, "Let us go into Judea again." His disciples expressed fear that Jesus would be stoned if he returned. Probably only Jesus' popularity with the common people had saved his life in Jerusalem before; perhaps his opponents had been gathering strength while he was away from the city. But Jesus told the disciples that his friend Lazarus was dead and that he must go to him. For once, Peter was not the first to speak up. It was Thomas, too often ridiculed in history as the doubter of the resurrection, who spoke in support of the decision: "Let us also go," he said to the other disciples, when they wavered, "that we may die with him."

They all set out for the village of Bethany, a small settlement just at the edge of the Judean desert on the eastern slope of the Mount of Olives. When they reached the little town, mourners had gathered to comfort the grieving sisters. Martha was able to greet Jesus, but Mary was so distraught she had to be encouraged to come outside the house and go to Jesus, where she fell at his feet. Jesus also wept; then he led everyone to the tomb.

One can imagine the friends and relatives approaching the place, perhaps with the loud wails of mourning still resounding in their ears. The entrance of the tomb was blocked by a large stone. Surely, those present were astounded when Jesus

ordered, "Take away the stone." Martha, the practical sister, objected that Lazarus had been dead for four days and there would be an odor. The body, according to traditional practice, had been washed in scented oils and wrapped in fine linen, but the Jews did not embalm the dead. Nonetheless, Jesus insisted. After praying to God, he shouted, "Lazarus, come out." Still swathed in his linen grave clothes, the man stumbled into the light. It was the fulfillment of Jesus' promise to Martha that, if she believed, she would "see the glory of God."

Soon afterward, Jesus and the disciples went to Ephraim, an isolated hill town about 12 miles northeast of Jerusalem. Meanwhile, according to John, the raising of Lazarus set off an explosion of anger in the Sanhedrin. Such miracles would seduce the people to follow this leader into rebellion, it was feared, and provoke the intervention of the Romans. As the high priest, Caiaphas, summed it up: " . . . it is expedient for you that one man should die for the people, and that the whole nation should not perish." At this point, prerogatives of power and concern for the public order seemed to be the overriding issues.

The decision was made to bring about Jesus' death with due speed. According to John, orders were given by the chief priests and Pharisees that anyone knowing Jesus' whereabouts should notify them immediately so that they could arrest him. It probably seemed obvious to Temple officials that a leader like Jesus would not neglect the opportunity to appear in the city as the multitudes arrived for Passover.

As these steps were being taken, Jesus was preparing his disciples for the events to come. According to Luke 18:31–33, he was very explicit: "Behold, we are going up to Jerusalem, and everything that is written of the Son of man by the prophets will be accomplished. For he will be delivered to the Gentiles, and will be mocked and shamefully treated and spit upon; they will scourge him and kill him, and on the third day he will rise." The mystery of this

statement was heightened by Jesus' enigmatic self-designation, "Son of man." The meaning of the term is still debated by believers today. It might have referred to an account of the vision in the Book of Daniel about a heavenly figure who would be given "everlasting dominion." It might have been used to dispel people's preconceived notions about a Messiah. Often Jesus used the term "Son of man" when speaking of the suffering he would endure. It seems to be a succinct way of conveying the idea of a suffering Messiah.

Triumphal entry into Jerusalem

Six days before Passover, Jesus returned to Bethany, where, John tells us, crowds of Jews came to see both him and Lazarus. According to Matthew, Jesus ordered two of his disciples to bring him an ass from Bethphage, a nearby settlement of Galileans. Word

The stones of Jerusalem and its suburbs hold poignant reminders of Jesus' great deeds. At the Pool of Bethesda (top right), a Roman-style bath that once stood just north of the city, Jesus healed a paralyzed man, commanding him to "Rise, take up your pallet, and walk." In Bethany, to the east, he raised Lazarus from the dead, ordering the tomb (possibly the one shown at right) to be opened, and declaring, "I am the resurrection and the life." While performing these acts of grace, Jesus also graciously received homage from others. The ruin shown above, also in Bethany, may have been the house of Simon the leper, where a woman anointed his head with costly ointment.

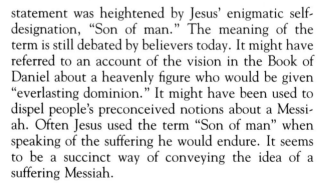

The tribute money each Roman subject owed the state was paid in coins like the silver denarius shown above, which is stamped with the profile of Tiberius Caesar; it was worth a single day's wage. Various Jewish coins also circulated in Palestine, but because of God's commandment against graven images, none carried a human face.

spread to the crowds that were gathering in Jerusalem for Passover that Jesus was also coming.

The next day, exuberant throngs gathered along the road to the city gates. Some were strewing fresh-cut spring fronds of palm. Others were spreading their garments on the road. In the midst of this unbridled enthusiasm Jesus appeared riding on the ass. The gesture was clear and challenging to all the political authorities in Jerusalem. He was, according to Matthew, dramatizing the prophecy of a messiah's arrival suggested in Zechariah 9:9: "Lo, your king comes to you; triumphant and victorious is he, humble and riding on an ass."

The occasion was ebullient enough to alarm some of the Pharisees, for the roads leading to the holy city echoed with such delirious cries as "Hosanna! Blessed is he who comes in the name of the Lord! Blessed is the kingdom of our father David that is coming!" According to a ninth-century tradition, Jesus entered Jerusalem from the east through the Golden Gate, which leads directly to the Temple Mount.

Cleansing the Temple

The Gospel of Mark tells us Jesus went to the Temple after his triumphal entry into Jerusalem and looked around at everything. He probably saw all the merchants and money changers, who were present in larger numbers than usual and more actively recruiting business from the throngs who had come to celebrate Passover later in the week. Because it was already late, Mark tells us, Jesus went to Bethany with his Apostles for the night. But the anger at the excessive commerce he had seen going on within the Temple walls must have seethed inside him.

In the morning, on the return trip to Jerusalem, Jesus passed a fig tree, and because he was hungry, he looked for fruit on it. But it was not the fig season, and the tree bore only leaves. In his anger Jesus cursed the tree. And when they reached the Temple, he gave further vent to the anger that had been boiling in him since the day before. He began to drive out all those who sold or bought, and he turned over the tables of the money changers and the seats of those who sold pigeons for Temple offerings. And he said, "Is it not written, 'My house shall be called a house of prayer for all the nations'? But you have made it a den of robbers." The chief priests and scribes were particularly alarmed by all of this, but they were afraid that the people would turn on them if they arrested Jesus, so they secretly plotted against him and bided their time.

Jesus continued teaching in the Temple and returned to Bethany that night. The next morning, on his way back to Jerusalem, he passed the same fig tree he had previously cursed, and Peter pointed out that it had withered overnight. Jesus told Peter that if he had enough faith he could move mountains. "Whatever you ask in prayer," Jesus said, "believe that you have received it, and it will be yours. And whenever you stand praying, forgive, if you have anything against any one; so that your Father also who is in heaven may forgive you your trespasses."

A money changer counts his stack of coins in this third-century A.D. relief, while a customer prepares to negotiate a loan. Banking and currency transactions were open-air activities in Roman times, with the money changers setting up tables and displaying their wares like any other tradesmen.

"Render to Caesar"

The excitement surrounding Jesus' entry into Jerusalem seems to have petered out quickly. There was no great thunderclap of immediate change. Matthew and Luke tell us that Jesus returned to his practice of discoursing and debating in the Temple, while John reports that he was troubled and spoke of his rejection by the people of Israel. As before, there were attempts to trap him into self-incriminating statements. This was not merely a matter of having Jesus lose a debate. Though the conundrums posed by the Pharisees and scribes were sometimes sincere, they were often invitations to flirt with death.

In one instance, Jesus was asked if it was right that the Jews pay tribute money to Caesar, the oppressor and idolator. If Jesus agreed that it was, he would seem to support tyranny, a position that would undoubtedly anger the people. But if he condemned the tribute, he could be held accountable by the Romans for disloyalty. In reply, Jesus asked to see a coin used to pay the tax; his answer was all the more memorable because of its concrete nature. The silver denarius, a coin minted at Lyons in Gaul, would not be common in Palestine; it showed a portrait of the Emperor Tiberius. "Whose likeness and inscription is this?" asked Jesus. There was only one possible answer: "Caesar's." Jesus' conclusion dumbfounded his opponents; it was both politically and spiritually unexceptionable. "Render to Caesar the things that are Caesar's, and to God the things that are God's." Frustrated in their aims by replies of such disarming wit, long-time enemies united against Jesus; Pharisees, Sadducees, and Herodians all came after him. The die was cast.

Within the confines of the Temple, money changers exchanged foreign coins brought by overseas pilgrims for Jewish shekels. The shekel was needed to pay Temple dues and to purchase lambs and pigeons on sale there for use in sacrifices. Although the money changers and animal sellers performed a practical service, Jesus was angered by the commercialization of the sacred precincts of his "Father's house." According to John, he made a whip of cords and drove them out with it.

The Church of St. Mary of Zion in Jerusalem is traditionally accepted as the site of the house in which Jesus and his disciples celebrated the Last Supper. The actual location of the Last Supper has been the subject of much controversy, but after the Crusades, this shrine was built, and one of its rooms, the Cenaculum, was set aside to commemorate the event. The Gothic arches of the Cenaculum are typical of the architecture of the Middle Ages.

Betrayal and thoughts of the end

But it was from the inner circle that the most devastating betrayal came. Considered by some to be the most astute among the disciples in business matters, Judas Iscariot, who, John tells us, had acted as treasurer for the frugal group, secretly lost faith. Had he, perhaps like many in the joyful crowds that had welcomed Jesus into the city a few days earlier, become disillusioned because Jesus had not seized power? For a sum of money, according to Matthew, Judas agreed on Wednesday to help his teacher's enemies find their prey when the time was ripe. It is unlikely that the money was temptation enough, in itself. The 30 pieces of silver mentioned by Matthew was traditionally the price of a slave, but in Roman times it would only pay for a new tunic. Judas' true motives have been lost to history, but

perhaps his defection was a kind of barometer of the public mood in Jerusalem. As Passover approached, it seemed clear that the popular enthusiasm in support of Jesus had crested. Other forces were on the rise.

Even as danger grew, however, Jesus was reminding his disciples that things were not what they might seem. Yes, he would be killed and seem to be defeated, but a great destruction would follow. Back and forth daily, the group climbed to the sprawling precincts of the Temple and spent the daylight hours among the imposing marble columns. But, Jesus warned, "There will not be left here one stone upon another, that will not be thrown down." More dire and incredible pictures of the future! The disciples, at this point, must have been overburdened with all that had taken place, and so were unable to take in right away all that Jesus said: the coming trials, the meaning of Jesus' rejection and foreshadowed death, and finally, the prediction that Herod the Great's Temple would be pounded to rubble. This was not the normal stuff of messianic hopes. Perhaps some would still be alive in A.D. 70 to witness Jerusalem's destruction; as many as 80,000 troops under the future emperor Titus would set fire to the city after a siege of many months.

With his impending death on his mind, Jesus also warned his disciples to prepare for their own deaths, for they knew neither the day nor the hour when they would be called, according to the Gospel of Matthew. Jesus described the day when the Son of man would gather everyone before him and, like a shepherd, separate the sheep from the goats. At that time, he would welcome to eternal life all those who had fed the hungry, given drink to the thirsty, welcomed the stranger, clothed the naked, and visited the sick and imprisoned, because "as you did it to one of the least of these my brethren, you did it to me." Conversely, he would condemn to everlasting fire all those who failed to perform such merciful acts, because "as you did it not to one of the least of these, you did it not to me."

Two days before Passover, according to Mark, while Jesus was dining at the house of Simon the leper in Bethany, a woman came in with an alabaster flask of expensive ointment of pure nard and poured it over Jesus' head. Some of those present objected to the waste, reasoning that the ointment could have been sold for more than 300 denarii and the money given to the poor. (A single denarius was a day's wage for a laborer.) But Jesus reproached them, saying, "She has done a beautiful thing to me. For you always have the poor with you, and whenever you will, you can do good to them; but you will not always have me." The woman, Jesus informed them, had anointed his body beforehand for burial.

The Last Supper

On Thursday evening, Jesus met with his Twelve Apostles in an "upper room," the guest room of someone whose identity is unknown. There they shared the meal that history knows as the "Last Supper." Matthew, Mark, and Luke indicate that it was a traditional Passover *seder*. John places the meal one day before Passover, a time that some scholars feel more comfortable with, as they hold that the trial that was to follow in the night and early hours of the morning would never have been held on Passover. In any event, Jesus gave the meal an entirely new significance. There was such a heightened level of sharing with him that for the disciples after his death it became a permanent symbol of their bond with their Lord; it was to be continually reenacted as "the Lord's Supper."

At the beginning of the meal, according to John 13:3–15, Jesus set an example for his disciples by exchanging his role as their master and teacher for that of a household slave. He wrapped himself in a towel, poured water into a basin, and began to wash their feet. When the startled disciples did not know

"The Son of man came not to be served but to serve," Jesus once told his followers, "and to give his life as a ransom for many." And at the Last Supper, as Jesus washed the feet of his astonished disciples, he gave this saying new meaning, urging them, in effect, to serve one another as he served them. His gesture was a dramatic reversal of roles. Washing the wayside dust from another's feet was an act of hospitality commonly performed by a servant.

Large foot basins of stone or ceramic—like this one from the second century B.C.—stood near the entranceway of all but the poorest Middle Eastern houses. A newly arrived guest would rest his foot on the brace in the center, while his host's servant bathed it with water.

The ancient olive trees of this garden (above) on the Mount of Olives mark it as the probable site of Gethsemane, where Jesus led his disciples after the Last Supper. (The name of the garden means, literally, "oil press.") To reach Gethsemane from the house where he had dined, Jesus probably descended from Mount Zion by a steep path, which was later made into a stepped road (right), and then left the city, and crossed the Kidron Valley.

how to respond, Jesus made clear the paradigm of service that he intended: "If I then, your Lord and Teacher, have washed your feet, you also ought to wash one another's feet."

The portion of the meal that was to become central in Christian worship is described in the accounts of Matthew, Mark, and Luke. At some point during the meal, Jesus took the loaf of unleavened bread, gave thanks to God, broke it apart, and gave it to the disciples. "This is my body," he said. Later, he took a cup of their wine, gave thanks, passed it for all to drink, and said, "This is my blood of the covenant, which is poured out for many" (Mark 14:22-24). By referring to the "blood of the covenant" Jesus was recalling the scene at Mount Sinai in Exodus 24 when the covenant that God made with his people when he delivered them from Egypt was sealed.

For these disciples, the Passover celebration of that deliverance would never be the same again. The festival of remembering the past had become focused on the future, and Jesus emphasized that future, according to Mark, by telling the Apostles, "Truly, I say to you, I shall not drink again of the fruit of the vine until that day when I drink it new in the kingdom of God."

Passover is generally a festive occasion, a treasured highlight of the year. The Talmud calls it "as delectable as the olive." This night, however, was characterized by somber reflection. Jesus spoke of his coming death and, in one horrifyingly crystalline moment, announced that someone in the room would betray him. It would be the man "who has dipped his hand in the dish with me." When Judas took a piece of bread—from Jesus' own hand, according to John—there was no outcry. Once again, the disciples seemed incapable of understanding what was happening. Jesus, consciously accepting what must be, said to Judas, "What you are going to do, do quickly." Judas immediately withdrew.

In the tender moments of fellowship that followed Judas' departure, Jesus spoke of the love his disciples must have for one another. In this banquet setting they were probably reclining on couches in the Roman manner. This was the calm before the storm. Sated, reflective, taking in their teacher's thoughts as oil lamps flickered in the cool spring night, they asked questions of Jesus and pledged firm loyalty. Jesus predicted that, on the contrary, the devoted Simon Peter, although he professed his readiness to die for Jesus, would deny knowing him three times before the cock crowed the following morning. Clearly, the pace of events would quicken.

In these last hours, Jesus focused the Apostles' minds on what could sustain them. They must learn to find their greatness and leadership in serving. They must be sustained even in their troubles by confidence in a kingdom that is the gift of God. They must believe that he would return to them and trust the Holy Spirit to guide them after he was gone.

In a long discourse, found in John, Jesus commanded his disciples to "love one another as I have loved you. Greater love has no man than this, that a man lay down his life for his friends. You are my friends if you do what I command you." The way was not going to be easy for them, but Jesus promised them a profound and unshakable peace. "In the world you have tribulation," he said as one who was about to be betrayed, "but be of good cheer, I have overcome the world."

Jesus then "lifted up his eyes to heaven," according to John, and prayed for the Apostles, whom he was sending into the world just as the Father had sent him into the world. "Sanctify them in the truth," he prayed; "thy word is truth." He also prayed for those who would believe in him through the teachings of the Apostles, "that they may all be one; even as thou, Father, art in me, and I in thee, that they also may be in us, so that the world may believe that thou hast sent me."

Agony in the garden

Soon the Apostles accompanied Jesus out of the city through the Kidron Valley northeast to a garden on the Mount of Olives called Gethsemane. It may have been an olive grove owned by a follower. Jesus and his disciples had often rested there before. He told his disciples to wait for him while he went off to pray, taking Peter, James, and John with him. Then, greatly distressed and troubled over the ordeal soon to begin, Jesus told the three to remain there and watch, and he went a little farther off, alone. He did not wish to die. Falling on the ground, he prayed, "Abba, Father, all things are possible to thee; remove this cup from me; yet not what I will, but what thou wilt." After praying, he returned to his followers. Pushed to their physical, emotional, and mental limits by the week's events, they had fallen dead asleep. And he said to Peter, "Simon, are you asleep? Could you not watch one hour? Watch and pray that you may not enter into temptation; the spirit indeed is willing, but the flesh is weak." After going off to pray twice more and finding the Apostles asleep each time, Jesus told them, "Rise, let us be going; see, my betrayer is at hand."

Suddenly, the little garden was filled with light and noise. Bearing torches, clanging their weapons, a crowd of armed men, including Temple guards, swarmed up with Judas at their head. In the traditional manner of greeting a venerable teacher, Judas moved to kiss Jesus. Thus was Jesus revealed to his pursuers, who promptly arrested him. Jesus made no attempt to resist, but Peter drew a sword and cut off the ear of one of the high priest's slaves. But Jesus said, "No more of this!" and healed the slave's ear.

Jesus before Annas and Caiaphas

Having thus begun, the course of events moved quickly. The dark, silent night of the ancient city was disturbed many times before daybreak. Exactly what happened during that night and the following

After praying in Gethsemane, Jesus was confronted by "a band of soldiers and some officers from the chief priests and the Pharisees," who had been led there by Judas. Armed "with lanterns and torches and weapons," they seized Jesus and led him to the high priest's house. After being questioned, Jesus was brought before Pontius Pilate, guarded by Roman soldiers as shown above.

day is, however, notoriously difficult to reconstruct, since the Gospels vary considerably in describing the order of events. In the Gospel of John the sequence begins as Jesus was taken to the wealthy neighborhood of Mount Zion to the house of Annas, a former high priest and father-in-law of the then high priest Caiaphas. This important leader and artful politician "questioned Jesus about his disciples and his teachings" as though there were something secret about them. Jesus protested that he had always spoken openly in the synagogues and Temple. "Ask those who have heard me, what I said to them; they know what I said." At that retort, an officer struck Jesus for his insolence, but the questioning proceeded no further. Annas sent Jesus bound to Caiaphas, and thence he was dispatched to the Roman prefect, Pontius Pilate, for trial. What transpired between Caiaphas and Jesus is not told in John. Instead we are told how Peter denied his association with Jesus three times, as predicted, before the cock crowed. Thus the Gospel of John describes no trial of Jesus before any sort of formal Jewish court, only a session of questioning by Annas, the former high priest.

Matthew and Mark place the emphasis elsewhere. After his arrest, Jesus was led before Caiaphas, the high priest, who had assembled the chief priests and elders and scribes. There, in the middle of the night, the Sanhedrin held a trial. According to Mark, only false witnesses came forward, and their various testimonies did not agree. Matthew asserts that two agreed in testifying that Jesus claimed to be able to destroy the Temple of God and build it in three days. In spite of such testimony, however, ultimately the trial centered on a single question put to Jesus by the high priest, "Are you the Christ, the Son of the Blessed?" According to Mark 14:62, Jesus replied, "I am; and you will see the Son of man seated at the right hand of Power, and coming with the clouds of heaven." Both the words *Blessed* and *Power* were understood to mean God. The statement was taken as blasphemy, evidently as a human claim to divinity, and Jesus was condemned to death. While Jesus was on trial inside, Peter was in the courtyard. At the same time that Jesus confessed and was condemned, Peter three times denied knowing him, and broke down and wept. In the morning the Sanhedrin, after a consultation, handed Jesus over to Pilate.

Luke offers a third perspective on events. After his arrest, Jesus was brought to the high priest's house and held in the courtyard through the night. Peter was also there by the fire that was kindled in the courtyard, and the test of his loyalty took on special poignancy. Even with Jesus nearby, Peter could not summon the strength to identify himself as his disciple. Twice he denied any knowledge of Jesus, and as he was yet uttering the words of his third denial, "the cock crowed. And the Lord turned and looked at Peter. And Peter remembered the word of the Lord, how he had said to him, 'Before the cock crows today, you will deny me three times.' And he went out and wept bitterly." When morning came, Jesus was finally led before the Sanhedrin. Again, Luke emphasizes that their single concern was whether he claimed to be the Christ and the Son of God. "If I tell you," Jesus replied, "you will not believe. . . ." Luke records no formal verdict but states that the whole company brought Jesus before Pilate.

To this day, scholars debate about whether the Sanhedrin had the authority to put a person to death for a capital offense. It is only certain that in most cases the right of the sword lay with the Roman prefect, and that he could intervene in any case as he so chose.

The cock that crowed at Peter's denial of his Lord appears in this 11th-century representation. Cockcrow signified a specific time of night, marking the dark hours just before dawn.

Pilate and Herod Antipas

The Roman prefect, Pontius Pilate, was known to despise the Jews and their beliefs; his only concern was to keep peace and exploit the region. When Jesus was brought before him, he was hardly concerned with whether Jesus was making blasphemous claims against the God of the Jews. He wanted to know one thing: "Are you the King of the Jews?" The question was almost a code for any of the numerous rebels against Rome who had arisen in Palestine—like the many others Pilate was holding for execution at that very time. Without protesting his innocence, Jesus answered ambiguously, "You have said so," but then responded to no further charges.

The Gospels, in one way or another, describe Pilate as reluctant to execute Jesus. It may be that Pilate was genuinely puzzled by this prisoner. John tells of the dialogue between the two men when Jesus asserted that, although his kingdom was not of this world, he was in fact born to be a king and to bear witness to the truth. The Roman asked, perhaps with world-weary skepticism and a sense of irony gained in the intrigues of politics, "What is truth?"

It may also be that Pilate was caught between his contempt for this Jew so insolent that he would not answer a question and his contempt for the Jewish leaders who brought him to trial. Pilate's reputation for dealing with the Jews was not good. Philo of Alexandria characterized his conduct as prefect as full of "briberies, violence, robberies, outrages, wanton injuries, executions without trial constantly repeated, and ceaseless and supremely grievous cruelty." According to such testimony, Pilate would evidently as soon execute this Jew as swat an insect, but he may not have wished to be seen as doing anything that favored the Jews. Ultimately, the Roman governor of Syria ordered Pilate back to Rome to stand trial for crimes in office.

In any event, the Gospels several times emphasize that Pilate found no capital offense in Jesus but despite that judgment ordered him to be executed. That Pilate was toying with this affair is perhaps suggested by the interlude described by Luke in which Pilate sent Jesus over to see Herod Antipas, who had come to Jerusalem from Galilee to celebrate Passover.

Herod, according to Luke, was delighted to have Jesus brought before him. Quite simply, he wanted to see a miracle; perhaps he wanted to lay to rest his fears that Jesus was a resurrected John the Baptist. Jesus, who had once referred contemptuously to the ruler as "that fox," refused to speak. Infuriated, Herod encouraged his soldiers to mock the prisoner, and as the cream of the jest, he had Jesus clothed in "gorgeous apparel," which might have been a royal robe. The tetrarch passed the burden of decision back to Pilate. Even so, according to Luke, "Herod and Pilate became friends with each other that very day, for before this they had been at enmity with each other."

For the moment, Pilate decided to thwart the desires of the priestly aristocrats to get rid of Jesus, by adopting a ploy, which quickly turned against him. According to the Gospels, it was the custom for the Romans to acknowledge the Jewish celebration of Passover by pardoning one condemned criminal. A rebel named Barabbas, who had been actively involved in an insurrection against Rome, was under sentence of death for murder at the time. Pilate, perhaps hoping to play on Jesus' well-known popularity in order to get the crowd to approve of executing the rebel, offered the crowd the choice of releasing Barabbas or Jesus, "the King of the Jews." Faced with the possibility of gaining the release of an active anti-Roman rebel, the crowd shouted, "release to us Barabbas." Taken aback by the turn of events, Pilate evidently thought better of his scheme and pushed for the release of the man who was in his eyes less dangerous. In Mark's account, "Pilate again said to them, 'Then what shall I do with the man whom you call the King of the Jews?' And they cried out again, 'Crucify him.' And Pilate said to them, 'Why, what evil has he done?' But they shouted all the more, 'Crucify him.' "

The determination of the crowd had become fixed on the release of Barabbas, though in the bargain that meant the execution of Jesus. Ultimately, Pilate gave up on his plan. Sensing that a riot was brewing, according to Matthew, he had a basin of water brought in and publicly washed his hands, saying, "I am innocent of this man's blood; see to it yourselves." Pilate then gave the order to release Barabbas and execute Jesus.

Scourging and crucifixion

Crucifixion, described by the Roman orator Cicero as "the most cruel and hideous of punishments," was reserved in Palestine for criminals without Roman citizenship, usually only for rebels against the state, delinquent slaves, or the most barbarous of offenders. It was a horrible example of a punishment designed to deter crime. Perhaps invented in a somewhat different form by the Persians and spread in the Middle East by Alexander the Great, this method of execution was refined by the Romans to produce a very slow and extremely painful death.

First, the condemned prisoner would be stripped, bound to a post, and given 39 or possibly more strokes with a short leather whip, the *flagrum*. The thongs of the *flagrum* held tiny lead balls and sharp bits of sheep bone to bite into the flesh. Generally, two soldiers took turns administering the strokes. The intent was to cause so much blood loss, pain,

The Antonia Fortress just northwest of the Temple Mount served as a barracks for Roman troops, and it was probably here that Jesus was taken to face trial before Pontius Pilate; its massive walls and four lofty towers appear above in an artist's scale model. It is possible that the soldiers played dice (above right) and other games of chance in their off-duty hours, scratching the markings for these contests in the paving stones. The example at right is from the central courtyard area, where Jesus' trial was probably held.

and circulatory shock that the victim would be near death; Josephus noted that certain rebel Jews had been "torn to pieces by the scourge before being crucified." The torture would so weaken the condemned that his time on the cross would be shortened, possibly an unintentional mercy. In Jesus' case, there would have been the added rigors of a sleepless night, physical and emotional abuse, appearances before the various tribunals, and walks from place to place totaling perhaps two and a half miles. Released from the whipping post, Jesus was garbed in a scarlet robe, crowned with a circlet of spiky thorns, probably of the jujube tree common to Judea, and spat upon by the soldiers.

At this point, according to John, Pilate reappeared to utter the phrase "Behold the man!" He seems to have wanted the crowd to see the effects of their choice. He also seems to have wanted to shift to the crowd his own responsibility for the execution.

The Way of the Cross

By custom, the prisoner had to carry the *patibulum*, or crossbar, of his own cross through the streets to the place of execution, which in Jerusalem was a bare hill outside the city walls called Golgotha, "the place of a skull." There, a sturdy wooden post was permanently positioned, ready to be used as the *stipes*, or upright beam, of the cross.

A succession of shrines marks Jesus' final passage through the streets of Jerusalem. After being condemned to death and flogged, Jesus was given the heavy horizontal beam of his cross to carry. A Franciscan friary (right) now stands on the spot on which these events are believed to have occurred, and a Franciscan shrine commemorates the place where a Jewish bystander relieved Jesus of his burden (below). According to tradition, Jesus fell three times on his way to Golgotha. The last fall is commemorated in a place outside the city gates, now occupied by a 13th-century Coptic monastery (below, at right).

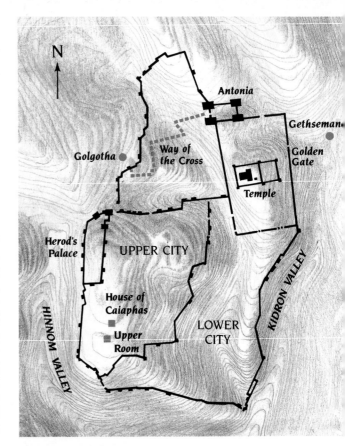

According to tradition, after h[is] trial and sentencing at the A[n]tonia Fortress, Jesus, burden[ed] with a heavy cross, stagger[ed] toward Golgotha, the site of t[he] crucifixion, a distance of just [a] third of a mile. This rout[e,] called the Way of the Cross [or] Via Dolorosa, is indicated [on] the map above. Yet some schola[rs] believe that Pilate condemned J[e]sus in Herod's palace, on t[he] western edge of Jerusalem.

Stumbling over the rough pavement, Jesus was weighed down by the thick wood beam of the *patibulum*, which was up to six feet in length and as much as 125 pounds in weight. The type of wood used to make the cross is unknown. Whatever the material, Jesus, already weakened by exhaustion and loss of blood, was apparently unable to carry it. The soldiers impressed a bystander, a Diaspora Jew named Simon from the North African region of Cyrene, "who was coming in from the country," and commanded him to carry it for him, following behind the weak and bleeding figure of Jesus. The distance covered was about a third of a mile.

A great multitude of people followed Jesus, including a number of women who wept for him. Jesus at one point turned to these women and told them to weep for themselves rather than for him, citing the proverbial saying, "For if they do this when the wood is green, what will happen when it is dry?" Apparently, Jesus was bitterly commenting on his suffering—if he, who was innocent, was tortured so cruelly, what would be the fate of a guilty Jerusalem?

When Jesus reached the summit of Golgotha, from which could possibly be seen the panorama of the city that had rejected him, he was stripped of his garments and knocked to the ground. His arms were then stretched out over the *patibulum*. Judging from skeletal remains of crucifixion victims of the period that have been discovered in Jerusalem, long iron nails were driven between the bones of his wrists into the wood of the *patibulum*, probably piercing the median nerve in the wrists and causing intense pain. Four soldiers then lifted the *patibulum* up and fixed it onto the upright *stipes*. (The *patibulum* would have been cut to fit snugly over the *stipes*, forming a T-shaped cross.) Then Jesus' feet may have been nailed to a wooden foot rest, called the *suppedaneum*, or against the *stipes* itself.

Above Jesus' head was attached the *titulus*, a sign proclaiming the victim's name and crime. In Jesus'

case, Pilate had taken a final, perhaps ironic, stab at the Jewish subjects he despised. The titulus read, "Jesus of Nazareth, the King of the Jews." (According to John it was written in Greek, Latin, and Hebrew, but by "Hebrew" John probably meant the common language of the local Jews, which was Aramaic.) The priests had objected that the inscription should explain that Jesus had only *said* he was king, but Pilate dug in. "What I have written," he replied, "I have written." Beneath this mocking *titulus*, Jesus began his ordeal, according to Mark, about 9:00 A.M., the third hour of the day.

Jesus on the cross

Briefly, some members of the aristocracy appeared and ridiculed Jesus. Soldiers, who had taken his clothes and were gambling for them, raucously suggested, "If you are the King of the Jews, save yourself!" For many Jews, the hopes that had been associated with Jesus seemed permanently dashed. The expectations of former days seemed ridiculous.

Grieving, shocked followers were also there, including many women who had followed Jesus from Galilee as his disciples. With them was Mary, Jesus' mother, whose words and actions are not reported. When Jesus saw his mother standing near the cross with the unidentified "disciple whom he loved," traditionally thought to be John, he told the two to become as mother and son to each other.

On either side of Jesus hung two "robbers," possibly other rebels like Barabbas, also in the throes of crucifixion. One wretch mocked Jesus, but the other expressed faith in him and was promised Paradise that very day.

Of the hours of suffering we have few details. During the ordeal, nerve injury probably produced fiery pain, which shot through Jesus' arms, and muscle cramps, which caused him even more distress. It is known that insects frequently bored into the lacerations of the crucified, and birds of prey

"Hail, King of the Jews!" cried the soldiers mocking Jesus, after they had circled his brow with a coronet of plaited thorns. There are many species of thorny shrubs or small trees that thrive in Judea, each armed with a battery of painful spines, and scholars are divided as to which type the soldiers used. This is one species that grows in the region.

might rip at the eyes, ears, and nose of the immobile prisoners. Thirst would become unbearable, as the body dehydrated. In fact, according to the Gospel of John, Jesus' only admission of discomfort was a single cry, "I thirst." He was given vinegar or wine on a sponge. According to John, it was "vinegar on hyssop." (Hyssop was a plant used in purification rites.) According to Mark, Jesus had also been offered "wine mingled with myrrh," which would have acted as a sedative, but he did not take it. The myrrh was also a reminder of one of the gifts brought to the infant Jesus by the Magi, which has been seen as a symbol of his humanity and suffering.

A major effect of crucifixion was a type of respiratory failure. As the body hung, taxing the muscles, it became increasingly difficult for the crucified person to exhale. Carbon dioxide would not be fully expelled. The victim would thus be gradually asphyxiated. It is thought that death was occasionally hastened, when a criminal proved especially hardy, by crucifracture, or breaking each leg below the knee. The condemned, having lost the ability to push himself upright to aid his breathing, soon suffocated.

Death and burial

But Jesus died at about three in the afternoon, an unusually short period on the cross. "It is finished," he said and, according to John's Gospel, "gave up his spirit." Darkness had covered the "whole land" since the sixth hour, or noon, the Gospels tell us, and at the ninth hour, when Jesus died, the earth shook and the curtain of the Temple was "torn in two, from top to bottom." To the saddened followers assembled at Golgotha, the great promise of their teacher's life had ended in shame and horror. No one, according to the evidence, had yet recognized the true significance of the day now revered by Christians as Good Friday, although many present knew that something momentous had occurred when Jesus died. The centurion who stood facing

him at that moment was moved to say, according to Mark, "Truly this man was the Son of God!"

Joseph of Arimathea, a wealthy man who had followed Jesus in secret, obtained Pilate's permission to bury Jesus. Joseph, a member of the Sanhedrin who, according to Luke 23:51, "had not consented to their purpose and deed" apparently owned a new rock tomb in a garden not far from Golgotha. According to John, he was joined by Nicodemus, a

Jesus' tomb, some Christians believe, may have been this cave just north of the old city wall, found in 1867 by a German missionary. It had been used for burials as early as 800 B.C.

thoughtful Pharisee who had discoursed on spiritual concepts with Jesus under cover of darkness. Some of the women followers and relatives keeping vigil at the cross might have joined them and helped wrap the corpse in linen and spices. They laid the body in the tomb and sealed the entrance with a large stone. As the Sabbath began, Jesus' disheartened followers returned through the evening gloom to the city.

Resurrection and ascension

No one was prepared for the stunning revelations that began to spread throughout the community of believers within 48 hours or less. Early Sunday morning, by Mark's account, Mary Magdalene, Mary the mother of James, and Salome (three of the women who were disciples of Jesus) went to the tomb after

A view of the crypt shows the hewn stone shelves on which the dead were laid. Another possible tomb site is in the Church of the Holy Sepulchre, located on Golgotha.

sunrise. The Sabbath was over, and they meant to anoint Jesus' body with more spices. Mark tells us that the women considered how to get help to roll the heavy stone from the front of the burial chamber. Suddenly, they noticed that it had already been moved out of the way. Entering the tomb, they saw a young man in a white robe seated there. "Do not be amazed," he said, "you seek Jesus of Nazareth, who was crucified. He has risen, he is not here."

The women kept this news to themselves at first, but gradually it got out. Jesus may have appeared almost immediately to Mary Magdalene. When Jesus approached her as she wept outside the tomb, according to John's Gospel, Mary thought her risen Lord was the gardener. It was only when Jesus tenderly addressed her by name that she recognized him and hailed him as teacher.

Luke reports that when the women announced this good news to the Apostles, they thought it was an idle tale and did not believe. During that first day and the days that followed, however, because of appearances and visions, the whole company that had followed Jesus came to the unshakable faith that he was indeed alive. They experienced his presence, heard his words, and on one occasion had him cook fish for them for breakfast. John tells us that when the disciple Thomas expressed doubt about his resurrection, Jesus invited him to touch the wounds he sustained on the cross. "Have you believed because you have seen me?" Jesus asked. "Blessed are those who have not seen and yet believe."

This was a time of consolidating faith, of ensuring that Jesus' words would spark a movement in his name. One day, according to Luke, he led his followers to the Mount of Olives, blessed them, and "was carried up into heaven." The disciples were left with many questions. What would it all mean that so many months before they had been chosen on the shores of Galilee? But joy and expectation filled them as they waited for the future to unfold.

"And he was in the wilderness forty days, tempted by Satan; and he was with the wild beasts; and the angels ministered to him." Mark 1:12–13. Painting by Duccio, Italian artist of the 13th and 14th centuries.

"For God so loved the world that he gave his only Son, that whoever believes in him should ... have eternal life."

During his brief time on earth, Jesus taught, worked miracles, suffered, died, and rose from the dead. No one knows precisely what he looked like, but artists through the centuries have provided us with their views of Jesus the man and of some of the events of his life.

"And passing along by the Sea of Galilee, he saw Simon and Andrew the brother of Simon casting a net in the sea; for they were fishermen. And Jesus said to them, 'Follow me and I will make you become fishers of men.'" Mark 1:16–17. Sixth-century mosaic from Ravenna, Italy.

"And after six days Jesus took with him Peter and James and John his brother, and led them up a high mountain apart. And he was transfigured before them, and his face shone like the sun, and his garments became white as light. And behold, there appeared to them Moses and Elijah, talking with him." Matthew 17:1–3. Twelfth-century stained glass panel at Chartres Cathedral, France.

"Seeing the crowds, he went up on the mountain, and when he sat down his disciples came to him. And he opened his mouth and taught them, saying: 'Blessed are the poor in spirit, for theirs is the kingdom of heaven. Blessed are those who mourn, for they shall be comforted. Blessed are the meek, for they shall inherit the earth. . . .'" Matthew 5:1–5. Detail from a painting by the French artist Claude Lorrain (1600–1682).

"And when he had ceased speaking, he said to Simon, 'Put out into the deep and let down your nets for a catch.' And Simon answered, 'Master, we toiled all night and took nothing! But at your word I will let down the nets.' And when they had done this, they enclosed a great shoal of fish; and as their nets were breaking, they beckoned to their partners in the other boat to come and help them. And they came and filled both the boats, so that they began to sink." Luke 5:4–7. Detail from a 13th-century stained glass window in Canterbury Cathedral, England.

"And when he got into the boat, his disciples followed him. And behold, there arose a great storm on the sea, so that the boat was being swamped by the waves; but he was asleep. And they went and woke him, saying, 'Save, Lord; we are perishing.' And he said to them, 'Why are you afraid, O men of little faith?' Then he rose and rebuked the winds and the sea; and there was a great calm." Matthew 8:23–26. Illustration from an 11th-century German manuscript.

"And he came and touched the bier. . . . And he said, 'Young man, I say to you, arise.' And the dead man sat up, and began to speak." Luke 7:14–15. Detail from Christ Raising the Son of the Widow of Nain by Domenico Fiasella (1589–1669).

"Jesus said to them, 'Fill the jars with water.' . . . When the steward of the feast tasted the water now become wine . . . [he] said, 'Every man serves the good wine first . . . but you have kept the good wine until now.'" John 2:7–10. Ivory plaque from the sixth-century Byzantine throne of Archbishop Maximianus.

"And Jesus said to him, 'Receive your sight; your faith has made you well.' And immediately he received his sight and followed him, glorifying God." Luke 18:42–43. Detail from an altar panel by Duccio, Italian artist of the 13th and 14th centuries.

"As they were going away, behold, a dumb demoniac was brought to him. And when the demon had been cast out, the dumb man spoke." Matthew 9:32–33. Illumination from the 12th-century Winchester Bible.

"And taking the five loaves and the two fish he looked up to heaven, and blessed and broke them, and gave them to the disciples to set before the crowd. And all ate and were satisfied. And they took up what was left over, twelve baskets of broken pieces." Luke 9:16–17. A 14th-century mosaic at Istanbul.

"And they brought the colt to Jesus, and threw their garments on it; and he sat upon it. And many spread their garments on the road, and others spread leafy branches. . . . [and] cried out, 'Hosanna! Blessed is he who comes in the name of the Lord!' " Mark 11:7–9. Russian icon.

"And he came out, and went, as was his custom, to the Mount of Olives; and his disciples followed him. . . . And he withdrew from them about a stone's throw, and knelt down and prayed, 'Father, if thou art willing, remove this cup from me; nevertheless not my will, but thine, be done.' " Luke 22:39–44. Miniature from a late 15th-century French prayerbook.

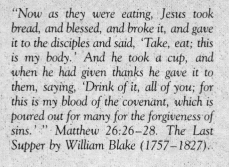

"Now as they were eating, Jesus took bread, and blessed, and broke it, and gave it to the disciples and said, 'Take, eat; this is my body.' And he took a cup, and when he had given thanks he gave it to them, saying, 'Drink of it, all of you; for this is my blood of the covenant, which is poured out for many for the forgiveness of sins.'" Matthew 26:26–28. The Last Supper by William Blake (1757–1827).

"While he was still speaking, there came a crowd, and the man called Judas, one of the twelve, was leading them. He drew near to Jesus to kiss him; but Jesus said to him, 'Judas, would you betray the Son of man with a kiss?'" Luke 22:47–48. Fresco by the 13th- and 14th-century Italian painter Giotto.

"And they crucified him, and divided his garments among them, casting lots for them, to decide what each should take." Mark 15:24. Disrobing of Christ by the Spanish painter El Greco (1541–1614).

"And there was darkness over the whole land . . . and the curtain of the temple was torn in two. Then Jesus, crying with a loud voice, said, 'Father, into thy hands I commit my spirit!' And having said this he breathed his last." Luke 23:44–46. Nineteenth-century African ivory crucifix.

"And he bought a linen shroud, and taking him down, wrapped him in the linen shroud, and laid him in a tomb which had been hewn out of the rock." Mark 15:46. Tabernacle made in Limoges, France, in the 13th century, showing the deposition from the cross and scenes after the resurrection.

" 'Do not be amazed; you seek Jesus of Nazareth, who was crucified. He has risen, he is not here; see the place where they laid him.' " Mark 16:6. Illumination from a 14th-century Hamburg missal.

"Then he led them out as far as Bethany, and lifting up his hands he blessed them. While he blessed them, he parted from them, and was carried up into heaven." Luke 24:50–51. The Acension by Rembrandt (1606–1669).

"When he was at table with them, he took the bread and blessed, and broke it, and gave it to them. And their eyes were opened and they recognized him; and he vanished out of their sight." Luke 24:30–31. The Supper at Emmaus by the Spanish painter Diego Velázquez (1599–1660).

Chapter Ten

Spread of the Gospel

Jesus' followers spread his message, first to other Jews and then to Gentiles, and Paul founded Christian communities throughout the Roman Empire. Despite repressions and bloody persecutions, the church grew. Eventually its converts included Constantine the Great, the first Christian Roman emperor.

Standing trial before the Sanhedrin, the supreme court of Jewish law, were a dozen men—Jesus' 11 surviving Apostles and a man named Matthias, who had been chosen to replace Judas Iscariot. The offense of which they were accused was disobedience to the Sanhedrin's explicit injunction against preaching the message of Jesus' life, his death, and especially his resurrection. The story of their trial is told in Acts 5:27–42.

"We strictly charged you not to teach in this name," said Caiaphas, the high priest, "yet here you have filled Jerusalem with your teaching and you intend to bring this man's blood upon us."

"We must obey God rather than men," answered Peter, speaking for the group. That statement, with its implication of privileged knowledge of God's will, was a blatant affront to the authority of the Sanhedrin, the body that was commissioned to uphold the rule of God, and by extension, to the law itself, the linchpin of Jewish religion and custom. Peter's explanation did nothing to

As the Apostles Peter and John were going to the Temple to pray, they met a man in his forties, lame from birth, and Peter healed him. News of the miraculous cure brought a crowd to Solomon's Portico, and Peter preached to them. He told of Jesus' resurrection and said that it was the fulfillment of ancient prophecy "from Samuel and those who came afterwards." They were arrested and ordered by the Sanhedrin not to speak or teach in Jesus' name.

The Story in Acts of the Apostles

The Acts of the Apostles, a continuation of the Gospel According to Luke, tells of the spread of the Christian faith from Jerusalem to the heart of the empire—Rome. It was probably written toward the end of the first century A.D., perhaps 50 or 60 years after the earliest events it recounts. It was intended to serve less as a complete historical account than as a statement, for the sake of the budding church of its time, of those memorable aspects of the church's early years that were most important to its growth.

The book is a succession of dramatic episodes, each rich with the kind of human detail that lends life to a story. But it is tantalizingly incomplete in many other details that would help us, from our distant perspective in time, to fully appreciate the momentous events it records.

lessen the offense. With growing outrage, the members of the Sanhedrin heard him say that the 12 men, along with the Holy Spirit, "whom God has given to those who obey him," were witnesses to God's having exalted Jesus "at his right hand as Leader and Savior."

The Holy Spirit and the trial

The reference to the Holy Spirit would not have mystified the members of the Sanhedrin, for they knew that the Spirit had filled the prophets from ancient times onward. But when the Apostles claimed that the Spirit was speaking to them, the Sanhedrin was angered. Not only were these men referring to an executed criminal as though he were a unique agent of God's will, but they were insinuating that the members of the Sanhedrin, lacking this Holy Spirit, were themselves disobedient toward God. Surely the offenders would have been punished

had not a Pharisaic scholar named Gamaliel risen to speak to the council.

Gamaliel was the most honored sage and teacher of his time, said by later tradition to have been the grandson of another respected teacher, Hillel, and his words bore great weight. Having ordered the Twelve removed from the chamber, he addressed the assembly, as Acts 5:35–39 reports.

"Men of Israel," he cautioned, "take care what you do with these men." He went on to cite other popular leaders who had gathered large followings, but whose movements had come to naught after their death. "So in the present case I tell you, keep away from these men and let them alone; for if this plan or this undertaking is of men, it will fail; but if it is of God, you will not be able to overthrow them. You might even be found opposing God!"

And so the Twelve were merely beaten, charged once more not to speak in the name of Jesus, and released. "And every day in the temple and at home," according to Acts 5:42, "they did not cease teaching and preaching Jesus as the Christ."

A special Pentecost

Acts makes it clear that such a confrontation as the trial before the Sanhedrin was inevitable from the day that the Twelve had been changed from Jesus' followers to emissaries and witnesses for him. This had occurred in Jerusalem during the Festival of Shavuot (the Greek term for Shavuot is Pentecost), 50 days after the Passover seder that had preceded Jesus' trial and crucifixion.

In the interval since that shared meal, the members of the group had experienced despair at their master's death, had found renewed hope in his resurrection, and had been filled with awe and elation at his ascension, described in Acts 1:9–11. Obeying his last instructions to them, they remained in Jerusalem and awaited the Holy Spirit he had promised to send.

Ten days after the ascension, they were gathered together to observe the day of Pentecost according to ancient law. Like the year's other great pilgrimage festivals, Pentecost was a time when devout Jews from far and near made their way to Jerusalem, and the city's population swelled by thousands. It was a joyous time, marking the end of the spring grain harvest, and it was customarily celebrated with fresh loaves of leavened bread made from the season's harvest and often featured free-flowing wine.

The Apostles may have been preparing for the feast when an event occurred that was to give a new meaning to the word *Pentecost* for all time to come.

As described in Acts 2, a roar like the "rush of a mighty wind" swept through the house where they were assembled. It must have been an awesome sound, for a "multitude" hurried toward it. "Tongues as of fire" rested on the Apostles, and "they were all filled with the Holy Spirit and began to speak in other tongues," amazing the growing crowd of onlookers. And most astonishing of all was that each person who heard them, though the listeners had come "from every nation under heaven," understood the words as though they were spoken in his own native language. The curse of the tower of Babel, it seemed, had been temporarily lifted for the sake of the message that these men were proclaiming.

Peter rose to the miraculous occasion and addressed the throng, telling them that they were witnesses to the fulfillment of prophesies from the

The name Gamaliel ranks high among Jewish leaders of the first three centuries A.D. Gamaliel II, right, grandson of the man who defended the Apostles before the Sanhedrin, worked to preserve the Jewish nation and the Torah after Jerusalem's destruction. His great-grandson, Gamaliel III, is believed to be buried in the tomb above, at ancient Beth-she'arim, northeast of Caesarea.

Book of Joel that God would pour out his Spirit "upon all flesh" to the accompaniment of signs and wonders, and telling them further that the crucified Jesus was the Christ. Peter's exhortations, following closely on what had clearly been signs and wonders, set in motion a wave of response that resulted in the baptism of some 3,000 people on that day, all promising to devote themselves to the Apostles' teaching and fellowship.

From then on, the Apostles preached unceasingly to all who would listen throughout the crowded city, their words given weight and emphasis by further signs and wonders, such as Peter's miracluous cure of a lame beggar at the Temple's Beautiful Gate, recounted in Acts 3. This event attracted a large crowd, which had pushed its way into Solomon's Portico, the vast colonnade along the east side of the Court of the Gentiles, to hear Peter preach. Angry Temple officials arrested Peter and his companion, the Apostle John, but not before they brought more thousands of Jews to believe in Jesus as the Messiah.

The following day, the two Apostles—"uneducated, common men"—stood before the august Sanhedrin for the first time and were charged not to speak or teach in the name of Jesus. Although the two refused to accept the command, the Sanhedrin,

Of central importance to the early growth of Christianity was the conviction that Jesus, through his death and his resurrection, had fulfilled God's covenant with Abraham and thus transformed the law, opening the faith of Israel to all humanity. This conviction is expressed on the fourth-century sarcophagus shown above: Jesus, standing on the arch of heaven, hands a scroll of law to Peter while looking toward Paul, Apostle to the Gentiles.

fearing the reaction of the people, who "praised God for what had happened," released them. But the teaching, the miraculous signs, and the conversions went on, even in the face of new arrests, including the one that culminated in the trial of all the Apostles before the Sanhedrin. The teaching was to continue until the gospel—the good news—of Jesus had spread throughout the land, the Roman Empire, and eventually, the world.

Seeds of Christianity

At first the Apostles and their growing band were but one among many Jewish sects that flourished during the first century A.D. They were distinguished largely by the fact that they persisted in teaching in Jesus' name. They did not call themselves Christians (it would be years before the term was coined), but simply followers of the Way. Their activities were centered in Jerusalem, and they continued to offer sacrifice at the Temple and to observe the laws of Judaism.

But they differed greatly from other sects in one important respect: they believed that, with the resurrection of Jesus, a new age had dawned—an age that would be the fulfillment of all the hopes of Israel. And they expected Jesus to return, possibly at any moment, ushering in the kingdom of heaven. Their shared experience of the Holy Spirit was, to them, the indisputable sign that the transformation of the world had begun. It was a gift to be shared with everyone, and they were driven by an urgent need to share it while there was yet time.

These early believers in Jesus formed a community of strong mutual support, selling their possessions and pooling the proceeds for sustenance while their leaders devoted their time and energies to preaching the Way. Their communal meals, in remembrance of the Last Supper that the Apostles had shared with Jesus, were central to their lives. This daily breaking of bread together, during which stories of their ab-

sent yet ever-present Lord were retold, was probably—along with the baptism of new followers—the only ritual that set them apart. And even these two rites they shared, in form if not in content, with the Essenes and other Jewish sects.

Although the followers of the Way included Galileans, Judeans, and others whose primary language was Aramaic—as was true of the Twelve Apostles themselves—there were also many Hellenist Jews, Greek speakers whose roots were in the lands of the Diaspora. These Hellenist Jews were to be crucial to the development and spread of Christianity. For some the journey to Jerusalem for Pentecost that fateful spring had changed their lives forever. Some had come from cosmopolitan communities in Palestine, such as Caesarea, Sebaste, and Ascalon; others had come from the far-off lands of the Diaspora. Some remained in Jerusalem, and others took the message of Jesus back home with them.

Jewish identity in the Diaspora

The differences between the Greek-speaking Hellenist Jews and the Aramaic-speaking local Jews went far deeper than language. The Hellenists were heirs to a long tradition of separation from the soil of Israel and Judea and from the Temple's sacrificial rituals. Over the centuries since the Babylonian exile, their ancestors had striven to maintain their identity as Jews and to hold fast to the ancient law in the far-flung cities where they put down roots. Lacking the central focus of the Temple, their lives had centered on their synagogues. These places of worship had come to serve their communities in many ways: they were schools, law courts, and centers of social and intellectul exchange.

Each community of the Diaspora had been influenced to some extent by the culture within which it existed. All had been additionally influenced by the flood of Greek culture that had spread throughout the Middle Eastern and Mediterranean

Recently discovered ruins near the rural community of Bova Marina, at the southern tip of the Italian peninsula, may be the oldest synagogue yet found in Europe. The upper layers of the site, accidentally uncovered by a road construction crew in 1983, are of a fourth-century synagogue, but exploratory diggings reveal a much older structure beneath. The Jews of the Diaspora kept their faith alive by establishing synagogues in their new lands.

from the one God to all people throughout the world. They sought to observe the law in their own daily lives. At the same time, they strove to minimize those aspects of Judaism that separated it from other people and to emphasize those things that linked their religion and way of life with the best of Hellenistic culture and philosophy.

On the other side were Jews who treasured the uniqueness of their heritage and sought to isolate themselves from the threatening cultures that surrounded them. They cultivated a distinct way of life, and they venerated the Temple and all it stood for as a symbol of their heritage—the God-given law that set them apart fom all others.

Meanwhile, Jerusalem was still the center of Jewish life, the place where foreign influence, even when imposed by conquerors, remained essentially alien, and thus resistible. All the debates of the Diaspora had found their way to Jerusalem in intensified form. Nevertheless, most Judeans, being physically closer to the roots of their ancient traditions, were able to cope with the tensions that the debates caused. The Temple was no distant dream to them, no idealized symbol, but a solid reality in their lives. This reality remained an anchor for their faith.

Religious rivalry in Jerusalem

By the time of Jesus, the imposed orderliness of the Roman Empire had made communication between Jewish communities faster and easier than ever before and had also made it possible for great numbers of Hellenist Jews from the Diaspora to return to the homeland of their ancestors. In the concentrated religious atmosphere of Jerusalem, issues that had long been discussed in scattered communities could become volatile causes for confrontation.

In keeping with their own traditions, many Hellenist Jews had organized synagogues based on their origins in the Diaspora—Acts 6:9 lists "the synagogue of the Freedmen [probably mostly former Jewish slaves who

worlds. But in the synagogues of each community the Jews had continuously identified and measured these influences and tried to cope with them in terms of the law and their own ancestral identity.

Inevitably, conflicts had arisen within and among the various congregations, often centering on the acceptable role of Jews in a Gentile society. The law did not deal with this subject directly, given as it had been to Jews seeking to establish a Jewish land. Thus over the centuries interpretations had been made— attempts to reconcile the letter of the law and the real situations that people faced in their daily lives. Although the range of these interpretations led to a seemingly infinite variety of debatable points, the questions often boiled down to just two opposing attitudes.

On one side, it appears, were those who saw the entire Diaspora as, in the words of Isaiah, "a light to the nations," bearing the message of righteousness

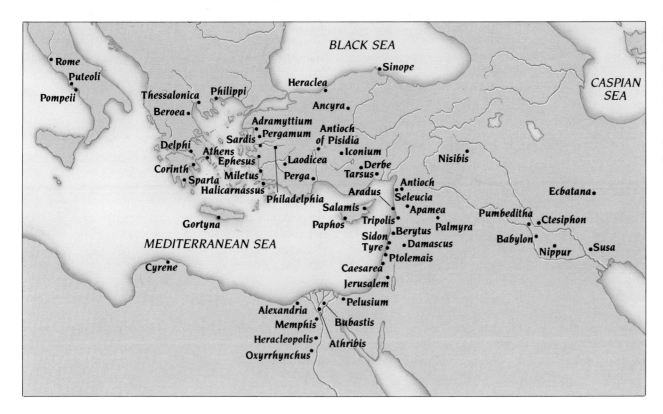

Although Jewish culture and religion centered on Jerusalem, the communities of the Diaspora, or dispersion, were scattered throughout the eastern part of the Roman Empire, as shown in the map at left. Over the centuries the people of these communities struggled with the many problems of living by Jewish law amid Gentile societies.

had returned to Palestine] . . . and of the Cyrenians, and of the Alexandrians, and of those from Cilicia and Asia." Here the old issues that had sometimes divided Diaspora Jews were argued with new heat.

The New Testament gives glimpses of these debates, especially as they were intensified by the proclamation of Jesus as the Messiah. Clearly, the nature of the law, the importance of the Temple—indeed, the fundamentals of Judaism—were at stake.

For some Hellenist Jews, the symbolic value of the Temple loomed large. Anything that threatened or denigrated their beautiful ideal—the center of the presence of God in the world—might ultimately destroy the law and bring down God's vengeance.

Opposing these tradition-minded Jews were those who felt that the law's most vital quality was at once more personal and more universal than Temple ritual expressed. Some even questioned the relevance of ancient sacrificial rites to their time and their lives, and many believed strongly that the God who had given the ancient law was a universal deity whose presence could by no means be limited to the Temple and whose laws were the laws of all nature.

In life, Jesus had probably had little impact on Hellenist Jews. But the message of his death and resurrection and the startling proclamation of forgiveness of sin in his name quickly took root among them.

It was evidently Hellenist followers of the Way who saw the most radical significance of that proclamation of forgiveness. If it was true, it meant that the Temple and its sacrifices, including the solemn rituals of the Day of Atonement, were no longer crucial. The visitation of the Holy Spirit underscored for them that the very meaning of the law was transformed. Whether this transformation was a terrible threat or a glorious promise depended entirely upon an individual's point of view.

Stephen, the first Christian martyr

One who embraced the new sect was Stephen, one of the seven disciples, all with Greek names—*Stephen* means "crown"—who had been chosen to minister to the Hellenist community after tensions had arisen between Greek-speaking and Aramaic-speaking members of the young sect. Stephen disputed with members of several Hellenist synagogues and ran afoul of many tradition-minded Jews who feared the loss of both the Temple and the law.

We can judge the intensity of their fear by the severity of their reported actions against him. First they instigated a campaign of slander to stir up public opinion, and then, accusing him of blasphemy and of speaking against the Temple and the law, they denounced him before the Sanhedrin.

Stephen's speech to the council, as recorded in Acts 7:2–56, began with a summary of the origins of the law and of God's covenant with the Jews, but it turned radical. In building the Temple, Stephen said in effect, Solomon had not served God, for "the Most High does not dwell in houses made with hands." He then attacked his judges directly. "You stiff-necked people," he called them, "uncircumcised in heart and ears, you always resist the Holy Spirit. As your fathers did, so do you. Which of the prophets did not your fathers persecute? And they killed those who announced beforehand the coming of the Righteous One, whom you have now betrayed and murdered, you who received the law as delivered by angels and did not keep it." It was a furious diatribe, certain to elicit a strong response.

"Behold," Stephen continued, "I see the heavens opened, and the Son of man standing at the right hand of God." He might well have said more, but his listeners "cried out with a loud voice and stopped up their ears and rushed together upon him," and Stephen was stoned to death.

Stoning was an ancient form of execution, but in Stephen's case, it seems not to have been a deliberate sentence but an act of pure rage.

Saul the persecutor

According to Acts, Stephen's martyrdom sparked a "great persecution," which was apparently directed especially against Hellenist followers of the Way in Jerusalem. The targets of the persecution fled from the city under the onslaught. The Apostles, however, did not flee, and the Aramaic-speaking brotherhood to whom they ministered evidently continued to flourish.

One of the most active persecutors was a Hellenist Jew named Saul, who, according to Acts, had been a consenting witness at Stephen's stoning.

Born into a family of tentmakers in Tarsus—the capital of Cilicia, about 10 miles inland from the southeastern coast of present-day Turkey—Saul had come to Jerusalem as a youth to study under Gamaliel. He was a bilingual Jew, speaking both Greek and Aramaic, who had inherited from his father the legal status of Roman citizenship.

According to Saul's own later words, recorded in Galatians 1:14, "I advanced in Judaism beyond many of my own age among my people, so extremely zealous was I for the traditions of my fathers." When he saw those traditions being threatened by such Hellenist Jews as Stephen, he felt that he had no choice but to try his best to stop them.

The fury of Saul and those like him had an effect they did not anticipate, for it caused the word to be carried wherever the scattered followers of the Way went. Acts 8:5–13 tells of Philip, one of the six

The death of Stephen, the first Christian martyr, was more of a mob action than a legal execution. In preaching Jesus' message, Stephen aroused fears and kindled antagonisms that were rooted in the disputes of the Diaspora. His stoning started a persecution in Jerusalem, which was apparently directed against Hellenist, or Greek-speaking, disciples and carried out by other Hellenist Jews, such as Saul, shown as a witness.

Hellenists who had been chosen with Stephen, preaching the Way and making converts in Samaria. Others must have preached in other places, for communities of followers were established among the Jews of Rome, Antioch, Alexandria, Damascus, and many other cities of the Diaspora.

The conversion of Saul

One of the most dramatic events recounted in Acts, one that was to become a turning point in the move of Christianity beyond the embrace of Judaism, was the revelation experienced by Saul as he traveled north from Jerusalem to Damascus. According to Acts 9, Saul had nearly reached Damascus, an important city of Syria, intent on rooting out followers of the Way from the synagogues there, when he was knocked to the ground and blinded by a blaze of light. Then he heard a voice say, "Saul, Saul, why do you persecute me?"

"Who are you, Lord?" asked the stricken Saul.

279

According to Acts 9:23–25, Saul's enemies in Damascus plotted to kill him and "were watching the gates day and night" to prevent his escape. Finally, he was lowered outside the city wall in a basket, as depicted at left in a 12th-century mosaic from Monreale Cathedral in Sicily. St. Paul's Window, above, is traditionally identified as the spot where the dramatic incident took place.

"I am Jesus, whom you are persecuting," said the voice; "but rise and enter the city, and you will be told what you are to do."

Saul let the men traveling with him lead him to Damascus, where he apparently spent three days in a kind of stupor. Then a follower of the Way named Ananias restored his sight, and "something like scales fell from his eyes." Saul the persecutor was baptized and immediately began a new life as the man who would be known to history as the Apostle Paul.

It was a total reversal of intention, though not of character. In his own later description of what had happened to him, he was to speak of his revelation as the ancient prophets had spoken of their calls,

identifying himself as "an Apostle of Christ Jesus by the will of God." He was still unstinting in his service to God's will, but his understanding of that will had been completely changed. Rather than seeking to preserve the exclusiveness of the traditions to which he had been so devoted, he was to spend the rest of his life reaching outward to include all humanity, Jew and Gentile alike, in the new community of believers. He was never to look back, never to long for what he had been nor to question what he had become. He threw himself into his new mission of spreading the faith as zealously as he had previously tried to suppress it.

Saul spoke in the synagogues of Damascus, proclaiming Jesus as the son of God. Many of his listeners, who had expected to hear just the opposite message, were baffled and enraged by his words. He was finally forced to flee a plot against his life.

Acts 9:26 says that he went to Jerusalem to join the Apostles and that they were afraid of him. But according to his own words in the Letter to the Galatians, after his revelation he spent three years in Arabia (the kingdom of the Nabateans, south of the Dead Sea) and was back in Damascus before going to Jerusalem, where he stayed but a short time and saw only the Apostles Peter and James. In any event, he soon departed for his home in Cilicia, sailing from Caesarea to Tarsus, to continue the work that was to occupy him for the rest of his life.

Peter's vision

The Apostles continued to preach throughout Judea, Galilee, and Samaria. They still worked only among other Jews and drew little attention from the Roman authorities, who took notice of Jewish sects only insofar as they caused trouble.

In the cities near the Mediterranean coast, the Apostles began to encounter interested Gentiles. Acts 10 gives great significance to one such encounter. It tells of a vision that Peter had while he was in Joppa, staying in the home of a tanner named Simon. He saw something descending from heaven "like a great sheet," which contained all sorts of animals, birds, and reptiles. A voice commanded him to eat, but he objected, saying that he had "never eaten anything that is common or unclean"—that is, forbidden by Jewish law.

"What God has cleansed," the voice replied, "you must not call common." As though for emphasis, the command was repeated, not once, but twice, and then the sheet was lifted to heaven.

As Peter pondered the meaning of his vision, three men arrived, saying that they had been sent by Cornelius, a Roman centurion who lived in Caesa-

rea, some 35 miles to the north, to bring Peter to him. Although Cornelius was a Gentile, Peter went to him, interpreting his vision to mean that he "should not call any man common or unclean."

Cornelius was one of the many Gentiles described in Acts as "God-fearers." These were people who did not become full converts, or proselytes, to Judaism but who were attracted to the monotheism, ethical rigor, and compassion of the religion. Though they remained uncircumcised and unobservant of Jewish dietary regulations, many like Cornelius joined in the prayers of the synagogue and gave to the poor, as Jews were taught to do.

Cornelius had assembled a group of like-minded friends, and he asked Peter to tell them "all that you have been commanded by the Lord." Peter told Jesus' story, ending with the statement that "every one who believes in him receives forgiveness of sins through his name." And as he spoke, according to Acts 10:44, "the Holy Spirit fell on all who heard the word." The group spoke in tongues (the experience of speaking in ecstatic, incomprehensible language) as Peter and the Apostles had done before them, and Peter baptized them all.

Upon his return to Jerusalem after spending several days as Cornelius' guest, Peter was criticized for going to a Gentile's house and eating with him. He told of his vision and of how the group had received the Holy Spirit. Acts 11:17 records that he said: "If then God gave the same gift to them as he gave to us when we believed in the Lord Jesus Christ, who was I that I could withstand God?" A great step had been taken in opening the new faith to the entire world.

The first Christians

Although most of the followers of the Way still continued to preach only to Jews, news came to Jerusalem from Antioch, the capital of Syria, that

Tiberius   Caligula   Claudius

The emperor Tiberius (above left) ruled Rome from A.D. 14 to 37. A skilled administrator, he instituted strict economies that enriched the treasury, but he became tyrannical and reclusive. It was during his reign that Jesus taught and died. His successor, Caligula (center), squandered in less than a year all the money that Tiberius had saved. He declared himself a god and demanded that his statue be installed at the Temple in Jerusaem. After his assassination in A.D. 41, his uncle Claudius (right) was proclaimed emperor and ruled until A.D. 54.

numerous Gentiles had been converted there. A Cypriot Jew named Joseph Barnabas was dispatched from Jerusalem to Antioch to investigate the claim. He liked what he saw and welcomed great numbers into the community of believers there. He and Saul, whom he brought from Tarsus, remained in Antioch for a year to teach new believers about Jesus and to shape the framework of the growing missionary movement.

It was in Antioch, according to Acts 11:26, that the followers of the Way were first called Christians—the word was derived from the Greek *christos,* or "anointed one," equivalent to the Hebrew *messiah.* It may have been used derisively since anointing with oil, a hallowed tradition to Jews, had no spiritual significance to Greek-speaking Gentiles or to Romans. Moreover, since the ending of the word *Christian* is Latin in formation, some scholars have even argued that it may have first been used by Roman police officials to keep track of members of a new movement.

Rome and religion

The Roman Empire was changing at the heart, losing some of the impetus that had driven its earlier growth. The Mediterranean region, long since reorganized along Roman lines, presented problems of administration and order but no true threats and few opportunities for conquest. The defense of outlying territories had little effect on life in the capital. The emperor Tiberius had spent most of the final decade of his reign in seclusion while functionaries administered the empire. He died in A.D. 37 and was succeeded by his great-nephew, Gaius—now better known by his childhood nickname, Caligula.

At first Caligula's reign seemed rich with promise. He was young, energetic, popular, and aggressive. But he proved to be a madman, arbitrary and capriciously cruel, obsessed with a vision of himself as a living god. As the heir of Julius Caesar and Augustus, both of whom had been deified in death, he declared himself immortal and demanded that he be worshiped beside all other gods throughout the empire. Though his reign was short, the results of this demand had long-term repercussions.

Rome's policy of religious toleration had done much to promote peace in its provinces and territories (see Chapter 8). Caligula's violation of that policy inflamed festering resentments in Judea. The resentment lingered, despite Caligula's death at the hands of his own guards in A.D. 41.

He had ordered a huge gilt statue of himself erected in the Temple in Jerusalem. When the Roman governor in Syria asked him to reverse the order because of the massive resistance of the Jewish people, Caligula sent a message to the governor commanding him to commit suicide. Caligula's assassination came in time to avert both the suicide and the making of the statue, but the fact that the order for the statue had been given and might have been obeyed moved Judea a little closer to violence and open rebellion.

Another Herod

One of Caligula's orders was to affect the future of Judaism and the rapid spread of Christianity in unforeseen ways. This was the appointment in A.D. 37 of his friend Herod Agrippa I, grandson of Herod the Great, as king over the lands that Herod Agrippa's recently deceased uncle, Herod Philip, had ruled as tetrarch. Two years later, Caligula took the territories of Galilee and Perea from another uncle, Herod Antipas, and gave them to Herod Agrippa as well.

Herod Agrippa was visiting in Rome when Caligula was assassinated, and he aided the aging Claudius in solidifying his hold on the imperial throne. One of Claudius' first official acts as emperor was to reward this loyalty. Herod Agrippa was appointed king over Judea and Samaria, giving him sway over most of the territory that his grandfather had ruled.

Raised in Rome but very conscious of his Jewish heritage, Herod Agrippa openly favored the Pharisees, and his support became more active as his power grew. This open espousal of the Pharisee cause, perhaps inspired as much by dreams of a resurgent Jewish nation as by religious persuasion, placed the power of his throne in opposition to the sects that the Pharisees viewed as radical.

Herod Agrippa soon began a persecution of the followers of the Way, presumably because he saw them as a threat to his ambitions for Jewish nationalism. James the son of Zebedee was beheaded, and Peter was jailed; Acts 12:7–11 tells how "an angel of the Lord" appeared and released him from prison. Peter apparently went into hiding for a time, and the leadership of the Jerusalem community of believers fell to another James, identified by Paul as "the Lord's brother." His loyalty to Israel and his scrupulous observance of Mosaic law undoubtedly did much to keep the peace between the followers of the Way and the Jewish community in which they lived.

Herod Agrippa died in A.D. 44 while presiding over a festival of games in Caesarea. Soon after having been hailed as divine by the crowd, he had been gripped by a sharp pain—smitten by the Lord, says Acts, "because he did not give God the glory."

The return of Roman rule

Rome resumed direct rule of Palestine. Cuspius Fadus, the procurator who replaced Herod Agrippa, was the first of a series of governors who had little interest in or sensitivity to the concerns of the Jewish people. For example, Fadus attempted to take the high priest's ceremonial robes back into custody (they had been released early in Caligula's reign for the first time since Herod the Great had seized them more than 70 years earlier), but was overruled by Claudius. Once again a threat, though unrealized, aroused public resentment against Roman rule.

Later, when a would-be prophet named Theudas led his followers to the banks of the Jordan, planning to part the waters as Joshua had done, Fadus sent cavalry to capture them. Much of the band was killed, and Theudas was beheaded. His head was paraded to Jerusalem as a trophy and a warning. The effect of the grisly display was probably to steel the resolution of zealous Jews, and uprisings continued to plague the procurators who succeeded Fadus.

Christians, magicians, and philosophers

In many cities of the empire, including Rome itself, followers of the Way were reaching out to Gentiles as Jews had never done before. The young movement was in danger of fragmentation. Included in its growing membership were communities of Jews, of Gentiles, and of mixed populations. All were united in their faith in Jesus, but many were divided by their understanding of how that faith affected their relationship to the traditions of Israel. Moreover, in the cities where they flourished, Christians faced the pressures of competition from other teachers and preachers, ranging from popular philosophers to magicians and proponents of mystery cults.

Saul continues his mission

It was this confused and potentially chaotic situation that confronted Saul when, not long after Herod Agrippa's death, he and Barnabas, along with John Mark, set off from Antioch for Barnabas' home island of Cyprus. Saul was already seeking strategic places in which to establish Christian communities, in fulfillment of the call that he had received on the road to Damascus.

According to Acts 13:5–8, they began by preaching among Jews in the synagogues of Salamis, Cyprus' largest city. They probably continued to preach in synagogues as they traveled the length of the island. The practice whereby members of the congregation would address the gathering in the course of services was part of the synagogue's historic role as the center of education in Jewish communities. It became an essential element in the spread of the gospel.

At Paphos, the capital of Cyprus, on the western coast, Saul was summoned by the Roman proconsul, Sergius Paulus. With the proconsul was a Jewish magician—a man who claimed to be able to influence people's destiny by the use of charms and magic—who called himself Bar-Jesus, or the son of Jesus. The proconsul "sought to hear the word of God" from Saul, apparently in order to judge between his teachings and those of the magician.

Saul met the challenge directly and, according to Acts 13:11, cursed the magician with temporary blindness that resembled the blindness Saul himself had experienced after his revelation on the road to Damascus. The proconsul was won over, giving Saul his first victory in a strictly Roman situation. It is significant that Acts 13:9 uses Saul's Roman name, Paul, for the first time in describing this confrontation and never again calls him by his Jewish name. From this point on, the story in Acts is about the planting of a new faith among Gentiles in cities of the Roman Empire.

Paul the Apostle

From Cyprus, Paul and his company sailed to Asia Minor. They traveled north into the mountains to Antioch of Pisidia, one of at least 16 cities named Antioch in the empire. In this thriving Roman colony, as in other cities he visited, Paul spoke first in the synagogue, telling Jews and God-fearing Gentiles alike that forgiveness of sin was proclaimed through Jesus and that "by him every one that believes is freed from everything from which you could not be freed by the law of Moses" (Acts 13:39). His words were apparently attentively received, for he was asked to speak again the following week.

On that occasion, says Acts 13:44, "almost the whole city gathered together to hear the word of God." But tradition-minded Jews, who saw the substantial threat to their community in Paul's words, tried to turn the meeting into a debate. Paul responded by quoting Isaiah, "I have set you to be a light for the Gentiles, that you may bring salvation to the uttermost parts of the earth" (Acts 13:47).

Paul made many converts among the Gentiles of Pisidian Antioch, which only increased the animosity of his opponents. They, too, had sought to be a light for the Gentiles. They had attracted God-fearers—some of whom went on to become full proselytes to Judaism—by teaching observance of the Torah and worship of the one God. Now, in the name of the God of Israel, Paul was undermining their own long-standing work by putting forward an executed criminal as the Messiah and by offering the Gentiles salvation without requiring observance of the law. Paul and Barnabas were driven from the district. They went on to other cities of Asia Minor, followed by angry Jews who sought to stop them, as they saw it, from further perverting the law.

Acts 14 says that in Lystra, a Lycaonian city that boasted of its temple to Zeus, Paul cured a cripple, and the people hailed him and Barnabas as incarnations of Hermes and Zeus. A sacrifice was prepared in their honor. The missionaries put a stop to it, but the suggestion of idolatry was enough to fuel the rage of their opponents. Paul was stoned and left for dead.

He survived this and other attacks, however, and before his return to Antioch he revisited the Christian communities he had founded, to evaluate their situation, strengthen their resolution, and further inspire them with the universality of Jesus' message.

Conference in Jerusalem

Before A.D. 50, the stresses that were inherent in Paul's mission to the Gentiles reached the point of crisis. The emperor Claudius had expelled the Jews from Rome, possibly prompted by the activities of Christians—Suetonius, a Roman historian, later wrote that the Jews had been stirred up by an agitator named "Chrestus." This expulsion certainly included Jews who were also Christians and indicates that the Roman authorities did not yet distinguish the Christians as a separate group.

Meanwhile, Jewish Christians from Judea had come to Antioch in Syria to teach that only those who were circumcised could be saved in Jesus' name. From their viewpoint, since Jesus was the Messiah promised to Israel, there was no tension between the new faith and the Torah. Circumcision was, and must remain in their eyes, the sign of God's "everlasting covenant" with Abraham. This direct contradiction of Paul's teaching threatened to split the church in two, and so a conference of the Apostles and elders had been arranged in Jerusalem to settle the question.

Paul told the conference of the work he had been doing and persuaded them that he was, indeed,

Paul forces Peter to eat—this detail from a 17th-century Beauvais tapestry illustrates the dispute that took place in Antioch over sharing meals with Gentiles.

serving the will of God by opening the faith to all humanity. The members of the group gave one another "the right hand of fellowship," and it was decided that Paul was to continue his missionary work among the Gentiles while Peter would lead the proclamation of the faith to the Jews. It was as much a compromise as a decision, for the rift remained and would surface in the future. Soon, a confrontation with Peter, described later by Paul in Galatians 2, demonstrated that the question was far from resolved.

Peter came to Antioch and shared communal meals with Jews and Gentiles alike. But later, when Judeans came who followed the dietary laws, he "drew back," probably insisting that Gentiles should also follow these laws if the two groups were to break bread in fellowship together. It may have been meant as an act of diplomacy, but Paul would have none of it. "If you, though a Jew, live like a Gentile and not like a Jew," he demanded, "how can you compel the Gentiles to live like Jews?"

Paul's letters

Paul was to spend the rest of his life establishing Christian churches in cities of the Mediterranean world and guiding their development, both with personal visits and with letters. Acts tells of some of the places he went, and draws gripping pictures of many of the adversities and persecutions that he overcame. But it is from his own letters that we gain a deeper insight into the nature of the problems he faced in forging a fellowship out of a widespread collection of Christian communities.

Paul may have written many letters that did not

survive. All those that were preserved were written in response to specific situations, often in answer to questions; but in addressing questions at hand, Paul also developed the central core of the new faith.

The church in Corinth

Paul had special concern for the church he founded in the lively and vital seaport of Corinth. Located on the narrow isthmus that connects southern and central Greece, the city was a crossroads for the empire. Between its two busy harbors, one facing east and the other west, cargo was moved on a wooden railway, and a constant flow of travelers and sailors kept the population in vigorous flux.

Like many other wealthy seaports, Corinth was both a hotbed of vice and a center for the exchange of fashionable "truths." Paul knew that the message of Jesus would be carried throughout the empire from a church established there. But though the city was fertile soil in which to plant a church, it was also rocky soil, and Paul had no easy task to ensure that the church he planted there would be firmly rooted.

He stayed more than a year and a half on his first visit, plying his trade as a tentmaker while he preached, organized, and wrote letters to other churches. He faced formidable competition, not only from his opponents in the Jewish community but from the proponents of a wide range of religions and philosophies, both Western and Eastern.

There were cults of Aphrodite, Astarte, Demeter, and a host of other deities, some of which offered orgiastic revels in the course of worship. There were mystery cults—including some that were beginning to spread alongside Christianity—that promised a rapturous afterlife to initiates, often without concern for moral or ethical behavior. And there were popular philosophers, most notably Cynics, Stoics, and Epicureans, preaching morality based on ethical systems of behavior with little foundation in religion.

The effect of the popular Greek philosophies was

During his three missionary journeys, Paul stopped in many cities. Upon his return to Jerusalem, Paul was accused of defiling the Temple and was later sent to Rome, his fourth and final journey (map, opposite).
Above: *The ruins of a Roman aqueduct in Pisidian Antioch, an important military center visited by Paul on his first journey.*
Right: *A harbor on Rhodes, the island where Paul stopped near the end of his third journey.*
Facing page, left: *The ruins of a Roman salt factory on Malta, where Paul spent three months after being shipwrecked.*
Far right: *The Church of the Blessed Virgin Mary of the Golden City in Paphos, Cyprus. Local tradition has it that Paul was tied to one of these Roman pillars and flogged.*

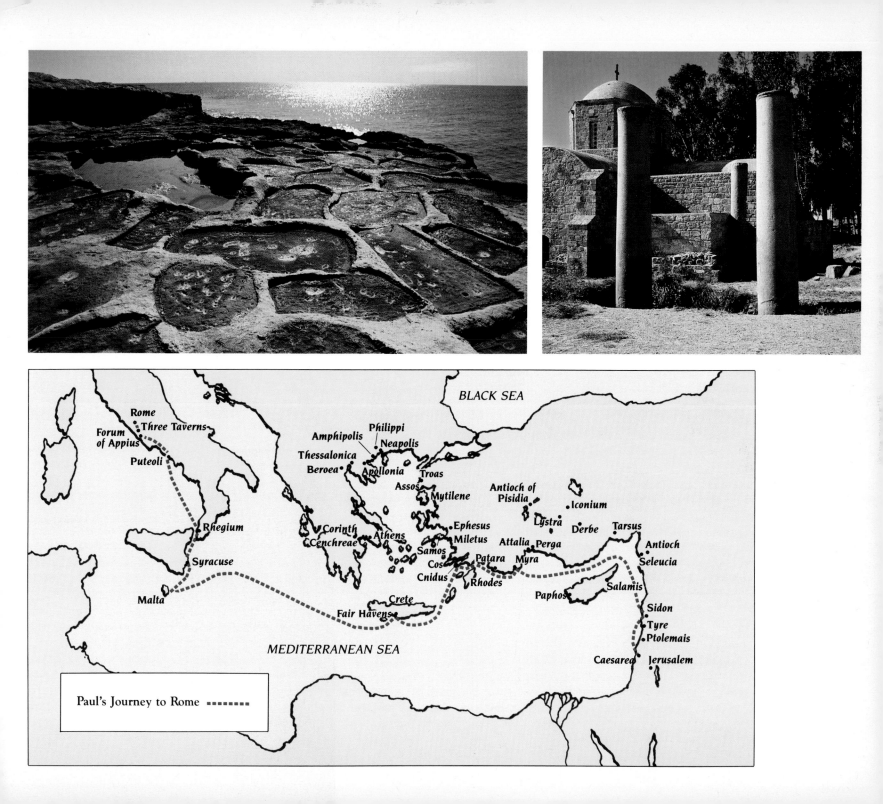

Paul's Journey to Rome ....

The boy Jesus visits the Temple in ▶
Jerusalem at Passover, c. A.D. 6.

Tiberius succeeds Caesar Augustus ▶
as Roman emperor 14–37.

◀ Council in Jerusalem decides
circumcision is not a prerequisite for
conversion to Christianity c. 50.

Simon bar Kokhba leads second Jewish ▶
revolt against Rome 132–135;
Roman general Severus defeats the
Jewish rebels, who are dispersed;
Judea is renamed Syria-Palestina;
Jerusalem becomes a Roman city 135.

Nero rules as Roman ▶
emperor 54–68;
Rome burns; Christians
are blamed 64.

Jesus is baptized and begins his ministry; ▶
John the Baptist is beheaded c. 26.
Pontius Pilate becomes prefect of Judea 26.

◀ Paul is taken to Rome in c. 60. After
imprisonment in Rome, Paul is executed c. 62.
Gessius Florus becomes last prefect of Judea 64.
First Jewish revolt against Rome begins 66.

Jesus is crucified c. 29. ▶

◀ Vespasian reigns as Roman emperor 69–79.
Roman commander Titus captures
Jerusalem and destroys the Temple 70.
Masada falls after mass suicide of
Jewish freedom fighters 73.

Stephen is martyred; Paul converts ▶
to Christianity c. 34.

Caligula reigns as Roman ▶
emperor 37–41.
Claudius rules as Roman
emperor 41–54.

Titus is Roman emperor 79–81. ▶

Herod Agrippa I, becomes king of Judea 41; ▶
Upon Herod Agrippa I's death, Judea
becomes a Roman province ruled by a
Roman prefect 44.

Domitian reigns as Roman ▶
emperor 81–96.

Vespasian 69–79

Trajan rules as Roman ▶
emperor 98–117.

*Bronze coin of Pontius Pilate
struck in Jerusalem in A.D. 31*

Paul begins missionary journeys c. 46. ▶

Hadrian reigns as Roman ▶
emperor 117–138.

Emperor Claudius expels Jews from Rome c. 49. ▶

1 B.C.   A.D. 50   A.D. 100

These few centuries were times of profound change in the Mediterranean world. They encompassed the death and crucifixion of Jesus Christ, the struggle for power within the ever-weakening Roman empire, the destruction of Jerusalem, and the founding and spread of a new faith that came to be known as Christianity.

particularly pervasive. Even though a person might not support the Stoic principle of *logos* (universal reason) or hold to the Epicurean principle of *ataraxia* (calmness leading to inner harmony and happiness), such concepts were part of the common tongue, and everyone's thinking was shaped by them to some extent—just as 20th-century thinking is shaped by such Freudian concepts as the ego and the subconscious mind.

Through the years, Paul maintained contact with the Christians of Corinth. He paid at least one personal visit, sent representatives such as Titus and Timothy, and kept up a lively correspondence. In

his writings to the Corinthians he repeatedly expressed his concern at the way they were being influenced by the turbulent moral and intellectual atmosphere in which they lived. The letter we know as 1 Corinthians was written in response to a message; in the view of many scholars, 2 Corinthians is probably composed of several letter fragments that were copied onto a single scroll at some later date.

First and second letters to the Corinthians

In 1 Corinthians Paul began with an appeal that the fellowship remain united in faith and not allow itself to be split into disputing factions. The letter dealt

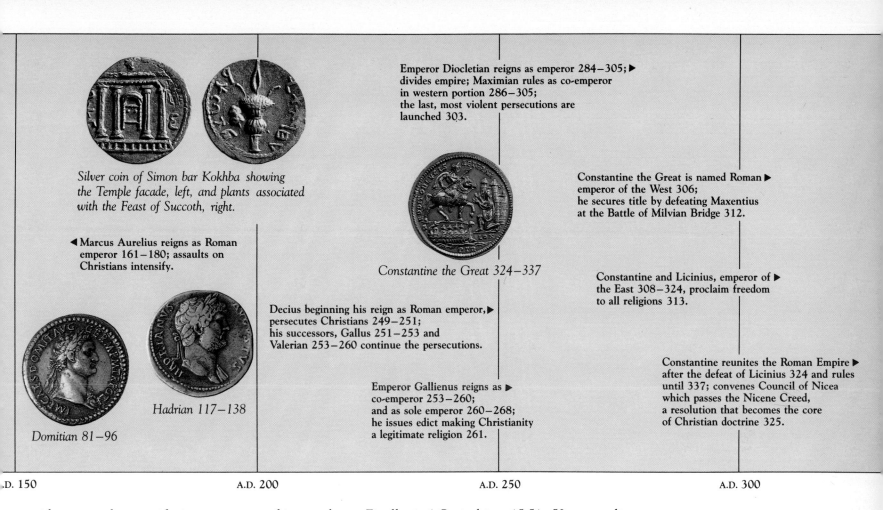

Silver coin of Simon bar Kokhba showing
the Temple facade, left, and plants associated
with the Feast of Succoth, right.

◄ Marcus Aurelius reigns as Roman
emperor 161–180; assaults on
Christians intensify.

Domitian 81–96

Hadrian 117–138

Emperor Diocletian reigns as emperor 284–305; ►
divides empire; Maximian rules as co-emperor
in western portion 286–305;
the last, most violent persecutions are
launched 303.

Constantine the Great 324–337

Decius beginning his reign as Roman emperor, ►
persecutes Christians 249–251;
his successors, Gallus 251–253 and
Valerian 253–260 continue the persecutions.

Emperor Gallienus reigns as ►
co-emperor 253–260;
and as sole emperor 260–268;
he issues edict making Christianity
a legitimate religion 261.

Constantine the Great is named Roman ►
emperor of the West 306;
he secures title by defeating Maxentius
at the Battle of Milvian Bridge 312.

Constantine and Licinius, emperor of ►
the East 308–324, proclaim freedom
to all religions 313.

Constantine reunites the Roman Empire ►
after the defeat of Licinius 324 and rules
until 337; convenes Council of Nicea
which passes the Nicene Creed,
a resolution that becomes the core
of Christian doctrine 325.

A.D. 150   A.D. 200   A.D. 250   A.D. 300

with many other specific issues: reports of immoral
behavior and of lawsuits among the fellowship, questions about marriage, about eating food that had
been sacrificed to idols (pagan temples were the
source of much of the meat sold in the city's markets), about speaking in tongues, and about methods
of worship. In addressing these questions, Paul repeatedly counseled self-control and the importance
of building up the community. Above all, he
stressed the essential simplicity of the faith and of
the love that unified the Christian fellowship. "So
faith, hope, love abide, these three; but the greatest
of these is love" (1 Corinthians 13:13).

Finally, in 1 Corinthians 15:51–53, responding to
questions about resurrection, he expressed a kernel
of faith that would grow into a cornerstone for the
developing church: "Lo! I tell you a mystery. We
shall not all sleep, but we shall all be changed, in a
moment, in the twinkling of an eye, at the last
trumpet. For the trumpet will sound, and the dead
will be raised imperishable, and we shall be
changed. For this perishable nature must put on
the imperishable, and this mortal nature must put
on immortality."

Many vexing difficulties with which Paul had to
deal in Corinth seem to have come from other

Paul's letters were written on papyrus, made from the 8- to 20-foot-tall Cyperus papyrus, like those above in the Huleh Swamp, Israel. The pith of the stem was cut into strips, which were laid side by side, overlapping slightly. More strips were laid across them, and the whole was beaten into a durable whitish sheet. Such sheets were attached end to end to make scrolls—Paul's Letter to the Romans would have needed a scroll some 13 feet long. It was probably rolled and sealed like the scroll at right. In later centuries papyrus sheets were made into booklike codices. At the far right is a page of Philippians 4:2–12 from a third-century A.D. codex.

Christian teachers who came there and were heeded. These men apparently carried letters of recommendation extolling their own goodness and justifying their claims to spiritual leadership. They disparaged Paul as a man of little power, a financial burden on the other churches, and an unskilled speaker, who could write forceful letters but who offered no tangible proof of the truth of his message.

In 2 Corinthians, Paul responded with pleading, with anger, with irony, with threats, with promises, and always with love. In defending himself and his teaching, he stressed that the legitimacy of the gospel could not depend on the authority of any teacher, but on the overriding truth of the sacrifice of Jesus. "For the love of Christ controls us, because we are convinced that one has died for all; therefore all have

died. And he died for all, that those who live might live no longer for themselves but for him who for their sake died and was raised" (2 Corinthians 5:14–15).

Letter to the Galatians

In the course of Paul's second missionary journey, he traveled through the province of Galatia, in the region of today's Ankara in central Turkey. Again, as in Corinth, other Christian missionaries arrived who sought to undo his work. They apparently represented Jewish Christians who believed that all Gentiles had to become proselytes to Judaism if they were to be Christians. In his letter to the Galatians, probably written about A.D. 55, Paul once again had to deal with the issues that had been raised in the Jerusalem conference.

Paul began the letter by telling of his own "former life in Judaism," of the revelation he experienced, and of his early conflicts, including the conference in Jerusalem and the confrontation with Peter. He went on, in Galatians 2:19, to state his faith—"For I through the law died to the law, that I might live to God." Then he asserted, for all time, Christianity's fulfillment of and separation from Judaism.

The key, he said, lay in the promise God had given to Abraham and his offspring; the law, he wrote, "was added because of transgressions, till the offspring should come to whom the promise had been made" (Galatians 3:19). Jesus, he said, was the promised offspring, and so "in Christ Jesus neither circumcision nor uncircumcision is of any avail, but faith working through love" (Galatians 5:6). "For

By A.D. 100 Christianity had spread throughout much of the Roman Empire, and the refusal of Christians to acknowledge the gods of Rome was seen as a threat to the empire's stability. The maps above and at left show the location of known churches of the time. Many were related to Jewish communities of the Diaspora, but—thanks to Paul and other missionaries, such as Timothy and Titus—many others were Gentile congregations.

Symbols of Christianity

Although most symbols adopted by early Christians had ancient antecedents in Judaism and other cultures, they became invested with special significance. The cross—symbolic of Jesus' death and resurrection—also formed an X, the first letter of the word *Christ* in Greek. It was similar to the Egyptian ankh, symbolic of life, and the ancient hooked cross, and both forms came to be part of its mystique. Another symbol with multiple meanings was the fish: it stood for baptism in living water, and it recalled Jesus' promise to make the disciples "fishers of men." But most significant to Christians during Roman persecutions was the fact that the letters of *ichthys*, the Greek word for "fish," formed an acronym for "Jesus Christ, God's Son, Savior." Images of Jesus as shepherd and as sacrificial lamb both draw on Jewish roots, as do the bread and wine of the eucharist. Other common symbols include the peacock, emblem of paradise, and the vine, emblem of immortality.

The Lamb of God displays the flag of victory in this terra-cotta wreath by the 15th-century Italian sculptor Luca della Robbia.

A fish and three Maltese crosses on a fourth-century gold ring.

The hooked cross appeared as a decoration on an eighth-century B.C. Greek vase. This shape was used by early Christians as a disguised cross during the time of persecutions.

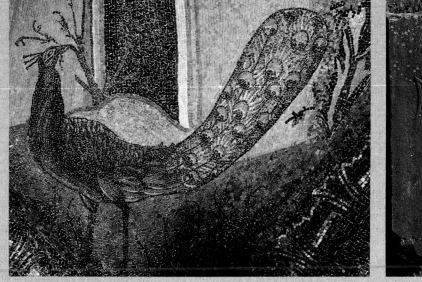

This peacock is part of a 14th-century mosaic in Istanbul's Mosque of Kari.

Latin cross from fourth-century Ephesus.

The monogram cross, shown above in an early Christian mosaic found in Carthage, incorporates chi and rho, *the first two letters of the word* Christ *in Greek. The distinctive Celtic cross, right, its four arms radiating out from the circle of immortality, may have begun as a variation.*

Russian Orthodox crucifix, crafted of silver gilt, has three transoms, or crosspieces, the lowest one slanted.

The fifth-century Byzantine pendant was probably worn on a neck chain.

The ninth-century Byzantine crucifix is cloisonné— enamel on metal.

the whole law is fulfilled in one word, 'You shall love your neighbor as yourself' " (Galatians 5:14).

Paul continually stressed his own frailties, weaknesses, and defeats, not his achievements or virtues, and in so doing he shaped a doctrine that would remain essential to Christianity's future growth: the polarity between human weakness and the strength of God. In Paul's letters the transcendant symbol of the cross, representing the singular sacrifice that embodied this polarity, was given its place as the standard of Christianity.

Imprisonment and death in Rome

After an intense career proclaiming the new faith, Paul spent his final years as a Roman prisoner. In A.D. 60 he was arrested in Jerusalem, where he had gone with money collected among Gentile Christians for the impoverished community of disciples in Judea. Wrongly charged with bringing Gentiles into the Temple's inner precincts, he was set upon by an angry crowd. Roman troops rescued him and took him into custody. After a series of long delays, he asserted his right as a Roman citizen to be heard by the emperor and was sent to Rome under guard.

Although the ship carrying Paul and his Roman guards was wrecked in the course of the journey, the company eventually reached the city. It had long been a goal of Paul's to preach in the center of the empire and to share fellowship with the large Christian community that existed there. Acts 28:30–31, the book's last two verses, say that he spent two whole years under house arrest in Rome, "and welcomed all who came to him, preaching the kingdom of God and teaching about the Lord Jesus Christ quite openly and unhindered."

Paul may have had some faith in Roman justice, but in spite of that, he was probably condemned and beheaded in Rome about A.D. 62. Roman justice had taken an unexpected turn owing to the unpredictable nature of imperial succession.

Paul's reputation as the Apostle to the Gentiles preceded him to Jerusalem, and when he was falsely accused of bringing Gentiles into the Temple, "all the city was aroused, and the people ran together; they seized Paul and dragged him out of the temple, and at once the gates were shut." Acts 21:30. The Roman soldiers who rescued him had no idea who he was or what he had done. They bound him in chains and, to protect him from the angry mob, carried him.

Persecution by Nero

The emperor Nero, who had succeeded his great-uncle and adoptive father Claudius in A.D. 54, was a patron of the arts, an uninhibited hedonist, an ardent admirer of all things Greek, and a strong proponent of the traditional gods and the cult of emperor worship. In the early years of his reign, he had brought about—through education, public spectacle, and even new legislation—a general enthusiasm among Romans for his tastes. But he went too far, making himself a buffoon by singing and reciting his own poetry in contests that no one dared to let him lose, and a menace by using the great power of his office to indulge his whims.

When Rome was destroyed by fire in A.D. 64, and the rumor spread that the emperor himself had set it so that he could rebuild the city to his own tastes, Nero needed a scapegoat upon whom to divert public fury. The Christians were made to order. They were intensely disliked by many Romans—not only because they, like the Jews, were "atheists," who refused to acknowledge the gods of Rome—but because they often tried to foist their beliefs on others. They were considered guilty of *odium humani generis,* or "hatred of the human race," for their active condemnation of the religious practices and moral standards of Roman society.

Moreover, though Nero was neither rational nor wise, he was astute enough to realize that, despite the many ties between Christianity and Judaism, the new faith was no longer simply a part of the older one, as Claudius had considered it to be. The Romans had long tolerated the particular ethnic traditions of the Jewish people and had usually avoided unprofitable attempts to force Jews to go against their ancestral laws by honoring other gods. But it had become clear—perhaps through the conflicts between Jews and Christians in Rome—that the Christians were not such a traditional, national group, but, in the words of the Roman historian

Tacitus, were a "mixed class" of Jews and non-Jews, who followed a "deadly superstition" and who practiced "abominations."

Arrests were made and, again according Tacitus, "those first were taken who confessed, then on their testimony a vast multitude was convicted, not so much on the charge of arson as of hatred of the human race. A sport was made of their execution. Some, sewn in the skins of animals, were torn apart by dogs. Others were crucified or burned, and still others, as darkness drew on, were used as torches. Nero devoted his gardens to the spectacle, provided a show in the circus, and himself, in the costume of a charioteer, rode around among the crowd."

No reliable evidence exists about the fate of Peter, who may have come to Rome during this period. Several early Christian writers said that he was martyred in Nero's Rome. If so, as the leader of the church, he would probably have been among the first taken, and his "confession" would have been nothing more than a proclamation of his faith. Later tradition has it that, like Jesus, he was crucified, but with his head downward at his own request.

Rebellion in Palestine

In Judea, the remarkably unwise, corrupt, and brutal government of several Roman procurators was driving more and more Jews toward intense anti-Roman nationalism. After the procurator Festus died in office, and before he could be replaced, the Sadducee high priest Ananus took the opportunity to bring James, the leader of Jerusalem's Christian fellowship, to trial and to execute him by stoning.

As Roman harshness increased, so too did the violence of resistance, led by the Zealots and other militant sects. The terror inspired among the upper classes by bands of *sicarii*, or "dagger men," who struck without warning, kidnapping or assassinating Romans and Jewish collaborators, made for a volatile atmosphere that needed only a spark to blaze.

The spark was struck in the spring of A.D. 66, when the long conflict between Jews and Greeks in Caesarea led to an incident in which some Greeks contemptuously performed a pagan sacrifice at the entrance to the synagogue. Violence broke out. Jewish leaders protested to the procurator, Gessius Florus. He had them arrested. In addition, he raided the Temple treasury for a large sum of money, and when the Jews protested this act, he sent in troops to sack parts of Jerusalem. Some 3,600 men, women, and children are said to have perished in the slaughter, and open rebellion erupted.

Early victories

Jewish forces at first achieved surprising success in Jerusalem. They drove the Roman troops out of the Upper City, put the Roman archives to the torch, and captured the Antonia fortress. To the south and east, the Roman-held fortresses of Machaerus and Masada were taken and looted for weapons to use in Jerusalem, and by late summer the city was entirely in Jewish hands. After fighting off an attack by the Twelfth Roman Legion, led by the Syrian governor Cestius Gallus, the rebels divided Palestine into seven military districts. So confident were they of victory that they began to mint their own coins.

Nero dispatched three Roman legions, which arrived in A.D. 67 under the command of General Titus Flavius Vespasianus, soon to become the emperor Vespasian. The legions cut a bloody swath through Galilee, and by the summer of A.D. 68 they had encircled Jerusalem and occupied nearly all the surrounding area. The general of the Jewish forces in Galilee, Joseph ben Matthias, was captured at Jotapata, but he lived to write the story of the war and of much Jewish history that preceeded it; he is known to us as the historian Josephus.

Nero was deposed by the Roman Senate on June 8, A.D. 68, and committed suicide the next day. Vespasian, the eventual winner of the fight for

Nero took the imperial throne in A.D. 54 at the age of 16, after his mother, Agrippina II, had poisoned her husband (and Nero's adoptive father), the emperor Claudius I. His reign was legendary for self-indulgence and brutality. He killed many of his family, including Agrippina, and was suspected of setting the fire that destroyed Rome in A.D. 64—for which he shifted the blame onto Rome's Christians. The Senate declared him an enemy of the people in A.D. 68, and he committed suicide.

The triumphal Arch of Titus in Rome was erected to commemorate the victory over the Jewish rebellion, achieved by Titus in A.D. 70 on behalf of his father, the emperor Vespasian. A relief on the arch, above, shows laurel-crowned Roman soldiers parading into Rome with the golden menorah and other plunder from Jerusalem's ruined Temple.

succession, departed for Alexandria, where he was proclaimed emperor in A.D. 69, leaving his son Titus to head the campaign in Judea.

The destruction of Jerusalem

Jewish forces, perhaps 25,000 strong but deeply divided into rival revolutionary parties, were poised to repel four legions of Roman soldiers, strengthened by the armies of allied kings. The Jews were confined to Jerusalem, Herodium, Machaerus, and the virtually impregnable fortress of Masada. By early June of A.D. 70, the Romans had breached two of Jerusalem's walls and taken control of the city's northern quarter. They erected a siege wall around the city with immediate effect: rations were soon desperately short. They took the Antonia fortress in late July, and the daily sacrifice in the Temple became a thing of the past. In August, Jewish defenders began giving way in the very Temple precincts. Finally the Temple complex was burned and razed.

After taking another month to capture the Upper City, Titus took the surviving populace into captivity. He then leveled virtually everything that remained standing in the city, leaving only part of the Citadel intact for use by his own troops. A year later, in A.D. 71, he staged a triumph in Rome, parading through the streets with high-ranking Jewish captives and treasures looted from the Temple.

Death at Masada

Meanwhile, a band of rebels clung unvanquished to the rock of Masada. Not until A.D. 73 were they overcome by the Romans' matchless skill at weaponry and engineering, but even in death they did not acknowledge defeat. The story of their end, the stuff of legend, lives on in the hearts of Jews to this day.

Flavius Silva, the new Roman procurator, first had a wall built around the base of the mountain to prevent the rebels from escaping or receiving aid. He then ordered the construction of a great ramp. After months of labor, it reached the height of the fortress, some 300 feet above the desert, allowing battering rams to breach Masada's wall. The defenders retreated behind a second wall, a wooden barricade, which the Romans set afire. When the soldiers broke through the charred timbers the next day, they found little but death. Some 960 men, women, and children had perished in a suicide pact rather than submit to Roman domination. Only two women and five children survived.

With the end of the Jewish rebellion and the destruction of Jerusalem and its Temple—following less than a decade after the loss of Peter, Paul, and James, the three pillars of the early church—the separation of Christianity from Judaism was nearly complete. Much of Jerusalem's Christian community had evidently fled the city before the siege, and few returned to Judea. The churches in Galilee and

Samaria survived, but the fellowship of Gentile Christians that Paul and his compatriots had created throughout the central regions of the empire became the body of the church. The Christian community in Rome, despite Nero's persecutions and others that would follow, became even more important, since the city was the heart of the empire.

Christian worship

Christian worship everywhere continued to reflect its roots in synagogues of the Diaspora. The believers met on the first day of the week for assemblies that emphasized prayer and instruction. The Greek translation of Jewish Scripture was read and interpreted; and gradually, whenever such Christian documents as Paul's letters were available, they too were read.

The Lord's Supper remained the central observance. It was part of an actual meal in which the sacrifice of Christ was reaffirmed, as were the fellowship and love of those who met in his name. But Paul's admonition to the Corinthians—that the meal was meant not to satisfy bodily hunger but to commemorate the dawn of a new age—was not forgotten. Sins were confessed so that the meal could be approached worthily, and thanks were offered. In time, the meal came to be called the Eucharist, from the Greek word for "giving thanks."

We catch some further glimpses of everyday Christian practices from an early church manual called the *Didache*, or "Teaching"—the full title was *The Lord's Teaching Through the Twelve Apostles to the Gentiles*. It was probably compiled in Syria before A.D. 100. From its pages we learn that Christians shared the Eucharist on the first day of the week, called "the Lord's Day of the Lord," and that they also practiced baptism, if possible by immersion in "living," or flowing, water. They recited the Lord's Prayer three times a day, fasted on Wednesdays and Fridays, and gave extensive support to prophets and teachers, who traveled from town to town.

Other insights into early Christian worship come from the writings of a convert to Christianity named Justin, who is commonly referred to as Justin Martyr because of the manner of his death. About A.D. 155,

Few tales of valor or ingenuity can match that of the siege of Masada. The well-supplied Jewish rebels could not be starved out, nor could the sheer cliffs be scaled in force. After building a series of camps (A, below) and a siege wall (B), the Roman commander, Flavius Silva, ordered construction of an earth and stone ramp (C), which took seven months to complete. When the troops broke through the walls, they found 960 defenders dead in a mass suicide. Today Masada, below left, is an Israeli shrine where army recruits are given the oath of allegiance.

he addressed to the emperor a defense of Christianity (*Apologia I*), in which he denied the charges of atheism and immorality that were commonly used against Christians. He also gave a description of many elements of Christian teaching and practice.

In describing Christian worship of his time, Justin told of extensive prayers, followed by the exchange of a kiss of peace. He said that there were readings from the "memoirs of the Apostles" (the Gospels) as well as from the Old Testament prophets "as long as time permits." The "president" of the congregation apparently delivered a kind of sermon, exhorting the assembly "to imitation of these noble things," and afterward the whole congregation shared in the Eucharist. Deacons even took the Eucharist to those members who were absent. No one, Justin emphasized, was eligible to share in the Eucharist unless he had assented to Christ's teachings, having been washed clean of his sins through baptism.

Growth of the church

To the Roman emperors who followed Vespasian and his son Titus—Domitian, Nerva, Trajan, and Hadrian—the fast-growing Christian Church was a matter of only occasional, but sometimes serious, concern. Among the governing classes and in much of the populace, Christianity was seen as an incredible superstition. People were often eager to believe the worst of these tight-knit communities, and lurid rumors fed the darkest public fears. People spoke of cannibalism (eating flesh and drinking blood) and of incest (brothers and sisters in secret meetings). Even when such rumors were not believed, the Christians' "atheistic" refusal to honor the gods who had blessed Rome and who maintained the prosperity of its people was a clear affront to the empire's well-being. It was during Hadrian's reign that the Roman biographer Suetonius listed the persecution of Christians as one of Nero's social reforms.

The emperor Domitian, who took the throne in A.D. 81, governed relatively well in some ways, but after a plot against him in A.D. 88, he became increasingly despotic and unpredictable. As Caligula had done before him, he proclaimed himself a lord and god, and in his final years he instituted a reign of terror that struck primarily at the upper classes but destroyed many other people as well. Domitian banished or executed those he saw as his enemies, including "philosophers," "atheists," and Jews. Among those exiled was a Christian named John, who, banished to the island of Patmos, wrote the Book of Revelation. References in that book to the "tribulation" of the "seven Churches that are in Asia" very likely pointed to repressions under Domitian.

In spite of rumors and repression, the church grew. It drew members largely from the lower classes, but its appeal crossed the empire's rigid class lines, so that its membership ranged from the lowliest slaves to high-ranking aristocrats. It has been estimated that by A.D. 100, as many as 300,000 believers were in the empire. The church was especially strong in certain regions—perhaps 80,000 Christians were concentrated in Asia Minor alone.

Sporadic repressions

It is from the Black Sea coast of Asia Minor that one of the most illuminating witnesses to the relation between the church and the empire comes to us, in the form of letters from a Roman named Pliny to the emperor Trajan. Pliny was the governor of Pontus and Bithynia, a region that was rife with unrest and corruption, and Trajan wanted him to bring affairs into order there. Trouble was often fomented by members of social, political, or religious clubs and organizations, many of which had become so worrisome that Trajan ordered Pliny to ban all such societies. He even refused to make an exception so that the people of the city of Nicomedia could organize a volunteer fire department.

All Christian congregations fell under the ban, of

The emperor Domitian, left, punished those who rejected the Roman gods. Trajan, above, persecuted Christians only if they were denounced and refused to recant. Hadrian, right, maintained Trajan's policy toward Christians. In A.D. 135 he quashed the second Jewish revolt; thousands of Jews were killed or enslaved, and Judea was renamed Syria-Palestina.

course, but that fact added only slightly to their tribulations; for, as Pliny's letters make clear, it was a capital offense simply to be "named" Christian. Many people were brought before the governor on the charge of being Christians. Some were accused by individuals, others by anonymous letters.

The illegal religion

In Pliny's own succinct words, "I asked them whether they were Christians, and if they confessed, I asked them a second and third time with threats of punishment. If they kept to it, I ordered them for execution." It was as simple as that. Those Christians who could claim Roman citizenship were dispatched to Rome for trial and execution.

Pliny's principal question was what he should do about those who had been Christians but who had renounced the faith. Many such apostates had, he wrote, "recited a prayer to the gods at my dictation, made supplication with incense and wine to your statue, . . . and moreover cursed Christ." Should they still be tried for crimes that they may have committed while they were Christians? Or was the offense simply to *be* a Christian—and if so, should renunciation justify release? Pliny was concerned "especially on account of the number of those in danger; for many of all ages and every rank, and also of both sexes are brought into present or future danger. The contagion of that superstition has penetrated not the cities only, but the villages and the country."

In his reply, Trajan set the policy that was to exist for many decades: There was to be no official persecution, but being a Christian was to remain a capital offense. "They are not to be sought out"; he wrote,

The Catacombs of Rome

The catacombs were underground cemeteries, or "places of rest," where the bodies of the Christian dead awaited resurrection in shelflike niches, sealed behind slabs of marble, slate, or earthenware. The Romans prohibited burial in populated areas, and so cemeteries were outside the city. Christian burials were probably in the ground or in mausoleums at first, but by the third century A.D., tunnels were dug in the soft tufa soil, which becomes rock-hard upon drying. By the fourth century, some 90 miles of labyrinthine galleries may have riddled the hills near Rome. Despite romantic legend, they probably never hid persecuted Christians. Catacombs were also dug in Naples, Malta, Tunisia, and other places.

Above: *The fish and anchor of this mosaic, from the Catacomb of Hermes in Tunisia, stand for Christ and his faithful followers.* Above left: *Catacomb of SS. Peter and Marcellinus in Rome.* Left: *Inscription from the tomb of a 21-year-old: "and in thy prayers thou pleadest for us, for we know thee in Christ."*

"but if they are accused and convicted, they must be punished—yet on this condition, that whoever denies himself to be a Christian and makes the fact plain by his action, that is, by worshiping our gods, shall obtain pardon on his repentance, however suspicious his past conduct may be."

Blood of the martyrs

The "name" of Christianity was banned, and any Christian was, at any moment, vulnerable to accusation by anyone who took offense against him for any reason. This situation made for sporadic periods of trouble and caused the churches to live defensively, so as not to endanger their members.

As more and more Christians died rather than renounce their faith, the importance of their sacrifice grew in the eyes of other believers. The legacy of Paul's teaching—that the heart of Christian faith lay in the crucifixion and resurrection of Jesus and that, as he wrote in Philippians 3:10, Christians could "know him and the power of his resurrection, and may share his sufferings, becoming like him in his death"—became a focal point of courage and of faith for all. Like Paul, the martyrs took joy in sharing Christ's sacrifice, and there were even those who welcomed death in order to achieve closeness with him. Year after year, decade after decade, they walked erect to their executions.

In later years, the martyrs' lives were considered appropriate material for sermons and homilies, and selections from the "acts" of the martyrs—accounts drawn from trial records, eyewitness testimony, and often pious imaginations—were read out at annual memorial services. There were other ways to remember the holy dead; in many places churches were later built at martyrs' graves, reminiscent of the old shrines to local heroes. Sometimes a shrine displayed a relic of its saint: a fragment of a tunic, a splinter of bone, an object he or she had used.

A contemporary view of the martyrs is given by the Greek satirist Lucian. For him, as for many in the Roman world, the actions of such people spoke less of bravery than of irrationality. "The poor wretches," he sneered, "have convinced themselves, first and foremost, that they are going to be immortal and live for all time. Therefore, they despise death and even willingly give themselves into custody, most of them. Furthermore, their first lawgiver persuaded them that they are all brothers of one another after they have transgressed once for all by denying the Greek gods and by worshiping that crucified sophist himself and living under his laws. Therefore they despise all things indiscriminately and consider them common property."

Christianity, the new force

Although the martyrs are today some of the most famous Christians of the second century and their importance to the development of the church cannot be denied, the fact is that the vast majority of Christians in most places and at most times lived at peace with their neighbors. Christianity continued to grow steadily, as Pliny clearly saw, and became too large a phenomenon to be seriously hurt by charges against individual Christians. Powerful bishops arose, as well as Christian scholars and teachers, and by no means were all of them executed as soon as they were known.

In a time when Judaism, after two unsuccessful revolts against Rome—the second had taken place in A.D. 132–135—was declining in its political importance, and when many pagans were growing increasingly dissatisfied with the traditional religions of Greece and Rome, the new faith filled a real need. Thousands flocked to it, no matter what the potential dangers might be. The church ceased to be defensive; it was becoming the new force to deal with. By the time the empire roused itself to do something serious about the growing movement, it was probably already too late to stop it.

The great persecutions

The first full-scale imperial attack on Christianity—and probably its severest test of survival—came about A.D. 250, when the emperor Decius set a deadline for all citizens to perform public sacrifice. Those who complied were to be issued a certificate testifying to their right to stay alive.

The growth of the church had brought in numbers of nominal Christians, who had no stomach for martyrdom, and many of them submitted. Others used bribery to procure *libelli*, as the certificates were called. Some Christians, such as the famous scholar Origen of Caesarea, were jailed and tortured.

Although it was Decius' intention to produce apostates rather than martyrs, many were executed. In parts of the empire, the persecutions were success-

Constantine the Great, the first Christian emperor, re-united the Roman Empire in A.D. 324 and moved its capital to Constantinople. Though he called himself a Christian, abolished crucifixion, and transformed the church from an outcast sect to an institution of wealth and power, he himself was baptized only on his death-bed in A.D. 337.

ful, in that they led to substantial defections from Christianity, but there was no effective follow-up to Decius' victory. Many Christians found it possible simply to stay in some form of hiding for a time before returning to their former lives.

Persecution continued under the emperors Gallus and Valerian, but in A.D. 261, Valerian's son Gallienus at last added Christianity to the list of *religiones licitae*, or legally tolerated religions. Ironically, although the period of tolerance lasted some 40 years, it was but a prelude to one of the bloodiest of all persecutions, initiated by the soldier-emperor Diocletian, who seized power in A.D. 284.

Diocletian's edicts

About two years after taking the imperial throne, Diocletian divided the empire into two parts, East and West, appointing two "senior" emperors, the augusti, and two "juniors," the caesars. He himself was augustus of the East. Diocletian's aim was reform of the government and the military. With these reforms under way, the emperor's anger was aroused about A.D. 298, when Christian members of the court made the sign of the cross during the taking of the omens—examining the entrails of a sacrificial animal. The omens were not good, and so Diocletian instituted a purge of Christian courtiers and soldiers.

Some Romans also blamed the empire's dire economic troubles on the Christians, and in A.D. 303 the first of four edicts was promulgated, all of which were aimed at exterminating the religion entirely. Diocletian's first decree banned religious gatherings, called for the destruction of churches and the surrender of books, and stripped Christians of many civil rights. A second decree threw Christian clerics into prison. A third provided for their release if they offered sacrifice and their deaths if they refused. The fourth edict, issued in A.D. 304, was a blanket demand that "all the people" offer sacrifice; the alternatives were death or hard labor.

Constantine the Great

Persecution continued under Galerius in the East and Constantius in the West until, in A.D. 311, Galerius wearily decreed the toleration of Christianity in his realm. In A.D. 312 Constantius' son, Constantine, defeated Maxentius, the son of an earlier augustus of the West, in the Battle of the Milvian Bridge near Rome, to secure his own succession in the West.

It was reported that Constantine prayed before the battle to the "supreme god" in an effort to ward off Maxentius' supposed magical powers. He was rewarded with the vision of a flaming cross in the midday sky, bearing the inscription *In hoc signo vinces* ("In this sign you shall conquer"). Constantine was also said to have dreamed that Christ counseled him to inscribe the symbol *chi rho* (the first two letters of the word *Christ* in Greek) on his soldiers' shields.

Whatever the realities of vision and dream, the historical fact is that Constantine won the battle and the Western throne, and he attributed his victory to the Christian God. In A.D. 313, he and Licinius, his counterpart in the East, agreed on an edict promulgating universal religious tolerance.

In A.D. 324 Constantine defeated Licinius in a battle to reunite the empire. He transferred the seat of government from Rome to a new capital at Constantinople, a move that also left the bishop of Rome as one of the most powerful political figures in the Western empire. In the years that followed, Constantine built magnificent churches in many cities of the empire, including Rome and Constantinople, and endowed them lavishly with funds.

Constantine seems to have viewed Christianity as a potential unifying force in the empire, but there were ambiguities in his own attitude. Although he called himself a Christian, he was unbaptized, and he continued to strike the coins of his reign with the image of the sun god, Apollo. When he made the Christian day of worship an official holiday, he named it "the venerable day of the sun," or Sunday.

On Easter Day in A.D. 337, Constantine was at peace with church and empire as he opened yet another of the churches with which he had beautified his luxurious new capital at Constantinople. This one was dedicated to the Holy Apostles. In the days that followed, the emperor fell ill. Visits to health-giving baths proved fruitless. As Pentecost approached, he made his peace with God, divided his empire among his three sons, and asked the bishop of Nicomedia to receive him formally into the church. He was baptized, and—still wearing the white robe of a Christian neophyte—he died on May 22, Pentecost Sunday, a little more than 300 years after the Holy Spirit's descent upon the Apostles during that fateful Pentecost in Jerusalem.

Constantine's legacy

Constantine had brought the church and its leaders into the powerful circles of the empire as never before. He had convened the great council of bishops at Nicaea, which formulated the original Nicene Creed and set forth a pattern of organization for the church's leaders. He had helped churches to regain the wealth and property that they had lost during the years of persecution. He had also begun to use the power of the state to aid one side against the other in theological debates within the church—heresy became an offense against the state.

Since its beginning among the uneducated disciples of a wandering Jewish teacher, the church had endured many tests, including long inner struggles and brutal persecutions from the outside. Now it was set on a new course and faced a new test.

Would it be able, without losing its unique spiritual identity, to form the foundation of an entire complex society as it replaced or incorporated the ancient traditions of Greece and Rome—and eventually of vast areas of the world?

Places in Bible Times

Christianity was a new idea in the first century A.D., but the cities and villages in which it took root had ancient pasts. The story of Christianity's development is often entwined in the history of these towns. It is the story of Nazareth, the rural hillside village of Jesus' youth, and of Capernaum, the center of Jesus' Galilean ministry, and of Bethany, the site of one of his greatest miracles. The well-known cities of the Middle East play a role here: Jericho, one of man's oldest permanent settlements; Caesarea Maritima, where Herod the Great constructed the largest port in Palestine; Antioch, where Christianity began to emerge as an independent religion separate from Judaism; and Damascus, the site of Paul's conversion. It is the story of Paul's travels to Ephesus, where his missionary success caused a riot among the followers of the fertility goddess Artemis, and of his church at the port of Corinth, a city famous for its loose morality. And finally, it is the story of Jerusalem and Rome. By Jesus' time, Jerusalem had been the capital of Judaism for over 1,000 years; eventually it also became sacred to both Christianity and Islam. Rome began by persecuting Christians, and yet the Christian church there flourished to become the dominant institution of the Middle Ages and the successor to the Roman Empire itself.

Alexandria

"Spiritual center of the Hellenistic world," Alexandria boasted the most famous library of ancient times. This beautiful city, founded in Egypt on the Mediterranean at the western edge of the Nile Delta by Alexander the Great in 332–331 B.C., was also a thriving commercial center. Busiest of ancient ports, it exported so much Egyptian wheat to Rome that it was called the "granary of the empire." Among its architectural achievements was the towering 400-foot-tall lighthouse on the nearby island of Pharos, one of the Seven Wonders of the Ancient World. Also remarkable was its elegant main street, the Canopic Way, a 200-foot-wide boulevard stretching for 3½ miles.

Scarcely mentioned in the Scriptures, this city of perhaps a million souls in Roman times was home to a community of Jews. The Jewish philosopher Philo of Alexandria tried to reconcile Judaic beliefs with Greek philosophy, but the most lasting achievement of scholarship in the city was the Septuagint, a rendering of the Old Testament into Greek that was used by New Testament writers and the early church. According to tradition, the Apostle Mark made his first convert in Alexandria in A.D. 45.

Antioch

According to tradition, the city where Christianity and Judaism began to separate was Antioch, the capital of Rome's province of Syria. It was there that Jesus' followers were first called Christians and that the mission to non-Jews began in earnest. The growth of a large Gentile congregation led the leaders of the early church to decree that a person could become a Christian without first being a Jew.

Antioch was founded about 300 B.C. by a successor of Alexander the Great, Seleucus I Nicator, and named for his father, Antiochus. Famous for its architecture, which included a theater, a public bath, a basilica (law court), and a two-mile-long colonnaded street complete with street lamps, the city also had a reputation for the variety of vices that flourished around the sanctuary of Apollo and Artemis. By the first century A.D., Antioch had become the third largest city in the Roman Empire, surpassed only by Alexandria and Rome.

During the persecution that followed the murder and martyrdom of Stephen, many of Jerusalem's Jews escaped to Antioch and formed the nucleus of the emerging Christian church there. Barnabas and Paul spent a year together in the city, and Antioch continued to serve as Paul's base during his travels. Traditionally the physician Luke, who may be the author of Acts and the Gospel that bears his name, is thought to have been a resident of Antioch, and possibly the Gospel of Matthew was written there.

Ascalon (Ashkelon)

One of the oldest cities in the Holy Land, Ascalon was rumored to be the birthplace of King Herod the Great. He lavished "baths, sumptuous fountains, and colonnades" upon it, according to Josephus, even though this Mediterranean seaport, about 12 miles north of Gaza, was not under his control.

An abundance of wells had attracted settlers to the site as early as the end of the third millennium B.C. In the Old Testament, Ashkelon (as it was then known) was one of the five Philistine city-states opposed to the Israelites during the period of the Judges, and Samson killed 30 of the enemy there, according to Judges 14:19. The city was destroyed by Nebuchadnezzar II in 604 B.C. As later conquerors swept back and forth across the Middle

East, however, the people of Ascalon (as it was called in the Greco-Roman period) survived by means of adroit diplomacy, even convincing the Romans to declare the town "free and allied." During the first Jewish revolt against Rome (A.D. 66–70) the Jews partially destroyed the city.

Athens

The Athens that Paul visited on his second missionary journey, about A.D. 50, was only a shadow of the Athens that 500 years earlier had been the chief city of Greece and Europe's greatest cultural center. The energy that had produced the Parthenon and other temples, the dramas of Sophocles, the sculptures of Phidias, the philosophy of Socrates, and the Athenian naval empire had long since dissipated. Yet Athenians took pride in their rich past, and their city was still a celebrated intellectual center, where a variety of religions flourished and where new ideas were eagerly discussed.

It was among those sophisticated Athenians that Paul encountered perhaps his most difficult audience. He was infuriated by the Athenians' idolatry in their worship of many gods, and they in turn treated Paul as simply another sophist, or traveling lecturer, preaching "foreign divinities." Arguing in the marketplace, as Socrates had done centuries earlier, and in the synagogue, Paul addressed the Athenians in an atmosphere of intellectual give-and-take to which they were accustomed. In a speech before the city's leaders, he spoke of God as the sole divinity, the creator of the entire universe, separate from the temples and graven images that men might build for themselves. He also spoke of Jesus and of the resurrection, but many of the Athenians mocked his words.

Azotus (Ashdod)

Like its sister city, Ascalon, Azotus was an important early center of eastern Mediterranean trade. Situated 3 miles inland and about 10 miles north of Ascalon, it was a way station on the Via Maris trade route. According to ancient Hebrew tradition, Ashdod (as it was then known) was originally peopled by Anakim, or "giants." In Old Testament days it was one of the five Philistine cities and a powerful enemy of the Israelites. It was the Philistine capital in Nehemiah's time, and for a while "Ashdodite" was synonymous with "Philistine."

Herodotus cites a seventh-century B.C. Egyptian siege of the town as probably the longest ever—29 years. Like other Middle Eastern cities, Azotus (the Greco-Roman name for Ashdod) felt the lash of more than one conqueror, but it remained a strong rival to Jewish interests until it was captured and devastated during the Maccabean period. It was rebuilt by the Romans and placed under the control of Herod the Great, who presented it as a gift to his sister Salome. Jews and Gentiles lived together in the former Philistine stronghold. According to Acts 8:40, the Apostle Philip was first to preach the gospel there, probably about A.D. 38.

Bethany

In Jesus' time, just as today, Bethany was a suburb of Jerusalem, located less than two miles from the eastern slope of the Mount of Olives. From there Jesus began his triumphal journey into Jerusalem on Palm Sunday. The village was also the home of some of his closest friends. Martha and Mary lived there with their brother Lazarus, whom Jesus raised from the dead. According to Luke, after the resurrection Jesus led the disciples to Bethany, and from there he ascended into heaven. Prior to A.D. 385 a church was built over the crypt that according to tradition held his body.

Bethlehem

Bethlehem, a hillside Judean village south of Jerusalem, was sacred to the Jews for centuries before Jesus was born there. The tomb of Rachel, Jacob's wife and the mother of Joseph and Benjamin, is located there. It was there that Ruth lived with her husband Boaz, there that their descendant David was born, and there that he was anointed king of Israel. In the eighth century B.C., the prophet Micah proclaimed that a new leader would be born in Bethlehem, a descendant of David who would return the Hebrews to their former glory after they had endured humiliation and exile. Seven hundred years later, many Jews still took this prophecy seriously—among them, according to Matthew, Herod the Great, who on learning from the Magi that the Messiah had been born, ordered that every male child in the region of Bethlehem under the age of two should be executed.

Bethlehem's grandest building is the Church of the Nativity, which is built over the cave that at least since the second century A.D. has been the traditional site of Jesus' birth. In the fourth century the great scholar Jerome resided there and completed the Latin translation of the Bible that still serves as the standard Roman Catholic text.

Caesarea (Caesarea Maritima)

Caesarea was a new city in Judea in the first century A.D., and in some ways it was an image of its builder, King Herod the Great. Like him, it had no significant roots in the Hebrew past. Like him, it rose through ingenuity and sheer force of will to dominate a landscape that by nature was ill suited to it. And like him, it was Jewish only in location—its spirit longed for Rome.

The site on which Caesarea stood was originally settled in the third century B.C. by Phoenicians. They built a small, fortified anchorage there, the best they could on the straight coast, by nature so unsuited to a port. Their settlement was called Strato's Tower, in honor of one of the Phoenician kings of Sidon. During the next centuries the small port was captured by the Hasmonean ruler Alexander Janneus and then by the Roman general Pompey. Herod was given the site by Augustus, and in the 12 years from roughly 22 to 10 B.C. he built a new and magnificent city there, naming it Caesarea in honor of the emperor.

Everywhere it reflected on a grand scale the Roman values that Herod so admired. The harbor was lined with white marble buildings, their walls reflecting the sun. In other parts of the city a typically Roman theater, hippodrome, palace, and colonnaded street were built. The Roman prefects, including Pontius Pilate, resided there, and it was clearly a center of Hellenism near the heart of the Hebrew world.

Although Jesus never visited Caesarea, it was, along with Jerusalem, a major city of the world he inhabited, and it is mentioned often in the New Testament. The Apostle Philip lived and preached there. It was there that Peter, after having had a vision that he should bring Jesus' teaching not only to Jews but also to Gentiles, converted the centurion Cornelius. Several times Caesarea was Paul's point of departure or arrival for his journeys to the west. It was in Caesarea that Paul was brought as a prisoner before the Roman governor Felix following the riots in Jerusalem; there that he was imprisoned for two years; there that he had an audience with the governor Festus, King Herod Agrippa II, and his sister Berenice; and from there that he embarked for his final trial at Rome. In A.D. 44 King Herod Agrippa I died there suddenly and mysteriously, just moments after a crowd had hailed him as a god.

In A.D. 60 the emperor Nero denied the Jews equal rights with the Hellenized Syrian population. This helped lead to riots between the Jews and the Syrians, which erupted into the first Jewish revolt in A.D. 66. During this war Caesarea served as the center of operations for Vespasian's and Titus' Roman troops. In the Roman victory celebration at the war's end, 2,500 Jewish prisoners were killed.

Caesarea Philippi

Jesus and his disciples came to the villages near Caesarea Philippi at the end of his ministry in Galilee. It was there that Jesus asked the disciples who they thought he was, and that Peter identified him as Christ. It was also there that Jesus announced his coming death to the disciples, and perhaps for the first time they began to understand the true nature of his kingdom.

Caesarea Philippi had an unusually beautiful setting. It stood at an elevation of 1,150 feet on a terrace at the base of Mount Hermon and offered a sweeping view of the upper Jordan Valley. The Jordan River has one of its primary sources there in a peaceful cave that is noted as "a natural place of worship." It is almost certain that ancient Semitic deities were honored there long before the Greeks erected a shrine and dedicated the cave to the Hellenic nature god Pan (the city's ancient name was Paneas) and the nymphs sometime after Alexander the Great conquered the area in 332 B.C.

The city was also strategically located. On the plain below it the Seleucids defeated the Ptolemies and took control of Judea in 200 B.C. During Roman times Emperor Augustus gave the city to Herod the Great. After Herod's death it passed to his son Herod Philip, who enlarged it, renamed it to honor the emperor and himself, and made it his capital. During the first century A.D., the city was primarily pagan. Roman troops gathered there during the first Jewish revolt (A.D. 66–70).

Capernaum

Capernaum was home to Jesus during his ministry in Galilee. Located on the northwestern shore of the Sea of Galilee near the main road from Damascus to Egypt, surrounded by the lush and fertile valleys for which the region is so famous, Capernaum was the area's major town. It was a community of fishermen, farmers, and small merchants. The New Testament references to a centurion and tax collectors in Capernaum suggest that it may have had a garrison of Roman soldiers and a customs house, probably because it was near the border between Herod Antipas' territory and the region to the east controlled by his brother Herod Philip. Certainly Capernaum was larger and more worldly than nearby rural Nazareth, where Jesus grew up.

For many years, scholars debated Capernaum's exact location. Recently there has been general agreement that it is the modern Tell Hum, where ruins of a large, ornately decorated synagogue pre-

sumably dating from the second or third century A.D. have been excavated. Ancient peoples often built new temples on the sites of old ones, and it may be that these ruins stand on the site of an earlier synagogue in which Jesus preached. Nearby, beneath the ruins of a fifth-century church, archeologists have unearthed what they believe is the Apostle Peter's house (see reconstruction on page 230), Jesus' home during his stay in the city.

Corinth

The Greek city of Corinth was so iniquitous that its name became the root of a Greek verb meaning to "indulge in base debauchery." Yet in the year and a half Paul spent among the people of this rowdy shipping center, he established one of his greatest, if most troublesome, churches. It was no accident that several of Paul's epistles were written from there, including the Letter to the Romans.

Ancient Corinth stood on the 3½-mile-wide isthmus that connects central and southern Greece, roughly midway between Italy and Asia Minor. It flourished as one of the Mediterranean's grandest commercial centers until the Roman invasion of Greece in 146 B.C., when the general Lucius Mummius leveled nearly the entire city and sold all the surviving inhabitants into slavery. For a century the ruins remained deserted, a terrifying monument to Rome's ruthless omnipotence. Finally, in 44 B.C., Julius Caesar reestablished the city as a Roman colony. Corinth's advantageous location accelerated its growth. Immigrants came from Italy and the eastern Mediterranean. By 27 B.C. it was the capital of the Roman province of Achaia; by the time Paul visited around A.D. 50, it may have had a population of 600,000.

Its cosmopolitan character made Corinth a city of cults, where religions from as far away as Egypt and Phoenicia were observed. Pilgrims seeking cures visited the shrine of Asclepius, the god of healing; often they left behind as votive offerings terra-cotta models of the parts of their bodies they believed the god had cured. The city's chief shrine, however, was dedicated to the Greek goddess of love, Aphrodite. Standing atop the 1,886-foot-high Acrocorinth, the temple was served by sacred prostitutes and was a major contributor to the city's licentious reputation.

While living in Corinth, Paul supported himself as a tentmaker and stayed with Aquila and Priscilla, a husband and wife, also tentmakers, who had been forced from Rome when Claudius expelled all Jews from the city, probably in A.D. 49. Typically, Paul was persecuted in Corinth by the more orthodox members of the Jewish community, who believed that his new teachings were heresy. They brought him before the Roman proconsul, who dismissed the case, holding that the issue involved merely the interpretation of Judaism, a religion the Romans had licensed, and not the introduction of a new religion, an act that indeed did violate Roman law. Paul continued to live in Corinth but eventually decided to move on to Ephesus.

Paul's ministry in Corinth had been primarily among the poor. The letters Paul wrote to the congregation there, which survive in part in the two Letters to the Corinthians in the New Testament, reveal Paul's frustration and concern about this factionalism within the church. After leaving Corinth he visited the city again in an attempt to resolve these conflicts, and it is clear that the church he established there was among those he cherished the most.

Damascus

A prominent Syrian trade center, Damascus is associated with Paul's conversion. Among the oldest continuously inhabited cities in the world, it had a rich and colorful history long before Paul visited it.

Damascus lies in an oasis on the edge of the Syrian desert east of Mount Hermon. In ancient times two major trade routes intersected there: the Via Maris, which connected Mesopotamia with the Mediterranean, and the King's Highway, which ran from northern Syria to Arabia and the Red Sea. Damask cloth, woven in reversible patterns,

and Damascus steel were among its major exports.

Abraham rescued his nephew Lot from invading eastern kings near Damascus, and around 1000 B.C. David conquered the city. Damascus regained its independence during Solomon's reign and became the dominant city in Syria. Over the next several centuries, it was conquered in turn by Assyrians, Persians, and Alexander the Great, before it waned in importance when the Seleucids moved Syria's capital north to Antioch. Brought under Roman control by Pompey in 64 B.C., the city was later given by Mark Antony to Cleopatra, but Augustus recovered it for Rome.

A large Jewish population lived in Damascus, and many of Jesus' followers sought refuge there during the persecution in Jerusalem following the murder and martyrdom of Stephen. Paul at that time viewed Christianity as a dangerous heresy and was among its most violent opponents. He obtained from Jerusalem's high priest a legal commission to go to Damascus and root out the new faith. As he approached the city, however, he was struck blind. He was taken into Damascus, where the disciple Ananias restored his sight. Paul then was baptized and began preaching Jesus' message in synagogues throughout the city until his life was threatened. The disciples, however, helped their former persecutor to escape in the dead of night by lowering him over the city's wall in a basket.

At the height of the first Jewish rebellion against Rome in A.D. 66–70, Damascus was the site of a tragic persecution in which as many as 10,500 Jews may have been killed. According to Muslim tradition, it is the site where Jesus will return at his second coming to destroy the Antichrist.

Emmaus

Luke 24:13–31 contains a touching story about two disciples' personal experience of Jesus' resurrection. Cleopas and a companion are walking from Jerusalem to the village of Emmaus on Easter Day. Suddenly they are joined by a stranger, who seems unaware of Jesus' crucifixion. The two disciples tell

the stranger of Jesus' death, of the visions reported at his tomb, and of some of the disciples' failing hope for his resurrection. But the stranger becomes angry at the mention of this lack of faith, and as they walk he interprets Scripture about the coming of the Messiah. Approaching Emmaus toward evening, the two disciples invite the stranger to stay with them. At dinner he breaks bread, and as they take it, according to Luke, "their eyes were opened and they recognized him" as Jesus himself. Jesus then vanishes as mysteriously as he appeared.

It is not completely clear which modern town should be identified with ancient Emmaus. No fewer than four sites have been proposed. One of them, Qalonyeh, bases its claim on the fact that it may be the Emmaus mentioned by the Jewish historian Josephus as the site where Roman veterans were settled. A second, Abu Ghosh, about 9 miles from Jerusalem, was where some detachments of Rome's Tenth Fretensis Legion were stationed. A third, El-Qubeibeh, was the site of a Roman fort named Castellum Emmaus. Perhaps the most likely candidate, however, is Amwas, or Nicopolis, as it has been called since the third century A.D., when it was rebuilt. Pilgrims to the Holy Land as early as the fourth century A.D. accepted this as Emmaus, and it does have one distinguishing landmark to support its claim. The Greek name *Emmaus* is based on a Semitic word that means "warm wells"; and indeed Amwas has two wells of lukewarm water. The problem with this site is that it seems to be too far from Jerusalem. The most reliable ancient texts of Luke's Gospel state that Emmaus was about 60 stadia (about 7 miles) from the city, while Amwas is more like 160 stadia (about 17 miles). There are, however, ancient texts of Luke's work that give the distance to Emmaus as 160 stadia, although these texts are thought by some scholars to be suspect.

Ephesus

Famed throughout the world for its magicians and mammoth pagan sanctuary, the splendid Aegean port of Ephesus was nonetheless the site of one of

Paul's most successful missions. Ephesus stood on the River Cayster in Asia Minor only a few miles from the coast. This location made it a major trade center connecting the sea routes to the west with the land routes to the east. During the first century A.D. it was the fourth largest city in the Roman Empire and may have had a population of a quarter of a million. Architecturally the city was magnificent. Its main thoroughfare has been called "the most splendid street of the Roman Empire." Thirty-six feet wide and nearly a third of a mile long, it was lined with ornate roofed colonnades.

The city's most famous landmark was the Temple of Artemis, dedicated not to the virgin huntress of Greek and Roman mythology but to a more ancient, many-breasted, Asiatic fertility goddess of the same name. The temple was almost as long as a modern football field and four times the size of Athens' Parthenon. Containing more than 100 columns 6 feet in diameter and more than 55 feet high, it was considered one of the Seven Wonders of the Ancient World.

Shortly after Paul arrived in this exotic city, many of the residents mistook him for yet another magician with a new kind of magic.

Paul spent more than two years in Ephesus. At first he spoke in the synagogue; but after a falling-out with Jewish leaders, he used a rented room. To support himself he worked from dawn to midday, the usual business hours. He then devoted the afternoon, when most people were resting, to his ministry—which proved to be successful.

Ironically, it was this very success that drove Paul from Ephesus. Local silversmiths made much of their living manufacturing pagan figurines and selling them at the Temple of Artemis. As Paul gained more converts, he was increasingly a threat to the smiths' business. Finally their fears, fueled by religious zeal, erupted in a riot. Not long thereafter, Paul left Ephesus for Macedonia.

On his way back to Jerusalem some time later, Paul bypassed Ephesus, stopping instead at Miletus to the south. There he met with the elders of the Ephesian church and in a moving speech bade farewell to the mission in Asia.

Nevertheless, Ephesus went on to have a rich Christian heritage. According to one tradition, it was the city to which John, the disciple "whom Jesus loved," migrated with the Virgin Mary after the crucifixion. The basilica of St. John the Divine, built there in the sixth century A.D., supposedly stood on the site of John's tomb. In A.D. 431 a famous ecumenical church council met in Ephesus to debate the relationship between Jesus' human and divine natures.

Gadara

A center of Greek culture in Palestine before the time of Jesus, Gadara is mentioned in the Bible only in the Gospel accounts of a demon-possessed man (or two demoniacs, in Matthew's version). When Jesus exorcised the supernatural tormentors, they passed into a herd of swine and drove the beasts into the Sea of Galilee. Although the town was situated some five miles southeast of the Sea of Galilee, its territory may have reached as far as the shore of the lake. Coins have revealed that shipping was a commercial activity of the town.

At one time the capital of Gilead, Gadara was one of the original members of the Decapolis. It remained a predominantly Greek city when captured by the Romans and given to Herod the Great by Augustus.

Herodium

King Herod the Great built Herodium as a luxurious desert retreat and a citadel atop a hill southeast of Jerusalem. The city was one of a chain of fortresses, including Masada, that lay in readiness in case the Jews ever revolted against their powerful king.

According to Josephus, "this stronghold resembled a town" because of the numerous and varied structures in the citadel. The natural hill had been artificially heightened, a double circular wall surrounded the summit, and four watchtowers were erected at the cardinal points of the compass.

Around the base of the hill, Josephus reported, Herod had palaces constructed for housing friends and his possessions. Possibly, the king was interred at his request in a mausoleum in Herodium when he died in 4 B.C. So far his tomb has not been found.

The later history of the complex was brief and bloody. Captured by the Zealots in the first Jewish revolt (A.D. 66–70), it was overrun by the Romans in A.D. 72. Recent archeological evidence indicates that it was used as a supply depot by Bar Kokhba's men during the second Jewish revolt against Rome in A.D. 132–135.

Jericho

Archeologial evidence of village life in Jericho stretches back 10,000 years, making it one of the oldest cities in the world. But its actual location has changed at least twice. The Jericho Jesus visited was not the Old Testament city Joshua had destroyed; rather, it was a new city a mile or so to the south, where Herod the Great built his winter capital. Although Jericho and Jerusalem are only 14 miles apart, the two cities have markedly different climates, especially in wintertime. Jerusalem stands at an elevation of about 2,500 feet in the Judean highlands; its winters are damp and chilly. Jericho, on the other hand, is the lowest city in the world. It is built along a wadi, at the southern end of the Jordan Valley, and the winters there are balmy.

Jericho was surrounded by an oasis, the result of plentiful springs and an elaborate irrigation system built in the second century B.C. by Israel's Hasmonean rulers, who also wintered there. The countryside is lush with greenery, and the balm from Jericho was one of Judea's most highly valued exports.

In this luxuriant setting Herod built one of his most beautiful estates (see reconstruction on page 68). Many of the structures were built of "Roman concrete," a style of masonry in which concrete is poured over a stonework lattice and then plastered and decorated. Herod died there in 4 B.C.

The Gospels mention that Jesus came to the city toward the end of his ministry, as he journeyed from Galilee to Jerusalem. But surely he must have visited it earlier. The traditional site of his baptism is about five miles to the east in the Jordan River, and Jebel Quruntul, the supposed site of his temptations by Satan in the wilderness, dominates the plain a few miles to the northwest. Jesus' famous parable of the Good Samaritan is set five miles from Jericho in a narrow pass on the desolate mountain road leading from Jericho to Jerusalem.

While Jesus was in Jericho, he ministered to both the rich and the poor. On the way into the city he healed a blind beggar, and later he stayed with the tax collector Zacchaeus, among the wealthiest men in the city.

During the first Jewish revolt (A.D. 66–70) Roman troops under Vespasian were stationed in Jericho. It is likely that troops from there destroyed the Essene community at Qumran. After the fall of Jerusalem at the end of the first Jewish revolt, Jericho declined rapidly. Hostilities flared there again during Bar Kokhba's rebellion in A.D. 132–135, but by that time Jericho was just a small garrison town. Slowly over the next centuries the city became deserted. Drifting desert sands reclaimed the once-fertile plain, covering the pools and palaces that had been Herod's pride.

Jerusalem

Located high in the Judean hills, Jerusalem has none of the geographical advantages that in ancient times were common prerequisites for a great city: it lacked good agricultural land; it had no valuable mineral deposits; it was not a strategic military center; and it was eight miles from the main east-west trade route through the region.

Before David conquered Jerusalem around 1000 B.C. and made it the capital of the United Kingdom of Israel and Judah, the city was not sacred for the Jews. Archeological remains date its early settlement to at least the fourth millennium B.C., and there are historical records of a city there in the 19th century B.C. According to tradition, Jerusalem's chief hill was where Abraham went to sacri-fice his beloved son Isaac, a site later marked by the Temple. In the 13th century Joshua led the Hebrew invasion of Canaan, but the Hebrews did not drive out Jerusalem's Jebusite inhabitants. David established the city as the capital of a new combined kingdom.

David brought the Ark of the Covenant to Jerusalem and housed it in a tent, just as it had been housed in a tent during the Hebrews' nomadic wanderings. What happened to the Ark after Solomon's reign is vague. Generally, scholars assume that it was destroyed by Babylonian troops when they leveled Jerusalem and took the Hebrews into exile in 587 B.C..

The Jews began to return to Jerusalem in 538 B.C., and under the leadership of Zerubbabel they rebuilt the Temple. After Alexander the Great's conquest about 333 B.C., the Jews were again split into factions, some of them wanting to adopt Hellenistic ways, others determined to maintain religious purity. When the Seleucids demanded worship of pagan gods in 167 B.C., the Maccabean revolt erupted; their Hasmonean descendants ruled a free Jewish state until the Roman conquest in 63 B.C. Herod the Great was brought to power by the Romans in a struggle against the last Hasmoneans, and it was Herod who built the grandest Temple in the city's turbulent history.

After Jesus' crucifixion and the stoning of his disciple Stephen by a crowd of hostile Jerusalem Jews, Christians centered their activities in Antioch, to the north. The enmity between these two groups marked the beginning of the emergence of Christianity as a separate religion.

During the first Jewish revolt of A.D. 66–70, the Jews again liberated Jerusalem, but with the subsequent Roman victory most of the city was destroyed and the Temple was burned. In A.D. 132 a second revolt broke out, led by Bar Kokhba. After two years the Romans suppressed this rebellion also, banned all Jews from the city, and reestablished it as the colony of Aelia Capitolina. (See also Chapter Five, "Jerusalem, the Holy City.")

Joppa (Jaffa)

The name *Joppa* comes from the Hebrew word for "beauty," and certainly this hilltop city high above the Mediterranean must have offered a beautiful view of the pounding sea. Here a natural breakwater protects a small harbor that was among Palestine's earliest ports. Evidence of a fortress at Joppa dates back to the 18th century B.C.

The city is mentioned often both in history and legend. The Egyptians conquered it about 1468 B.C., supposedly by smuggling soldiers through its defenses in baskets. It is also the setting for a Greek myth about Perseus' rescue of the Princess Andromeda from a sea monster. As late as Roman times, shrewd Joppa showmen were still profiting from the display of "monster bones" and "Andromeda's chains." In the 10th century B.C., Solomon apparently developed Joppa's harbor, and it became the main port through which cedar was shipped from Lebanon to Jerusalem for construction of the Temple. According to the Bible, Jonah set sail from Joppa in an attempt to avoid God's command, only to be swallowed by a whale.

In 701 B.C. the city was conquered by the Assyrians and later by Alexander the Great. It came under Herod the Great's rule in 37 B.C., yet he decided to build his major harbor farther north at Caesarea. In the New Testament, Joppa is associated with the Apostle Peter. There he raised Tabitha from the dead and had a vision in which God told him that all foods were ritually pure, which Peter interpreted to mean that Jesus' message should be taken not just to the Jews but to all mankind.

During the first Jewish rebellion against Rome (A.D. 66–70), Joppa was a stronghold for Jewish patriots, and the Roman general Vespasian destroyed the city in A.D. 68.

Lydda (Lod)

Lydda, the Hellenistic name for Lod, is an ancient city built by the tribe of Benjamin on the southern edge of the Plain of Sharon. Strategically situated where the main Joppa-Jerusalem highway crossed a major route between Egypt and Babylon, it endured destruction several times and always reemerged as a modestly prosperous commercial center. It was famous for its purple-dyed cloth. The great Maccabean rebellion began just a few miles to the east in the village of Modein.

It was in Lydda that Peter performed one of his miracles, curing a man who had been paralyzed for eight years. News of the miracle spread quickly to Joppa and led Peter into a more extended ministry at Caesarea.

Lydda was destroyed during the first Jewish revolt of A.D. 66–70 and then resettled by the Romans. One of Lydda's legends concerns Saint George, the famous dragon killer and patron saint of England. According to story, he was buried in Lydda after he had served in a Roman legion, converted to Christianity, and was martyred for his faith early in the fourth century A.D.

Lystra

Settled as early as 3000 B.C., Lystra, a Lycaonian city in Asia Minor, was by the first century A.D. the major Roman stronghold against the mountain tribes of the region. Fleeing the hostility of Jewish opponents in Iconium to the north, Paul and Barnabas came to Lystra. At first they were worshiped as gods, but in the end Paul was stoned as a rebel.

It was there that Paul and Barnabas performed one of the most astounding miracles recorded in Acts: healing a beggar who had been crippled since birth. This miracle convinced the Lystrans that the two missionaries were the Greek gods Zeus and Hermes, who, according to local legends, had visited the area as men twice before. To prevent the Lystrans from honoring them with sacrifices, Paul and Barnabas protested the sacrilege and tore their own clothing, a reaction to blasphemy that may have been required by Jewish tradition. A short time later, Jewish opponents arrived from Pisidian Antioch and Iconium and incited the townspeople against the missionaries. Paul was stoned and left for dead; but he recovered, and he and Barnabas

fled to Derbe. Nonetheless, Paul returned to Lystra twice more and made one of his most faithful converts there—Timothy, who became a significant missionary.

Malta

In ancient times the rocky Mediterranean island of Malta was called Melita, perhaps from a Phoenician word meaning "escape"—a fitting name, since the island was often a haven for storm-tossed mariners. One traveler who benefited from its shelter was Paul. After two weeks in the grip of a frightening storm, the cargo ship carrying Paul as a prisoner from Caesarea to Rome was wrecked in a bay on the island's northeastern coast, possibly at the present-day St. Paul's Bay.

According to Acts, while gathering firewood shortly after the wreck, Paul was bitten by a snake, yet he remained unharmed. This led many to believe that Paul was a god. Today there are no poisonous snakes on Malta, and it may be that the snake that attacked Paul was from a local species that bites but has no poison fangs.

Malta was also the site of one of Paul's miracles of healing. It was there that his prayers and the laying on of hands cured the chief magistrate's father of fever and dysentery, ailments common on the island, perhaps caused by an organism in goat's milk.

Paul and his companions remained on Malta for three months awaiting the end of the winter storm season. Despite the length of Paul's stay and the strong impression he made, he apparently did no preaching there, possibly because he could not speak the Maltese language.

Masada

No site is more dramatically associated with Jewish resistance to Roman rule than the fortress of Masada—the 20-acre plateau atop a steep rock outcropping on the western shore of the Dead Sea that stands hundreds of feet above the surrounding terrain. The first person to fortify it was probably Alexander Janneus, the Hasmonean king who ruled

Judea from 103 to 76 B.C. But it was Herod the Great who turned it into one of the most formidable strongholds of the ancient world. It was designed to be both comfortable and impregnable, immune to direct assault and the insidious ravages of siege.

Beginning in A.D. 6, Masada may have been occupied by the Romans. They were holding it in A.D. 66 at the start of the first Jewish revolt, when the Zealots, Jewish insurgents devoted to a strict interpretation of the ancient Hebrew law, captured it by trickery. Even after Jerusalem fell in A.D. 70, the Zealots continued to occupy the fortress. Then in A.D. 72 the Roman prefect Flavius Silva led the Tenth Legion, supported by the forced labor of tens of thousands of prisoners of war, in an assault on the citadel, a final attempt to end the resistance to Roman rule. Sure that the defenders could not escape, the Romans decided to wait until morning before launching their assault.

But in that night, these Jews, who had struggled so fiercely and so long for independence, decided one last time to defy Rome's will. Inspired by their leader, Eleazar, 960 of the Zealots chose death rather than Roman oppression. When the Romans stormed the citadel the next morning they were greeted by an eerie silence. Finally they found the only survivors—2 women and 5 children who had hidden in an aqueduct.

Megiddo

A city of northern Palestine, Megiddo became a symbol for the final catastrophic battle between the forces of good and evil, described in Revelation 16:14–16. The prophetic term *Armageddon* is a corruption of the Hebrew phrase *Har Medigddo*, meaning "Mountain of Megiddo." It was that hill that made the town a military prize throughout its troubled history. Because it overlooked the Jezreel Valley (or Plain of Esdraelon) and thus controlled two of the ancient Middle East's most strategically important routes—the Via Maris, which connected Egypt in the south with Syria and Mesopotamia to the north, and the route linking eastern Palestine with the Mediterranean—Megiddo was the conqueror's key to northern Israel. Therefore, from its beginning about 3000 B.C. until it was mysteriously abandoned in the fourth century B.C., the city knew almost no peace.

As a Canaanite stronghold, Megiddo apparently resisted Joshua's troops successfully but fell to David. In the ninth century B.C. its famous water system was constructed, which safely brought fresh water from outside the city walls even during siege. Designated one of the royal "chariot cities" for the quartering of crack horse-drawn troops, the town had stables for 492 steeds in King Ahab's army. After many vicissitudes Megiddo became militarily unimportant around the seventh century B.C.

Nazareth

"Can anything good come out of Nazareth?" Nathanael asked, according to John 1:46, when he was invited to join Jesus' disciples. The question, though it may seem arrogant and narrow-minded, was not completely inappropriate, for the Galilean village where Joseph worked as a carpenter, where Mary received the announcement that she would be the virgin mother of God's child, and where Jesus grew to manhood was indeed remarkably insignificant. Although Nazareth certainly existed prior to Jesus' birth, it is not mentioned by any ancient writers before the writers of the Gospels. Outside of Christian literature, there is no mention of it until A.D. 135.

The Nazareth of Jesus' youth was a secluded and quiet village, clinging to a sheltered slope in the foothills of Lower Galilee. No major roads passed through it, and it seems to have been an outlying settlement of larger towns nearby, particularly Japhia, Chesulloth, and Sepphoris. Some scholars speculate that the name *Nazareth* is derived from the Hebrew word for "guard place," suggesting that the village may have arisen merely as an outpost of a nearby town. Nazareth's growth was further limited by a poor water supply. Only one spring surfaced there, and the villagers probably augmented it by cutting cisterns into the hillside's soft limestone.

Nonetheless, Nazareth was a magnificent place in which to grow up, especially for a child with imagination and a sense of his people's heritage. The heights above the village command a view of a landscape rich in history. To the south is the Plain of Esdraelon, the scene of King Josiah's defeat at Megiddo and of the Maccabean struggle for freedom; farther south is Mount Gilboa, where King Saul was defeated by the Philistines; to the east is the Jordan Valley, and to the northeast the Sea of Galilee; to the west, Mount Carmel and the Mediterranean.

Jesus' ministry in Nazareth was brief and decidedly ineffective, prompting his famous remark that a prophet is not honored in his own land. After one of his sermons, according to Luke, his listeners were so angered that they dragged him to the top of the village hill and attempted to throw him over the precipice.

Paphos

The capital of Roman Cyprus, Paphos had long been famous as a cult center for the worship of Aphrodite, the Greek goddess of love, who according to legend was born nearby from the sea.

Cyprus was the first stop on the mission of Paul and Barnabas and may have been chosen because it was Barnabas' home. The missionaries were received graciously by the Roman proconsul there, but they were accosted by the Jewish magician Bar-Jesus, who was a teacher in the proconsul's household and probably saw the missionaries' teachings as threatening to his position. According to Acts, Paul temporarily blinded the magician; but some scholars have suggested that this is a legend based on the fact that Paul's discussion of religion showed Bar-Jesus' spiritual blindness. It was on Cyprus that Paul for the first time in Acts is referred to as Paul rather than Saul.

Patmos

One of the Aegean islands used by the Romans for banishment, Patmos was the scene of the mystical visions described by John in Revelation 1:9. He writes that he was there "on account of the word of God and the testimony of Jesus," presumably for prophesying the return of his lord. Banishment was a standard punishment for any kind of prophecy, whether Christian, pagan, or Jewish; the Romans considered the practice as reprehensible as astrology and magic. Accordingly, John's life on Patmos, a rocky, volcanic island only 10 miles long and 6 miles wide at the broadest point, probably consisted of hard labor on a chain gang. Generally, the sentence was the equivalent of life imprisonment. Yet a well-established tradition of the early church holds that John was sent there in A.D. 95 by the emperor Domitian and released only 18 months later by the new emperor, Nerva.

Pergamum

Perhaps the most spectacularly beautiful of Hellenistic cities in Asia Minor, Pergamum became the seat of Roman power in Asia. For early Christians, it was a dangerous place because of its primacy in the cult of the emperor, part of the state religion of Rome. In 29 B.C. the first officially sanctioned imperial cult temple was built in honor of Augustus and Roma; later temples were built to celebrate the divinity of Trajan and Caracalla. The first Christian martyr to Nero's policy in Asia may have been executed in Pergamum.

Built in Asia Minor about 15 miles from the coast of the Aegean Sea but reachable by ship on the River Caicus, Pergamum was a marvel of city planning, with distinguished public buildings erected on artificial terraces set against the slopes of a dark granite mountain. Its library, second only to the ancient world's largest in Alexandria, was a famous center of classical learning. The English word *parchment* comes from the Latin *pergamentum*. It is derived from the city's name and refers to the sheepskins used as writing material there. Pergamum also had a shrine to the Greek god of healing, Asclepius, which attracted the afflicted from many parts of the ancient world.

To believers in Jesus, Pergamum was first and

foremost a hotbed of paganism and tyrannical power. In Revelation, John wrote that "Satan's throne" could be found there, perhaps equating imperial Rome with God's traditional adversary.

Philippi

The first Macedonian city visited by Paul was Philippi. This small inland military center was named for Philip II, the father of Alexander the Great. Philip conquered the area in 356 B.C., drawn by its strategic importance and valuable gold mines. The plain outside the city was famous as the battle site where Octavian and Mark Antony defeated Brutus and Cassius in 42 B.C., during the Roman civil war. Many of the town's inhabitants were descendants of Antony's followers, whom Octavian had forced to leave Italy after he defeated Antony and Cleopatra for sole control of the empire. As a result, there were few places in the eastern Mediterranean that possessed a stronger sense of connection to Rome.

Philippi is one of the few cities Paul visited where he was persecuted not as a Christian but as a Jew. Paul was brought before the city authorities on the charge that he was an anti-Roman propagandist, who was not merely practicing Judaism, which was allowed by Roman law, but actively proselytizing converts to the faith and thus threatening the state religion of emperor worship. An angry crowd gathered. Paul and his companion, Silas, were stripped, beaten, and thrown into jail, their feet placed in stocks. That evening a violent earthquake shook the prison, opening the cells and breaking the chains of all the inmates. In despair, the warden, who could be executed if his prisoners escaped, was preparing to kill himself, when Paul stopped him, saying that all the prisoners had remained in the jail. The warden was amazed. He took Paul and Silas to his home, bathed their wounds, and fed them—and he and his family were baptized. The next morning Paul and Silas were released.

Paul returned to the home of Lydia, a God-fearing Gentile working in Philippi as a dealer in goods of purple dye. Like many women in this part of the world, she took an active part in the Christian community. Early in Paul's visit she converted to Christianity and was one of the leaders of the church there. From her home, Paul bid the small Philippian church he had formed farewell and departed for Thessalonica.

The church Paul established at Philippi was strongly devoted to him personally. When Paul was imprisoned—probably in Rome, but perhaps in Caesarea or Ephesus—they sent an emissary to his aid. Moved by their concern, Paul sent the emissary back with the Letter of Paul to the Philippians that appears in the New Testament. In it Paul encouraged the Philippians' continued belief in Jesus by the model of his own faith despite adversity.

Pisidian Antioch

Mountainous Pisidia was never entirely subdued by any of the armies that invaded Asia Minor throughout its history. Around 300 B.C. the Seleucids established a military outpost on its border with Phrygia. The city they built stood on a well-protected plateau overlooking the River Anthius. They named the city Antioch—one of 16 cities in their empire named in honor of Antiochus, the father of their dynasty's founder, Seleucus I.

When Paul and Barnabas ventured to Pisidian Antioch some 350 years later, they found the local situation little changed from Seleucid times. Traveling through a dangerous pass in the Taurus Mountains that was often beset by bandits, they arrived at what was then a Roman outpost, different from its Seleucid predecessor but militarily the same in its function of subduing the surrounding countryside. Despite its Romanization, the city still held signs of its indigenous Phrygian culture. One striking building was a temple dedicated to the god Men, who was represented by a bull's head and was associated with the fertility goddess Artemis. At the synagogue in Pisidian Antioch, Paul delivered sermons concerning Jesus' role in Judaism and the inclusion of Gentiles in the faith, issues that ultimately separated Christianity from its Judaic origins.

Ptolemais (Acco)

The ancient port city of Ptolemais was one of Palestine's very few good harbors. Enjoying "all possible advantages of both sea and land," according to one early traveler, the town lay on the coastal plain north of Mount Carmel. Situated on the Via Maris trade route, Ptolemais principally served the needs of Galilee and the Jezreel Valley but was considered a key entry point for invading armies. It was near Acco (as it was called in the Old Testament) that Elijah slew the false prophets of Baal, achieving both a real and symbolic triumph of monotheistic ideas over paganism. As Christianity began to spread throughout the Middle East, the city's inhabitants were among the early converts to the new religion. According to Acts 21:7, Paul visited with them on his third voyage.

Qumran

Late in the winter of 1947 a Bedouin shepherd, searching for a lost goat amid the marl cliffs of the Judean Wilderness just northwest of the Dead Sea, came upon the most ancient manuscripts we have for many of the books of the Old Testament. The Dead Sea Scrolls also contain the enigmatic record of a strict Jewish sect that had its headquarters at nearby Qumran at the time of Jesus.

The site at Qumran was first settled in the eighth century B.C.. It may be the City of Salt mentioned in the Book of Joshua as one of the six cities of the wilderness. This settlement, however, was abandoned toward the end of the sixth century B.C. Then around 150 B.C., during the reign of the Maccabees, the site was repopulated by Essenes, members of a Jewish sect who were outraged by the secularization of Judaism during the Maccabean Wars. Separating themselves from the Temple, these purists retreated to the Judean Wilderness, where they awaited the end of the world, a time when evil would be destroyed and their righteousness would triumph.

The Qumran complex was destroyed, probably by the earthquake of 31 B.C., and it remained unoccupied until the end of Herod the Great's reign. Resettled perhaps sometime between 4 and 1 B.C., it flourished again until the first Jewish revolt (A.D. 66–70). It was occupied by Vespasian's troops in June of A.D. 68 and remained a Roman garrison at least until the fall of Masada in A.D. 73. Presumably it was during the Jewish war that the scrolls from the great library there were hidden in surrounding caves in an attempt to protect them from Roman capture or destruction. Sixty years later Qumran's abandoned buildings served as hideouts for Bar Kokhba's rebels during the second Jewish revolt (A.D. 132–135), and letters signed by Bar Kokhba himself have been found in caves some 10 miles south of Qumran. The village has remained empty ever since.

Rome

Rome's earliest history is lost in the colorful mists of legend, but it is nearly certain that as early as the eighth century B.C. simple villages existed on the hills of Rome and the surrounding plain of Latium. In 509 B.C. these Latins, as the people were called, rebelled against their Etruscan overlords and established an independent republic. Burned by the Gauls in 390 B.C., Rome was rebuilt during the next century and expanded its influence throughout the western Mediterranean.

This expansion brought conflict with Carthage, a major power on the north African coast. Rome finally defeated Carthage in 202 B.C. and during the next 50 years spread its empire eastward through Macedonia and Greece. But external conquests led to internal strife. For about a century, from 133 to 27 B.C., the city was plagued by civil wars during which the only real power rested with military commanders and their personal armies. During this period Julius Caesar increased Rome's dominion, and his own personal power, by brilliant military campaigns in Gaul and Spain, while Pompey subdued the eastern Mediterranean, including Syria and Palestine. When the inevitable clash between these two great generals came, Caesar emerged victorious and ruled Rome as a dictator for five years, until his assassination in 44 B.C. by a group headed by Brutus and Cassius, who favored a return to a republican form of government. The republicans were defeated by Caesar's grand-nephew and adopted son, Octavian, and by Mark Antony, who governed together until they themselves clashed. Octavian's victory at Actium over the troops of Antony and the Egyptian queen Cleopatra in 31 B.C. gave him complete control of Rome. In 27 B.C. he changed his name to Augustus and was crowned as the first Roman emperor.

It was during Augustus' 41-year reign that Jesus was born. Although Jesus never visited Rome, his message apparently reached there soon after his crucifixion. It was probably carried by Jewish pilgrims returning from Jerusalem to Rome's large Jewish community, which may have had roots going back to the mid-second century B.C. In A.D. 49–50 the emperor Claudius expelled all Jews from Rome because of disturbances among them regarding the teachings of "Chrestus," a name that some scholars believe may be a garbled reference to the teachings of Jesus. By A.D. 64 Christians were sufficiently distinct from Jews there that the emperor Nero could make them scapegoats accused of starting the fire that destroyed much of the city. During this persecution a multitude of Christians suffered bizarre and excruciating deaths.

Our information on Peter at Rome is sketchy. According to legend, he was executed there during Nero's persecution by being crucified upside down. Either his death or his burial is supposed to have taken place on Vatican Hill, where the Church of St. Peter now stands.

Paul's relation to the Roman church has better historical grounding, although the details are unclear, particularly concerning the last years of his life. It is certain that he was brought there for trial, and it is generally agreed that he was sentenced to death and beheaded. His traditional burial site lies on the Ostian Way. It is marked by the Basilica of St. Paul Outside the Walls.

Despite sporadic persecutions, the number of Christian converts in Rome kept growing. At first these Christians had no churches, and services were held in parishioners' homes, but by the third century actual churches were being built, most often in the poorer and more densely populated parts of the city. From the mid-third century to A.D. 313, there were a series of systematic persecutions by the emperors. This conflict between the church and the state came to an end only when Christianity was legally tolerated and protected by the Edict of Milan, issued in A.D. 313 by the emperor Licinius and by Constantine, the first Christian emperor. With the conversion of the emperor to the Christian faith, the church soon became the dominant religious institution throughout the empire.

Samaria (Sebaste)

High on an easily defensible hill, the city of Samaria is apparently the only major city the ancient Hebrews founded. It was built by King Omri around 880 B.C. to serve as the capital of the Kingdom of Israel in the north, a capital that would vie in grandeur with Jerusalem in the Kingdom of Judah to the south. Samaria was the site of some of the most wanton sacrilege recorded in the Old Testament. There King Ahab and his Phœnician wife, Jezebel, erected a temple to Baal; there they were confronted by the prophet Elijah; and there their dynasty was overthrown in a furious revolution led by Jehu, who, according to 2 Kings, slaughtered the worshipers of Baal and turned the god's temple into a latrine. Jeroboam II, Jehu's great-grandson, ruled Samaria for 41 years and was one of Israel's greatest kings. The city continued as the capital of the northern kingdom until it fell to the Assyrians in 721 B.C. after a three-year siege. Part if not all of it was burned before the Assyrian king Sargon II deported more than 27,000 Israelites, rebuilt the city, and repopulated it with Gentiles.

During the following centuries Samaria was conquered by the Babylonians, then the Persians, and then the Macedonians. Between 108 and 106 B.C. the Hasmonean leader John Hyrcanus I conquered the pagan city and made it part of his Jewish kingdom. Pompey captured it for Rome in 63 B.C., and later the emperor Augustus made a gift of it to Herod the Great, who renamed the city *Sebaste,* the Greek translation of "Augustus."

In the time of Jesus, the Samaritans occupied a kind of cultural middle ground between Judaism and paganism. They worshiped the Hebrew God, kept the Sabbath, and practiced circumcision, but they did not recognize Jerusalem as a sacred city, and they accepted only the first five books of the Bible as Scripture. The Jews despised them for their lax observance of the Hebrew law. Jesus visited the area, and it was a suitable place for the Apostle Philip to center his ministry, making it one of the first places where Jesus' message was taken outside of Jerusalem proper. Philip was joined later by Peter and John, and together they gained many followers for the new faith. Among these was a magician named Simon, who may have been trying to establish himself in Samaria as the Messiah, in open rivalry to Jesus. This fact perhaps explains why Luke bothers to mention Simon and his conversion in Acts. Simon tried to buy from the Apostles the power they had because of their faith in God; thus the sin of attempting to buy divine favor or ecclesiastical office was named simony.

Early in the first Jewish revolt (A.D. 66–70) Sebaste was burned by Jewish rebels, but after the Roman victory the Temple of Augustus was rebuilt and paganism flourished, especially during the period of prosperity the city enjoyed under the emperor Severus in the decades around A.D. 200. When Christianity became the official religion of Rome, Sebaste became the seat of a bishop; nonetheless, pagan sentiment remained strong.

Sardis

Dramatically positioned on a mountain pinnacle in western Asia Minor, Sardis first became famous as the capital of the ancient kingdom of Lydia, whose last and most notorious ruler was the proverbially wealthy Croesus. Gold could be found in a nearby river, and the first coins were minted there. Rich and arrogant, Croesus was defeated by the Persian king Cyrus because, assuming his citadel to be impregnable, Croesus saw no reason to post guards. The Persians climbed and conquered, and made the town their most important settlement in all of Asia Minor. The Romans built a new city of Sardis below the mountain. Trade and industry thrived, and a remarkable temple was raised to honor the goddess Artemis.

In Revelation, Christ tells John to write a letter warning the congregation at Sardis that they are spiritually dead and should be alert for his return. Not long afterward Christianity did begin to take hold. The Temple of Artemis became a church. A second-century leader, Bishop Melito, was a scholar and pastor who became one of the most important figures in the growth of the early church.

Sidon

With its sister city, Tyre, the Phoenician seaport of Sidon was an important trading and political power throughout most of biblical history. Called "Great Sidon" in the Old Testament, the remarkable little city-state sent the first Phoenician ships out on the open seas; indeed, as we learn from several references in Homer, Sidonians were the first Middle Eastern people to establish relationships with the ancient Greeks. Its exports of cedarwood and such luxury products as goldwork, embroidery, and copper goods helped it to prosperity, but it is perhaps best remembered for the trade monopoly in red and purple dyes made from the murex sea snail.

Not surprisingly, success did not make the people of Sidon modest. In a notable misjudgment, the Sidonians decided to revolt against Persia in 351 B.C. Perhaps 40,000 people were killed as the city was burned to the ground. Resilient Sidon came back to life, however, and the city was prospering in Roman times. According to Luke and Mark, Jesus visited Sidon and preached to its people.

Smyrna (Izmir)

Home to one of only two churches that John praises in Revelation, the large Aegean port city of Smyrna in Asia Minor was extremely dangerous to early Christians. John, noting the believers' material poverty in contrast with their great spiritual wealth, warns of persecutions. In fact, the large Jewish community in the beautiful and cosmopolitan city was aggressively hostile toward the message of the Gospels. Some of its members were so eager to martyr the city's elderly bishop Polycarp about A.D. 156 that they broke the Sabbath to gather wood for the pyre that would burn him alive.

The port began as a Greek colony and was thriving about 600 B.C., when the Lydian king Alyattes conquered it and dispersed its citizens. Almost 400 years later Alexander the Great's successors built a new city on the site, and its citizens boasted of living in a town that had "died and lived again." Smyra developed into a magnificent city, with an acropolis atop 400-foot Mount Pagos. Its many grand public buildings included the Homerium, a temple commemorating one traditional belief that Homer was born there. To ancient eyes, the walls and structures of the acropolis resembled a crown; the image was therefore familiar on coins and public monuments. The beleaguered Christians, however, transformed the crown of Smyrna into a religious message, remembering John's words, the "crown of life."

Tarsus

The city of Tarsus in Asia Minor was Paul's birthplace, the site of his very early youth, and the place to which the Apostle returned for perhaps 10 years some time after his conversion to Christianity. There, among the mixed population of this cosmopolitan commerical center, he had an excellent opportunity to discuss Jesus' teachings with both Jews and Greeks—an invaluable preparation for his later ministry to the Gentiles.

Standing in a fertile plain along the Cydnus River, Tarsus had both easy access to the Mediterranean and proximity to the Cilician Gates, the pass through the Taurus Mountains along the major trade route from Syria to central Asia Minor. For centuries its favorable location had made it the chief city of Cilicia and a meeting ground of East and West. Cleopatra and Mark Antony met for the first time in Tarsus' thriving port.

The city was also a center of learning and had a university that served local students. After the Roman emperor Augustus came to power, Tarsus was administered by his tutor, the Stoic philosopher Athenodorus, a native of the city. Some scholars have seen Stoic influences in Paul's interpretation of Jesus' teachings.

Thessalonica

In Thessalonica, Macedonia's capital, Paul ministered amid the bustling variety of an urban port peopled largely by laborers and artisans of diverse ethnic and religious backgrounds. The church he established there, despite its varied congregation, was among his most stable and devout.

From the beginning, Thessalonica had been a city of the uprooted. It was founded about 316 B.C. by Cassander, the husband of Alexander the Great's half-sister, Thessalonica, for whom it was named. Cassander created the city by destroying 26 nearby villages and resettling their inhabitants around the excellent natural harbor at the head of the Thermaic Gulf. The city grew to become, with Ephesus and Corinth, one of the Aegean Sea's most important ports.

Paul and his companions, Silas and Timothy, traveled to Thessalonica after their imprisonment in Philippi, some 90 miles to the east. The city they entered was a free city, its right to self-government having been granted by Antony and Octavian as a reward for loyalty during the Roman civil war that followed Julius Caesar's assassination in 44 B.C. The city's freedom was perhaps nowhere more evident than in the number of religions that flourished there. There was also a Jewish synagogue in Thessalonica, and it was there that Paul and his compan-

ions founded its church. But soon, as usual, the new faith they preached brought them into conflict with the orthodox Jewish leaders. Paul continued his ministry among the Gentiles, both the "God-fearers," who although not Jews had turned from the confusing welter of pagan divinities to worship the one Hebrew God, and outright pagans who had no association with Judaism.

Paul was forced to leave the city when the Jewish opposition raised a mob against him and dragged his host, Jason, before the civil authorities, charging that Paul and his companions encouraged insurrection against Rome with their teaching that Jesus was king. Apparently, Paul's followers were compelled to post a bond, which would be forfeited if there was further trouble from Christians.

Silenced, the evangelists moved on to Beroea, a city some 45 miles to the west that also had a synagogue. But Paul's Thessalonian opponents followed him even there and incited a mob that drove him from that city. Paul fled southward to Athens and from there to Corinth, where around A.D. 51 he composed the two letters to the Thessalonian church that are included in the New Testament.

Tiberias

Although Jews initially shunned Tiberias, a major city in Galilee, it later became one of the great centers of Hebrew culture. The city was founded by Herod Antipas, a son of Herod the Great, in the early decades of the first century A.D. Named for the emperor Tiberius, Tiberias served as the capital of Herod's tetrarchy of Galilee and Perea. Although it was built on an acropolis overlooking the Sea of Galilee, the city was nonetheless almost 700 feet below sea level, and its climate was often hot, humid, and oppressive. The steamy atmosphere was made worse by sulfur springs in nearby Hammath, famous in ancient times just as they are today for their healing powers. Early in the city's construction, workers uncovered a cemetery from the ancient settlement at Hammath. This made Tiberias unclean in the eyes of devout Jews, and Herod

Antipas had trouble populating the new city; many of the inhabitants were brought there by force. In Jesus' time the population was almost entirely Gentile, which may be why Jesus never visited there, although his Galilean ministry was centered at Capernaum, only some 10 miles to the north.

The city surrendered to Vespasian during the Jewish revolt against Rome in A.D. 67. After the destruction of Jerusalem during the second Jewish revolt in A.D. 135, Tiberias emerged as one of the major centers of Hebrew culture in Palestine.

Tyre

Ruler of the sea for much of the first millennium B.C., the Phoenician seaport of Tyre was built on a rocky island about half a mile off the coast 25 miles south of Sidon. Tyre's venturesome sailors astonished the ancient world, sailing as far west as Spain and Britain and even circumnavigating Africa in 600 B.C.. They established commercial ties with every nation known in their day.

For a brief period there were good political relations between the cheerfully materialistic Phoenicians and the Hebrews who had come into Canaan. King Hiram of Tyre was a friend of David's and sent expert carpenters and masons along with the highly prized cedars of Lebanon to build a palace in Jerusalem. Solomon, too, received the precious lumber and skilled craftsmen to help in the construction of the Temple. The idolatry of the Phoenician princess Jezebel, wife of Ahab of Israel, soured relations, however, and Tyre, along with Sidon, became a favorite target of Hebrew wrath.

Tyre was conquered by Alexander the Great in the fourth century B.C. During the Roman period Tyre regained much of its former glory, exporting glassware, pottery, wines, and purple dyes. Jesus preached in the area, and citizens of Tyre often traveled to nearby Galilee to hear him speak. According to Acts 21:3–4, Paul and Luke spent seven days with the small but established Christian community there while waiting for a ship to be unloaded.

Biblical Citations

This list provides the chapter and verse of biblical citations used in the text. Boldface numbers indicate the page in the book where the quote appears. If the citation is given in the text, it is not repeated here. All quotes, unless otherwise noted, are from the Revised Standard Version.

13 "In those days a decree went out from Caesar Augustus that all the world should be enrolled. . . . And all went to be enrolled, each to his own city." Luke 2:1, 3. **15** "they were both righteous before God, walking in all the commandments and ordinances of the Lord blameless." Luke 1:6. **15** "filled with the Holy Spirit," Luke 1:15. **16** "Adam, the son of God." Luke 3:38. **16** "Hail, O favored one, the Lord is with you!" Luke 1:28. **16** "Son of the Most High; . . . and of his kingdom there will be no end." Luke 1:32, 33. **16** "The Holy Spirit will come upon you, and the power of the Most High will overshadow you;" Luke 1:35. **16** "For with God nothing will be impossible." Luke 1:37. **16, 17** "just man . . . unwilling to put her to shame, . . . 'Joseph, son of David, . . . save his people from their sins.' " Matthew 1:19, 20, 21. **17** "shall be established for ever." 2 Samuel 7:16. **17** "leaped . . . filled with the Holy Spirit . . . 'Blessed are you among women, and blessed is the fruit of your womb!' " Luke 1:41, 42. **17** "My soul magnifies the Lord." Luke 1:46. **17** "For behold, henceforth all generations will call me blessed;" Luke 1:48. **18** "His name is John." Luke 1:63. **18** "the prophet of the Most High;" Luke 1:76. **24** "out in the field, keeping watch over their flock by night." Luke 2:8. **24** "Be not afraid; . . . a Savior, who is Christ the Lord." Luke 2:10, 11. **25** "a babe wrapped in swaddling cloths and lying in a manger." Luke 2:12. **25** "Glory to God in the highest, and on earth peace, good will toward men." Luke 2:14, King James Bible. **25** "kept all these things, pondering them in her heart." Luke 2:19. **26** "Lord, now lettest thou thy servant depart in peace." Luke 2:29. **26** "a light for revelation to the Gentiles, and for glory to thy people Israel." Luke 2:32. **26** "wise men from the East came to Jerusalem, saying, 'Where is he who has been born king of the Jews? For we have seen his star in the East, and have come to worship him.' " Matthew 2:1–2. **26** "who has been born king of the Jews?" Matthew 2:2. **28** "a ruler who will govern my people Israel." Matthew 2:6. **28** "search diligently for the child," Matthew 2:8. **30** "Out of Egypt have I called my son." Matthew 2:15. **30** "A voice was heard in Ramah, wailing and loud lamentation, Rachel weeping for her children; she refused to be consoled, because they were no more." Matthew 2:18. **32** "I bring you good news of a great joy . . . for to you is born this day in the city of David a Savior, who is Christ the Lord." Luke 2:10, 11. **46** "make of you a great nation, and I will bless you, and make your name great," Genesis 12:2. **46** "Depart, go up hence, you and the people whom you have brought up out of the land of Egypt, to the land of which I swore to Abraham, Isaac, and Jacob," Exodus 33:1. **49** "By the waters of Babylon, there we sat down and wept, when we remembered Zion. . . .If I forget you, O Jerusalem, let my right hand wither!" Psalm 137:1, 5. **54** "Let every one who is zealous for the law and supports the covenant come out with me!" 1 Maccabees 2:27. **60** "graven image," Exodus 20:4. **92** "no favor in his eyes because he has found some indecency in her," Deuteronomy 24:1. **101** "beside the palace of Ahab king of Samaria." 1 Kings 21:1. **101** "The Lord forbid that I should give you the inheritance of my fathers." 1 Kings 21:3. **119** "Three times a year all your males shall appear before the Lord your God." Deuteronomy 16:16. **124** "And David dwelt in the stronghold, and called it the city of David." 2 Samuel 5:9. **126** "No, but I will buy it of you for a price; I will not offer burnt offerings to the Lord my God which cost me nothing." 2 Samuel 24:24. **126** "the city which the Lord had chosen out of all the tribes of Israel, to put his name there." 1 Kings 14:21. **138** "The Lord bless you from Zion! May you see the prosperity of Jerusalem all the days of your life! May you see your children's children! Peace be upon Israel!" Psalm 128:5–6. **144** "in the temple, sitting among the teachers, listening to them and asking them questions;" Luke 2:46. **144** "all who heard him were amazed at his understanding and his answers." Luke 2:47. **144** "Son, why have you treated us so? Behold, your father and I have been looking for you anxiously." Luke 2:48. **145** "How is it that you sought me? Did you not know that I must be in my Father's house?" Luke 2:49. **145** "kept all these things in her heart." Luke 2:51. **148** "Hear, O Israel: The Lord our God is one Lord;" Deuteronomy 6:4. **171** "ship of Adramyttium;" Acts 27:2. **200** "Repent, for the kingdom of heaven is at hand." Matthew 3:2. **200** "Even now the axe is laid to the root of the trees; every tree therefore that does not bear good fruit is cut down and thrown into the fire." Matthew 3:10. **200–202** " 'Who are you?' . . . 'I am not the Christ'. . . . 'What then? Are you Elijah?' . . . 'I am not.' 'Are you the prophet?' . . . 'No.' . . . 'Who are you? Let us have an answer for those who sent us. What do you say about yourself?' . . . 'I am the voice of one crying in the wilderness, "Make straight the way of the Lord," as the prophet Isaiah said.' " John 1:19, 20, 21, 22, 23. **201** "the jungle of the Jordan?" Jeremiah 12:5. **202** "Behold, I will send you Elijah the prophet before the great and terrible day of the Lord comes." Malachi 4:5. **202** "I will raise up for them a prophet like you from among their brethren; and I will put my words in his mouth, and he shall speak to them all that I command him." Deuteronomy 18:18. **202** "A voice cries: 'In the wilderness prepare the way of the Lord, make straight in the desert a highway for our God.' " Isaiah 40:3. **202** "You brood of vipers!" Matthew 3:7. **202** "Who warned you to flee from the wrath to come? Bear fruit that befits repentance, and do not presume to say to yourselves, 'We have Abraham as our father';" Matthew 3:7–9. **202** "I baptize you with water for repentance, but he who is coming after me is mightier than I, whose sandals I am not worthy to carry; he will baptize you with the Holy Spirit and with fire. His winnowing fork is in his hand, and he will clear his threshing floor and gather his wheat into the granary, but the chaff he will burn with unquenchable fire." Matthew 3:11–12. **203** "Therefore justice is far from us, and righteousness does not overtake us; we look for light, and behold, darkness, and for brightness, but we walk in gloom. We grope for the wall like the blind, we grope like those who have no eyes; we stumble at noon as in the twilight, among those in full vigor we are like dead men." Isaiah 59:9–10. **203** "For behold, the Lord will come in fire, and his chariots like the stormwind, to render his anger in fury, and his rebuke with flames of fire." Isaiah 66:15. "Let every one who is zealous for the law and supports the covenant come out with me!" 1 Maccabees 2:27. **206** "You shall have no other gods before me." Exodus 20:3. **207** "mighty warriors of Israel, every one who offered himself willingly for the law." 1 Maccabees 2:42. **207** "many of those who sleep in the dust of the earth shall awake, some to everlasting life, and some to shame and everlasting contempt. And those who are wise shall shine like the brightness of the firmament;" Daniel 12:2–3. **207** "Repent, for the kingdom of heaven is at hand." Matthew 3:2. **212** "a kingdom of priests and a holy nation." Exodus 19:6. **213** "They do all their deeds to be seen by men; for they make their phylacteries broad and their fringes long," Matthew 23:5. **214** "they preach, but do not practice." Matthew 23:3. **214** "sit on Moses' seat;" Matthew 23:2. **217** "the way of the Lord;" John 1:23. **222** "would gladly have fed on the pods that the swine ate;" Luke 15:16. **222** "He who has two coats, let him share with him who has none; and he who has food, let him do likewise." Luke 3:11. **222** "who comes after me," John 1:27. **223** "This is he of whom I said, 'After me comes a man who ranks before me, for he was before me.' " John 1:30. **223** " 'I need to be baptized by you, and do you come to me?' . . . 'Let it be so now; for thus it is fitting for us to fulfil all righteousness.' " Matthew 3:14, 15. **223** "he saw the heavens opened and the Spirit descending upon him like a dove; and a voice came from heaven, 'Thou art my beloved Son; with thee I am well pleased.' " Mark 1:10–11. **226** "a very high mountain, . . . all the kingdoms of the world. . . . 'All these I will give you, if you will fall down and worship me.' . . . 'Begone, Satan!' " Matthew 4:8, 9, 10. **227** "with the wild beasts;" Mark 1:13. **228** "being glorified by all." Luke 4:15. **228** "fishers of men." Matthew 4:19; Mark 1:17. **228** "the kingdom of heaven is at hand." Matthew 4:17. **228** "Go; your son will live." John 4:50. **233** "Let us go on to the next towns, that I may preach there also; for that is why I came out." Mark 1:38. **234** "whom Jesus loved," John 21:20. **234** "show us the Father, . . . He who has seen me has seen the Father;" John 14:8, 9. **234** "Can anything good come out of Nazareth?" John 1:46. **234** "Follow me." Matthew 9:9. **234** "tax collectors and sinners?" "I came not to call the righteous, but sinners." Matthew 9:13. **234** "the Twin," John 21:2. **235** "A prophet is not without honor, except in his own country, and among his own kin, and in his own house." Mark 6:4. **236** "Think not that I have come to abolish the law and the prophets; I have come not to abolish them but to fulfil them." Matthew 5:17. **236** "Love your enemies and pray for those who persecute you," Matthew 5:44. **236** "But if any one strikes you on the right cheek, turn to him the other also;" Matthew 5:39. **236** "be perfect, as your heavenly Father is perfect." Matthew 5:48. **236** "You cannot serve God and mammon." Matthew 6:24 and Luke 16:13. **236** "and all these things shall be yours as well." Matthew 6:33. **238** "Are you he who is to come, or shall we look for another?" Matthew 11:3 and Luke 7:19. **238** "A reed shaken by the wind? . . . A man clothed in soft clothing? . . . and more than a prophet." Luke 7:24, 25, 26. **240** "when you leave that town shake off the dust from your feet as a testimony against them." Luke 9:5. **242** "And I tell you, you are Peter, and on this rock I will build my church, and the powers of death shall not prevail against it. I will give you the keys of the kingdom of heaven, and whatever you bind on earth shall be bound in heaven, and whatever you loose on earth shall be loosed in heaven." Matthew 16:18–19. **243** "Get behind me, Satan!" Matthew 16:23. **243** "If any man would come after me, let him deny himself and take up his cross and follow me." Matthew 16:24. **243** "until the Son of man is raised from the dead." Matthew 17:9. **243** "he set his face to go to Jerusalem," Luke 9:51. **243** "Let the children come to me, do not hinder them; for to such belongs the kingdom of God. Truly, I say to you, whoever does not receive the kingdom of God like a child shall not enter it." Mark 10:14–15. **243** "And Jesus looking upon him loved him, and said to him, 'You lack one thing; go, sell what you have, and give to the poor, and you will have treasure in heaven; and come, follow me.' " Mark 10:21. **243** "It is easier for a camel to go through the eye of a needle than for a rich man to enter the kingdom of God." Matthew 19:24; Mark 10:25; Luke 18:25. **244** "With men it is impossible, but not with God; for all things are possible with God." Mark 10:27. **244** "there is no one who has left house or brothers or sisters or mother or father or children or lands, for my sake and for the gospel, who will not receive a hundredfold now in this time, houses and brothers and sisters and mothers and children and lands, with persecutions, and in the age to come eternal life. But many that are first will be last, and the last first." Mark 10:29–31. **245** "How is it that this man has learning, when he has never studied?" John 7:15. **245** "If you are the Christ, tell us plainly." John 10:24. **245** "Is not this the man whom they seek to kill? And here he is, speaking openly, and they say nothing to him! Can it be that the authorities really know that this is the Christ?" John 7:25–26. **246** "Let us go into Judea again." John 11:7. **246** "Let us also go, that we may die with him." John 11:16. **246** "Take away the stone." John 11:39. **246** "Lazarus, come out." John 11:43. **246** "see the glory of God?" John 11:40. **246** "it is expedient for you that one man should die for the people, and that the whole nation should not perish." John 11:50. **247** "Rise, take up your pallet, and walk." John 5:8. **247** "I am the resurrection and the life;" John 11:25. **248** "Hosanna! Blessed is he who comes in the name of the Lord! Blessed is the kingdom of our father David that is coming!" Mark 11:9–10. **248** "Is it not written, 'My house shall be called a house of prayer for all the nations'? But you have made it a den of robbers." Mark 11:17.

248 "whatever you ask in prayer, believe that you have received it, and it will be yours. And whenever you stand praying, forgive, if you have anything against any one; so that your Father also who is in heaven may forgive you your trespasses." Mark 11:24–25. 249 "Whose likeness and inscription is this? . . . Render to Caesar the things that are Caesar's, and to God the things that are God's." Mark 12:16, 17. 249 "Father's house." John 2:16. 250 "there will not be left here one stone upon another, that will not be thrown down." Matthew 24:2 and Mark 13:2. 250 "as you did it to one of the least of these my brethren, you did it to me." Matthew 25:40. 251 "as you did it not to one of the least of these, you did it not to me." Matthew 25:45. 251 "She has done a beautiful thing to me. For you always have the poor with you, and whenever you will, you can do good to them; but you will not always have me." Mark 14:6–7. 251 "the Son of man came not to be served but to serve, and to give his life as a ransom for many." Matthew 20:28. 252 "Truly, I say to you, I shall not drink again of the fruit of the vine until that day when I drink it new in the kingdom of God." Mark 14:25. 252 "who has dipped his hand in the dish with me;" Matthew 26:23. 252 "What you are going to do, do quickly." John 13:27. 253 "love one another as I have loved you. Greater love has no man than this, that a man lay down his life for his friends. You are my friends if you do what I command you." John 15:12–14. 253 "In the world you have tribulation; but be of good cheer, I have overcome the world." John 16:33. 253 "lifted up his eyes to heaven" John 17:1. 253 "Sanctify them in the truth; thy word is truth." John 17:17. 253 "that they may all be one; even as thou, Father, art in me, and I in thee, that they also may be in us, so that the world may believe that thou hast sent me." John 17:21. 253 "Abba, Father, all things are possible to thee; remove this cup from me; yet not what I will, but what thou wilt." Mark 14:36. 253 "Simon, are you asleep? Could you not watch one hour? Watch and pray that you may not enter into temptation; the spirit indeed is willing, but the flesh is weak." Mark 14:37–38. 253 "Rise, let us be going; see, my betrayer is at hand." Mark 14:42. 253 "No more of this!" Luke 22:51. 254 "a band of soldiers and some officers from the chief priests and the Pharisees, . . . with lanterns and torches and weapons," John 18:3. 254 "questioned Jesus about his disciples and his teaching." John 18:19. 254 "Ask those who have heard me, what I said to them; they know what I said." John 18:21. 255 "the cock crowed. And the Lord turned and looked at Peter. And Peter remembered the word of the Lord, how he had said to him, 'Before the cock crows today, you will deny me three times.' And he went out and wept bitterly." Luke 22:60–62. 255 "If I tell you, you will not believe;" Luke 22:67. 255 "Are you the King of the Jews?" Matthew 27:11; Mark 15:2; Luke 23:3; John 18:33. 255 "You have said so." Matthew 27:11; Mark 15:2; Luke 23:3. 255 "What is truth?" John 18:38. 256 "that fox," Luke 13:32. 256 "gorgeous apparel," Luke 23:11. 256 "Herod and Pilate became friends with each other that very day, for before this they had been at enmity with each other." Luke 23:12. 256 "release to us Barabbas" Luke 23:18. 256 "Pilate again said to them, 'Then what shall I do with the man whom you call the King of the Jews?' And they cried out again, 'Crucify him.' And Pilate said to them, 'Why, what evil has he done?' But they shouted all the more, 'Crucify him.' " Mark 15:12–14. 256 "I am innocent of this man's blood; see to it yourselves." Matthew 27:24. 257 "Behold the man!" John 19:5. 259 "who was coming in from the country," Mark 15:21 and Luke 23:26. 259 "For if they do this when the wood is green, what will happen when it is dry?" Luke 23:31. 259 "Jesus of Nazareth, the King of the Jews." John 19:19. 259 "What I have written I have written." John 19.22. 259 "If you are the King of the Jews, save yourself!" Luke 23:37. 259 "disciple whom he loved" John 19:26. 260 "I thirst." John 19:28. 260 "vinegar on hyssop" John 19:29. 260 "wine mingled with myrrh;" Mark 15:23. 260 "Hail, King of the Jews!" Mark 15:18; John 19:3. 260 " 'It is finished'; . . . and gave up his spirit." John 19:30. 260 "torn in two, from top to bottom." Mark 15:38; Matthew 27:51. 260 "Truly this man was the Son of God!" Mark 15:39. 260 "Do not be amazed; you seek Jesus of Nazareth, who was crucified. He has risen, he is not here;" Mark 16:6. 261 "Have you believed because you have seen me? Blessed are those who have not seen and yet believe." John 20:29. 262 "For God so loved the world that he gave his only Son," John 3:16. 271 "from Samuel and those who came afterwards;" Acts 3:24. 273 "tongues as of fire, . . . other tongues, . . . from every nation under heaven." Acts 2:3, 4, 5. 274 "uneducated, common men," Acts 4:13. 275 "praised God for what had happened." Acts 4:21. 276 "a light to the nations," Isaiah 42:6. 278 " 'Behold, I see the heavens opened, and the Son of man standing at the right hand of God.' . . . cried out with a loud voice and stopped their ears and rushed together upon him." Acts 7:56, 57. 279 " 'Saul, Saul, why do you persecute me?' . . . 'Who are you, Lord?' . . . 'I am Jesus, whom you are persecuting; but rise and enter the city, and you will be told what you are to do.' " Acts 9:4, 5–6. 280 "something like scales fell from his eyes" Acts 9:18. 280 "an Apostle of Christ Jesus by the will of God," 2 Corinthians 1:1. 281 "like a great sheet," Acts 10:11. 281 "never eaten anything that is common or unclean" Acts 10:14. 281 "all that you have been commanded by the Lord." Acts 10:33. 281 "every one who believes in him receives forgiveness of sins through his name." Acts 10:43. 283 "because he did not give God the glory;" Acts 12:23. 284 "sought to hear the word of God." Acts 13:7. 285 "everlasting covenant" Genesis 9:16. 285 "the right hand of fellowship," Galatians 2:9. 285 "If you, though a Jew, live like a Gentile and not like a Jew, how can you compel the Gentiles to live like Jews?" Galatians 2:14. 291 "former life in Judaism," Galatians 1:13. 298 "seven churches that are in Asia:" Revelation 1:4.

Bibliography

GENERAL

ACHTEMEIER, PAUL J. *Harper's Bible Dictionary.* San Francisco: Harper & Row, Publishers, Inc., 1985.

AHARONI, YOHANAN. *The Land of the Bible.* Philadelphia: The Westminster Press, 1979.

AHARONI, YOHANAN. *The Macmillan Bible Atlas,* rev. ed. New York: Macmillan Publishing Co., Inc., 1977.

ALEXANDER, DAVID, and PAT ALEXANDER. *Eerdmans' Handbook to the Bible.* Tring, England: Lion Publishing, 1973.

AMIRAN, DAVID H.K., and others, eds. *Atlas of Israel.* Jerusalem: Ministry of Labour, Survey of Israel, 1970.

BAHAT, DAN. *Carta's Historical Atlas of Jerusalem.* Jerusalem: Carta, the Israel Map & Publishing Company, 1983.

BALY, DENIS, and A.D. TUSHINGHAM. *Atlas of the Biblical World.* New York: The World Publishing Company, 1971.

BEITZEL, BARRY J. *The Moody Atlas of Bible Lands.* Chicago: Moody Press, 1985.

Bible Today, The Jerusalem Version. London: Marshall Cavendish Ltd., 1970.

COOK, S.A. *The Cambridge Ancient History,* Vols. 9–12. Cambridge, England: Cambridge University Press, 1966.

CORCOS, GEORGETTE, and others, eds. *The Glory of the New Testament.* Jerusalem: The Jerusalem Publishing House, Ltd., 1983.

CORCOS, GEORGETTE, and others, eds. *The Glory of the Old Testament.* New York: Villard Books, 1984.

CORNELL, TIM, and JOHN MATTHEWS. *Atlas of the Roman World.* New York: Facts on File, Inc., 1982.

ELIOT, ALEXANDER. *Myths.* New York: McGraw-Hill Book Company, 1976.

ENCYCLOPEDIA JUDAICA. Jerusalem: Keter Publishing House Jerusalem Ltd., 1972.

GEHMAN, HENRY SNYDER, ed. *The New Westminster Dictionary of the Bible.* Philadelphia: The Westminster Press, 1944.

GRANT, FREDERICK C., and H.H. ROWLEY. *Dictionary of the Bible,* 2nd. ed. Edinburgh: T. & T. Clark, 1963.

HAREUVENI, NOGAH. *Nature in Our Biblical Heritage.* Kiryat Ono, Israel: Neot Kedumim Ltd., 1980.

HAREUVENI, NOGAH. *Tree and Shrub in Our Biblical Heritage.* Kiryat Ono, Israel: Neot Kedumim Ltd., 1984.

HUNTER, ELOISE, and others, eds. *Bible Encyclopedia for the Family.* Nashville: Thomas Nelson Publishers, Inc., 1982.

The Illustrated Bible Dictionary. Wheaton, Ill.: Tyndale House Publishers, 1980.

KRAELING, EMIL G. *Rand McNally Bible Atlas.* Chicago: Rand McNally & Co., 1962.

LIFE MAGAZINE EDITORIAL STAFF. *The World's Great Religions.* New York: Time Inc., 1955.

MAY, HERBERT G. *Oxford Bible Atlas,* 2nd ed. New York: Oxford University Press, 1974.

MILLER, MADELEINE S., and J. LANE MILLER. *Encyclopedia of Bible Life.* New York: Harper & Row, Publishers, Inc., 1944.

MILLER, MADELEINE S., and J. LANE MILLER. *Harper's Encyclopedia of Bible Life,* rev. and ed. Boyce M. Bennett, Jr., and David H. Scott. San Francisco: Harper & Row, Publishers, Inc., 1978.

MOLDENKE, HAROLD N. *Plants of the Bible.* New York: The Ronald Press Co., 1952.

New Catholic Encyclopedia. New York: McGraw-Hill Book Company, 1967.

PACKER, JAMES I., and others, eds. *The Bible Almanac.* Nashville: Thomas Nelson Publishers, Inc., 1980.

PARRINDER, GEOFFREY. *Religions of the World.* New York: Grosset & Dunlap, Inc., 1971.

READER'S DIGEST EDITORS. *Atlas of the Bible.* Pleasantville, N.Y.: The Reader's Digest Association, Inc., 1981.

ROGERSON, JOHN. *Atlas of the Bible.* New York: Facts on File, Inc., 1985.

ROWLEY, H. H. *Dictionary of Bible Place Names.* Greenwood, S.C.: The Attic Press, Inc., 1970.

SHAMIS, GIORA, and DIANE SHALEM. *The Jerusalem Guide.* Jerusalem: Abraham Marcus Limited, 1973.

SHEPHERD, WILLIAM R. *Historical Atlas.* New York: Barnes & Noble, Inc., 1964.

SMITH, GEORGE ADAM. *The Historical Geography of the Holy Land.* New York: Harper & Row, Publishers, Inc., 1966.

SPEAKE, GRAHAM, ed. *Atlas of the Bible.* New York: Facts on File, Inc., 1985.

STEINSALTZ, ADIN. *The Essential Talmud.* New York: Bantam Books, Inc., 1977.

VAN DER HEYDEN, A.A.M. *Atlas of the Classical World.* New York: Thomas Nelson and Sons, Ltd., 1959.

WRIGHT, GEORGE ERNEST, ed. *Historical Atlas to the Bible.* Philadelphia: The Westminster Press, 1956.

ZOHARY, MICHAEL. *Plants of the Bible.* New York: Cambridge University Press, 1982.

BIBLES AND COMMENTARIES

CATHOLIC BIBLICAL ASSOCIATION of AMERICA, trans. *The New American Bible.* Nashville: Thomas Nelson Publishers, Inc., 1983.

The Holy Bible, King James Version. New York: American Bible Society, 1966.

Illustrated New Testament. Collegeville, Minn.: Liturgical Press, 1974.

The Interpreter's Bible. Nashville: Abingdon Press, 1951.

The Interpreter's Dictionary of the Bible: An Illustrated Encyclopedia. Nashville: Abingdon Press, 1962.

MAY, HERBERT G., and BRUCE M. METZGER, eds. *The New Oxford Annotated Bible with the Apocrypha, Revised Standard Version.* New York: Oxford University Press, Inc., 1977.

ALAND, KURT. *Synopsis of the Four Gospels.* New York: United Bible Societies, 1982.

ALBRIGHT, W.F., and C.S. MANN. *The Anchor Bible, Matthew.* Garden City, N.Y.: Doubleday & Company, Inc., 1971.

BOUCHER, MADELEINE I. *The Parables.* Wilmington, Del.: Michael Glazier, Inc., 1981.

DORÉ, GUSTAVE. *The Doré Bible Illustrations.* New York: Dover Publications, Inc., 1974.

DRANE, JOHN W. *Jesus and the Four Gospels.* New York: Harper & Row, Publishers, Inc., 1979.

EDWARDS, O.C., Jr. *Luke's Story of Jesus.* Philadelphia: Fortress Press, 1981.

ELLISON, JOHN W., comp. *Nelson's Complete Concordance of the Revised Standard Version Bible,* 2nd ed. rev. Nashville: Thomas Nelson Publishers, Inc., 1972.

FITZMYER, JOSEPH A. *The Anchor Bible, The Gospel According to Luke (I–IX).* Garden City, N.Y.: Doubleday & Company, Inc., 1981.

MUNCK, JOHANNES. *The Anchor Bible, The Acts of the Apostles.* Garden City, N.Y.: Doubleday & Company, Inc., 1981.

READER'S DIGEST EDITORS. *Family Guide to The Bible.* Pleasantville, N.Y.: The Reader's Digest Association, Inc., 1984.

UNGER, MERRILL F. *The New Unger's Bible Handbook.* Chicago: Moody Press, 1966.

HISTORY AND ARCHEOLOGY

ACKERMAN, ANDREW S., and SUSAN L. BRAUNSTEIN. *Israel in Antiquity: From David to Herod.* New York: The Jewish Museum, 1982.

AVIGAD, NAHMAN. *Discovering Jerusalem.* Nashville: Thomas Nelson Publishers, Inc., 1983.

AVI-YONAH, MICHAEL. *Encyclopedia of Archaeological Excavations in the Holy Land.* Englewood Cliffs, N.J.: Prentice-Hall, Inc., 1976.

AVI-YONAH, MICHAEL, ed. *The World History of the Jewish People, Vol. 7, The Herodian Period.* Tel Aviv: Jewish History Publications Ltd., 1975.

BARTLETT, JOHN R. *Jews in the Hellenistic World.* New York: Cambridge University Press, 1985.

BOWERSOCK, G.W. *Roman Arabia.* Cambridge, Mass.: Harvard University Press, 1983.

BRUCE, F.F. *Jesus and Paul, Places They Knew.* Nashville: Thomas Nelson Publishers, Inc., 1983.

CASSON, LIONEL. *The Ancient Mariners: Seafarers and Sea Fighters of the Mediterranean in Ancient Times.* New York: The Macmillan Company, 1959.

CASSON, LIONEL. *Ancient Trade and Society.* Detroit: Wayne State University Press, 1984.

CASSON, LIONEL. *Ships and Seamanship in the Ancient World.* Princeton, N.J.: Princeton University Press, 1971.

CASSON, LIONEL. *Travel in the Ancient World.* London: Samuel Stevens, 1974.

COLLINS, JOHN J. *Between Athens & Jerusalem: Jewish Identity in the Hellenistic Diaspora.* New York: Crossroad Publishing Co., 1983.

DAVIES, J.G. *The Early Christian Church.* Grand Rapids: Baker Book House, 1965.

DAVIES, W.D., and others, eds. *The Cambridge History of Judaism.* Cambridge, England: Cambridge University Press, 1984.

DE VAUX, ROLAND. *Ancient Israel,* Vol. 2, *Religious Institutions.* New York: McGraw-Hill Book Company, 1961.

ENSLIN, MORTON SCOTT. *Christian Beginnings.* New York: Harper & Brothers, Publishers, 1938.

FINEGAN, JACK. *The Archeology of the New Testament.* Princeton, N.J.: Princeton University Press, 1969.

FREYNE, SEÁN. *Galilee from Alexander the Great to Hadrian 323 B.C.E. to 135 C.E.* Wilmington, Del.: Michael Glazier, Inc., and Notre Dame, Ind.: University of Notre Dame Press, 1980.

FREYNE, SEÁN. *The World of the New Testament.* Wilmington, Del.: Michael Glazier, Inc., 1980.

GRANT, MICHAEL. *The Jews in the Roman World.* New York: Charles Scribner's Sons, 1973.

GRANT, ROBERT M. *After the New Testament.* Philadelphia: Fortress Press, 1967.

GRANT, ROBERT M. *Augustus to Constantine.* New York: Harper & Row, Publishers, Inc., 1970.

GRANT, ROBERT M. *Early Christianity and Society.* San Francisco: Harper & Row, Publishers, Inc., 1977.

HARRISON, R.K. *Major Cities of the Biblical World.* Nashville: Thomas Nelson Publishers, Inc., 1985.

JOSEPHUS, FLAVIUS. *Jewish Antiquities,* Books IX-XI. Cambridge, Mass.: Harvard University Press, 1937.

JOSEPHUS, FLAVIUS. *The Jewish War,* Books I-III. Cambridge, Mass.: Harvard University Press, 1927.

KENYON, KATHLEEN M. *Jerusalem, Excavating 3000 Years of History.* New York: McGraw-Hill Book Company, 1967.

KOESTER, HELMUT. *Introduction to the New Testament.* Vol. 1 Philadelphia: Fortress Press, 1982.

LIEBERMAN, SAUL. *Hellenism in Jewish Palestine,* 2nd. ed. New York: The Jewish Theological Seminary of America, 1962.

LING, ROGER. *The Greek World.* New York: E.P. Dutton & Co., Inc., 1976.

MACMULLEN, RAMSAY. *Christianizing the Roman Empire, A.D. 100-400.* New Haven, Conn.: Yale University Press, 1984.

MAZAR, BENJAMIN. *The Mountain of the Lord.* Garden City, N.Y.: Doubleday & Company, Inc., 1975.

MILLARD, ALAN. *Treasures from Bible Times.* Tring, England: Lion Publishing, 1985.

MORTON, H.V., and RENÉ BURRI. *In Search of the Holy Land.* New York: Dodd, Mead & Company, Inc., 1979.

MURPHY-O'CONNOR, JEROME, O.P. *The Holy Land.* Oxford, England: Oxford University Press, 1980.

NEGEV, AVRAHAM, ed. *Archaeological Encyclopedia of the Holy Land.* New York: G.P. Putnam's Sons, 1972.

NEUSNER, JACOB. *From Politics to Piety: The Emergence of Pharisaic Judaism,* 2nd. ed. New York: KTAV Publishing House, 1979.

PACKER, JAMES I., MERRILL C. TENNEY, and WILLIAM WHITE Jr., *The World of the New Testament.* Nashville: Thomas Nelson Publishers, Inc., 1982.

PACKER, JAMES I., MERRILL C. TENNEY, and WILLIAM WHITE Jr., *The World of the Old Testament.* Nashville: Thomas Nelson Publishers, Inc., 1982.

PEARLMAN, MOSHE, and YAACOV YANNAI. *Historical Sites in Israel,* rev. ed. New York: Simon and Schuster, 1969.

PETERS, F.E. *The Harvest of Hellenism.* New York: Simon and Schuster, 1970.

PETERS, F.E. *Jerusalem.* Princeton, N.J.: Princeton University Press, 1985.

READER'S DIGEST EDITORS. *Great People of the Bible and How They Lived.* Pleasantville, N.Y.: The Reader's Digest Association, Inc., 1974.

RHOADS, DAVID M. *Israel in Revolution: 6–74 C.E.* Philadelphia: Fortress Press, 1976.

ROSTOVTZEFF, M. *Social and Economic History of the Hellenistic World.* Oxford, England: Clarendon Press, 1967.

SAFRAI, S., and M. STERN. *The Jewish People in the First Century.* Amsterdam: Van Gorcum, 1976.

SCHALIT, ABRAHAM, and others, eds. *The World History of the Jewish People,* Vol. 6, *The Hellenistic Age.* Tel Aviv: Jewish History Publications Ltd., 1972.

SCHÜRER, EMIL. *A History of the Jewish People in the Time of Jesus.* Ed. NAHUM N. GLATZER. New York: Schocken Books, Inc., 1961.

SHANKS, HERSHEL. *Judaism in Stone.* New York: Harper & Row, Publishers, Inc., 1979.

TCHERIKOVER, VICTOR. *Hellenistic Civilization and the Jews.* New York: Atheneum, 1970.

TOYNBEE, ARNOLD. *The Crucible of Christianity.* New York: World Publishing Company, 1969.

WRIGHT, G. ERNEST. *Biblical Archaeology.* Philadelphia: The Westminster Press, 1962.

YADIN, YIGAEL. *Bar-Kokhba.* New York: Random House, 1971.

BIOGRAPHIES

BARCLAY, WILLIAM. *Jesus of Nazareth.* London: Collins + World, 1977.

CRAVERI, MARCELLO. *The Life of Jesus.* New York: Grove Press, Inc., 1967.

GOODSPEED, EDGAR J. *Paul.* Nashville: Abingdon Press, 1947.

GRANT, MICHAEL. *Herod the Great.* New York: American Heritage Publishing Co., Inc., 1971.

PEROWNE, STEWART. *The Life and Times of Herod the Great.* New York: Hodder and Stoughton Ltd., 1956.

STAUFFER, ETHELBERT. *Jesus and His Story.* New York: Alfred A. Knopf, Inc., 1960.

JESUS: HIS LIFE AND TIMES

BROWN, RAYMOND E. *The Birth of the Messiah.* Garden City, N.Y.: Image Books, 1979.

DANIEL-ROPS, HENRI. *Jesus and His Times.* New York: E.P. Dutton & Co., Inc., 1956.

GUIGNEBERT, CHARLES. *Jesus.* New Hyde Park, N.Y.: University Books, Inc., 1959.

GUIGNEBERT, CHARLES. *The Jewish World in the Time of Jesus.* New Hyde Park, N.Y.: University Books, Inc., 1959.

JEREMIAS, JOACHIM. *Jerusalem in the Time of Jesus.* Philadelphia: Fortress Press, 1969.

KOTKER, NORMAN. *The Holy Land in the Time of Jesus.* New York: American Heritage Publishing Co., Inc., 1967.

PAX, WOLFGANG E. *In the Footsteps of Jesus.* New York: Leon Amiel Publisher, 1976.

SCHULTZ, HANS JURGEN. *Jesus in His Time.* Philadelphia: Fortress Press, 1971.

SCHÜRER, EMIL. *The History of the Jewish People in the Age of Jesus Christ (175 B.C.–A.D.135).* Rev. and ed. GEZA VERMES and others. Edinburgh: T. & T. Clark Ltd., 1979.

TERRINGO, J. ROBERT. *The Land & People Jesus Knew.* Minneapolis: Bethany House Publishers, 1985.

WILKINSON, JOHN. *Jerusalem as Jesus Knew It.* London: Thames and Hudson Ltd., 1978.

DAILY LIFE

BOUQUET, A.C. *Everyday Life in New Testament Times.* New York: Charles Scribner's Sons, 1953.

CONNOLLY, PETER. *Living in the Time of Jesus of Nazareth.* Oxford, England: Oxford University Press, 1983.

DANIEL-ROPS, HENRI. *Daily Life in the Time of Jesus.* New York: Hawthorn Books, Inc., 1962.

HEATON, E.W. *Everyday Life in Old Testament Times.* New York: Charles Scribner's Sons, 1956.

LOCKYER, HERBERT. *All the Trades and Occupations of the Bible.* Grand Rapids: Zondervan Publishing House, 1969.

NATIONAL GEOGRAPHIC SOCIETY. *Everyday Life in Ancient Times.* Washington, D.C.: National Geographic Society, 1951.

NATIONAL GEOGRAPHIC SOCIETY. *Everyday Life in Bible Times.* Washington, D.C.: National Geographic Society, 1968.

PACKER, JAMES I., MERRILL TENNEY, and WILLIAM WHITE, JR. *Daily Life in Bible Times.* Nashville: Thomas Nelson Publishers, Inc., 1982.

VAN DEURSEN, A. *Illustrated Dictionary of Bible Manners and Customs.* New York: Philosophical Library, Inc., 1967.

ART

AVI-YONAH, MICHAEL. *Views of the Biblical World,* Vol. 5, *The New Testament.* Jerusalem: The International Publishing Co., Ltd., 1961.

BERNARD, BRUCE. *The Bible and Its Painters.* New York: Macmillan Publishing Company, 1984.

BUECHNER, FREDERICK, and LEE BOLTIN. *The Faces of Jesus.* Croton-on-Hudson, N.Y.: A Riverwood/Simon and Schuster Book, 1974.

EIMERL, SAREL, and the EDITORS of TIME-LIFE BOOKS. *The World of Giotto.* New York: Time Inc., 1967.

JOBÉ, JOSEPH. *Ecce Homo.* New York: Harper & Row, Publishers, Inc., 1962.

JONES, CLIFFORD M. *New Testament Illustrations.* Cambridge, England: Cambridge University Press, 1966.

LESSING ERICH. *Jesus: History and Culture of the New Testament, A Pictorial Narration.* New York: Herder and Herder, 1971.

LOOK MAGAZINE BOOK DIVISION. *The Coming of Christ.* New York: Cowles Magazines and Broadcasting, Inc., 1963.

Acknowledgments

The editors are grateful to the following individuals and organizations for their help in the preparation of this book.

Prof. Nahman Avigad, *The Hebrew University of Jerusalem*
Daniel Blatt
Carol and Lee Boltin
Werner Braun
Prof. Lionel Casson, *New York University*
Deanna Cross, *Metropolitan Museum of Art, New York*
Colonel John R. Elting, U.S. Army (Ret.)
Joan Evanish, *The Biblical Garden, The Cathedral*

Church of St. John the Divine, *New York*
Helen Frenkley, *Neot Kedumim Ltd., Kiryat Ono, Israel*
Sonia Halliday
Robert Harding Picture Library, London
David Harris
Dr. F.N. Hepper
Michael Holford
Israel Government Tourist Office, New York
Barbara Jago, *Magnum Photos, New York*
Dr. A. Thomas Kraabel, *Vice President and Dean, Luther College, Decorah, Iowa*
Aaron M. Levin

Irene Lewitt, *Israel Museum, Jerusalem*
Garo Nalbandian
Dr. Ehud Netzer, *Institute of Archaeology, The Hebrew University of Jerusalem*
Richard T. Nowitz
Lisa Pollenberg, *Art Resource, New York*
Zev Radovan
Dr. J. Ringel, *Director, The National Maritime Museum, Haifa*
Raffi Safieh
Ronald Sheridan's Photo Library, London
Dr. James F. Strange, *University of South Florida, Tampa*

Credits

ART: David Blossom **241.** George Buctel **61, 88, 277, 291.** Peter Connolly from LIVING IN THE TIME OF JESUS OF NAZARETH by Peter Connolly, published by Oxford University Press, © Peter Connolly 1983. **130, 136, 141, 176.** Lane Dupont **15** bottom, **78-79.** Wallace H. Fax **95, 206.** George S. Gaadt **36-37.** Larissa Lawrynenko **100-101.** Victor Lazzaro **15** top and right, **19, 27, 66, 68-69, 121, 154, 156-157, 175, 181, 201, 216, 230-231, 239, 258, 290.** Dennis Lyall **12-13, 118-119, 170-171.** Jerry Pinkney **20-21, 90-91, 114, 198-199.** Walter Rane **139, 153, 211, 279, 294.** Ray Skibinski **41, 52-53** maps, **107, 131, 179, 287, 297.** John Thompson **62-63, 98, 223, 249, 251, 254, 270-271.** Richard Williams **86-87, 110, 146-147, 224-225.** Ben Wohlberg **28.**

PHOTOGRAPHS

Picture Editor: Robert J. Woodward
Associate Picture Editor: Richard Pasqual

2-3 Garo Nalbandian. **3** *right* Zev Radovan. **4** From the Collections of the Israel Department of Antiquities, photo Israel Museum, Jerusalem/David Harris. **11** Scala/Art Resource, N. Y. **14** Erich Lessing/Magnum. **17** Erich Lessing/Magnum. **19** *top left* Erich Lessing/Magnum; *middle left & bottom* Daniel Blatt. **22** The Ancient Art & Architecture Collection. **23** *top* Erich Lessing/ Magnum; *bottom* Daniel Blatt. **24** Raffi Safieh. **25** Micha Bar-Am/Magnum. **26** Lick Observatory Photograph. **27** *top* The Robert Harding Picture Library. **29** *upper left* The Metropolitan Museum of Art, Harris Brisbane Dick Fund, 1954; *bottom left* The Robert Harding Picture Library; *bottom right* F. Nigel Hepper. **31** C. Thomson/The Image Bank. **32** Scala/Art Resource, N. Y. **33** *left* Scala/Art Resource, N. Y.; *right* © The Pierpont Morgan Library 1986 (M. 6, f. 41). **34** *right* Kunsthistorische Museum, Vienna; *remainder* Sonia Halliday. **35** Scala/Art Resource, N. Y. **38** Richard T. Nowitz. **39** The Granger Collection, New York. **40** *left* The British Museum/Michael Holford; *middle* Alinari/Art Resource, N. Y.; *right* Erich Lessing/Magnum. **41** *bottom* Giraudon/Art Resource, N. Y. **42-43** NASA Photograph © Pictorial Archive (Near Eastern History) Est., P. O. B. 19823, Jerusalem. **44** F. Nigel Hepper. **45** *left* Micha Bar-Am/Magnum; *top right* David Harris; *bottom right* Daniel Blatt. **46** René Burri/Magnum. **47** *top left* Werner Braun; *bottom left* Nathan Benn/Woodfin Camp & Associates; *top right* Daniel Blatt; *bottom right* Richard T. Nowitz. **48** *top* Erwin R. Goodenough, *Jewish Symbols in the Greco-Roman Period,* Bollingen Series XXXVII, Vol. 11: *Symbolism in the Dura Synagogue.* Copyright © 1964 by Princeton University Press. Photograph by Fred Anderegg. Plate VII reprinted by permission of Princeton University Press/Art Resource, N. Y.; *bottom* Erich Lessing/Magnum. **50** Scala/Art Resource, N. Y. **55** Erich Lessing/ Magnum. **56** Alinari/Art Resource, N. Y. **57** *left* Alinari/Art Resource, N. Y.; *top middle* Museum of Antiquities, Newcastle/ Michael Holford; *center* The British Museum/Michael Holford;

bottom middle From the Collections of the Israel Department of Antiquities, photo Israel Museum, Jerusalem/David Harris; *remainder* Zev Radovan. **59** Jean Dieuzaide. **60** *top* The Robert Harding Picture Library; *lower* The Jewish Museum/Art Resource, N. Y. **64** Zev Radovan. **65** *left* Richard T. Nowitz; *right* The Ancient Art & Architecture Collection. **67** *top left* Erich Lessing/Magnum; *bottom left* Sonia Halliday; *top right* Harry Thomas Frank; *bottom right* Richard T. Nowitz. **68** *top left* Zev Radovan. **70** Zev Radovan. **71** *bottom* Louis Goldman/Photo Researchers; *top* Zev Radovan. **73** *bottom left* The Ancient Art & Architecture Collection; *remainder* From the Collections of the Israel Department of Antiquities, photos Israel Museum, Jerusalem/David Harris. **74** The Ancient Art & Architecture Collection. **75** Scala/Art Resource, N. Y. **76** From the Collections of the Israel Department of Antiquities, photo Israel Museum, Jerusalem/David Harris. **77** *top* The Ancient Art & Architecture Collection; *bottom* Zev Radovan. **79** *top right* Zev Radovan; *bottom* The Jewish Museum/Art Resource, N. Y. **80** Richard T. Nowitz. **81** *bottom left* The British Museum/Michael Holford; *remainder* Erich Lessing/Magnum. **82** *upper* Rheinisches Landesmuseum Trier; *bottom left* Israel Museum Shrine of the Book, photo Israel Museum, Jerusalem/David Harris. **83** *left* From the Collections of the Israel Department of Antiquities, photo Israel Museum, Jerusalem/David Harris; *right* The British Museum/ Michael Holford. **84** *top* Erich Lessing/Magnum; *bottom* Scala/Art Resource, N. Y. **85** Israel Museum, photo Israel Museum, Jerusalem/ Yakov Harlap. **92** Louis Goldman/Rapho/Photo Researchers. **93** Werner Braun. **94** Nathan Benn/Woodfin Camp & Associates. **95** *top right* Daniel Blatt. **96** *top* Werner Braun; *bottom* F. Nigel Hepper. **97** *bottom right* Zev Radovan; *remainder* Daniel Blatt. **99** *left* Israel Museum Shrine of the Book, photo Israel Museum, Jerusalem/David Harris; *right* © Gail Rubin 1976. **100** *top left & right* Garo Nalbandian; *bottom left* Werner Braun. **102** *top* Nathan Benn/Woodfin Camp & Associates; *bottom left* Louis Goldman/ Rapho/Photo Researchers; *bottom right* Sonia Halliday. **103** Garo Nalbandian. **105** *top right* Tor Eigeland/Black Star; *bottom left* Werner Braun; *remainder* Daniel Blatt. **106** Werner Braun. **107** *left* Sonia Halliday. **108** F. Nigel Hepper. **109** *top right* The Ancient Art & Architecture Collection; *bottom* Daniel Blatt; *remainder* Zev Radovan. **111** Daniel Blatt. **112** Daniel Blatt. **113** The Ancient Art & Architecture Collection. **115** *top* Kevin Fleming/Woodfin Camp & Associates; *bottom* Daniel Blatt. **116** Sonia Halliday. **117** Betsy Kissam/Brooklyn Botanic Garden. **120** Marvin E. Newman. **122** *top right* Richard T. Nowitz; *bottom left* © Gail Rubin 1976; *remainder* Zev Radovan. **125** *left* Werner Braun; *right* David Harris. **126** Werner Braun. **127** Georg Gerster/Rapho/Photo Researchers/ Courtesy of the Rockefeller Museum. **128** *left* Raffi Safieh; *right* Erich Lessing/Magnum. **129** Serraillier/Rapho/Photo Researchers. **131** *right* From the Collections of the Israel Department of Antiquities, photo Israel Museum, Jerusalem/David Harris. **132** Peter Larsen/Photo Researchers. **133** *top* Scala/Art Resource, N.Y.; *lower* Sonia Halliday. **134** Werner Braun. **135** *left* Zev

Radovan; *right* David Harris. **137** Israel Museum Shrine of the Book, photo Israel Museum, Jerusalem/David Harris. **141** *bottom* Richard T. Nowitz. **142** Zev Radovan. **143** *left* Sonia Halliday; *right* Marvin E. Newman. **145** Aaron M. Levin. **148** *left* Zev Radovan; *right* David Harris. **149** *left* Neot Kedumin, The Biblical Landscape Reserve in Israel; *right* Peter Larsen/Photo Researchers. **150** *left* Zev Radovan; *right* Sonia Halliday. **152** The Ancient Art & Architecture Collection. **155** Erich Lessing/Magnum. **157** *top right & bottom right* The Ancient Art & Architecture Collection; *middle right* David Harris. **158** *top* Zev Radovan; *bottom* The British Museum/Michael Holford. **160** *left* Nogah Hareuveni/Neot Kedumin, The Biblical Landscape Reserve in Israel; *right* © Cecile Brunswick. **161** The British Museum/Michael Holford. **162** Erich Lessing/Magnum. **163 & 164** The Ancient Art & Architecture Collection. **165** Scala/Art Resource, N. Y. **166** *top* Collection of Studium Biblium Franciscanum/Photo by Garo Nalbandian; *bottom* Richard T. Nowitz. **167 & 168** The Ancient Art & Architecture Collection. **172** John Bryson/The Image Bank. **173** Bob Ivey/Ric Ergenbright Photography. **176** *top* Marvin E. Newman/The Image Bank. **178** *upper left* David Harris; *remainder* The Ancient Art & Architecture Collection. **179** Zev Radovan. **180** Alinari/Art Resource, N. Y. **182** *left* Sonia Halliday; *right* Scala/Art Resource, N. Y. **182** The Ancient Art & Architecture Collection. **184** Gabriel Covian/The Image Bank. **185** *top left* The Bettmann Archive; *top right* Peter S. Thacher/ Photo Researchers; *bottom left* Marvullo; *bottom right* The Granger Collection, New York. **186** From the Collections of the National Maritime Museum, Haifa. **188–189** *bottom* Alinari/Art Resource, N. Y. **189** *right* C. M. Dixon. **190** *left* Scala/Art Resource, N. Y.; *middle* The Robert Harding Picture Library; *right* Dr. David Darom. **191** Sonia Halliday. **192** *left* Daniel Blatt; *right* Garo Nalbandian. **194** *top* A. A. M. van der Heyden; *bottom* Collection of Dr. and Mrs. Irving F. Burton. **197** The Ancient Art & Architecture Collection. **201** *left & middle* Garo Nalbandian. **202** *top* The Ancient Art & Architecture Collection; *bottom* From the Collections of the Israel Department of Antiquities, photo Israel Museum, Jerusalem/Nir Bareket. **204** Giraudon/Art Resource, N. Y. **209** *left* Sonia Halliday; *right* Richard T. Nowitz. **213** *left* Staatliche Graphische Sammlung, Munich; *right* Richard T. Nowitz. **214** Erich Lessing/Magnum. **215** David Harris. **216** *bottom left* David Harris; *top* Sonia Halliday. **218** The Ancient Art & Architecture Collection. **219** *top* Israel Museum, Jerusalem; *bottom* Israel Museum Shrine of the Book, photo Israel Museum, Jerusalem/David Harris. **220** Michael Holford. **221** The Ancient Art & Architecture Collection. **222** Nogah Hareuveni/Neot Kedumin, The Biblical Landscape Reserve in Israel. **226** Richard T. Nowitz. **227** *bottom* Richard T. Nowitz; *remainder* © Gail Rubin 1976. **228** Georg Gerster/Rapho/Photo Researchers. **229** *left* Werner Braun; *top right* Sonia Halliday; *bottom right* © Gail Rubin 1976. **230** *left* Richard T. Nowitz. **232** Georg Gerster/Rapho/Photo Researchers. **233** Garo Nalbandian. **236** *left to right:* The Ancient Art & Architecture Collection; F. Nigel Hepper; Werner Braun; Dr. David Darom. **237** *left* Sonia Halliday; *right* The Ancient Art & Architecture Collection. **240** Zev Radovan. **242** Sonia Halliday. **244** *left* Sonia Halliday; *right* Marvin E. Newman. **247** *left* John Bryson/Photo Researchers; *top right* Richard T. Nowitz; *bottom right* Sonia Halliday. **248** The Ancient Art & Architecture Collection. **250** Richard T. Nowitz. **251** *bottom* Erich Lessing/Magnum. **252** *top* Kjell B. Sandved/Photo Researchers; *bottom* Sonia Halliday. **255** The Ancient Art & Architecture Collection. **257** *lower right* Richard T. Nowitz; *remainder* Zev Radovan. **258** *bottom left* Hillel S. Burger; *top left & bottom right* Daniel Blatt. **260** *left* Daniel Blatt; *right* Michael Holford. **261** Michael Holford. **262** *top left* © The Frick Collection, New York; *bottom middle* Scala/Art Resource, N. Y. **262–263** *bottom* © The Frick Collection, New York; *top* © James R. Johnson. **264** *top left* Sonia Halliday; *bottom left* Howard Agriesti, Ringling Museums, Sarasota, Fl.; *top right* Bibliothek Darmstadt. **265** *top left* Sonia Halliday; *top right* Reproduced by courtesy of the Trustees, The National Gallery, London; *bottom left* Erich Lessing/Magnum; *bottom right* Scala/Art Resource, N. Y. **266** *left* Album Treasures from the Kremlin, Moscow/Courtesy of The Metropolitan Museum of Art, Photography by Sheldon Collins; *bottom* © The Pierpont Morgan Library 1986 (M. 292, f. 24v). **266–267** *top* National Gallery of Art, Washington, Rosenwald Collection. **267** *bottom left* Scala/Art Resource, N. Y.; *right* Michael Holford. **268** *left* Lee Boltin; *right* The Metropolitan Museum of Art, Gift of J. Pierpont Morgan, 1917. **269** *top left* © The Pierpont Morgan Library 1986 (M. 892, f. 1); *bottom left* The Metropolitan Museum of Art, Bequest of Benjamin Altman, 1913; Scala/Art Resource, N. Y. **273** *left* A. A. M. van der Heyden; *right* Bibliothèque Nationale, Paris. **274** *left* Michael Holford; *right* C. M. Dixon. **276** Robert Suro/NYT Pictures. **280** *left* C. M. Dixon; *right* A. A. M. van der Heyden. **282** *left to right:* Zev Radovan; Giraudon/Art Resource, N. Y.; SEF/Art Resource, N. Y. **285** Beauvais Cathedral/Emile Rousset. **286** *top* Sonia Halliday; *bottom* Aaron M. Levin. **287** *left* Paolo Curto/The Image Bank; *right* Sonia Halliday. **288** *right* Zev Radovan; *remainder* Israel Museum, Jerusalem. **289** *top left & right* Zev Radovan; *remainder* The Ancient Art & Architecture Collection. **290** *top left* Werner Braun; *right* Chester Beatty Library. **292** *top left* Scala/Art Resource, N. Y. *top right* The Ancient Art & Architecture Collection; *bottom left* C. M. Dixon; *bottom middle* Erich Lessing/Magnum; *bottom right* Sonia Halliday. **293** *top left* Bardo Museum, Tunis/Michael Holford; *top right* Porterfield-Chickering; *bottom right* The Ancient Art & Architecture Collection; *remainder* Victoria and Albert Museum/Michael Holford. **295** SEF/Art Resource, N. Y. **296** The Ancient Art & Architecture Collection. **297** *left* Marvin E. Newman. **299** *left to right:* Scala/Art Resource, N. Y.; SEF/Art Resource, N. Y.; Zev Radovan. **300** *top left* Scala/Art Resource, N. Y.; *remainder* C. M. Dixon. **302** The Ancient Art & Architecture Collection. Back cover *top* The Ancient Art & Architecture Collection.

Index

Page numbers in **bold** type refer to captions.